W9-BBB-564

Freedom
Road

Freedom
Road

An American Family Saga from
Jamestown to World War

Ric Murphy

authorHOUSE®

AuthorHouse™
1663 Liberty Drive
Bloomington, IN 47403
www.authorhouse.com
Phone: 1-800-839-8640

Published by AuthorHouse 07/13/2015

ISBN: 978-1-4969-2051-5 (sc)
ISBN: 978-1-4969-2050-8 (e)

Print information available on the last page.

Any people depicted in stock imagery provided by Thinkstock are models,
and such images are being used for illustrative purposes only.
Certain stock imagery © Thinkstock.

This book is printed on acid-free paper.

Dedication

In honor of all of those who sailed to these lands before us
In honor of all of those who walked these lands before us
In honor of all of those who worked these lands before us
In honor of all of those who served to protect these lands for us
… and in honor of those who made this great nation what it is today

Table of Contents

List of Figures

Foreword

In sharing the story of the Cornwall Murphy family, the question is bound to come up as to the veracity of one African American family having such a rich and exciting family history. In responding to this question, a clear discussion of the genealogical and historical research techniques used in this narrative is as important and exciting as the story itself.

As most amateur genealogists soon learn, genealogical research is an exciting opportunity to reconnect with elderly relatives, record their stories and go back in time. When the initial research was conducted for Freedom Road, the Internet was only a concept. Resource tools such as online genealogical search engines were not in existence.

The majority of the genealogical research for Freedom Road was conducted during the 1980s, and primarily consisted of information supplied by living relatives, then cross-referenced with information primarily from colonial town records in Massachusetts, including certified birth, death and marriage records - and military and pension records from Massachusetts' military and pension records. Additional primary sources records included county estate, land, court, wills and tax records from colonial Virginia and North Carolina.

For the twenty years prior to publication, the primary information collected has been documented from eighteenth and nineteenth century records from Virginia and North Carolina. Most secondary source materials included abstracted deeds, orders, wills and tax records as compiled at a later date by a contracted third party who was neither present nor participated in the actual event. Secondary information has been most helpful in the collection of information from Virginia and North Carolina since primary data such as birth, death and marriage records were not recorded until the early twentieth century.

As the historical significance of the Cornwall Murphy family began to emerge, a mix of primary and secondary source records were used to connect the genealogical significance of the family with the much larger picture of the historical importance that the family played in more than four hundred years of American history dating back to the establishment of the Jamestown colony in Virginia. In constantly evaluating and re-evaluating primary and secondary research material collected, the emergence of selected historical reference materials began to support the information collected from the primary source records and the secondary source information.

As for the question of how is it possible for one African American family to have such a rich and exciting history, the answer is: It is a direct result of the enormous amount of information collected for the more than fifteen generations of the Cornwall Murphy family that covers more than five hundred years. That made it is impossible to tell the story and provide all of the primary and secondary footnotes for each family member and for each generation in the narrative. However, all of the primary, secondary and selected reference materials may be found in the Bibliography.

Acknowledgements

I would like to take this opportunity to thank all of the contributors who, over many years, helped to make this project possible: my grandparents, Harold and Marie Cornwall and Robert and Margret Murphy, whose willingness to share their personal stories and whose insight of the past provided a wealth of information to be shared in the future; the validation of stories provided by my great-great-cousin Pearl Ashport Brookes, my great-uncle Paul Chapman; and my great-aunts Claudia Dausuel, Cora Hilliard Lopez, Odie Rocha and Martha Royster, who each enabled me to bring life to these stories through old family photographs. I must also thank the insight of Bob Burns, Connie Curts, Douglas Cornwall, Brian Lawrence, Alan Murphy, and Eric St. John as they helped to perfect each version; the patience of Joan and Will Murphy, as they watched me work through many sleepless nights instead of spending quality time with them; and lastly, Alexis Bobrik as she carefully edited many manuscripts. A profound thank you to all.

Joan Cornwall and Bob Murphy
in Barnstable County, Massachusetts, circa 1950.

Introduction

When Bob Murphy and Joan Cornwall married, little did they know that they were bringing together two of the most historic African American families in American history, a history transcends three continents. It definitively captures the feudal wars in Africa, the religious clashes in Europe, the attempted extermination of the indigenous people of North America, and the racial conflict in America.

The Cornwall and Murphy families trace their remarkable historic roots through three distinct racial groups: their Native American ancestors from the Algonquian Nation on the United States Atlantic Seaboard; their ancestors from the eastern coast of Africa in the area now known as the Republic of Angola; and their European ancestors from England, Scotland, and Ireland.

Much has been written about the origins and history of Americans of African descent during the antebellum period and American Civil War, but very little history mentions follows the life and struggles of these American families from colonial Jamestown into the 21st century. *Freedom Road* fills that void in American history, following the Cornwall Murphy line from its 17th century roots into the present day.

Freedom Road is a compilation of individual stories that begins in Africa and the Gulf of Mexico in 1619, when a captured slave ship en route from Angola to the "New World." From there, it spans more than fifteen generations and three continents. Each family legend has been thoroughly researched to capture the historic times in which Cornwall Murphy family members lived and the challenges of which they endured and persevered. These legends and stories, passed from one generation to another, have now been artfully captured for future generations to enjoy and share. Each hero in the Cornwall Murphy family has been accurately captured to document the historical significance of these brave men and women, their contribution to the greatness of this nation, and to their enduring legacy for their descendants.

Hopefully, *Freedom Road* will help to reshape the world's view of African Americans and their positive impact on American life, culture and history. This story has been consolidated into five sections, summarizing the remarkable lives of an unbelievable African American family that would otherwise be lost to history, as are so many family histories.

In Part I: *American Colonization 1500–1700,* we learn how these founding African American families contributed to the survival of Jamestown in colonial Virginia and in the Plymouth Bay colony in Massachusetts. We discover how African American families help to pave the way and developed the colonial communities in Massachusetts, New York, Virginia and North Carolina for the millions of Americans and immigrants to follow.

In Part II: *The American Revolutionary War (1700–1800),* we are moved by the hopes, dreams and aspirations of the early African American pioneers who worked hard and believed in a justice system that protected the individual freedoms and rights of all Americans. We witness five family members who serve in the Continental Army (one European and four African American patriots) and go to war with England, in a fight that brought together men and women of African, European, and Native American descent for one purpose: American freedom. That freedom was tested when the United States was challenged by internal economic, political and racial struggles as the young nation attempted to take its place on the world stage. Meanwhile, Great Britain took advantage of these struggles, embroiling the young United States in a second war, the War of 1812.

In Part III: *The American Civil War* and the years preceding and following it *(1820–1870),* when the nation was evolving from a colony dependent of farmers and frontiersmen to a country of growing urban centers, where hard-fought freedoms were regionalized and marginalized, based on race, color and ethnicity. That resulted in an internal war, where brother fought against brother, where the north fought against the south, and where the agricultural planter was pitted against the urban industrialist. It also was where former slaves joined Union forces next to free African Americans from Massachusetts and Virginia to fight for freedom, equality and dignity.

In Part IV: *Industrial and Social Changes (1870 – 1910),* we witness how an African American family struggled in the aftermath of a war that tore the nation apart, and how the family was integrally entwined with the rapid changes of the American industrial revolution, the railroad industry, and the birth of new technologies. We see how they struggle and endure the segregationist Jim Crow policies that moved family members from their southern ancestral homes in search of more equal opportunities in the north.

In Part V: *International Wars and Internal Conflicts (1910-1975)*, we learn how international events helped shape the lives of this remarkable African American family, and how the combined families' earlier efforts to shape colonial laws eventually became the framework of the United States Constitution, the United States Bill of Rights, and the framework of the historic 1960s Civil Rights legislation.

Freedom Road is not only a story about a young couple who marries and brings together two historic families, but a story about the millions of people of African and Native American descent who helped to make America the great nation that it is today. It is also a heartwarming story that draws attention to, and educates us, about the major historical significance that African and Native American founding fathers and mothers played in the creation and design of this great nation. It has been edited for the privacy of descendants. It has been edited for the privacy of descendants. The family history is presented as a history book, not a genealogical book. It shares one couple's legacy – American History in context. Likewise, it demonstrates the influence people have when living normal daily lives, marrying, having children, taking a stand for one's political, religious, and moral beliefs, and experiencing society through its many changes in one's lifetime.

The family history is presented as a history book, not a genealogical book. It shares one couple's legacy to American History and demonstrates the influence people have when living normal daily lives, marrying, having children, taking a stand for one's political, religious, and moral beliefs, and experiencing society through its many changes in one's lifetime.

Part 1: American Colonization, 1500-1700

*The early people of the Americas were a convergence of three races
of people: the indigenous Native Americans, the Angolans from
Africa, and the multicultural Europeans.*

1.1   The Cornwall Murphy Family - A Tri-Racial Family

The marriage of Joan Cornwall of Brockton, Massachusetts, and Bob
Murphy of Boston, Massachusetts, brought together two of the most
interesting and historic African American families in modern day
history. Their ancestors are descended from the indigenous people of
North America, primarily from the Algonquian and Iroquois Nations
on the Atlantic seacoast; from the royal tribesmen of Africa, mainly
from the nation of Angola; and from Western Europe, particularly the
nations of England, Ireland, Scotland and Germany.

The ancestry of Joan Cornwall and Bob Murphy is a mosaic of
African, European and Native American bloodlines that spans
more than fifteen generations, and dates back to the global political,
economic and religious conflicts in England, Africa and the Americas.
This extraordinary family lineage and its remarkable descendants
have contributed to every major historical event in American history.

Descendants of the Cornwall Murphy family line challenged Virginia
and North Carolina's court systems in the early days of America,
fighting against unfair taxes and for property rights of Free People of
Color. Their ancestors confronted Boston's political leaders and church
elders for their conservative views on religion, the poor treatment of
the Native Americans, and the role of slavery in puritanical Boston
and colonial Virginia.

Joan Cornwall and Bob Murphy's ancestors were people with
unique pioneering spirits who challenged the inequities of early
American law, while still defending their country and its government
against its enemies. They contributed to the survival of the earliest
colonies in Jamestown, Virginia, and Plymouth Bay, Massachusetts,
not only as European newcomers, but also as Free People of Color from
Angola and indigenous Native Americans. They helped to shape the
colonial laws in Massachusetts and Virginia that eventually became

1

the framework for the United States Constitution, the United States Bill of Rights, and the 1960s Civil Rights legislation. As founders of our nation, they served with distinction in the Revolutionary War, the War of 1812, and the Spanish American War, as well as in World Wars I and II, and the Korean and Vietnam Wars.

The family of Joan Cornwall's father Harold R. Cornwall of Brockton, Massachusetts, originates in 14th century England, and continues through the religious strife between the British King Henry VIII and the commoners in 15th century England. Harold Cornwall's European ancestry is traced back to Mansfield Cornwall, who was the 9th generation great-grandson of Thomas Cornell and Rebecca Briggs of Fairstead Manor, Essex.

Harold Cornwall is also the 4th generation great-grandson of Ruth Raif, a young Native American girl from the Massachusetts' Wampanoag tribe of the Algonquian Nation. The state of Massachusetts is named for the tribe's leader, Chief Massasoit, who greeted the English Pilgrims in Plymouth in 1620. Harold Cornwall's Native American roots also date back to Hannah Cornwall, reportedly the daughter of the Chief of the Warren Springs tribe, of the Iroquois Nation. Hannah Cornwall's biracial son, Flushing Cornwall, was Harold's great-grandfather.

Harold Cornwall's African ancestry is traced through Flushing's wife, Ms. Harriet Brooker of Boston, Massachusetts. Harriet Brooker was the great-granddaughter of Benjamin Brooker, Cuffe Grandison, and Caesar Russell, three historic African men who served honorably in the American Revolutionary War, despite the growing numbers of African men and women being enslaved in America's southern colonies.[1] Harold's great-grandfathers were the first of more than ten million African men, women and children brought to American shores as chattel property.

The family of Joan Cornwall's mother Marie Howell originates with the African royal and mercantile families of Angola brought to Jamestown in early 1619 on the Spanish frigate *San Juan Bautista*. Marie Howell Cornwall of Brockton, Massachusetts, is the 9th generation great granddaughter of John Gowen of Luanda, Angola. The Gowen family is descended from one of the first enslaved Africans who were brought to Jamestown, Virginia in 1619 from the Portuguese colony in Angola.

The family of Bob Murphy's father Robert Murphy of Norfolk, Virginia, dates back to the late 1700s in Virginia, during the darkest period of American slavery. Robert Murphy's wife, Margaret Melton, was from Ahoskie, North Carolina. Her family is also descended from the royal and mercantile families of Angola, as well as from English and Scottish indentured women in the early 1700s. Margaret is the 2nd generation great granddaughter of Joshia Melton of Hertford County, North Carolina. The Melton family is descended from the African slaves brought to Jamestown, Virginia, from Angola in 1619. The Melton family intermarried with the Chowanoke and Meherrin Native American tribes of coastal North Carolina and Virginia, with white indentured women, and with the daughters and sons of white frontiersmen.

The families of Robert Murphy and his wife Margaret Melton Murphy, along with Marie Howell Cornwall, date back to the beginning of the original English settlement in North America, under the charter of the Virginia Company in Jamestown in 1607. The families descended from the Native American people who lived in the area of the original English settlements, which were divided into eight counties: Accomac (now Northampton County), Charles City, Charles River (now York County), Elizabeth City (now part of the City of Hampton), Henrico County, James City, Warwick (now another part of the City of Hampton), and Warrosquyoake (now Isle of Wright County). The land mass was easily accessible by boat via the northern and western tributaries of the James River, and the Chesapeake Bay on the east. Harold Cornwall's family dates back to the second English settlement under the charter of the Plymouth Bay Company in Plymouth in 1620, primarily in the counties of Essex, Plymouth and Suffolk.

The Cornwall and Murphy families descended from the original people of North America. The families descended from the Native American tribes of the Algonquian nation along the Atlantic seacoast, from the first Africans brought to America in Jamestown, and from the original English settlers who colonized Jamestown in Virginia then colonized Plymouth Bay in Massachusetts.

1.2   Descendants of Native American Ancestry

To better understand the genealogical history and importance of the Cornwall Murphy families, one must understand the historical prominence of Native Americans, the impact of the arrival of the western Europeans, and the introduction of Africans to the Native American tribal communities.

The population of America's indigenous people, commonly called Native Americans, grew from a few thousand inhabitants to approximately 20,000,000 people across the vast fertile lands of North and South America. In 1492, the year in which Christopher Columbus mistakenly "discovered" America, there were eight distinct Native American nations.

The Cornwall Murphy family is descended from the Native American Algonquian nation, which consists of many different tribes, including the Wampanoag of eastern Massachusetts, the Chickahominy of Virginia, and the Chowanoke and Cherokee of North Carolina. The family is also descended from the Iroquois nation, from the Warren Springs tribe in New York and the Meherrin tribe of Virginia and North Carolina.

Harold Cornwall was the 4th generation great grandson of Cuffe Grandison and his wife, Ruth Raif, who was a Native American directly descended from the Algonquian nation's Wampanoag tribe[2]. In 1620, the Wampanoag tribe greeted the English Pilgrims who sailed on the historic Mayflower in what is now known as the Town of Plymouth, Massachusetts. Harold Cornwall's 2nd generation great-grandmother, Hannah Cornwall, was a member of the Warren Springs tribe of Iroquois nation from Canada.

Robert and Margaret Melton Murphy, and Marie Howell Cornwall, are descended from the southernmost branches of the Algonquian nation, which consists of the Cherokee nation and the now-extinct Chowanoke nation, both of North Carolina. Margaret Melton Murphy is also descended from the Chickahominy of Virginia, who were affiliated with their Algonquian cousins, the Chowanoke of North Carolina.

In the middle of the doughnut-shaped Algonquian nation was the Iroquois nation, another nation of separate tribes. Prior to the arrival

4

of the Europeans, the Iroquois occupied much of southern Canada and most of present-day New York State, the western portion of Pennsylvania, the state of Maryland, and the western half of the Mid-Atlantic States. The Iroquois nation was one of the major rivals of the Algonquian nation, from the dawning of the Americas, through the Revolutionary War, all the way up to the War of 1812. Unlike the patriarchal Algonquians, the Iroquois nation was a matriarchal society in which property passed from mother to daughter. The Warren Springs tribe was affiliated with the Iroquois nation, and was located in central New York State.

The Native American ancestry for the Cornwall Murphy families is primarily from Native American women marrying and having children with European men, as well as with African men who were brought to the Americas as slaves between the mid-1600s and late 1700s. These men had children with the Native American women, and in time, also with white indentured women from Europe.

After his maiden voyage in 1492, Christopher Columbus, on his second voyage in 1493, brought with him more than 1,200 men from Spain, who were scattered throughout what was referred to as the West Indies." In order to survive, the Spaniards needed inexpensive labor for menial tasks, which included culling the forest to construct settlements, clearing areas to plant the fields, and eventually harvesting the crops. It was only a matter of time before the indigenous men were taken for slaves, the women were overpowered, and the valuable metals, minerals and other natural resources of the islands were confiscated in the name of Spanish exploration. In short order, the indigenous people began to suffer from the aggressive pursuit of valuable commodities that were subsequently sold in Spanish markets in Europe and traded for goods in Asia.

Due to Spanish colonization, many native people died on the West Indian islands, resulting in the introduction of native slaves from neighboring islands and, eventually, from the mainland. Native Americans began to hide from the Spanish explorers and slaveholders. Those who did not hide often died from the new diseases brought to them by the Europeans, or from the brutal treatment under the hands of their overseers. Their populations across all of the West Indian islands rapidly diminished in a short period of time. The large number of deaths led to the rapid decline in the availability of West Indian islands' slave labor. That decline, combined with European growing need for cheap workers, led to the introduction of slave labor from Africa. In 1498, on his third voyage, Columbus, having stopped at the Canary and Cape Verde Islands, began to import and introduce Africans to the West Indies, resulting in the creation of the transatlantic slave trade, and driving the demand for African slaves to an unprecedented level.

The initial introduction of African labor proved to be extremely beneficial to the Europeans, particularly because the African slaves could work in the tropical heat of the islands for long, backbreaking hours. African slave labor provided a quick remedy for the needs of the early Spanish as they ravaged the mines and virgin farmland of the West Indies. As European exploration became more profitable, the African continent was able to provide the vast numbers of required bodies to meet the growing needs for cheap labor.

Slavery was also widely practiced by various tribes on the African continent, particularly on the western coast of Africa. When warring groups took prisoners, it was much different in Africa than in America, where Native Americans often assimilated their enemies into their tribes rather than enslaving them. In Africa, tribes would often slaughter their enemies, or trade entire racial and religious groups to European slavers.

The sixteenth and seventeenth centuries were turbulent times for the coast of West Africa. Territorial wars brought the massive pillaging of villages for possible slave labor in the fields, and for the wide-scale trade and trafficking of human chattel to foreign lands. In order to eradicate their competitors and gain profit, tribal chieftains and warlords bargained with the European slave traders. They provided men, women and children to be bought and sold in the slave markets in Europe, the Caribbean islands, and eventually on the mainland of the "New World," the Americas.

African men were initially used in the New World to work in the fields and the mines. However, the subsequent usage of African slaves was for breeding purposes, ensuring a constant supply of women and children of African descendant. The Europeans learned early from their mistakes with Native American slavery: If they were to expand their exploration in the Americas, they would need a steady influx of African slaves.

When the Europeans first came to the Americas, there were eight well-defined Native American Nations.

The Algonquian nation, consisting of hundreds of distinct tribes, covered an area of modern day Canada and northeastern portions of the United States from the Atlantic seaboard to the Mississippi River, and down to the northern points of modern day North Carolina. The people of the Algonquian nation were nomads who hunted and gathered food in small family-related bands. They were a patriarchal society, where property and status passed from father to son. Since they lived on the eastern seacoast, they were the first major nation of indigenous people on the mainland to be directly impacted by the widespread encroachment of the Europeans.

Algonquian tribes on the southeastern seaboard became increasingly less tolerant of the invasion of these European explorers and the development of their settlements. As the explorers invaded Native Americans' land, the indigenous tribesmen reacted instinctively and tried to overrun the European camps. Customarily, aggression against a Native American village was met with strong resistance. The local tribesmen would either attempt to run the aggressors off, or try to capture them and integrate them into their village.

By the middle of the sixteenth century, the Native American tribes in what is now known as the state of Virginia belonged to three language families: the Algonquian, the Iroquoian, and the Siouan. The Algonquian tribes occupied the land in Virginia that was east of a line running from present day Washington, D.C. through Fredericksburg, Richmond, and Petersburg, Virginia, and into coastal North Carolina. By the end of the sixteenth century, the powerful Chief Powhatan had conquered most of the Algonquian tribes in modern-day Virginia, creating an empire that included more than thirty provinces under his rule.[3] The Powhatan Confederacy became one of the largest Algonquian tribes, and is believed to be the inspiration for the name of the Potomac River. Chief Powhatan's powerful reign continued through the beginning of the seventeenth century.

During the last quarter of the sixteenth century, the Powhatan Confederacy saw numerous European ships from Spain, France, and England pull into the Chesapeake Bay in search of fresh water, firewood, and trade. By 1607, Chief Powhatan was reported to be in his sixties.[4] Despite his advanced years, he was a skilled warrior with much experience in battle and in managing his growing empire. When the British arrived with three ships and more than a hundred passengers, they had little knowledge of Chief Powhatan or his 14,000 subjects, 3,200 of them warriors. Britain's goal, much like Spain before them, was to extract gold and silver from the land, and to develop vast personal fortunes from land acquisitions.[5]

Chief Powhatan realized that the British planned to take over his land, diminishing his power and control. He would not allow this to happen. The Powhatan Confederacy was the protector of its villages, their neighbors, and their families. It was their duty to stem the invading British tide.

Chief Powhatan moved his principal village to an area that is known today as Stafford County, Virginia. That is where one of the most famous kidnappings in American history took place when the English Captain Samuel Argall kidnapped Pocahontas, daughter of Chief Powhatan, in April 1613 and took her on board the Ship *Treasurer*.[6]

Upon learning of the whereabouts of Chief Powhatan's daughter, the English Captain set about a strategy to lure the young woman to an English vessel in the hopes of receiving special copper gifts - and in the hopes of kidnapping Pocahontas and ransoming her for the return of Argall's men that were being held by her father. During her capture, Pocahontas converted to Christianity and adopted the name Rebecca. Upon her release one year later, an "uneasy truce" was forged between the Powhatan Empire and the English settlers. At the age of nineteen, she married an Englishman by the name of John Rolfe, a twenty-eight year old widower. The following year, in 1615, she bore a son, named Thomas Rolfe. Pocahontas died in 1617. John Rolfe became an important figure in the purchase of the first African slave in the English colony, John Gowen, an ancestor to the Cornwall Murphy family.

The truce between the Powhatan Confederacy and the British was short lived. In 1622, Native Americans overran the Jamestown Colony. They killed many Europeans and took many of the African slaves as captives. The African slaves were taken to various Native communities, and then gradually integrated into the general population, forging a natural bond between the two races. Whether early Africans were captured by the Native Americans or escaped from their British slaveholders on their own, the Africans' introduction into the native population began the slow integration of the African and Native American races. As the two races bonded, biracial children were born in colonial Virginia. From these early unions came the ancestors of Margaret Melton of Ahoskie, North Carolina, whose family originated in the general area now known as Accomack County, Northampton County, and Southampton County, Virginia.

Despite their attack on Jamestown, not all Native Americans were hostile to the advances of the early European explorers. Ruth Raif, the 4th generation great grandmother of Harold Cornwall, was a Native American directly descended from the Algonquian Nation's Wampanoag tribe of eastern Massachusetts. Ruth Raif's Wampanoag tribe was part of one of the northern branches of the Algonquian people.[7] She was born in 1735, in the Town of Scituate, Massachusetts, originally part of the land owned by the Wampanoag's Tribe and later settled by the Pilgrims in Plymouth Bay Colony. Ruth married Cuffe Clapp Grandison, a man of African descent, who was a servant to Job Clapp of Scituate, Massachusetts.

The Algonquian Wampanoag Tribe was the original host to the Pilgrims that landed in Plymouth, Massachusetts, in 1620. It has been widely romanticized that the Wampanoag Nation provided aid and comfort to the sick and exhausted English Pilgrims, nursed them to health, and that a year after the Pilgrims' arrival, the Wampanoag's Chief Massasoit hosted a "dinner of thanks," or what is now known as the first Thanksgiving Dinner, on behalf of his Pilgrim guests. While this is not entirely accurate, Chief Massasoit did provide the Pilgrims with supplies to survive the winter, enabling the Pilgrims' survival and subsequent harvest the following year, after which they celebrated for three days. A truce of sorts was struck between the Wampanoags and the Pilgrims, but nearly four hundred years in the future, "Native Americans do not celebrate the arrival of the pilgrims and other European settlers…To them, Thanksgiving Day is a reminder of the genocide of millions of their people, the theft of their lands, and the relentless assault on their culture."[8]

1.3 John Geaween: First Recorded African Slave Who Also Became the First to be Freed

Americans, white and Black, find it very difficult to conduct genealogical research on their ancestors prior to the Civil War. Many Americans are descended from European immigrant ancestors who kept few to no vital records in their communities. Americans of African descent, by virtue of how their ancestors came to America - as slaves, against their will - find numerous obstacles to this genealogical research because their ancestral roots have been lost through the ages. Marie Howell Cornwall from Brockton, Massachusetts is unique in that she is able to trace her African ancestry to her 9th generation great-grandfather, the first African slave recorded in American history and the first to be freed in the British colonies - John Geaween, as his last name was initially spelled.

John Geaween (Gowen) was born in Angola, a Portuguese colony with a turbulent history of enslaving Africans to be sold in foreign markets. To better understand how John Geaween and some twenty odd Angolans arrived in colonial Jamestown, Virginia, in 1619, one must first look to the conflict in Europe, particularly on the Iberian Peninsula, and its effect on colonization in Africa.

The Catholic monarchies of Portugal and Spain shared the Iberian Peninsula. The two nations had quarreled for centuries and competed on land and sea. The Portuguese in the late 1400s were very similar to the Spanish colonization of the West Indian islands in the Americas. In 1483, nine years before Christopher Columbus discovered the West Indies for the Spanish King Ferdinand and Queen Isabella, Portuguese explorer Diogo Cão came upon a number of African kingdoms along the Congo River. One such kingdom was the Kingdom of Kongo.

The Portuguese, who initially were looking for African slaves for export, entered into a mutually peaceful partnership with the reigning King Nzinga Nkuwu of the Kongo. "They hoped that a diplomatic relationship with the Kongo, what they considered to be a powerful African Kingdom, would provide them with a profitable trade in gold, copper, silver and spices - but, instead, they learned that the most valuable item in the basically agricultural economy was the region's labour."[9]

After the Portuguese colonized the Kingdom of Kongo, King Nzinga Nkuwu, who had been baptized and taken the name of King João in honor of Portugal's King John I, requested that "his sons to be sent to Portugal to learn to read and write and to be Christians."[10] The African king hoped that "the foreigners would supply teachers and craftsman to educate and train his people, and that they would supply arms and mercenaries to strengthen his own army" against insurgents.[11]

Figure 1: Historic Dates for the Kingdoms of Kongo and Angola[12]

1180	Kingdom of Kongo founded
1442	First West African slaves taken to Lisbon, Spain.
1483	Portuguese navigator Diogo Cão discovers Kongo Kingdom.
1485	King Njinga Nkuwu of Kongo, baptized and rules as King João. I
1506	Death of King Njinga Nkuwu, son Njinga Mbemba rules as King Afonso.
1513	King Afonso I attacks rebel Ndongo Kingdom.
1518	Ndongo Kingdom requests independence from Kongo.
1520	King Afonso I of Kondo establishes Christianity as national religion.
1520	Portuguese missionaries sent to Ndongo to set up independence mission, unsuccessful.
1526	King Afonso I writes to Portugal's King complaining about African slave trade.
1543	Death of King Afonso I.
1545	King Diogo I crowned as new King of Kondo Kingdom.
1550	Independent Ndongo Kingdom founded.
1560	A second Portuguese mission, led by Paulo Dias de Novais, is sent to Ndongo.
1564	Portuguese explorer Dias de Novais secured a grant allowing him to colonize Angola (Ndongo).
1575	Portuguese under Dias de Novais founded Luanda, capital of Angola.
1589	Paulo Dias de Novais, supported by King Álvaro I of Kongo, sends a large army to attack Angola. Portuguese/Kongoese army defeated at the Battle of Lukala.
1595	The Pope declares Portuguese colony of Kongo to be an "episcopal see," the seat of the Catholic Bishop, with jurisdiction over both Kongo and Angola.
1599	Portugal and Ndongo sign a peace treaty and formalize relationships
1618	Governor Luis Mendes de Vasconcelos wages successful war on Ndongo
1619	Slave ship *San Juan Bautista* sets sail from Angola to Brazil
1619	*San Juan Bautista* is pirated; human cargo arrives in Jamestown, Virginia.

In 1506, King Nzinga Nkuwu passed away and his son, Mvemba Nzinga, inherited his father's kingdom, adopting the name King Afonso I. During the reign of King Afonso I, the relationship between the Kongo and Portugal had a definite price. "As early as 1512, the Portuguese Crown made clear that it expected payment for its services...and stated that ships returning to Europe be as heavily laden as possible with slaves as well as with copper and ivory in order to repay the necessary high expenses incurred" by Portugal to support the needs of the colony. [13]

By the early sixteenth century, the demand for African slave labor intensified. To secure the needed labor, Portugal attempted to expand its holdings and influence in the Kwanza Valley by pitting rulers of warring kingdoms against each other. As the Portuguese incrementally expanded their holdings in Africa, taking control of the land and governments, the royal families continued to feud as they had done for thousands of years. There was little incentive for the Portuguese to stop the brutal feuds for a divided population of native Africans was an easy population for foreign colonists to rule and control, and one of the more valuable exports for the Portuguese was human chattel. With each bloody war came the spoils of victory.

After each battle, hundreds, if not thousands of enslaved men, women and children were made available to be shipped to the ports of Brazil to work the sugar fields, to the West Indian Islands to mine the forest, or to European capital cities to provide hard labor. The Portuguese made money from selling the slaves, and made money from slave labor. The Kongo royal families made money by providing slaves from Africa's interior. Each bloodstained battle was a win-win proposition for the two allies.

Meanwhile, there was a rumor "that...rich silver deposits in the mountains around the upper Kwanza River helped the Portuguese to decide to try to conquer the kingdom of Ndongo" (present day Angola).[14] In 1518, the provincial Ndongo Kingdom requested from Portugal independence from the Kongo Kingdom.

Two years later the Portuguese sent Catholic missionaries to Ndongo as a first step towards independence, but the initial attempt failed. The Ndongo Kingdom was "inhabited by the Mbundu people and ruled by a dynasty of kings called Ngolas. The kingdom's capital was on the northern bank of the Kwanza River."[15] A second failed attempt by the Portuguese to establish formal ties with the Ndongo Kingdom occurred in 1557.

Figure 2: Portuguese attempt diplomatic ties with the African nation Ndongo

In 1557, a second attempt to establish diplomatic relations with Ndongo was attempted. Portuguese Paulo Dias, a Jesuit, and a party of seven sailed up the Kwanza River in a small boat. The barren coastal country gave way to more populace regions with rich valleys and lush vegetation. Numerous palm trees produced wine, oil and fruits, as well as building materials for houses. At the time of navigation, the party was welcomed by one of the Ngola's tribal chiefs. They marched for several days, passing through twenty villages before reaching the royal city. When they arrived they were received by an official…and accommodated in substantial straw huts. The city was large and well built. The Jesuits considered it not much smaller than their own city of Evora, Portugal.

Marq De Villers and Shelia Hirtle, Into Africa,
A Journey through Ancient Empires[16]

The Portuguese intruders once again were unsuccessful in colonizing the kingdom. In 1571, the "Portuguese crown…issued a charter to Paulo Dias de Novias to establish a colony on the Angola coast around the mouth of the Kwanza River," but in short order, Dias de Novias was displaced by the Angolans and sought refuge in Kongo.

In 1589, the Portuguese forces belonging to Dias de Novias and the forces from the Kongo attempted to restore de Novias to power. However, at the Battle of Lukala, the Portuguese and Kongoese both suffered heavy losses while fighting the Angolans.

An uneasy peace was established until another attempt at colonization was made in 1618 by Luis Mendes de Vasconcelos, a Portuguese-appointed colonial governor. He launched a very successful war against Ndongo. By 1619, the Ndongo Kingdom was badly beaten, and a year later it had to concede defeat, losing considerable land to the Portuguese.[17] It was during this final effort to colonize Angola that John Geaween, and more than 4,000 other Angolans from the royal village were captured and sold into slavery. From there, some twenty-odd captives found their way to the British colony of Jamestown, Virginia, after being pirated from the Spanish frigate, *San Juan Bautista*.

Figure 3: 4,000 Angolans Are Sold Into Slavery

"Mendes de Vasconcelos was sure that he could break through the military and diplomatic stalemate that had halted Portuguese advancement in Angola since their decisive defeat at the Battle of Lukala on December 29, 1589. He was so confident that, on receiving nomination as governor, he submitted a memorandum to the king announcing his intention to conquer the lands from one coast to the other and to join Angola with the equally new and uncertain Portuguese colony in what became Mozambique, thus opening a new route to India."

"The military forces unleashed by Mendes de Vasconcelos got out of hand. The Angolan Catholic bishop maintained that some 4,000 baptized Christians had been captured illegally and sent to the capital city Luanda. The people enslaved by Mendes de Vasconcelos' army were from the narrow corridor of land about thirty miles broad and some fifty miles deep between the Lukala and Lutete Rivers, a cool plateau region mostly over 4,000-foot elevation. Within this region most of the enslaved came from the royal district of Ndongo, the targeted region of both the 1618 and the 1619 campaigns, and the heartland of the area. As such, they were from urban backgrounds. Kabasa, the royal court, and nearby settlements formed a dense complex of towns in thickly populated country side. The royal district was not much different in 1618 than it had been in 1564 when it was first visited by the Portuguese who described the nucleated town of Angoleme as being as large as the Portuguese city of Evora. Aligned along streets inside a stockade interwoven with grasses were 5,000-6,000 thatched dwellings that probably housed 20,000-30,000 people. So many people were captured and designated for sale abroad during this brief time that shipping was inadequate to transport all the slaves captured. The *San Juan Bautista* was one of the thirty-six slave ships that left Luanda for Brazil on ports of the Spanish Indies in 1619."

John Thornton, *The African Experience of the "20 and Odd Negroes" Arriving in Virginia in 1619*[18]

As the *San Juan Bautista* left the waters of Luanda, Angola in 1619, it was heavy with the weight of more than 350 African slaves. Many of the captured men, women and children would never arrive at their designation of Vera Cruz, Mexico, and would eventually become the forefathers of today's Americans of African descent. Within a month at sea, many of the captives on board became ill and the ship's captain, Manuel Mendez de Acunha, was fearful that he would lose all of his human cargo. He decided to stop at the Caribbean island of wJamaica to obtain medicine and supplies, hoping to deliver as many of his human cargo to Vera Cruz as possible. Soon after departing from Jamaica, Captain Acunha realized he was being followed in the Gulf of Mexico by two pirate ships.

Figure 4: Angolan slaves sicken and die on slave Ship *San Juan Bautista*

"…Captain Acunha recorded that he "has many sick aboard, and many already died. Before the frigate crossed the Atlantic and reached the West Indies as few weeks later, more than one hundred on the *Bautista* had died of sickness. And, Vera Cruz, her intended destination was still nearly one thousand miles away. Fearing the entire shipment would be dead before reaching Mexico, Captain Acunha paused briefly in the Caribbean for medicine and supplies that he paid for with twenty-four 'slave boys he was forced to sell in Jamaica where he had to refresh.' Of the original 350 Angolans who crossed on the *San Juan Bautista* in the summer of 1619, only 147 would finish the voyage to Vera Cruz in August. However, not all of the slaver's losses were due to sickness. Leaving Jamaica in early July the slave ship had entered the gulf of Mexico between Cuba and the tip of the Yucatan Peninsula when on July 15, and less than five hundred miles from Vera Cruz, Captain Acunha, while glazing at a massive band of low, ominous clouds coming in from Africa, first noticed that he was being stalked by two pirate ships.

Tim Hashaw, *The Birth of Black America, the First African Americans and the Pursuit of Freedom at Jamestown*[19]

In mid-July, as the *San Juan Bautista* left Jamaica and approached the Gulf of Mexico, it was spotted by two pirate ships sailing between Cuba and the Yucatán Peninsula. Hoping the frigate carried gold and silver, the two man-of-war ships, the Dutch *White Lion* and the English *Treasurer*, gave chase, trapping the Portuguese ship in the Bay of Campeche.[20]

The large, slow-moving *San Juan Bautista* frigate was not designed to compete with the smaller and sleeker Dutch and British pirate ships. After several hours of cannon fire, Captain Acunha was forced to surrender his ship and his human cargo. Once the pirates boarded the *San Juan Bautista,* they were disappointed to discover that instead of gold and silver treasure, they had won a cargo of enslaved Africans being shipped from Luanda, Angola, to Vera Cruz, Mexico.[21] In order to make money off their human cargo, the pirates transported approximately twenty to thirty of the healthiest men, women and children to the British colony of Jamestown, Virginia, on the Chesapeake Bay.

One crucial source document that chronicles these events is found in the Spanish archives, a financial accounting ledger. The accounting ledger documents the events at sea and the purchase of the 350 slaves in Angola and their delivery, receipt and sale in Vera Cruz, Mexico on August 30, 1619.

Figure 5: Financial accounting of slaves purchased in Luanda, Angola

"Enter on the credit side the receipt of 8,657.875 pesos by Manuel Mendez de Acunha, master of the Ship *San Juan Bautista*, on 147 slave pieces brought by him into the aid port on August, 30, 1619 …on the voyage inbound, Mendez de Acunha was robbed at sea off the coast of Campeche by English (war ships). Out of 350 slaves, large and small, he loaded in said Loanda (200 under a license issued to him in Sevilla and the rest to be declared later) the English left him with only 147".

Engel Sluiter,
New Light on the "20 and Odd Negroes" Arriving in Virginia in 1619[22]

Of the thirty-six slave ships that arrived in Mexico, the *"San Juan Bautista* was the only slave ship among [those] arriving at Vera Cruz between 1618 and 1622 to be attacked, inbound from Angola."[23] Based on the ship's registries found in the Spanish archives, and during the same period of time, only six slave ships arrived at Vera Cruz, Mexico, each having loaded their "human cargo" in Sao Paulo de Loanda (also known as Luanda), Angola.

The transportation of these Africans to the Jamestown colony is colloquially known as the voyage of the "Black Mayflower." While no one ship can claim the actual title of "Black Mayflower," all three vessels, the Portuguese frigate the *San Juan Bautista,* the Dutch *White Lion,* and the British *Treasurer,* were instrumental in bringing the first widely recorded Africans from Angola to English-speaking America.

Figure 6: Spanish documentation confirms arrival of Africans to Virginia

Based on credible evidence from Spanish archives …the blacks brought to Virginia in a Dutch ship in 1619 almost certainly came directly, in two stages, from Africa. In the accounts of the income and outgo of the Vera Cruz treasury for the fiscal year, June 18, 1619 to June 21, 1620, is an account detailing receipts from head taxes paid on African blacks arriving at the that port. During that year, six slavers arrived at Vera Cruz. All had loaded their human cargo at Sao Paulo de Loanda, the capital of Portuguese Angola. Out of some 2,000 blacks they had taken aboard in Africa, 1,161 were delivered alive in Vera Cruz. The losses were caused not only by the rigors of the Middle Passage but also by shipwreck and in one case by corsair attack.

Engel Sluiter,
New Light on the "20 and Odd Negroes" Arriving in Virginia in 1619[24]

Colonel, John Rolfe, widower of Pocahontas, updated the Virginia Company in England on the colonists' activities in Jamestown. In his letter to Sir Edwin Sandys, Rolfe only briefly and casually mentions the arrival of "20 and odd Negroes" in Jamestown, presumably from the West Indies (the Caribbean). John Rolfe was purposefully vague with the owners of the Virginia Company because he knew that if the colonists engaged in any form of piracy, their exclusive Virginia Charter to colonize America would be in jeopardy. Trading in slaves could have jeopardized their charter as well.

Figure 7: The arrival of 20 and Odd Negroes

"About the latter end of August, a Dutch man of War of the burden of a 160 tunes arrived at Point-Comfort, the Commando name Capt. Jope, his Pilot for the West Indies one Mr. Maramaduke an Englishman. They met with the Trier in the West Indeyes, and yes determined to hold consort ship hitherward, but in their passage lost one the other. He brought not anything but 20 and odd Negroes, with the Governor and Cape Marchant bought for victualle (whereof he was in grate need as he pretended) at the best and easiest rate they could. He had a lardge and ample Comyssioin from his Excellency to range and to take purchase in the West Indes."

John Rolfe, January 1620, *The Records of the Virginia Company of London*
Susan Myra Kingsbury[25]

Since the institution of slavery was an integral part of African life, the Angolans quickly understood their circumstances in America - after all, they were now the victims of an institution that they themselves had practiced in their own kingdom. But the Angolans were not afraid of hard work. They demonstrated to the English that they were people of strong character, who in their prior lives had managed large commercial and agricultural projects and groups of people. Because of the colonial Portuguese government, the Angolans had familiarity with European farming tools and knew how to use them effectively. The original English colonists in Jamestown could not have had a better partner in the development of the English colony than their captured Angolan indentured servants.

Figure 8: The Africans Brought Specialized Skills and Knowledge

"Many of the Africans who came to Virginia during the seventeenth century brought along a specialized knowledge of agriculture and other practical skills that made a significant contribution to the developing colony. Of immediate use was their familiarity with the cultivation of tobacco".

Martha W. McCartney, *Jamestown People to 1800, Landowners, Public Officials, Minorities and Native Leaders*[26]

From 1619 to 1630, the Angolans were concentrated in the southeast Virginia counties of Southampton, York, James City and Charles City. The earliest Angolans labored on the farms and in the fields as indentured servants alongside indentured Europeans and Native Americans. In England, an indentured servitude was tantamount to an apprentice, where a young man could learn a trade from a tradesman and would commit a period of time under his apprentice in an indentured arrangement. In the early days of the colonies, African men worked until they paid off their indenture, and then were considered free People of Color. The first documented Free Person of Color was John Gowen whose last name was recorded as Graweere or Geaween in historical documents. John Gowen was purchased by William Evans in 1619. Given that William Evans was with John Rolfe to greet the pirate Ships *Treasurer* and *White Lion*, evidence suggests John Gowen was one of the first African slaves to be purchased in colonial America.

John Rolfe and William Evans may have had self-serving motives when they met the Ship *Treasurer*. Colonel Rolfe was very familiar with the captain and crew of the Ship *Treasurer*, for that was the ship that once held captive Pocahontas, the beloved daughter of Chief Powhatan. After Colonel Rolfe and Pocahontas married, the *Treasurer* also was the ship that transported them and their infant son to England in 1615. Rolfe and Evans had much to gain if they could acquire able - bodied workers off the ship - most importantly, land rights. England, through its London Company, wanted to rapidly build its American colony, and one of the quickest ways to achieve this was to send men, women and children to the colony. For every indenture contract that could be proved, the owner of the indenture was awarded land grants or patents for "headrights," which consisted of a 50-acre tract of land. By treating the first

Africans to arrive in the Jamestown colony as indentured servants rather than slaves, William Evans acquired a 50-acre tract of land for free.

On March 31, 1641, John Geaween, servant to William Evans, was granted his freedom by the Virginia Court in an unusual twist of events. [27] In 1640, a year before he was freed, there were only fifty Africans in the Jamestown colony, and this was the first record of any of them being freed in America.

Figure 9: William Evans purchases the Angolan, John Geaween

"In 1625, six years after the brief meeting with the *Treasurer* at Point Comfort, land documents reveal that [William Evans] had an African named John Graweere working on his thousand-acre plantation, which suggests that Graweere arrived in 1619 either on the *Treasurer* or the *White Lion*, since no other ship brought a large group of Africans before that time."

Tim Hashaw, *The Birth of Black America, the First African Americans and the Pursuit of Freedom at Jamestown*[28]

William Evans was considered to be one of the wealthiest men in colonial Jamestown. He owned the largest plantation on the Tappahannah River and lived next door to John Rolfe, the cultivator of the colony's first successful tobacco crop and the widower of Pocahontas. On the other side of the Evans' land was the plantation of Robert Shepherd, a Jamestown legislator. John Gowen had a son with Margaret Cornish, a young slave girl on the Shepherd plantation. While there is no known record of a marriage between the two, it is presumed that John Geaween and Margaret Cornish considered themselves married.

Before it was outlawed in 1705, some Jamestown slaveholders allowed Africans to raise cattle and crops of their own in order to earn money to purchase their freedom from indentureship. William Evans allowed John Geaween to work on the side to raise the necessary funds to free himself, - and his wife, and their son, Mahill Gowen, from Margaret Cornish's master, Robert Shepherd.

However, Margaret Cornish became pregnant again and when her second child was born, it was apparent that the child was interracial, and could not have been the biological son of her African husband,

John Gowen. As this was highly frowned upon in socially conservative colonial Jamestown, an investigation was launched.

It was soon determined that Margaret had not been sexually assaulted as may have been presumed, but was having an extramarital affair. Once the illicit affair became public, Margaret Cornish and prominent Englishman Robert Sweet, the father of Margaret's second child, were brought before the James City Court. On October 17, 1640, the two were found guilty on the charges of adultery.

Any case of adultery was cause for scandal in colonial Jamestown, but interracial adultery was an unheard of occurrence. Shamed by his wife's much-publicized affair, John Gowen went to court to obtain the immediate custody over his son, Mahill Gowen. Five months after the affair, John sold all of his livestock and worldly possessions, and went to his former wife's master, Robert Shepherd, to gain sole custody of Mahill and purchase his freedom.

Figure 10: John Geaween's wife becomes pregnant with another's child

"Whereas Robert Sweet hath begotten with a child a Negro woman servant belonging unto Lt. Sheppard, the court hath therefore ordered that the said Negro woman shall be whipped at the whipping post and the said Sweet shall tomorrow in the forenoon do public penance for his offence at James City church in the time of divine service according to the laws of England in that case provided."

Council and General Court Records,
The Virginia Magazine of History and Biography[29]

The torrid affair of Margaret Cornish and John Gowen's desperate efforts to free his son have become the legacy of these two ancestors of Marie Howell Cornwall and her 8th generation great-grandfather, Mahill Gowen of Jamestown, Virginia.[30] Despite the public rebuke, Margaret Cornish continued her relationship with Robert Sweet. They had four additional children, half siblings to Mahill Gowen. Although Margaret had more children with Robert Sweet, there are no public records to indicate that he ever moved forward to provide the necessary funds to purchase Margaret's freedom.

Figure 11: James City Courts free Mahill Gowen

"Whereas it appeareth to the court that John Gowen, being a negro servant unto William Evans, was permitted by his said master to keep hogs and make the best benefit thereof to himself provided that the said Evans might have half the increase which was accordingly rendered unto him by the said negro and the other half reserved for his own benefit: And whereas the said negro having a young child of a negro woman belonging to Lt. Robert Sheppard which he desired should be made a Christian and be taught and exercised in the church of England, by reason whereof he, the said negro did for his said child purchase its freedom of Lt. Sheppard with the good liking and consent of Tho: Gooman's overseer as by the deposition of the said Sheppard and Evans appeareth, the court hath therefore ordered that the child shall be free from the said Evans or his assigns and to be and remain at the disposing and education of the said Gowen and the child's godfather who undertaketh to see it brought up in the Christian religion as aforesaid."

Council and Jamestown General Court Records,
The Virginia Magazine of History and Biography[31]

When the James City courts freed five-year-old Mahill Gowen, they also freed his father John Gowen, making them one of the first, if not the first, Africans to be freed in America. However, John Gowen was unable to provide for his child full time, so Mahill Gowen was placed in the custody of Captain Christopher Stafford until his eighteenth birthday.

Captain Stafford passed away before Mahill came of age, so his indenture was placed with Stafford's sister, Anne Barnhouse. When Mahill turned eighteen, Anne Barnhouse released him - and his infant son, William Gowen, born by Anne Barnhouse's Slave Prosta Mnu - from servitude.

William Gowen's family line is especially difficult to research as the root for a vast number of different branches of the Gowen family tree. The spelling of the family surname changes often, and each generation tends to use the same first names.

Different spellings of the Gowen family names include Ganes, Gawn, Goen, Goin, Goyne, Gowan and Gowing, depending on how the name was pronounced in various regions of colonial Virginia and North Carolina.

Figure 12: Mihill (Mahill) Gowen and his son William set free

"Be it known that I Anne Barnhouse of Martins Hundred, Virginia widow for divers good causes and consideration hereunto hath given unto Mihill Gowen Negro he being at this time servant unto Robert Stafford a male child borne the 25 August 1655 of the body of my Negro Prosta being baptized by Mr. Edward Johnson 2 September 1655 and named William and I the said Amy Barnhouse doth bind myself, my heirs and Executive Administrators never to trouble or molest the said Mihill Gowen or his son William or demand any service of he said Mihill or his said son William".

York County, Virginia Wills, Deeds and Orders[32]

Upon his release from servitude, Mahill Gowen, now known as Michael, and his son William Gowen moved to James City County, and received a grant of land for forty acres in 1668.[33] Michael Gowen subsequently married an English woman and had three additional sons, Daniel, Christopher and Thomas.

Figure 13: Mihill Gowen receives Land Deed

"Mihill Gowree, 30 or 40 acres situated in Merchants Hundred Parish in James City County, formerly belonging to John James, deed, and by him purchased of Captain Richard Barnhouse and lately bound to escheat (forfeiture and reversion to the crown) and by a jury for said county under hand and seal of Colonel Miles Carey, 20 December 1666 and now granted to said Gowree 8 February 1668."

York County, Virginia Wills, Deeds and Orders[34]

Michael Gowen's son, William Gowen was born in August, 1655, by a young slave girl named Prossa Mnu, a servant to Anne Barnhouse. The following month, on September 25, the infant son was baptized by Mr. Edward Johnson.[35]

William Gowen "received a grant for land in Charles City County on April 20, 1687."[36] William's son Edward was born about 1681, presumably in Charles County, Virginia, where his father had acquired his land grant. Very little information is known about Edward Gowen, and what is known was almost lost to history because Gloucester County, where Edward eventually lived, suffered the tragic loss of all of its court records just before 1865 in Richmond, Virginia. In 1936, over a ten-year period based on available documents, the records were reconstructed and recorded.

Figure 14: Challenges of Researching Colonial Documents

"In the tidewater section of Virginia, where we speak of the 'lost counties as those having lost their county records, Gloucester is known as doubly 'lost', having twice experienced the loss by fire of all public records. This lamentable destruction first occurred in 1820, when all the history of her colonial past, as recorded in the Clerk's Office, was burned. From copies of old deeds and wills still to be found in a few private homes ... following the 1820 fire, many Gloucester residents took their family records and had them rerecorded by the county clerk. All of these re-recordings were again lost in 1865 at the burning of Richmond, where the re-recorded records were taken for safe keeping during the Civil War".

Polly Cary Mason, Records of Colonial Gloucester County Virginia[37]

The 1704 Gloucester Rent Roll lists Edward Gowing in Kingston Parish with 100 acres of land.[38] Gloucester County located in the Chesapeake Bay region is on the north side of the James River in close proximately to where Edward Gowing was born. It is presumed that since Edward, heretofore referred to as Edward "1" for clarity's sake because of the multiple generations with the same first name, was only renting his land. He eventually moved to Charles City, Virginia, around the time that his son Edward Gowen II was born - around 1700, presumably in Gloucester County, Virginia, where his father rented land.

The Gowen family was fortunate in that they were able to acquire land permits, buy land and rent sizable tracts of land during a period when the African slave trade was escalating. For a brief period in history, Africans and other indentured servants were treated equally, able to live freely with their colonial neighbors once their indentureship had ended.

The first African arrivals were looked upon as indentured servants, not as chattel property. They were able to buy their freedom after a work period of seven to ten years. The first Africans in the colonies, the Angolans, were able to fundamentally read and write, and practiced Catholicism, all of which made it difficult for the religious Englishmen to treat them as slaves. Without the indentured servants, specifically the Angolans and their knowledge of farming, the Jamestown colony might have failed.

Due to their tremendous service to the colony, ensuring the colonists' survival, the first Angolans were accepted into mainstream colonial culture. The Angolans intermarried with each other, white Europeans, and Native Americans - and their progeny became less African in appearance, and more American in attitude and expectations. However, as more Africans arrived in greater numbers, the English colonists began to look at future African generations not as worthy neighbors and partners, but as subservient workers.

Although the early generations of indentured and free Angolans worked side-by-side with their European neighbors, memories faded. Eventually, the status and good will towards the original Angolans deteriorated in the eyes of the growing European population in the Virginia colony. Seventy years after the Angolans were first accepted into the colony, the European colonists took specific and deliberate steps to restrict the freedom and civil liberties of their once trusted allies and their offspring.

Racial tensions surfaced and prejudices grew, and the search for affordable and abundant land opportunities pushed the free Angolan clans further and further south and west into the frontier lands. As they moved into the isolated frontier, their descendants continued to intermarry with available local Native Americans and unprejudiced frontier whites.[39] With these marriages, the Angolans, who culturally believed that a sign of wealth was to own vast tracks of land and to have large families, began to rapidly repopulate themselves as Free People of Color and acquired more and more frontier land.

Despite the emerging tension between the African and European cultures, Americans of African descent were crucial to the initial development and subsequent success of the European colonies in America. "To claim that the colonies would not have survived without slaves would be a distortion, but there can be no doubt that the development was significantly speeded by their labor. They provided the basic work force that transformed shaky outposts into areas of permanent settlement."[40]

1.4   Joshia Melton from Southampton County, Virginia

Another historic colonial family of the Virginia tidewater area was the family of Margaret Melton Murphy, who is descended from a once-powerful, Algonquian-speaking Native American tribe.[41]

The Chickahominy were affiliated with Chief Powhatan and lived on the James River in the area of present day Charles County. The Chickahominy people intermarried first with the original English settlers of Jamestown, and then, as the settlers migrated into the Native Americans' tribal lands, their sons and daughters also married people of English extraction. Likewise, as Africans were introduced into the frontier by the English, the Chickahominy people also intermarried with the Angolans.

The first documented member of Margaret Melton's family was her 3rd generation great grandfather Joshia Milton, who was born in 1742, in Southampton County, Virginia, originally part of the Isle of Wright County.[42] Little is known of Joshia's parents, but according to public records, his older brother Elisha Melton (Milton) was born in 1740, also in Southampton, Virginia. The preponderance of evidence suggests that Joshua and Elisha were the grandsons of Robert Melton and his wife, Mary Farar from Kent County - not far from the tribal lands of the Chickahominy and north of Isle of Wright County.

Robert Melton was the great-grandson of William Melton who was born in Lancashire, England in 1617. According to the Land Patents of Virginia, in 1638, William Melton came to America as a bonded servant to Colonel Edward Hill of Charles City, Charles County, Virginia, as his headright.[43]

Elisha Melton's son James enlisted in the Revolutionary War, and reportedly died at Boston's Bunker Hill, Massachusetts, from smallpox.[44] In a court deposition, his sister Ann stated that her brother, a free man of color, enlisted in the Revolution in Southampton County, served under Captain James Gray, and died of smallpox at Bunker Hill, which is located in Boston's Charlestown section of the city.[45] Coincidentally, some 200 years later, Margaret Melton Murphy - who moved to Boston to be with her two brothers and her sister, along with her high school friend, Estelle Dupree - often remarked that her family had felt some kind of bond with the city. Margaret Melton knew that she had a distant uncle who was in the Revolutionary War and that he had died somewhere in Massachusetts. Little did she know that less than ten miles away from her home in Boston's Roxbury neighborhood, her cousin, James Melton (three times removed), had died and was buried at Bunker Hill, some 725 miles from where both he and Margaret were born and lived in North Carolina, two centuries apart.

As one of the tri-racial families that originated in colonial Virginia, the Melton family descended from European men and women who eventually intermarried with African American and Native Americans, and their families formed communities of free interracial people.[46] These families were pioneers and they were the epitome of the American spirit. They were a strong, rugged people who were the first to settle in territories never explored by non-Native Americans.

As they moved into tribal areas, they eventually befriended and married within the local Native American villages. They married partners who helped them till the field, feed the animals and raise the children. These pioneering ancestors had the backbone to turn thick forests into vibrant communities. They did not concern themselves with the racial pedigree of their spouses or their neighbors. These were America's true pioneers. However, as they cleared their fields and their lands, and progressively moved westward, racial tensions developed with the new immigrants from Europe who followed them.

The Meltons and other tri-racial families taught their children the customs of and how to trade with their Native American cousins, how to respect and honor their African ancestors, and how to socialize with their European relatives. When these families came to town to shop and trade, they walked proudly down the streets with their multiracial children and grandchildren. As descendants of Africans who were taken against their will from Africa, of Native Americans whose land was taken away from them often by force, and of indentured Europeans who left their homeland because they were poor, these families embraced and practiced the concept of equality for all. Unfortunately, the Meltons - along with other early triracial families - eventually became the target of new racial laws in colonial Virginia.

The Meltons took their olive to copper skin color from their African and Native American ancestors, and they inherited their thin facial features and blue, green, or light brown eye color from their European ancestors. Some family members inherited their black, straight hair from their Native American heritage, while some got their curly hair from their African American heritage. The Meltons often joked that the texture and color of their hair came from any combination of any of the three heritages, and they were not sure which. The Meltons were truly reflective of a family of tri-racial heritage.

The Virginia Meltons were part of a rapidly growing population of tri-racial Americans in the south, who were neither slaves nor indentured servants. They became the original ancestors to a significant portion of the American populace prior to the large European migration to the colonies - and other areas of what would become the United States - in subsequent centuries.

The Melton families married in and were interrelated to the Ballard, Bunch, Chavis, Gibson, Gowen, Hall, Hillard, Howell, and Jones families. They owned and farmed their land. They were merchants, sailors, and frontiersmen. Because of their tri-racial color and heritage, they were able to expand into traditional Native American villages for shelter during times of hostility, and facilitated trade and commerce between the European colonists and the Native Americans. Over the next one hundred years, the Melton and other multiracial families homogenized in communities that they founded across the new frontiers in the southern and in the mid-Atlantic colonies, particularly in Maryland, Virginia, North and South Carolina, and eventually Tennessee and Kentucky.

As these triracial and Free People of Color expanded in numbers and influence, racial attitudes towards them changed resulting in the construction of laws that restricted their freedoms and their activities. As each generation mingled with other racial groups, the interracial heritage of the Melton family came to represent the exact "problem" about which the colonial Virginia and southern governments were concerned. Starting in Virginia, each southern colony took gradual but deliberate measures to restrict almost every activity of the Free People of Color, including what happened in their bedrooms.

In April 1691, the Virginia House of Burgesses passed a law forbidding a white man or woman from marrying "a negro, mulatto or Indian man or woman, bond or free." Those that did were banished from the "country" (colony). The law further stipulated that any white women having a "bastard" child by a Negro or mulatto had to pay fifteen pounds sterling, and that the child was to be bound to servitude by churchwardens until 30 years of age.[47]

Figure 15: An Act for Suppressing Outlying Slaves

Any "English or other white man or woman being free shall intermarry with a negroe, mulatto, or Indian man or woman bond or free shall within three months after such marriage be banished and removed from this dominion forever … if any English woman being free shall have a bastard child by any negro or mulatto, she pay the sume of fifteen pounds sterling, within one moneth after such bastard child shall be born, to the Church wardens of the parish where she shall be delivered of such child … and that such bastard child be bound out as a servant by the said Church wardens until he or she shall attain the age of thirty yeares, and in case such English woman that shall have such bastard child be a servant, she shall be sold by the said church wardens."

William W. Hening, *The Statutes at Large: Being a Collection of All the Laws of Virginia, from the First Session of the Legislature.*[48]

To make matters worse, in the same year, Virginia passed a law prohibiting whites from freeing any blacks or mulattoes without paying to have them physically removed from the colony, essentially stemming the tide of this rapidly growing, multiracial population of Free People of Color.

Even though southern colonial governments took severe measures if a white person married a mulatto, had a mulatto child, or tried to free a mulatto, there was no legal definition of "mulatto." This meant that severe actions and penalties were taken against a large variety of families and individuals, with no clear legal precedent. The laws were not only punitive, they were arbitrarily applied, and it was not until 1705 that a formal definition was provided. The definition was designed to permanently label any man or woman, no matter what their station in life, as a person who was not of pure blood - or, at least, not pure European blood.

Figure 16: Who Shall be Deemed Mulattoes.

"That the child of an Indian and the child, grandchild, or great grandchild, of a negro shall be deemed, accounted, held and taken to be a mulatto."

William W. Hening, *The Statutes at Large: Being a Collection of All the Laws of Virginia, from the First Session of the Legislature.*[49]

The law's intent was to ensure that multiracial families didn't try to conceal their mixed African and Native American racial heritage in order to pass for white and marry into the general population.

This, unfortunately, was the world that Joshia and Elisha Melton's family lived in, and the environment in which they raised their children and grandchildren. The Melton brothers and their progeny were defined and recorded in probate records, tax lists and in census records as mulattoes, a term that had a distinct impact on their lives.

The physical characteristics of the Melton family certainly set them apart from the greater community at large, particularly as they began to marry and repopulate themselves in larger numbers. The Melton family, much like many other triracial families, saw themselves as a bridge between the European and African American communities.

Whether the perception was met with the reality, the newly restricted multiracial families saw themselves as different from the newly arriving enslaved Africans, who were only a generation or two removed from the tribal conflicts in Africa. They also saw themselves as different from the newly arriving indentured European servants, despite being only a generation or two removed from the economically depressed ghettos and religious conflicts of Europe. However, they did see themselves as the convergence of the best of the cultures that Africans and Europeans brought to America, and better as a people because of it.

The Melton family and other Free People of Color were the epitome of the American pioneering spirit. As the laws of Virginia were changed specifically to restrict their civil rights, these Free People of Color took responsibility for their lives and for the future of their children. They constantly took risks by uprooting and relocating their families to undeveloped areas of the frontier, doing whatever it took to maintain their freedom.

Each time the Free People of Color evolved and improved their conditions, new laws were constructed to hold them back and restrict their success. Being a resourceful group, Free People of Color found ways to circumvent those laws, specifically by leaving the state of Virginia. However, as more and more Free People of Color left migrated to North Carolina, the North Carolina Assembly instituted its own racially charged laws, in an attempt to prevent the prosperity of the Free People of Color; the idea being there was no better place to hit them than in the pocketbook.

In 1715, the North Carolina General Assembly defined tithables (a taxable person) as "every white person male of the age of sixteen years and upwards, and all Negroes, Mulattoes, Mustees, male or female, and all persons of mixt blood to the fourth generation male and female of the age of twelve years and upwards shall be tithables."[50]

This meant that in any white household, only the white male was taxed, whereas in a black or mulatto Mulatto household, every family member, male or female, young or old, was taxed. Apparently, the white colonial settlers in North Carolina did not think the law was strong enough. In 1749, the North Carolina General Assembly amended the law to include "all mulattoes, mustees, quadroons and all persons of mixed blood to the fourth generation over the age of 12."

Additionally, to punish any white man who dared to marry a mixed blood wife, he had to pay a tax on his wife and any children over the age of 12.

Figure 17: A tax on interracial marriages and cohabitation

"all and every White Person, Male, of the Age of Sixteen Years, and upwards, all Negroes, Mulattoes, Mustees Male or Female, and all Persons of Mixt Blood to the Fourth Generation, of the Age of Twelve Years, and upwards, and all white Persons intermarrying with any Negro, mulatto, or Mustee, or other Person of mixt Blood, while to intermarry with no other Person or Persons whatsoever, shall be deemed Taxables..."

North Carolina General Statues.[51]

The North Carolina law exempted any white woman from being taxable and any white male under the age of sixteen from paying the poll tax. However, all mixed race women over the age of 12 were taxable, resulting in a huge and disparate financial burden on those families.

However, Free People of Color, including the Meltons, who were intelligent and knew how the system worked, manipulated it to their advantage. Since the laws in North Carolina were slightly different than in Virginia, the Melton men and other Free Men of Color were able to list their wives and children as white, so as to not to have to pay the tax on them. As more restrictive laws were passed, the Free People of Color exercised several forms of civil disobedience. For instance they refused to pay what they saw as a marriage tax, on the grounds that their wives and daughters were not property and were white.

These early progressive acts of civil disobedience would influence the thinking of future European colonists on issues surrounding taxation and representation, and individual human rights. The irony of this struggle was that from the early to mid-1700s, many of the wealthy southern land barons that supported the racial laws became some of Virginia's strongest political activists for independence and the issue of taxes imposed upon them.

These activists included George Mason, Thomas Jefferson, James Madison and George Washington, each from the state of Virginia. While defining their arguments for independence from England, they utilized many of the same principles articulated by the Free People of Color in their own states.

The Meltons married different racial groups, and they also married into other multiracial families, including the large Chavis family. According to African-American historian and researcher, Paul Heinegg, the Chavis family also originated in Virginia before 1650 and was listed as free, mixed-raced people in Amelia, Brunswick, Charles City, Henrico, James City, Prince George, and Surry counties in Virginia, as well as Edgecombe, Granville and Bladen counties in North Carolina. The earliest known member of the Chavis family, Elizabeth Chavis, petitioned the General Court of Virginia to release her son Gibson from an unlawful indenture on March 28, 1672. No race is indicated in the court record, but Gibson's descendants were mixed-race.[52]

The Meltons and other Free People of Color witnessed growing numbers of European immigrants arriving each month. European economies suffered from constant recessions and inflation during the seventeenth and eighteenth centuries, and European cities were overrun with the unemployed, the sick, and the hopeless. To the working poor in Europe, the opportunity to go to America, the possibility of land ownership, and improving the conditions of their lives and their families' lives weighed heavily on the decisions to enter into a legal contract for up to seven years of servitude in exchange for passage to America.

In order to grow the colonies and to take advantage of the many natural resources found in the New World, indentured servitude became a major source of inexpensive and reliable labor for the British colonies. Reportedly, more than half of all immigrants to the British colonies in North America during this period consisted of indentured servants, primarily from the British Isles of England, Ireland and Scotland. Many other indentured servants came from Germany.

Servitude for Americans of European ancestry in the north differed from servitude in the south. Indentured servants in the northern colonies lived mainly in the cities and towns of their contract holders, and they generally participated in the community as a whole. Indentured servants in the south primarily lived and worked on rural farms, generally lived in the same household of their contract holders, and had little contact or social interaction with the greater community. But regardless of location, the role of the European indentured servant in the early development of America was significant in building the country's economic foundation. The indentured Europeans served as a major source of early population in America, and they provided a stable work force in the areas of demographic expansion.

With large numbers of European immigrants arriving each month, the Meltons and Free People of Color experienced increasing hostility directed at them by the European colonists. Virginia granted more land patents than the other southern colonies, and cheap labor was needed to clear the forest and cultivate the land. The Free People of Color also noticed that as the number of large agricultural plantations increased, so did the number of African slaves doing the backbreaking work for their white masters. As the white community continued to grow in numbers and influence, more and more punitive laws were enacted by the government to restrict the freedom of Americans of African descent. These laws, however, did not apply to European indentured servants - unless they married outside their race.

The new racial laws not only infringed on the rights and lives of the Melton family, but also the ever-increasing population of African slaves. The laws were laced with racially charged language directed at all African and mixed race Americans. The cooperation of the original Africans and Europeans that lived in Jamestown was now forgotten by both the Free People of Color and the European colonists. The spirit of racial inclusion and diversity had come to an end.

The Meltons and other Free People of Color were constantly walking a fine line between several worlds and cultures. By the late 1600s, they realized that within a few short years, the strong ties between their different racial communities had been severed. White Virginians no longer looked at the Free People of Color as partners in building colonial governments and communities. The newly arrived African slaves looked at Free People of Color with puzzlement and often held them in disdain, jealous of their freedom. The Native Americans began to think that this group of free, multiracial people wanted to intermarry in order to acquire their shrinking Native tribal lands, causing animosity between the Free People of Color and their former Native American friends and extended family members. With the dawn of the early eighteenth century, multiracial Americans began to see a very different country - politically, socially, economically, religiously, and racially.

The families of Marie Howell Cornwall and Margaret Melton Murphy intersected in colonial Virginia long before the marriage of Joan Cornwall and Bob Murphy. As their colonial families migrated from Jamestown and York County, Virginia, each family took a different path through Virginia into North Carolina. If the descendants of Free People of Color were to remain free, they had limited options in terms of with whom they could marry and have children. Over the next four to five hundred years, the Howell and Melton families would cross paths with and marry into other family lines, including the Chavis and Gowen families.

1.5   Elizabeth Owell of York County, Virginia

The family of Elizabeth Owell, another early Angolan family, first appeared in the 1650s in early colonial Virginia records.

[53] Elizabeth Owell, was a servant to Mrs. Mary Timson in York County, Virginia, and was presented to the York County court and punished in 1695 for having "a bastard child by a 'Negro' for which she had to serve her mistress an additional two years of her indentured servitude."[54]

Figure 18: Virginia's African Population

Year	African Population	Year	African Population
1619	32	1640	50
1624	22	1649	300
		1671	2000

Formed in 1634, York County was one of the original counties in colonial Virginia, and included the historic area of Jamestown. At the time, the pool of potential African fathers was limited to fewer than a hundred men, each brought to Virginia from the area of Angola. While there is no documentation as to whom the father of Elizabeth Owell's daughter was, the evidence suggests that the father was one of the original Angolans brought to Jamestown. The veracity of the Howell family having lived in colonial Virginia is based on a number of 1650 colonial records, and that the family descended from early Angolans is based on the actual number of Africans in Virginia during the time period in which the family first appears in public records.[55]

Sir William Berkley, Virginia's colonial governor, provided insight and documentation as to the total number of residents in colonial Virginia, including the total number of indentured servants and the number of Africans. Sir Berkeley responded to a series of questions submitted to him by the British Lord Commissioners of Foreign Plantations as to the legal status and the racial composition of the colony. As part of his response in 1670, Sir Berkley stated that colonial Virginia had a total population of 40,000 inhabitants, of which 2,000 were slaves and 6,000 were indentured servants.[56]

Figure 19: Responses to Enquires to the Governor of Virginia

Question 15	"What number of planters, servants and slaves …?"
Answer:	"We suppose, and I am sure we do not much miscount, that there is in Virginia above forty thousand persons, men, women and children, and of which there are two thousand *black slaves*, six thousand *Christian servants* …"
Question 16	"What number of English, Scots or Irish have for these seven years past [1664–70] come yearly to plant and inhabite within your government; as also what *blacks* or *slaves* have been brought in within the said time?"
Answer:	"Yearly, we suppose there comes in, of servants, above fifteen hundred, of which most are English, few Scotch, and fewer Irish, and not above two or three ships of negroes in seven years."

William W. Hening, *The Statutes at Large: Being a Collection of All the Laws of Virginia, Colonial Extracts, in the Year 1670.*[57]

The earliest Africans arrivals in colonial Virginia lived as indentured servants, like other European indentured servants during the same period. Initially, all of them served their masters for the same amount of time, and were eventually awarded their freedom. However, in 1670, the status of any new Africans brought to colonial Virginia was clearly defined, and the formal institution of slavery was now formally established.

Figure 20: An Act for What Tyme Indians to Serve

"That all servants not being Christians imported into this colony by shipping shall be slaves for their lives; but what shall come by land shall serve, if boyes (sic) or girles (sic), until thirty yeares (sic) of age, if men or women twelve yeares (sic) and no longer."

William W. Hening, *The Statutes at Large: Being a Collection of All the Laws of Virginia, from the First Session of the Legislature.*[58]

It is plausible that Elizabeth Owell was an indentured African woman and not a slave, since her daughter, Judith Howell, and her descendants lived as a Free People of Color. However, since no race was listed in her 1695 court order, Elizabeth Owell may have been of European descent. In 1662, the Virginia House of Burgess passed a law transferring the legal status of the mother on to her children. This law, one of the earliest of the Virginia Slave Laws, passed before Judith Howell was born.

Figure 21: Negro Children to Serve According to the Condition of the Mother

> "all children bourne of negro women in this country shall be held bond or free only according to condition of mother, And that if any Christian shall commit fornication with a negro man or woman, hee or shee soe offending shall pay double the fines imposed by the former act."
>
> William W. Hening, *The Statutes at Large: Being a Collection of All the Laws of Virginia, from the First Session of the Legislature.*[59]

From the period of 1670 to 1690, the African population in Virginia exploded. The rapid growth of the African population in the earliest days of colonial Virginia was due to the repopulation of the Africans through interracial marriages and relationships. However, as time passed, the explosive growth was no longer the sole result of repopulation, but also due to the direct import of Africans from overseas.

1.6   Thomas and Rebecca Cornell from Essex, England

In today's complex world, where racial groups still struggle to find cultural ground, it is somewhat hard to understand how a well-established African American family can be descended from a prominent well-established European American family. However, Harold Cornwall, of Brockton, Massachusetts, is an African American descended from one of the original English colonial families from Massachusetts- by way of St. John, New Brunswick, Canada.

As a young child in the later part of the 18th century, Harold learned of distant ancestors who served in the Revolutionary War and had the name Cornwall. It was logical to assume that their family name could be a derivative of the name Cornwallis. At the time, many of Harold Cornwall's family thought they might be descendants of the British Lord General Charles Cornwallis, who was a significant player in American history. Lord Cornwallis was the commanding British General who fought the American colonists during the American Revolutionary War. As the architect of the failed British southern campaign, Cornwallis surrendered to American General George Washington in August 1781 after the Battle of Yorktown. As a child, Harold, as well as his siblings and cousins, were often teased about the name Cornwall, often called "Cornball" or "Stonewall." But the biggest insult was to be called "Cornwallis."

Although he was an African American, Harold Cornwall's European lineage is significant. His European ancestors were notable people from fifteenth- to seventeenth-century England. He was a direct descendant of Thomas Cornell and his wife Rebecca Briggs of Fairstead Manor in Essex, England.[60]

Thomas Cornell and Rebecca Briggs were descended from some of England's oldest recorded families. Thomas Cornell's family lineage dates back to 1460 to Terling, Essex, England, to Lawrence and Amy (Elroude) Cornwall.

Rebecca Briggs' lineage, at the time of this writing, continues to be debated in genealogical circles worldwide.[61] Her paternal great-grandparents were Edward Briggs (1526-1611) and his wife, Cecily More (1526-1615), according to records captured by Gertrude Elizabeth Guiteras in 1926.[62] Rebecca's great-grandmother's name, Cecily More has stirred profound historical and religious questions for genealogists.

Some genealogists proclaim that Rebecca Briggs' great-grandmother Cecily More was the granddaughter to Sir Thomas More, and other genealogists go so far as to assert that this particular Cecily More was the actual daughter of Sir Thomas More. The study of ancient genealogy is not a perfect science and in this particular case has resulted in a third group of genealogists that believe that Rebecca Briggs and her paternal great-grandmother, Cecily More, are of no direct relation to the Lord Chancellor Sir Thomas More.[63]

At the age of 17, Henry VIII ascended to the British monarchy upon the death of his unpopular father, King Henry VII, in 1509. Sir Thomas More became a trusted advisor and Lord Chancellor to King Henry VIII, who greatly admired Sir More's philosophies, particularly those expressed in his novel Utopia.[64] However, the King ultimately had Sir Thomas More executed because of a disagreement, and this action, in part, led to one of the most tumultuous periods in English history.

In order to solidify his position domestically, politically and internationally, after Henry VIII took the throne, the King immediately married Catherine of Argon, the daughter of the Catholic King

Ferdinand and Queen Isabella of Spain. Catherine only provided Henry with a daughter but was unable to bear him a son. So in 1529, Henry VIII requested that Pope Clement VII annul his marriage from the Catholic Catherine.

Henry VIII sent his trusted aide, Cardinal Thomas Wolsey, Lord Chancellor, to Rome to secure the annulment. When Cardinal Wolsey failed, he was stripped from his political office and was replaced by Sir Thomas More, as part of the English Reformation. When the Pope, head of the Catholic Church, refused to grant Henry VIII an annulment, the angry King seized the monasteries and other church properties, and established himself as the new head of the Church of England. The acts of King Henry VIII King Henry's acts "unleashed a century and a half of religious and political turmoil in England."[65]

Early in their association, Henry VIII had tremendous respect for Sir Thomas More and his popular political novel, *Utopia*, published in 1516, which described a fictional island in the Atlantic Ocean and the qualities of an ideal political, economic and religious community. The novel sparked intellectual thought and debate, and Sir Thomas More was credited with challenging the standard opinion of what an ideal country and world should be. The "fictional island" depicted a country like England as an ideal utopian society, capturing the best virtues of English life. There were elements of Thomas More's *Utopia* that Henry VIII and Anne Boleyn - his mistress who was reportedly sympathetic to the theological Protestant Reformation movement - found relevant and appropriate to the King's request for an annulment from the Catholic Catherine of Argon.

Upon Henry VIII's second marriage, to Anne Boleyn, the Parliament of England passed what has been referred to as the First Succession Act, forcing all of the King's subjects to swear an oath to the King as the Divine Ruler of the state and the church. The oath also stated that the King's unborn child - a daughter born to Anne Boleyn - would be the rightful successor to the throne. Anyone who refused to take this oath would be charged with treason.

After Pope Clement VII refused to approve the dissolution of the King's first marriage, many devout Catholics were appalled when the King arbitrarily annulled his marriage to Catherine of Argon and effectively declared his first daughter, Mary, an illegitimate child and thus ineligible as an heir to the throne. At the time, Sir Thomas More, Chancellor of England, was one of the most highly placed confidants of Henry VIII. But in May 1534, when requested to swear the oath to the King"s new royal succession, More refused. After being charged for acts under the newly enacted Acts of Treason, Sir Thomas More was swiftly, tried and condemned for defending the papacy and was beheaded for acts of treason on July 6, 1535.

To ensure that there would be no retaliation from sympathizers to Sir Thomas More, Henry VIII engaged in one of the most horrific and gruesome of medieval customs: He placed the severed head of Sir Thomas More on a stake at the gates of London Tower for all to see, and to understand what would happen to anyone else who dared the King.

Sir Thomas More was survived by his four children. After his beheading, Thomas More's daughter Margaret More Roper was able to retrieve his severed head before it was thrown into the River Thames, as was the custom.

King Henry VIII went on to marry four more times - after Anne Boleyn was falsely accused of treason, incest, and adultery, before being executed. During his reign, Henry VIII was considered a cruel and self-centered ruler, and he is remembered primarily for his six marriages, his quick temper and penchant for beheading those close to him, and the English Reformation. The acts of Henry VIII and the English Reformation movement created were the catalyst for religious and political protestors to embark on a migration to America in the mid-1660s.

While Harold Cornwall's Cecily More's ancestry will continue to be debated in genealogical circles as to whether or not she is the daughter, the granddaughter, a niece, or no relation at all to Sir Thomas More, she and her husband Sir Edward Briggs managed to live through one of the most tumultuous periods in England's history, raising their children in Norfolk County.

Cecily More and Sir Edward Briggs' great-granddaughter, Rebecca Briggs, married Thomas Cornell of London, England. Thomas Cornell was born on March 24, 1593 in Fairstead Manor, Essex, England, and died on February 8th 1655, at the Cornell Homestead in Portsmouth,

Newport County, Rhode Island.[66] Thomas and Rebecca Cornell were the first in their family to leave England and set sail for America. They were the 8th generation great-grandparents of Harold Cornwall of Brockton, Massachusetts.

The most definitive and compelling historical account of the Cornell family was a publication written by the Reverend John Cornell, one of their descendants.[67] Reverend Cornell meticulously recorded information on Thomas and Rebecca Cornell, chronicling the births, marriages, deaths, and the main events for the Cornells and their descendants, which spanned more than 250 years in England and America. Thomas and Rebecca Cornell came to America around 1638, eighteen years after the voyage of the Mayflower.

Although the Cornells did not come over on the Mayflower, they played a significant role in early colonial American history. In America, and possibly while they lived in England, the life of Thomas and Rebecca Cornell was deeply entwined with the life of Anne Maubury Hutchinson, who was the daughter of a radical Puritan minister named Frances Maubury, a vocal critic of the popular reign of Queen Elizabeth I (1533–1603), Henry VIII's second daughter. Following in the footsteps of her father, Queen Elizabeth I finally eradicated all Catholicism from England by eliminating her Catholic opposition and formally establishing the Protestant Church of England.

Queen Elizabeth maintained the rituals of the Catholic Church and installed herself as Supreme Governor of the church rather than the Pope.[68] Because of the Queen's actions, England was under constant military threats from their Catholic neighbors, Spain and France - both of which were supported by the Pope in Rome. Despite the initial spirit of unity and nationalism, a growing group of dissidents loyal to the Queen felt that she should have gone further by eliminating all vestiges of the Roman Catholic Church in England, including the religious rituals and pageantry of the Church.

As a young man, Reverend Frances Maubury, Anne Maubury Hutchinson's father, had strong conservative Protestant leanings and was constantly imprisoned for his vocal criticism of the Queen, as he thought she did not go far enough in her Protestant actions. He instilled these strong religious and political beliefs in his daughter.

As an adult, Anne, along with her husband William Hutchinson, became active participants in the Brownist movement. The movement, named after Robert Brown, consisted of Anglicans in England who opposed government interference in matters of the church, and wanted the monarchy out of church affairs. They were advocates of the congregational or local form of a small church control, rather than the structured central national control of church hierarchy managed by the monarchy.

As the Brownists attempted to set up local churches separate from the Church of England, movement leaders were exiled from England to the Netherlands. As Brownist followers continued to establish their separate churches, the English government began to impose stiff taxes on the Separatists for not attending the official Church of England. Queen Elizabeth considered any challenge to her authority over the church as an act of disloyalty to her and an act of treason to the government. The Separatist leaders, many of whom by now were exiled to the Netherlands, joined forces with the members of their congregation that remained in England to request a land permit to resettle in the New World. The Queen and her court could think of no better way to rid themselves of the Brownist problem than to let them sail as far away as possible. In 1620, the small band of Separatists sailed the vessel the Mayflower to America.

That first winter in America was hard on the religious Pilgrims, but the following years were encouraging to those of Plymouth Colony, and word got back to England and to other Separatists that religious freedom, clean air and land were bountiful in the New World. For those who remained in England, the religious conflict between the Church of England and the Separatist movement only worsened. When England's new monarch, King James I, took power, the Separatist opposition grew louder and in return the King threw more people in jail and imposed heavier fines and taxes. Anne and William Hutchinson, along with thousands of other middle to upper-class Englishmen, many the sons and daughters of Britain's nobility, and members of the mercantile class, decided to leave England before they lost their fortunes to the rising taxes or were imprisoned for their conservative Protestant views.

It is not clear whether or not Thomas and Rebecca Cornell personally knew Anne and William Hutchinson while in England, but two years after the Hutchinson's and their eight children left for America, the Cornells sailed for America in 1638. As with many other English settlers, the Cornells came to America with the clear objective of escaping the religious and political turmoil in England, and in the hopes of acquiring land permits. According to public records, Thomas Cornell first purchased property in the city of Boston, where he reportedly was an innkeeper, and sold wine and other strong beverages.[69]

Anne Hutchinson's arrival in Boston was met with religious and political controversy. Hutchinson continued with her activism, and split the city's establishment into two separate camps. Boston's political and religious establishment intentionally wanted to leave behind the rancor of the religious and political turmoil in England, but now Anne Hutchinson had brought these same divisive issues to the American shores.

Having learned the lessons of the Bible at an early age, Anne held weekly lessons for the women of Boston. Because of Anne's "hypnotic speaking ability," her eloquence, and her ability to interpret scriptures, her sermons soon included not just the local women but also their husbands.[70] Immediately upon her arrival, she challenged the rigid autocratic authority in Boston, by articulating and constantly reminding her neighbors of the reasons why many left England to come to America - the quest for religious freedom.

A small but growing band of dissenting Bostonians began to question the religious authority of the city's Puritan leaders. As the articulate and liberal-leaning Hutchinson began to question the religious teachings in the city, she encountered more and more disfavor from the political and religious leaders of Boston. She became a vocal critic of the establishment, supporting the rights of women, challenging the treatment of the local Native Americans, and daring to question the origins of Man. One of Anne Hutchinson's strongest supporters was John Briggs, brother-in-law to Thomas Cornell, and the brother of Thomas' wife Rebecca.

Because of her seemingly radical biblical teachings, Anne Hutchinson was soon labeled a heretic by Boston's conservative religious leaders. At trial, Hutchinson was found guilty and sentenced to spend time in jail. After her sentence, she was excommunicated from the Massachusetts Bay Colony. She resettled in an area of Rhode Island now known as Newport. Once Anne Hutchinson and her followers, including the Reverend Roger Williams, settled in Rhode Island, John Briggs persuaded Thomas Cornell and his family to resettle in the area as well. Shortly after arriving in Rhode Island, in 1642, Anne Hutchinson, along with John Briggs and Thomas Cornell, and a band of thirty-five other families, were given permission by the Dutch government in New Amsterdam to settle outside of the city-limits.

As Anne Hutchinson and her band of nonconformists began to develop the land in an area known today as Westchester, New York a serious war broke out between the settlers and the local Native American Siwanoys, a tribe of the Algonquian nation. When the Dutch governor tried to impose a tax on the Siwanoys and they refused, the governor decided to attack the various tribal communities and forcibly removed the Siwanoys from their land.[71]

In 1643, the Reverend Roger Williams sailed to England to obtain a petition to combine several townships in Rhode Island and make it a colony independent from the Massachusetts Bay Colony. The charter also provided that the residents of the Providence Plantation, as it was called, were free from religious persecution and free to practice their religious beliefs. This clause eventually served as the foundation for the First Amendment to the United States Constitution in 1789.[72]

Shortly after Reverend Williams returned from England, the Siwanoys launched a swift and brutal retaliatory attack on the European settlers, killing Anne Hutchinson, most of her neighbors, and all of her family, except her youngest daughter, Susan – who was captured by Siwanoy warriors and brought back to live amongst the tribe. She "spent eight or nine years with the Siwanoys and reportedly left the tribe reluctantly."[73]

The remaining settlers, including Roger Williams and Thomas Cornell and their families, fled to the city limits of New Amsterdam. The brutality of the attack caused Thomas and his family to retreat back to the safety of Rhode Island, and the family settled in Portsmouth, where they remained for a number of years. Ten years later, when peace was restored in New Amsterdam between the Dutch and the Siwanoys, the Cornells returned and settled in the area of Westchester County still known today as Cornell's Neck. But as fate would have it, after the family developed the land, another Native American and European war broke out, and for the second time, Thomas Cornell and his family fled to Rhode Island, where Thomas was eventually buried.

As Thomas and Rebecca moved back and forth, between Boston, Portsmouth, Rhode Island and New Amsterdam, their children grew up and got married. These children began their own families, establishing different family lines in multiple geographic locations throughout New England and New York. Thomas Cornell, the patriarch of the growing Cornell family, born at Fairstead Manor, Essex, England, and arriving with his family to America in 1633, died on February 8, 1655.[74]

However, the saga of Thomas and Rebecca Cornell did not end with Thomas' death. At the age of 73, in her homestead in Portsmouth, Rhode Island, Rebecca Cornell fell asleep while smoking her pipe, and burned to death in 1673. However, though it was presumed her death had been caused by smoking in bed, Rebecca's brother came forth with allegations of murder.

Rebecca's brother, John Briggs, the same John Briggs who was a close friend and confidant of Anne Hutchinson, testified that his nephew, Rebecca's second eldest son, Thomas Jr., murdered his mother, presumably to inherit her land and possessions. The elderly, religious Briggs astounded the community by testifying that he had a vision from his sister upon her death, in which she twice told him, "See how I was burned with fire," that he said was her claim to having been murdered.

Based on this testimony, and the fact that Thomas Jr. was the last one known to see his mother, Thomas Jr. was tried, convicted, and quickly executed for the alleged crime, his lifeless body hung in public display. Because of the overwhelming controversy caused by his trial, immediately after his execution, another jury was formed to retry Thomas Jr. Based on the evidence presented, the second jury found him not guilty of his mother's death, and he was posthumously acquitted.

The circumstances surrounding the unfortunate affair -Rebecca's death, her son's insistence of innocence, the uncle's testimony at the first trial and the quick acquittal at the second trail - created tremendous friction and guilt within the Cornell family. During the first grueling trial, Thomas Jr.'s wife, Sarah, was pregnant. When their daughter was born, Sarah named her Innocent, reflecting her belief in her husband's innocence. But even though Thomas Jr. was acquitted after his death, the expanded Cornell family was devastated and humiliated by the intrusive publicity of this very public series of events.

The trail pitted family members against one another, and against their uncle John Briggs - who reportedly was sent a message from his deceased sister, Rebecca. Some family members attempted to avoid the negative publicity, ridicule and innuendos by altering the spelling of their family name to distance themselves from the trial and the surrounding public ridicule. Many family members also tried to geographically distance themselves from the turmoil of the trial by moving away from Portsmouth, Rhode Island, deciding to move westward in search of their personal fortunes.

Some of the Cornell family branched out to northern parts of New England and to parts of Canada, while others moved back to what had been New Amsterdam - which was part of the Dutch colony, New Netherlands, that stretched from the western Long Island north along the Hudson River to near the modern-day border separating Massachusetts and Vermont. New Netherlands was captured by the British and New Amsterdam was renamed New York in 1664, nine years before Rebecca Cornwall's fiery death.

Other Cornell families moved into the Ohio Valley, while others family members moved to Maryland and points as far south as Virginia. Additionally, some Cornell families changed their surnames, variations included Cornwell and Cornwall.

Harold Cornwall's 6th generation great grandfather, Richard Cornell, was a younger brother to Thomas Jr. Richard was born in 1624 in England, and died in 1694 in Rockaway, New York. Like other family members, Richard and his wife, Elizabeth Jessup, had a large family, consisting of twelve children. According to public records, Richard had changed the spelling of the family name from Cornell to Cornwell, perhaps in an attempt to protect his family from the embarrassing trial of his brother and the discourse within the family resulting from his brothers hanging and subsequent acquittal.

Richard and Elizabeth Cornwell's son, Jacob Cornwell, was born in 1669 in the Township of Flushing, Long Island, New York, and died in 1694 in Rockaway, New York.[75] Jacob married Miss Hester Paine, who was born in 1680. Jacob and Hester Cornwell had eleven children. Their second child, Daniel, was born in 1702 in Flushing, New York. By the time Daniel Cornwell was born, the English colonies were beginning to survive and expand.

Compared to England, the weather and the growing seasons along the eastern seaboard of North America were conducive to farming; this led to an abundance of crops that sustained the rapidly growing population and was exported to Europe. The rivers, which led to the interior portions of the colonies, allowed commerce between small outposts and the larger cities and towns. The abundant natural resources promoted growth at every level. The strong oak, pine, lark and cedar trees were good natural wood for shipbuilding and regional commerce. The deep harbors promoted a thriving trans-Atlantic trade between the colonies, Europe and the West Indies. "Only one serious obstacle impeded colonial progress: an acute shortage of labor that everywhere retarded growth and local economies. A vast amount of work was required to exploit the resources of a new continent, and the supply of able workers was kept down by the refusal of European workers to accept a permanent wage-earning status."[76]

As a result of Europe's cities, towns and villages enduring economic, civil, religious and social strife during this period, the lure of going to America began to become powerful. With abundant land at inexpensive prices compared to Europe, the opportunity to own land instead of being part of a feudal society was the stimulus that started the migration of Europeans from all economic classes to America. From the mid to late 1700's, the Cornell family and other European immigrants thrived, expanded and explored new territories in the British colonies. The family now had several distinct lines across all of New England and was beginning to move into the mid-Atlantic colonies.

1.7 Cuffe and Flora Grandison from Scituate, Massachusetts

Another historic family in Plymouth County, Massachusetts, was that of Samuel Clapp. In 1645, Samuel's grandfather, Thomas Clapp, purchased twenty-four acres of farmland in the town of Scituate, a small farming and fishing community twenty miles southeast of Boston. Samuel Clapp, a shipping mogul, owned what was referred to as a "good barge called the *Adventure*, of burden about 'forty tun,' and did much for the shipbuilding industry" in the town.[77]

Although the family's wealth came from shipping, it is unclear how the family made its fortune, what they traded in the West Indies, or what they brought back to the colonies. While there is no documentation to suggest that Samuel actually traded in African slaves, two of his grandsons, Thomas and Joseph Clapp, each owned African slaves. Colonel Thomas Clapp was the owner of a young servant woman named Flora, and his brother Joseph Clapp owned a young servant man named Cuffe.[78]

In 1740, Thomas and Joseph Clapp's servants, Cuffe and Flora were married by "the Reverend Nathaniel Eells of the Second Parish Church in Scituate, Massachusetts, who at some point reminisced that their marriage ceremony was the 280th wedding that he officiated during his time as minister at the church."[79] Cuffe and Flora chose the surname Grandison, and were the 4th generation great-grandparents of Harold Cornwall of Brockton, Massachusetts.

The historic significance of a young slave couple being married by a minister of a church in 1740, especially in a church that whites attended, was unprecedented. In most parts of the country, until the 1860s, slave couples were not allowed to marry or have a formal marriage ceremony because slave masters believed that marriage was a legal bond between a man and a woman, and they were afraid that this bond might affect their legal rights as masters over their slaves. In slave communities across the county, the slave ceremony of "jumping the broom" was conducted to indicate that the couple was in a committed relationship. However, the marriage of Cuffe and Flora Grandison was historic in two very distinct ways.

First, it was unusual for a white church anywhere in the country, even in Massachusetts Bay Colony, to allow a slave couple to be married in it. In 1740, the Scituate Second Parish Church was originally a Congregational Church, which was the prominent church in colonial Massachusetts. European congregants were opposed to having slaves attend or marry in their churches, primarily because they believed that slaves were not equal to good Christian white people, and having slaves worship in the church contradicted the master-slave relationship. Thomas Clapp, the owner of Flora, and Joseph Clapp, the owner of Cuffe, along with other members of the Clapp family, must have been progressive thinkers who had sufficient influence within the town that they were able to facilitate the marriage of the young slave couple at the Second Parish Church.

The second reason this marriage was so significant was that the young black slave couple married despite the obvious hostility from certain townspeople who would have resented any slaves' desire and decision to marry. The couple felt it was important to take a stand and marry in the church. Although the young couple earned the respect of the Clapp family, Cuffe and Flora had to be able to present a strong argument to support the need to take a surname reflecting their bond to one another. The young couple decided not to take their masters' surname, Clapp, but chose instead to establish their own family name, Grandison.

The newly established Grandisons also had another thing going for them and the man who presided over the ceremony - the marriage was in Massachusetts. Had Reverend Eells attempted to perform the marriage in colonial Virginia, he would have violated colonial law. According to the 1691 law passed by the Virginia House of Burgesses, white men and women were prohibited from marrying "a negro, Mulatto or Indian man or woman, bond or free." If Reverend Eells performed the marriage ceremony in Virginia, he would have been banished from the colony. The institution of slavery and indentured servitude was very different in Massachusetts and the other northern colonies compared to the more repressive and restrictive southern colonies.

However, though in modern times colonial-era slavery tends to be remembered as being problematic only in the south, African men and women were held as chattel property against their will in the New England and mid-Atlantic colonies as well, albeit on a much smaller scale.

But whether in the north or the south, slavery was a cruel institution. African slaves and sometimes Native Americans were auctioned openly in the public squares of the northern port cities, such as Boston, New York and Philadelphia. Though the number of slaves sold in the north was substantially fewer in number than in the south, the inhuman treatment of the African men, women, and children was no less degrading than if they were being sold in the colonial southern port cities of Alexandria and Norfolk, Virginia, and Savannah, Georgia.

However, there was something different about slavery in the north. When African and Native American slaves were bought and sold in northern cities, they marched past the white steeples of Congregational and Methodist churches and the stoic wooden meetinghouses of the city's elders. Once they became integrated into the communities of their new homes, they walked through the same cobblestone town squares where the European colonists were openly debating the injustices being imposed on white colonists by the British monarchy and how their own rights and freedoms were being denied.

Ten years before Cuffe and Flora married in Scituate, the Massachusetts Bay Colony had approximately 5,000 slaves and an unspecified number of African indentured servants. Many of the slave men and women lived within the households of their masters and became integrated within the family, to varying degrees. Unlike the south, where African Americans lived in segregated slave quarters, far removed from the white community and labored primarily in the fields, northern slaves became part of the communities in which they lived. They were expected to learn trades that contributed to the growth and development of these communities.

When Thomas and Joseph Clapp helped facilitate the marriage of Cuffe and Flora in the Second Parish Church of Scituate, it's likely the young couple was well known in the small farming and fishing community. Cuffe could have worked with Thomas Clapp in one of his businesses, making it probable that he was well known, accepted and liked by the teetotalers of Scituate and the high society in the surrounding communities.

Thomas Clapp was an interesting character and had substantial influence in the town, primarily because he represented the members of his community and served in the Massachusetts General Court.

He was well known and at some point was shamed by the Puritan elders for the selling of "intoxicating liquors" in his community. He eventually sold his investment in the liquor business "to the American patriot Samuel Adams."[80] It is unclear if his recipes became part of the modern day and widely popular Samuel Adams Lager that is manufactured in Boston, Massachusetts. However, Thomas Clapp's recipes must have been exceptionally good in order to convince some of Scituate's citizens to buy his "intoxicating liquor."

In 1743, as a member of Massachusetts General Court, the personal relationship that Thomas Clapp had with Cuffe and Flora Grandison created a controversial legal problem for Thomas when Cuffe and Flora had their first child. When the couple married, they rejected their slave surname, Clapp, for their chosen surname of Grandison. When their first son Cuffe Junior was born, his parents obviously gave their son their new last name of Grandison. However, in doing that, a legal property issue came up as to whether or not Thomas Clapp had ownership or property rights over the new slave baby.

According to the town records, when the baby Cuffe Grandison Junior was born, it was originally listed in the Town of Scituate Records as "Couff Grandison son of Couff Grandison and Floro his wife." However, in reviewing the more than two-hundred year old written record, it appears that the original last name on the ledger for the infant child was changed from Grandison to Clapp. Beneath the original ledger, it is written, "Couff Clapp, son of Couff Clapp and Floro his wife." It is unclear whether Cuffe's given surname name as originally listed was crossed out shortly after the birth of the child or if during the past two-hundred years it was edited for clarification purposes to distinguish between father and son.

In 1755, the young Cuffe Clapp, a servant to another family member, Job Clapp of Scituate, Massachusetts, married Ruth Raif, a Native American of the Massachusetts' Wampanoag tribe of the Algonquian nation.[81] At the age of thirty-four, in 1777, Cuffe Grandison enlisted in the Revolutionary War under his legal name of Cuffe Clapp. However, after the war, he permanently changed his surname and took the family surname, Grandison. Since Cuffe's children were part African American and part Native American, it is unclear if at this point in time if they were considered slaves or servants of the Clapp family.

1.8   Caesar and Sally Russell from Beverly, Massachusetts

The Town of Scituate, Massachusetts, was on the South Shore of Boston; the Town of Beverly, Massachusetts, was a similar fishing and farming community on Boston's North Shore. Although the towns were forty miles apart, they were strikingly similar in many ways. Each derived its wealth from the maritime industry, and the ancillary trades of shipbuilding, off-shore fishing, and international commerce. In the late 1600s and the early 1700s in colonial Massachusetts, the ownership of African slaves was concentrated on Boston's north and south shore in coastal communities such as Scituate and Beverly, where wealthy families needed to augment their diverse needs for additional labor.

These were the same regions where early civil rights case law was established and the question of individual rights were openly and actively debated and challenged in both the white and in the Black communities. Beverly, Massachusetts, is the community where Caesar and Sally Russell, the 3rd generation great-grandparents of Harold Cornwall of Brockton, Massachusetts. The life of Caesar Russell was intertwined with the lives of three generations of the Thissel (or Thistle) family of Beverly, Massachusetts. This resulted in confusion as to the date of his actual birth and his age at the time of his death.

Caesar Russell's certified Commonwealth of Massachusetts Death Certificate states that he died at the age of 105 on October 20, 1861, in Taunton, Massachusetts, making his year of birth 1756. This record lists his birthplace as North Carolina. But in the city of his death, Taunton's official Registry of Deaths lists Russell as being 110 at the time of his death, placing his birth year to 1751. However, Caesar enlisted as a private in the Revolutionary War's Continental Army, where his date of birth was listed as 1765, which would have made him 96 at the time of his death. Though confusing, these records are intriguing. The mystery of Caesar Russell's birth begins with the European Larcom family of Beverly, Massachusetts.

The Larcom family lineage starts with Mordecai Larcom, born in 1629. Mordecai appeared in Ipswich, Massachusetts, in 1655, and soon after moved to Beverly, Massachusetts, where he obtained a land grant. According to Larcom family genealogy, Mordecai's grandson, David Larcom, married Anna Batchelder, widow of John Bryant. After Anna Batchelder passed away, David Larcom married Mary Herrick West, widow of Thomas West and daughter of Captain Henry Herrick.[82]

Mary Herrick West brought the Larcom family their first slave, a young girl named Juno. Captain Henry Herrick died in 1755 but had written a will the year before. The will left to his daughter, Mary Larcom, "13 pounds, 6 shillings and 8 pence, with a Negro girl now living with her named Juno." In 1756, Juno was married to Jethro, a "servant" of Jeffrey Thistle, and together they had twelve children.[83] The young slave girl, Juno Larcom, became a famous heroine in Massachusetts colonial history by articulating her individual rights, her rights as a mother, and the rights of her children over her slave master.

According to research, two of Juno Larcom's children were sold as slaves, evidenced by two preserved deeds of sale for these children; one is printed in the Essex Institute of Historical Collections, and the other is among the collections of the Beverly Historical Society. The first of these sales is dated July 30, 1757, and shows that "one Negro boy named Sesar aged about seven year" was sold for 30 pounds, 6 shillings and 3 pence to Thomas Davis, shoreman of Beverly. The second records the sale of "Negro Boy named Reuben Aged about Twelve years" to James Thistle for 46 pounds, 13 shillings and 4 pence on April 6, 1773.[84] When Juno Larcom's two sons were sold in 1757, she did the unthinkable for a woman of color anywhere in the country during this time period. She sued her master, David Larcom.[85]

When Juno's slave mistress, Mary Herrick West Larcom, died, her second husband, David Larcom, ran into financial difficulties. Larcom was looking for ways to generate funds to resolve some of his debts. He was fearful that his ownership of Juno's children and his ability to generate funds from their sale would be lost with the discussions and pending legislation on emancipation of African slaves in Massachusetts. Larcom reacted to this fear by selling Juno's older children, Sesar and Reuben, to nearby merchants. He then wanted to sell her remaining children because they would be "seasoned" by their northern experiences.

When Juno Larcom brought her suit against her master, she feared that her remaining children would be sold in the South for more money than could be generated in the North, and that she would never see her children again. Her lawyer, the famous John Adams (who later became the second President of the United States), argued that Juno's mother was Native American and that she was kidnapped as a child from North Carolina. Therefore, he proposed that Juno was not a slave but a victim of a kidnapping who had been held against her will. Adams argued that technically her children, by birthright, were not slaves and should not be taken from Juno and sold into slavery. This brave woman of color testified before the Massachusetts Supreme Court in 1774, and argued the complex issues of race, kidnap, and slavery. Before the case could be resolved, David Larcom passed away and the court case was dismissed. But it had the desired affect for Juno Larcom - her remaining children were not sold.[86]

Research shows that Caesar Russell lived and raised his children in Beverly, Massachusetts, the same place that Sesar Larcom was born. Though the spelling of the first name is different, this was not uncommon during the time period, particularly for African men. Additionally, surnames often differed between records, as many slaves' last names changed in accordance to their owners, and in Massachusetts, some slaves had the opportunity to choose their own surname. Given that Caesar Russell's date of birth is unclear, it is possible that this Sesar's birth date would match the date of Caesar Russell's birth.

Because Caesar Russell lived in Beverly, it is plausible that at the time of his death, someone from the Town of Taunton looked up the Massachusetts Vital Records for the Town of Beverly, surmised that this was the same Caesar and assumed that the two men were the same, and thus listed his year of birth as 1756. However, Sesar Larcom, son of Juno Larcom and Jethro Thistle, enlisted in the Revolutionary War, and "was lost at sea while serving as privateer cook in the Revolution."[87] In 1801, according to the Beverly, Massachusetts, Historical Society, Caesar Russell was found on the crew list of the Ship *Mary* as a cook. This ship's manifest listed Caesar Russell's birth year as 1766. The captain of the Ship *Mary* was John Thissel, Jr., (1773 - 1809) the grandson of James Thistle, who owned Jethro and subsequently purchased

Reuben, a son of Juno and Jethro and brother to Sesar. Though easy to confuse Sesar Larcom and Caesar Russell because of their first names and their various overlapping connections, based on military records and an independent ship manifest, it appears that the two were not the same man. However, there clearly was a relationship between both Sesar Larcom and Caesar Russell and the Thistle/Thissel family as late as 1801.

Based on other genealogical documents, Caesar Russell, who was the 4th generation great-grandfather of Harold Cornwall of Brockton, Massachusetts, was born somewhere in North Carolina in 1766. According to his Death certificate, Caesar's parents were Samuel and Grace Russell from North Carolina.[88] This would indicate that he was at least a second or third generation African American living in the colonies and that he must have been purchased in North Carolina, and was probably sold and brought to Massachusetts as a young child. Caesar was short in stature, only five-feet, four-inches tall. He was taught the fundamentals of reading and writing, evidenced by his ability to formally write his signature as an adult.

During the time in which Caesar lived, very few Americans knew how to sign their names. In documents in which his signature was required, Caesar Russell did not use a mark when signing his name, which was customary for many adults - white and black - during this time.

Had Caesar continued to live in North Carolina to adulthood, it would have been illegal for him as a slave to know how to read or write.

1.9   Peter and Elizabeth Rucker of Bayen, Germany

The extended family of Peter and Elizabeth Rucker were one of the largest landholding and slaveholding families in colonial Virginia, and their relationship to the Cornwall Murphy families is an interesting one. When conducting any form of scholarly research, researchers often hit upon a wall where they can go no further with their work. In genealogy, this means that family lines come to an end.

That was the case for the family of Lucy Rucker of Roanoke, Virginia, Robert Murphy's 2nd generation great-grandmother. With the use of DNA testing, the family line of Robert Murphy was definitively connected to the Ruckers.[89] Based on this and a preponderance of other evidence, it can be concluded that William and Catherine Rucker and one of their great-grandchildren are the ancestors to Lucy Rucker, an African American woman.

As Europeans with some financial means came to America and expanded their personal holdings, families such as the Ruckers rejected the free market wage system and expanded their wealth by relying on compulsory labor - indentured servitude for whites and slavery for blacks -to provide the day-to-day work force essential for their economic progress.[90] Because of the acute labor shortage, the introduction of large numbers of indentured poor Europeans and captive African slaves set the stage for the foundation of the Cornwall Murphy families in America, particularly for some of the branches of the family from the South.

The Rucker family was of French Huguenot origins, religious rebels who belonged to the Protestant Reformed Church of France. They believed in the principles of John Calvin, who was the inspiration for the religious movement of Calvinism. Because France was a strong Catholic nation, the Huguenots were persecuted for their religious beliefs, and by late the late 1600s, fled France for more sympathetic Protestant nations, such as the British colonies in America. Upon their arrival, they settled in different communities, including colonial Virginia.

Sudie Rucker Wood, a descendant of Peter and Elizabeth Rucker, wrote extensively about the Rucker Family. In her book, she explored the Rucker family where she explains that Peter Rucker, the first in the family to come to America, "may have been a French Huguenot, for he was naturalized with a number of Frenchmen."[91] However, based on contemporary research, it is now known that the Rucker family was of German heritage from Rothenberg, Bayern, Germany.

The only French connection the family had was the marriage of the German born Ambrose Levi Rucker to Elizabeth A Beauchamp, who was born in France in 1642. Their son, Peter Rucker, who was born in 1661, in Bayern, Germany, and his English-born wife, Elizabeth, were the first to arrive in America. The Ruckers, based on their religious beliefs, were German Calvinist Protestants who immigrated to the colonies with the French Huguenots.

At the time of his death in 1743, Peter Rucker provided tremendous insight into the size of his family and his personal possessions. In his will, he left all of his property and his slaves to his wife, and at his request, upon her death his assets were to be divided by each of his eleven named children. During his life, Peter and Elizabeth Rucker acquired substantial land holdings in Orange and Culpeper counties in Virginia. The area in which the family initially lived in Orange County, Virginia, was east of Rippon's Run on an area known as Friendly Acres. The village settled by the Rucker family became known as Ruckersville, named for Captain John Rucker in 1732. Peter and Elizabeth Rucker's son, John Rucker, and his wife Susanna Coghill lived and prospered in Orange County. [92]

According to one account, John Rucker was a colorful character. During an election for representatives to the House of Burgesses in 1741, the local Sherriff closed a polling location at the Court House because of general rowdiness. Upset that the polling had been temporarily shut down Rucker physically accosted the Sheriff, threw him out on the street, and commandeered the Court House's polling location. Once in control, he offered "several large bowls of punch" to any man who voted for his candidate. At the conclusion of election, John Rucker's candidate was declared a winner. [93]

John's will provides additional genealogical information for the Cornwall Murphy family. In his will, John Rucker listed the names of each of his eleven children; however, based on the science of DNA evidence, one of John's children is the biological grandparent of Lucy Rucker, Robert Murphy of Norfolk, Virginia's 2nd great-grandmother.

For African Americans conducting genealogical research, a colonial will such as John Rucker's can provide valuable information that can connect family lines and generations. John's will and the subsequent will of his wife Susanna reveal a detailed description of their personal holdings, including their substantial land holdings and their slaves.

The wills also document the Rucker family being one of colonial Virginia's largest slave-holding families during that time, thereby connecting Lucy Rucker, to the slave-holding Rucker family - not just as chattel property, but also as a descendant.

Figure 22: Will of John Rucker from Orange County, Virginia

In the Name of God Amen. I John Rucker of Saint Marks Parish in the County of Orange A Planter being weak in Body, but of Perfect Mind & Memory And knowing that it is appointed for all men once to Dye, Do make and Ordain this my last Will & Testament in manner and form following. IMPRIMIS I do order that all my just Debts & funeral Charges be paid & satisfied

Item. I give to my well beloved Wife, Susannah Rucker, four negros name by Bristol, Tony, Doll & Sue, and one third part of my household & Furniture & Stock, horses Excepted one horse I give to my wife named Roger, the four mentioned Negroes to remain my Wifes no Longer than her Widowhood after to be sold & divided as the rest of my Estate hereafter mentioned. Item I give to my son Peter Rucker one black horse, called Jockey & his Choice of my guns. Item I give to my Son John Rucker one grey horse called Oglesby and a gun the next choice after his Brother. Item I give to Thomas Wright Belfield one lot in Fred Kurg No. 5 to him and his Heirs forever.

My desire is that the one half of my land on the Branches of James's River may be sold by my Excr. for six months credit to the highest bidder Likewise my Wagon and five horses & horse kinds in the same manor in order to pay my debts, I likewise leave my Dwelling house and Land thereunto adjoining to be sold at the Direction of my Exec if my Debts can't be complyed with if they can the dwelling house and Land to Remain my wifes, dureing her Widowhood & If she marrys to be sold by way of auction.

Item I give to my well beloved Sons Peter Rucker, John Rucker, Ambrose Rucker, Benj a Rucker, Reuben Rucker, Isaac Rucker, Anthony Rucker & to their Heirs forever, half the Land I hold ln the Branches of James River to be equally divided between the seven brothers, the rest of my Estate I desire may be Equally divided among my beloved Children as follows, Peter Rucker, John Rucker, Sarah Rucker, Winniford Rucker, Ambrose Rucker, Benja Rucker, Reuben Rucker, Isaac Rucker, Anthony Rucker, Mildred Rucker, Pheby Rucker, to them and their Heirs forever, Item I give my Daughter Margaret Smith one shilling Stering, and lastly I do constitute and appoint my beloved wife Susanah Rucker my Exr and my beloved Son Peter Rucker, and my beloved friend George Taylor my whole and sole Exs of this my Last will & Testament, hereby Revoking and Disallowing all other Testament and Wills by me made Confirming this and no other to be my last Will and Testament. In witness whereof I have now unto set my hand & seal this XI day Jan 1742.[94]

Part 2: From the American Revolution to the War of 1812: The Cornwall Murphy Family Helps Build America

"Give me liberty or give me death."
Patrick Henry

2.1   An American Family's Patriotic Service in the Time of War

The forefathers of the Cornwall Murphy lineage fought in the colonists' Continental Army in order to free the young nation from British tyranny. They hoped to advance the unique American concept of political democracy, individual freedoms, and social equality. Five Cornwall Murphy ancestors, four of whom were of African descent, served in integrated military units with men of European descent. The American Revolutionary War was the only war in which white and black troops were integrated until the Korean War in the 1950s - almost 200 hundred after the Boston Massacre, where a man of color became the first casualty of the eight-year fight for freedom against the British.

Figure 23: Revolutionary War Military Honor Roll

Benjamin Brooker, Drummer Boy (June 1776 – June 1783)
Samuel Cornwell, Private, 5th New York Regiment (January 1776 – 1781)
Cuffe Grandison, Private, Massachusetts Independent Company (April 1777)
Edward Going, Private, 2nd North Carolina Regiment (September 3, 1778 – June, 1779)
Caesar Russell, Private, 4th Massachusetts Regiment (March 1781 – April, 1783)

The call for service in the Revolutionary War impacted each man and their families differently, but had especially profound implications for many men of African descent. For European colonists, the call to military service sought independence from British taxes, oppression, and tyranny. For those of African descent, including the more than 10,000 African men who served in the Continental Army, it meant the possibility of freedom from slavery. It provided men of African descent the dream of equality, the possibility of economic empowerment, and most of all, the dignity of being a free man and not the chattel property of others.

From the mid-seventeenth to the mid-eighteenth century, the political, social and economic interests of the thirteen American colonies and the British sovereignty drifted apart from one another. The colonies were becoming wealthier, and the British government wished to tax this prosperity in order to expand Britain's wealth, influence and power internationally. The British Parliament also needed the American colonies to pay for the costs of the French and Indian War. The British government had helped fund the colonists' very expensive seven-year war against the French and their Indian supporters, causing the British economy to suffer a significant financial loss. To combat this loss, King George III, in conjunction with the British Parliament in 1765, imposed a widely unpopular Stamp Act, taxing the stamps that colonists placed on every document used to conduct any business.

Across all thirteen colonies, the colonists vehemently protested the taxation from the British Parliament, and boycotted British imported goods so as to avoid paying the tax. The successful boycott and protests against the Stamp Act added to England's already overburdened economy. Britain reluctantly acquiesced to the American colonies and eliminated the Stamp Act.

Nonetheless, the British were not happy with their American colonies. They complained that the colonists were willing to take financial aid when they needed it for the French and Indian War, but refused to pay their fair share of the debt incurred. So, England decided to impose a number of measures to assert its control and authority over the colonies. However, each measure was met with strong resistance from the colonists.

In 1768, in an effort to demonstrate their power over the colonies, the British government stationed soldiers in the city of Boston. Outrage sparked between the soldiers and the local residents, and left five civilian men dead in an event known as the Boston Massacre. The first man to die for American freedom and independence was a man named Crispus Attucks, a runaway slave of African and Native American descent. Boston, Massachusetts, was the epicenter for much of the initial opposition to the British. The events in Boston and the slaughter of Crispus Attucks and four other brave American civilians stirred colonial Americans to action.

Bostonians of European descent, many only a few generations removed from their native countries, were resolute - they wanted total, irrevocable independence from Great Britain. Bostonians of African descent, many of whom were only a generation or two removed from Africa, simply wanted their freedom from bondage and slavery. The Boston Massacre served as a catalyst for the battle between the British Empire and its colonial governments in America. The political and economic conflicts that led to the Revolutionary War provided all Americans - white and black, African and European - an opportunity to serve their country. The phrase coined by the American patriot Patrick Henry, "Give me liberty or give me death!" was a call heard throughout the American colonies, including in the homes of African Americans.

Americans of African descent were especially driven to fight for independence, as freedom from British tyranny could also mean freedom from slavery. After the death of Crispus Attucks at the Boston Massacre, African Americans in Boston and other parts of New England quickly took up the cause for American sovereignty. They too wanted a voice in the discussion of independence, and they wanted to be able to take up arms to defend themselves, their families, and their country. In communities all across Massachusetts and other parts of New England, men of African descent were asked to make the ultimate sacrifice and join with their European neighbors in fighting for their country and in supporting the militia. The cry for independence was universal - black and white.

The Boston militias were integrated troops, with European and African men fighting side-by-side. Men of African descent fought bravely in some of the earliest of battles of the Revolutionary War, including the Battle of Lexington and Concord, and the Battle of Bunker Hill.

During the Battles of Lexington and Concord, Peter Salem, a freed slave, stood against the British on the village green in Lexington when the battle broke out, later described in a poem by Ralph Waldo Emerson that included the phrase, "the shot heard around the world." One of the last men wounded in the Battle at Lexington was Prince Estabrook, an American of African descent from the town of West Lexington.

Two months after the British retreated from the Battle of Lexington and Concord, where they were outmaneuvered by the well-trained Minute Men, they attacked an American position outside Boston at the Battle of Bunker Hill. Peter Salem was once again in battle, along with at least twenty other African Americans. The brave Peter Salem was honored for firing the shot that killed Major John Pitcairn, the British officer who led the Redcoats, when they attacked Salem's small unit at Lexington, Massachusetts.[95] Another causality at Bunker Hill who died and was buried at the site, was James Melton of North Carolina, a distant cousin (three times removed) of Margaret Melton Murphy.

As the political rhetoric grew, white Bostonians discussed openly their desire for freedom and independence from Britain. African men and women, free and slave, couldn't help to imagine what it might mean to be free from England, and to be free from slavery. They were cautiously optimistic that after the war, they too could be free men and women. Freedom became a cornerstone for political dialogue within the African American community in Massachusetts, and it began to spread south in the communities of Free People of Color throughout the rest of the New England colonies. As African American shipmates traveled up and down the eastern seaboard, they shared with other men of color the situation in Boston and the progressive thinking in Boston's African American communities across the state of Massachusetts. African men and women understood the true meaning of liberty, for their personal freedoms and their own self-preservation, and eagerly took up the cause and arms for American independence.

The war grew from skirmishes in Massachusetts to a broader conflict throughout the colonies, and the politics of race and the role of African American men in the war effort changed dramatically. Southern states were outright fearful of African men being armed, particularly in the states that had large numbers of African slaves. General George Washington and the Continental Congress issued a Proclamation prohibiting slaves from entering the newly formed Continental Army.

However, British generals had noticed the bravery of the African American men. There was no way the generals could ignore it because some of the major casualties among British troops were due to

American men of color. If the British generals could have gotten these men to fight for them and not against them, they could have caused a rift between the colonies as well as strengthened their own troops. On November 7, 1775, the Royal Governor of Virginia, John Murray, Earl of Dunmore, who knew about the southern colonies' racial fear and weakness, offered absolute freedom to any slave or indentured servant who supported the British in their war effort. By the end of the war, more than 15,000 soldiers of color accepted Dunmore's offer and joined the British Army.[96]

General George Washington, a Virginia slaveholder, initially continued to side with the southern states and refused to allow men of color - slave or free - to enlist in the Continental Army. But once he learned that Dunmore would lift the ban on Blacks enlisting in the British army and provide "freedom to all slaves who would join the King's army," George Washington and other members of the Continental Army had to rethink their position. In December 1775, when it was apparent the number of white soldiers was not enough for significant military strength, General Washington decreed that any slaves who served one year in the Continental Army would be granted their freedom and five shillings for each month of service rendered. This act encouraged thousands of enslaved and free men of African descent to take up arms for the cause of American freedom and independence.

While some records documented more than 6,000 soldiers and seaman of African, Native American, or Mixed heritage served the cause for American Independence, it is likelier that more than 10,000 of these men took up arms and fought for the Continental Army and Navy during the American Revolution.[97] In recent years, scholars and historians have discovered that between ten and twenty percent of the 200,000 Continental Armed Forces consisted of African American, Native American and Mixed-race colonists. Whether they were free, slave, or an indentured servant, African American patriots fought side by side with white soldiers - each seeking independence from British rule and domination. Scholars and historians agree that the Revolutionary War would not have been won without the brave and historic participation of these forgotten men and women.

In the spring of 1776, King George III, impatient and tired of the rebellious colonies, sent more than 130 warships and more than 25,000 British soldiers to New York Harbor. The goal was to stop the insolent colonists, enter New York, and split the colonies in two, the political thinkers in Philadelphia and the military insurgents in Boston. A colony physically divided would be easier to conquer. But because of King George's actions, the young nation's Founding Fathers crafted a Declaration of Independence from Britain and become a new nation known as the United States, on July 4, 1776. The Declaration of Independence redefined the conflict between the thirteen American colonies and Great Britain.

The thinking of the colonial leaders was that the King would now have to accept American independence. However, King George III was now more determined than ever to get the Americans and their treasonous leaders back under his control.

The Declaration of Independence was a declaration of war, igniting a chain of events that would forever change America, and the destiny of the Cornwall Murphy family, for generations to come.

2.2   Samuel Cornwell, Private in the 5th New York Regiment

By 1776, five generations of Thomas and Rebecca Cornell's descendants were well established in the American colonies. While there may have been British sympathizers amongst the Cornell family, the political, financial and economic interests of the family were no longer intimately tied with their ancestral home in Great Britain, but to their new home in America.

At the outset of the war, the Continental Congress in Philadelphia, Pennsylvania, selected General George Washington as the commander of the Continental Army. He had the enormous charge of bringing together thirteen disparate colonies and winning the war against England, all while protecting his men in battle. A group of those men were provided by members of the Cornell family, who were willing to sacrifice their lives for American freedom - and by extension, the freedom of People of Color across the new nation. From the very beginning, there was one soldier who was with the commander-in-chief nearly the entire time. That solider was Private Samuel Cornwell, the 1ˢᵗ generation great-grandson of Thomas and Rebecca Cornell of Portsmouth, Rhode Island. Samuel Cornwell was also the 3ʳᵈ generation great-great grandfather of Harold Cornwall of Brockton, Massachusetts.

Samuel Cornwell fervently believed in American independence and joined the Continental Army as one of the first soldiers in the war effort, six months before the signing of the Declaration of Independence. On January 29, 1776, Samuel Cornwell entered the Continental Army as a private in the regiment commanded by Colonel Burrell from the state of Connecticut. Samuel Cornwell was not only one of the first soldiers to enlist in the Continental Army he also served in some of the most important and historic battles of the war. Private Cornwell had the distinct honor of serving in the regiments that were led by General George Washington - from the horrific conditions at Valley Forge in Pennsylvania, until the surrender of General Cornwallis at Yorktown in Virginia.[98]

At the beginning of the war, before Samuel Cornwall was in the regiment led by General Washington, the Continental Congress tried to convince their Canadian neighbors that they should join them in rebellion against the British. However, the French Catholic clergy advised the Canadian leadership that the predominately-Catholic country would not be served well under the control of the conservative Protestant American colonies.[99] When the Canadians rebuffed the overture of the Continental Congress, the Americans decided to conquer and permanently annex the Canadian territories. While in the new nation's Capital City, Philadelphia, Pennsylvania, Colonel Ethan Allen and Colonel Benedict Arnold tried to convince the leaders of the young government to heed their advice and let them lead the military command on the raid on Canada. Instead, General Philip Schuyler and Brigadier General Richard Montgomery were chosen to lead the military effort.[100]

"A misguided venture from the start, the campaign was one in which just about everything that could go wrong did."[101] In the winter of 1775, Private Samuel Cornwell, along with 1,000 other cold, weary, and hungry men, marched to Canada and participated in the Battle of Quebec. Samuel Cornwell was "there at the time that Brigadier General Richard Montgomery was killed," shortly after the battle began.[102] The devastating death of the American Brigadier General Montgomery was one of the first significant causalities of the war. The battle in Canada did not go well for the Continental Army, which exacerbated the sour relationship between Canada and the United States and set the stage for another major conflict some thirty-five years later, the War of 1812, in which Samuel Cornwell would again be an active participant.

After the Battle of Quebec, Samuel Cornwell continued to serve in the same regiment for the remainder of his enlistment until he was discharged from service at Whitehall in the state of New York, at Lake Champlain. While Samuel was at Whitehall, the Continental Army, under the command of Colonel Benedict Arnold, was trying to protect its northern flank by building forces along the Canadian border.[103] The Americans knew that the British would eventually invade them from the north.

After he was discharged at Whitehall, Samuel Cornwell reenlisted and joined the company of Captain John Lloyd's, then went on to the State of New Jersey where he joined General Washington's army. Washington arrived in New York as the British were moving in on New York Harbor. Once the British ships landed and their soldiers came to shore, they quickly took control of the city of New York and most of the surrounding area. The British army chased the Continental Army northwest of the city, splitting the militia in two and separating Washington from his northwest flank, the troops of which were tasked with leading their British pursuers away from the leader of the Continental Army.

On September 11, 1777, General Washington realized that the British intended to attack the American capital city of Philadelphia, Pennsylvania, starting the operation at Chadd's Ford. Washington brought his troops, which included Private Cornwell, to a location that was thought to provide a strategic advantage for the Americans. The two armies clashed on the banks of the Brandywine Creek, but the Continental Army was no match for the skilled British soldiers. As the Americans held their lines, they were ambushed by a second British army from the rear. Washington and his army had to retreat before being overrun by the British, and the Founding Fathers had to escape Philadelphia before the city was captured.

After these early defeats General Washington and his advisors had no choice but to analyze their previous military tactics. As a result, they became better at strategic and military planning, and devised strategies to think more like their enemies in an effort not to be caught off guard. General Washington was learning how to utilize the local militia units so that they could complement the limited resources of his own troops. He used the winter of 1777 to re-engineer his military strategies and to reorganize his troops in the field.[104] After the British General, Sir William Howe, outmaneuvered General Washington and seized the American capital, General Washington and his troops camped at Valley Forge, northwest of Philadelphia, Pennsylvania, in the winter of 1777.

Private Samuel Cornwell survived the harshest military environment of the entire war, the historic encampment at Valley Forge. After experiencing an unusually cold autumn, the men arrived at Valley Forge and needed to build -long-standing shelters against the upcoming winter months. They settled in and "began to build a city of over 1,000 small cabins or huts".[105] Without sufficient supplies and tools, the men endured severe hardships. Their living conditions were deplorable. The soldiers had no materials to absorb the dampness from the floors, and the shelters provided insufficient heat to keep them warm.

The exhausted, hungry soldiers were wracked with diseases such as typhus and smallpox. The suffering of the soldiers was echoed by the rotting carcasses of the horses that had died of exposure and illness. Many of the soldiers speculated that the conditions of camp were even worse than fighting or dying on the battlefield.

On December 23, 1777, General Washington penned a letter to Henry Laurens, President of the Continental Congress: "Sir...I am convinced beyond a doubt that unless some great and capital change suddenly takes place...this Army must inevitably...starve, dissolve, or disperse, in order to obtain subsistence in the best manner they can."[106] This cry for help brought some relief, but conditions in the camp continued to deteriorate. Morale declined, fights broke out, and men were abandoning the camp. On top of all this, the enemy was winning the war.

General Washington was most concerned with the army's food shortage.[107] Samuel Cornwell and the other men were suffering a major food scarcity due to a breakdown in the supply chain. Not enough food was delivered to feed the number of men stationed at Valley Forge, and when more food did arrive, it was often spoiled and inedible. The men were asked to ration food and often went hungry. These men were not only starving, but freezing, as well in their damp huts without warm clothing. These circumstances caused the men to feel the bite of the winter's chill all the more painfully.

General Washington knew that if he was to succeed, he would need the help of an experienced foreign solider, a man who could take control of the administrative and logistical aspects of the war. Washington wanted a tactician who could establish a supply system that delivered the necessary goods to the troops, as well as a system that provided for military training and discipline. Washington also needed to take steps to reduce or even eliminate desertion, disease, and death among his own troops, in addition to eliminating the constant threat of a British attack on his incredibly demoralized troops.

Figure 24: Observation of Life at Valley Forge 1777-1778

"There comes a Soldier - His bare feet are seen thro' his worn out Shoes - his legs nearly naked from the tatter'd remains of an only pair of stockings - his Breeches not sufficient to cover his Nakedness - his Shirt hanging in Strings - his hair dishevell'd - his face meagre - his whole appearance pictures a person forsaken & discouraged. He comes, and crys with an air of wretchedness & despair - I am Sick - my feet lame - my legs are sore - my body cover'd with this tormenting Itch - my Cloaths are worn out - my Constitution is broken - my former Activity is exhausted by fatigue - hunger & Cold - I fail fast I shall soon be no more! and all the reward I shall get will be -'Poor Will is dead.' ..."

Dr. Abilgence Waldo, a surgeon with the Continental Army[108]

In February 1778, the Continental Congress sent a new recruit to General Washington at the suggestion of Benjamin Franklin. The new recruit's name was Friedrich Wilhelm Augustus von Steuben, reportedly a military officer in the Prussian army. Von Steuben traveled to Paris in the summer of 1777, met with the American envoy Benjamin Franklin, who was in France to negotiate military support, and discussed the possibility of the French working with the Continental Army in America. Upon arrival at Valley Forge, Steuben had no papers to attest to the veracity of his military standing, only a bejeweled cross that represented an honored knighthood in the Prussian army. General Washington took a bold military move in soliciting the help of Friedrich Wilhelm Augustus von Steuben, subsequently known as General Baron von Steuben, the drillmaster of Valley Forge.

General Baron von Steuben's experience as a member of the Prussian Army gave him a wealth of knowledge that was unheard of in the American army of the time period. His vast knowledge of military structure was sorely needed if the thirteen colonies were to succeed against the military force of Great Britain. With his expert military training, Von Steuben brought to the American soldiers the technical and tactical knowledge necessary to create an effective army and to eventually win the war.[109] Von Steuben did not speak English, but his French was such that he could communicate with some of the officers. Washington's *aide-de-camp*, Alexander Hamilton, assisted in translations.[110] While Hamilton as well as Nathaniel Greene, helped Steuben draft a comprehensive training program for the soldiers.[111]

General Washington needed to build a military from the bottom up, as his army had no structure and his men had no training. General Washington's military consisted of idealistic young men who only knew how to shoot at rabbits behind their families' barns, and farmers who could only commit to a few months of service at a time before they would have to go back to their farms and tend to their crops during the harvest season. These soldiers were poorly trained and lacked the necessary discipline and direction to win a war against the British.

Figure 25: Steuben Screamed but Things Happened

At the time of von Steuben's arrival at Valley Forge…"to the eye of a professional soldier, Valley Forge was a miserable sight. The systems of drill were as varied as the units drilling. Dress, equipment, security regulations were not alike, nor even similar, in any two regiments …thinking and writing in French, Steuben wrote the first American Army Manual, a combination Infantry Drill Regulations, Field Service Regulations and guide for officers. With this book the American Army was born".

Major Fred J., Wilkins, *Steuben Screamed but Things Happened and an Army Was Born at Valley Forge Just One Hundred and Seventy Years Ago*[112]

Steuben's training programs, were known collectively as the "Regulations for the Order and Discipline of the Troops of the United States" or the "Blue Book".[113] included guidelines for camp sanitation and weapons firing procedures. It served as the foundation for the complex military operations that Washington needed for his army to succeed. Steuben's military and organizational skills dramatically improved the conditions for Samuel Cornwell and the troops at Valley Forge. Steuben reassigned the duties of logistical support and supply chain management, ensuring that the troops were fed and clothed. He trained the troop leaders and instituted daily drills and marching procedures to keep the men busy. He developed operational exercises so that the men would be better prepared for offensive and defensive combat maneuvers.

The lives of thousands of men, including Samuel Cornwell, were saved from hunger, disease and military mishaps by the clear and swift actions of General Baron Von Steuben and the protocols he instigated. Generations of Americans, including the descendants of Samuel Cornwell, would not be here today had General Steuben not improved the basic sanitary and military conditions at Valley Forge.

Figure 26: An Army Was Born at Valley Forge

During the winter of 1777-1778, the "Revolution seemed to be heading for a frozen, miserable end. The British in Philadelphia were unconcerned and inactive"…the British believed that before "winter would run its course, the rebellion would freeze or starve or die of pertinence. Untrained in sanitation, lacking medical care, the Colonials were losing more men from disease than bullets. And the British sat in their warm quarters planning to round up the survivors when the snow melted. Yet the spring thaws found an Army at Valley Forge, thanks to the ability and zeal of Frederick von Steubin, the man who founded the American Army".

- Major Fred J., Wilkins, Steuben Screamed but Things Happened and an Army Was Born at Valley Forge Just One Hundred and Seventy Years Ago[114]

During his military service to the Continental Army, Private Samuel Cornwell, Harold Cornwall's 3rd generation great-grandfather, participated in some of the most critical battles during the Revolutionary War, including the Battle of Quebec, the Battle of Brandywine, the march from Valley Forge to the New Jersey offensive to protect the city of New York, and, near the end of his military career, his participation in and as a historic witness to the surrender of the British General Cornwallis at Yorktown.

2.3   Benjamin Brooker, a Drummer Boy from New Haven, Connecticut

For many American men, young and old, the thought of going to war with Britain was exciting. Great orators spoke in communities all across the colonies, encouraging Americans to take up the cause and join the war effort. There were many historic moments that led up to the Revolutionary War and hundreds of thousands of patriotic men and women who supported the war effort. But adults were not the only patriots in the war. There were also thousands of children across the thirteen colonies that supported their fathers, brothers, uncles, grandfathers and neighbors in various capacities during the war.

Children supported the war effort by taking care of sick soldiers, managing their family farms, and enlisting in the army. One of the youngest Americans to enlist in the service of the Continental Army was a ten-year-old boy of African descent named Benjamin Brooker, another 3rd generation great-grandfather Harold Cornwall. According to his pension record, Benjamin (known as Benjamin Cain before the war) lived with a man named Samuel Brooker, who left such a profound impact on Benjamin that as an adult, he changed his surname from Cain to Brooker, and named his second son Samuel.

Benjamin Brooker was born in 1766 in New Haven, Connecticut, and enlisted in the Continental Army as a drummer boy on June 15, 1776.[115] He served in Captain William Clark's company, and as a private in Captain Seth Turner's company, which was part of the regiment under the command of Colonel Thomas Marshall.[116]

Typically, the drummer boys were twelve to sixteen years old, but some boys as young as eight managed to enlist. The perceived glamour of being a drummer boy was enough to encourage an enthusiastic boy such as Benjamin to exaggerate his age to eleven, and since military recruiters were desperate to sign up men and boys for the cause, no one seriously questioned him. After all, drummer boys never served in the military for long, regardless of how old they were when enlisted.

Continental Army recruiters preferred to enlist "street kids" as young drummer and bugle boys, to avoid upsetting any potential grieving mothers. These children often were orphaned, abandoned, or wards of the church. They were given up by their young unwed mothers, who had been ostracized by their families and could barely take of themselves. Many of these unwed mothers would leave their hometowns to have their babies, and would then leave the babies with the local churches. This was before most communities had formal orphanages.

There is no evidence that Benjamin Brooker was orphaned, abandoned or living on the streets. He was probably just simply an idealistic young boy who probably thought it would be fun or exciting to join the army and play the fife or drums. But, like so many other naive young boys, he too would grow up many years before his time. The initial allure of being a drummer or bugle boy often wore off once the stark realities of war set in.

As a drummer boy, Benjamin's responsibility was to maintain a rhythm for the soldiers marching or charging the opposing army's front line. Since the drummer boys led the advancing troops in battle, they were often the first to be killed by opposing snipers on the battlefield. The young drummer boys in the Drum and Bugle Corp were the signal corps of the Army who alerted the troops when to move forward or when to retreat. The Drum and Bugles Corp were crucial in military maneuvers because the tactics at the time were to form a line and fire in a volley for maximum impact of the bullets. The drummer boys were a critical component of the on-the-field military strategy, particularly with an advancing line.

The enemy combatants would intentionally aim their fire directly at the young drummer boys and cause the advancing line to fall out of step, losing any competitive advantage that they might have had. Most drummer boys had little to no musical training. They had to learn on the job. They needed to be tall and strong, and coordinated enough to drum and march at the same time. Many of the boys learned how to hold the drum and play the bugle, which meant that they were constantly on call, required to play their instruments around the clock and at a moment's notice.

From the very beginning of the war, General Washington, his military commanders, and his strategists understood that they were at a huge disadvantage. The British army had military protocol, war strategies and trained men, all combining to create what was considered the mightiest army in the world. And although their uniforms were bright red, they were confident in their military prowess and had no fear of being seen from a mile away. The British were experienced with using psychological strategies against their opponents, and they intended to use their arsenal of tricks to disarm their American military opponents before they even went into battle.

By contrast, the Continental Army consisted of men with little to no training in military combat. Many of the men were young and inexperienced, some were old and out of shape, and almost all of them lacked the military discipline that a solider would have after years of military training. Their experience with weaponry was limited to game shooting, and while some of the frontiersmen had experience in fighting aggressive neighboring Native Americans, their battle experience was very different than what was found in the well-armed and trained Royal Army. And the American commanders had no tricks up their sleeves, psychological or otherwise, that would offset their weaknesses.

Benjamin Brooker and the other drummer boys served a strategic military objective. Their drumbeats helped the officers in the field to communicate with their troops. The troops understood that each drum roll represented a different military command that they were trained to follow. For example, the basic *tap-tap-tap* of the drum roll would instruct the men to line up in a simple military formation and stand behind the drummer boy.

When Benjamin Brooker started the "long drum roll" on the battlefield, he was signaling to his troops that it was time to attack the enemy. However, the British knew this signal, and waited patiently to hear the long drum roll. Then the snipers would set their sights on the vulnerable drummer boys, and shoot to kill. Many battlefields were lined with the lifeless bodies of the youngest casualties of war, the brave drummer and bugle boys.

Benjamin Brooker was first assigned to the New York Militia, Duchess County Regiment II. He mustered out of the Continental Army from the town of Hull, Massachusetts. Northeast of Hull was a strategic naval community for the Continental Army, the Massachusetts Bay. The command that Benjamin served, located twenty miles south of the city of Boston by land and only five nautical miles by water, would protect the city's southern flanks. The regiment was tasked primarily with guarding Fort Independence, located on an island in Boston Harbor, was a strategic location for the army to protect Boston and its surrounding communities from a possible British sea attack.

Once the British left Boston, they never returned to attack Boston from the harbor side, so Benjamin and his regiment saw very little combat in the war. Benjamin was most fortunate to escape death, given the high fatality rate of drummer boys.

Though drummer boys played a vital role in the troops' success, they were still very young, so they often were looked after by older men in the troops. Being a young boy of African descent, Benjamin was probably watched over by some of the older men of African descent. One such man was Cuffe Clapp Grandison of Scituate, Massachusetts.

2.4 Cuffe Grandison, Private in a Massachusetts Independent Company

While joining the Continental Army was an adventure for Benjamin Brooker, for African American men in the colonies the call to military service was an opportunity to address the oppression of white rule - American or European - and to seek personal independence and freedom from the bonds of slavery and indentured servitude. Serving in the Continental Army gave African American men their first chance of equality with their white compatriots.

Once General Washington lifted the ban for African American men to serve in the Continental Army, African men all across the colonies joined in anticipation of establishing their freedom. In the town of Scituate, Massachusetts, three patriotic brothers of African descent enlisted in the Continental Army: Cuffe, Charles and Simeon, the sons of Cuffe and Flora Grandison. At the time of the Revolutionary War, some Grandison family members were already Free People of Color, while others were still servants to the Clapp family of Scituate. Cuffe and Flora Grandison's oldest son, Cuffe, who enlisted as Cuffe Clapp, and was later known as Cuffe Grandison, was the 4th generation great-grandfather to Harold Cornwall.

For any family, white or black, to have three sons serve their country was a significant feat, but for the Grandison brothers - Cuffe, Charles and Simeon- the call to military service was even more significant. Cuffe and Flora became Free People of Color around the time of the war, but the younger Cuffe was probably not a free man, hence his original surname, Clapp. The status of Charles and Simeon are undetermined. However, regardless of their status, it was important for the Grandison brothers to be viewed by their community as equal citizens and not just as second-class citizens or chattel property.

Their first step to full equality and independence was to join the Continental Army and to permanently secure their freedom from slavery. Charles and Simeon Grandison both enlisted on February 14, 1777, and both served at the same time in the 11th Massachusetts Regiment, under the command of Colonel Ebenezer Francis.

As part of the New York campaign, the British decided that the best way to win the war against the rebellious colonists was to separate the New England colonies from the southern colonies by taking control of the Hudson River. This separation was designed to stop the commercial and communication links between Boston and Philadelphia. The first point of attack in this strategy was at the American's Fort Ticonderoga, near a narrow part of Lake Champlain in upper New York.

On July 5, 1777, British General John Burgoyne and more than 8,000 soldiers surrounded the understaffed Fort Ticonderoga and its 2,500 Continental soldiers. Charles and Simeon Grandison participated in the Saratoga campaign, where on the morning of July 7, 1777, the Continental Army was forced to retreat from Fort Ticonderoga. The British Army took command of the Fort without firing a single shot, and the Grandison brothers, along with the rest of the American Army, escaped without injury. As the Continental Army retreated from Fort Ticonderoga, they stopped at a farming village in Hubbardston, Vermont. Colonel Francis and his men were responsible for delaying the approaching British forces while the main Continental Army escaped further south. The Grandison brothers fought at the Battle of Hubbardston, where Colonel Francis was killed.

Upon the death of Colonel Francis, the 11th Massachusetts Infantry came under the command of Colonel Seth Warner's Regiment in Vermont. The brothers then became part of the infamous band of soldiers known as the "Green Mountain Boys." Although they lost the Battle of Hubbardston and were overtaken by the British, they succeeded in their mission to delay their opponents, successfully protecting the larger contingent of retreating Continental forces.

The Green Mountain Boys were a rugged group of men who prided themselves on being fiercely independent. Before the war, the Green Mountain Boys was a loose band of rowdy soldiers who came together to protect the territory between New York and New Hampshire known as the Vermont Republic.[117] They now were responsible for defending their fellow soldiers against the strongest army in the world. In this group, the Grandison brothers would learn a lot about themselves, the rugged lifestyle in the Vermont Mountains, and the men that protected them.

After securing Fort Ticonderoga, the British intended to secure the vital Hudson River. As the British moved south to attack Philadelphia, Colonel Seth Warner suspected that British General John Burgoyne would look for supplies in a community that Colonel Warner was all too familiar with - his hometown of Bennington, New York. The Grandison brothers, along with the Green Mountain Boys, were on the move, marching toward Bennington. On August 16, 1777, the British army and General John Burgoyne suffered one of their first major defeats in the war at the Battle of Bennington.

The Battle of Bennington was a strategic success for the Northern Continental Army, and this victory changed the course of the war, giving the Americans a much-needed morale boost. British General John Burgoyne lost a significant number of his troops and his supplies had dwindled, a combination that prevented the British from taking control of the Hudson River and strengthening their position southward. It forced the British to realize that taking New England and punishing the rebels in Boston would not be an easy feat. The British generals were forced to reengineer their strategy for taking New England after their embarrassing loss at Bennington only reinforced their desire to divide the colonies. The British troops advanced towards the mid-Atlantic and southern colonies, where they felt that their military strategies would be easier to accomplish.

In 1777, at the age of thirty-four, Cuffe, the oldest Grandison brother, enlisted in the Continental Army under the name of Cuffe Clapp, the name given to him at birth by his slave master. As Massachusetts continued to reinforce its batteries, Cuffe Grandison served as a private in Captain Newcomb's independent company that was stationed close to home at Hull, Massachusetts.[118] Though it was a private organization, Newcomb's company was considered part of the Massachusetts militia. Massachusetts wanted to be continuously prepared in case Britain decided to leave New York Harbor and come back to Boston Harbor to attack the city. The coastal community of Hull provided a tremendous strategic location for monitoring an advancing British fleet. Cuffe Grandison and the other seamen of Hull and its surrounding coastal communities were well familiar with the coastal waters and could provide an early warning to Boston and its citizens, as well as serve as a temporary military deterrent to the British.

In 1779, as the war moved towards a Southern Campaign, far from the corners of western and upstate New York, General Washington moved to take action against the constant raids on communities supporting the rebellion against Britain and the destruction of American supply lines by British Loyalists and Native Americans from the Iroquois nation. American Generals John Sullivan and James Clinton, with a contingent of more than 4,400 soldiers engaged in warfare against the Iroquois, destroying everything in their path.

On September 2, 1779, Charles and Simeon, along with an unspecified number of other Continental soldiers, were taken prisoner by British sympathizers.[119] Being captured is a precarious situation for any soldier, but it was even riskier for the rebellious Americans, as they could be charged with treason against the British government. For the African American soldiers, it could be a fate far worse: They not only feared being charged with treason and hanged, they also knew they could be sent to any of the dangerous sugar plantations in the West Indies and sold into slavery.

While in captivity, in order to prevent the Continental Army or other Green Mountain Boys from finding them, the British sympathizers hid the Grandison brothers and the other captives in the thick forests of upstate New York. The captured Continental soldiers were severely mistreated and malnourished, but they were not turned over to the British government. Charles and Simeon were released on June 11, 1780, as part of a prisoner exchange of "officers and other infantry men belonging to Col. Seth Warner's Massachusetts 11th regiment."[120]

2.5 The Ballard, Melton and Rucker Families in the Southern Campaign

As frontier families - such as the Ballard, Chavis, Gowen, Howell, Melton, and Rucker families in Virginia and North Carolina - repopulated themselves, they expanded not only their number of relatives, but their landholdings. Their ancestral families originated in the 1600s in the eastern Virginia coastal counties of Brunswick, Charles City, Elizabeth City, Henrico, Isle of Wight, James City, Northampton and York County. With each subsequent generation, the families succeeded in obtaining valuable land permits further and further into the western frontier land. These families cleared the land, tilled the fields, and turned thick virgin forests into productive farmland. They traveled the crooked Native American pathways in the woods and fished the bountiful streams along the riverbanks. They worked long, hard hours and fought to keep their land.

The Ballard, Chavis, Gowen, and Melton families were part of the groups against whom the racial codes passed by the Virginia House of Burgesses were directed. As each family became more racially integrated, they had to move from their established homes in the Virginia Tidewater region, to the northern and eastern counties of North Carolina. But although the Meltons and their extended families had left one home, they were determined to establish permanent roots in their new communities, even if it meant suffering through British invasion.

As the Ballard, Chavis, Gowen, and Melton families migrated further south and west they became some of the founding families of the newly incorporated Virginia counties of Brunswick, Greenville, Orange, and newly incorporated North Carolina counties of Southampton, and Gates, Granville, Guilford, Hertford Northampton and Rockingham.

These areas had been largely exempt from battle while the war effort was contained to a northern strategy, but that was about to change.

In January 1780, the British decided to change their military strategy and leave the comfortable surroundings of New York Harbor. Instead of heading north, they launched a southern offensive, and sailed towards the port city of Charleston, South Carolina. Charleston was one of the richest port cities on the continent, had an ideal deep-water harbor and was the fourth largest city in the colonies. England hoped that the significant population of Loyalists, colonists they perceived to be sympathetic to and supportive of England, would work to their advantage. The British commanders mistakenly believed that since the southern colonies in general, and South Carolina in particular, were loyal to the British crown, a southern offensive would be a much easier feat than in the North.[121]

The British, under the command of General Henry Clinton, landed more than 8,000 soldiers south of Charleston and marched northward to take the port city. After a six-week- long offensive, the Continental Army was no match for an aggressive British attack. Once the British took control of Charleston, they launched their Southern Campaign. General Clinton and his navy left Charleston Harbor and returned north to New York harbor. Military control transferred to British General Charles Cornwallis.

Under the leadership of General Cornwallis, the British troops marched northward through the swamps and backcountry of South Carolina to take the remainder of the southern colonies. However, they were often encumbered by minor but very costly battles with the scrappy South and North Carolina militias. The British believed that once they arrived in South Carolina and took control of Charleston, the Loyalists would come to their defense and assist them in bringing the war to a speedy end. However, "of the many mistakes Britain made with her American colonies, none was more costly or had more far-reaching consequences than her assumption that numerous southern Loyalists would without encouragement" support the war effort against the American rebels.[122]

As Cornwallis became entangled with the guerrilla tactics of the Carolinas' backcountry militias, many British soldiers were killed, which cost the army its valuable competitive edge. Cornwallis also lost important military supplies in the muck of the swamps, and the sweltering heat caused a significant decrease in troop morale. General Cornwallis needed to change course and strategy. Throughout the war, the British were masterful in using psychological warfare to their advantage at every opportunity. For the Southern Campaign, the British decided that they needed to separate the loyalties of the wealthier southern colonists from the poorer common man. To accomplish this, the British would play upon the biggest fear of the southern gentry: the freeing and arming of their African slaves.

Once British Army General Henry Clinton arrived back in New York from Charleston and heard of the challenges that Cornwallis was having in the Carolina swamps, he issued the Phillipsburg Proclamation, which stated that any slaves that escaped their American masters and joined the British army would be freed, given protection, and given their own land.

Although it was initially reported that more than 30,000 slaves escaped from their plantations to take advantage of the Phillipsburg Proclamation, General Clinton's action ultimately backfired on the British.[123] As thousands of African slaves were escaping from plantations all across the south, particularly from the Carolinas, the unrest between the British Loyalist and the American Patriots only increased. Furthermore, Free People of Color who already owned land feared that their property would be seized by the British, who would then give it to newly freed slaves. The Free People of Color also feared that as free Africans, they would be considered "Black Loyalist," despite having been Free People of Color before the Phillipsburg Proclamation.

White neighbors, Patriots and Loyalist, fought hand-to-hand in each other's backyards. Hungry and lost runaway slaves, unfamiliar with the terrain, were crisscrossing the countryside. Free People of Color, who feared losing their freedom to British proclamations, took up arms against anyone who came on their property. It was anarchy all across the Carolinas, entirely disadvantageous to a British army that was used to military control and structure.

This was not what the British had hoped for, particularly since they were chasing militia throughout unfamiliar, dangerous terrain while civil disorder was erupting all around them. Once again, the psychological warfare employed by the British was not meeting their expectations. Their tactics against the Americans only caused the American militia to grow in ranks and in anger. The Southern Campaign's effort to free the slaves in order to aid the British backfired: It only added more and more white soldiers to the American militia.

The British progress was further hampered as the newly freed and runaway slaves affixed themselves to the British troops and formed caravans behind the marching soldiers, slowing their progress through the thicketed forests. The British were already short on supplies and now had more mouths to feed and bodies to clothe. The Redcoats were fighting an unconventional guerrilla campaign in the swamps and the thick of the southern forests, and this was not the type of warfare to which they were accustomed. At this juncture, General Cornwallis understood that the Southern Campaign was not going well from any tactical standpoint, and another major military course correction was in order.

Hearing of the British General Cornwallis' dilemma, the Continental Army sent General Nathaniel Greene to support the southern militia and confront Cornwallis, further entangling him and his army in the thick of the Carolina swamps. Following the example of local Native American warriors, General Greene forced the British General to chase him throughout the Carolinas, causing the British troops to go deeper and deeper into the wilderness, and further and further from supplies and reinforcements. The ever-elusive General Green and his men escaped North Carolina into Virginia without being captured, which only added to General Cornwallis' frustration.

2.6   Edward Gowen, Private in North Carolina Regiment

During the winter between 1780 and 1781, General Greene and his rebel troops regrouped in Halifax, Virginia, the ancestral home of Margaret Melton Murphy's family. On February 22, 1781, General Green positioned his men to confront and taunt Cornwallis and his men, who were now tired, weary of the Carolina swamps, and weakened by the disease-carrying mosquitoes. However, though temporarily overwhelmed by the Carolinas' unfamiliar terrain, the British army gradually untangled itself from the forests and swamps, and moved onward to the Virginia and North Carolina Chesapeake Bay tidewater regions.

As the two powerful armies approached and prepared for war, local families prepared, too, and decisions needed to be made quickly. Political allegiances had to be established. And most importantly, provisions needed to be prepared in the event of a lengthy war. One such family was that of Edward Going (as spelled on his military papers), the 4th generation great-grandson of John Gowen of Jamestown, Virginia.

Edward Goings' first appearance on the Revolutionary War roster was on September 3, 1778, where he enlisted to serve as a Continental solider for nine months in Bute County, North Carolina. Based on the transcript, he was a thirty-five year old private, born in Virginia and was five feet, seven inches in height. According to his Pension Affidavit, Private Going joined the North Carolina 5th Regiment under Colonel William Eaton and was stationed for about two months in Halifax, Virginia before he marched from Leesburg to the Savannah River in Georgia. From there he marched upstream to a place called the Black Swamp, where he fell ill. He was hospitalized in Charleston for several months, after which he was discharged and sent home. He mustered out in June, 1779.[124]

After being home for about two years, Edward Going rejoined the Continental Army in Louisburg Township in Franklin County under the command under Captain Benjamin Eaves. His regiment eventually joined the Army commanded by General Nathaniel Green.[125] With General Green playing a tactical cat-and-mouse game with the British, the tidewater families prepared for the inevitable - the convergence of war in their own backyards.

Once his troops and the local volunteers were in place and ready for combat, General Green crossed the Virginia side of the Dan River back into North Carolina. He was prepared to draw General Cornwallis into a battle in an area known as the Guilford Courthouse, which was strategically favorable to the American troops. On March 15, 1781, one of the bloodiest battles of the war erupted at the Guilford County Courthouse, in Greensboro, North Carolina. Although the British were the technical winners of the battle, they suffered one of the greatest psychological losses of the war. With his troops battered, hungry, and physically drained, Cornwallis made the tactical decision to leave North Carolina for Virginia.

In 1781, the news of the mass casualties from the Southern Campaign and the military stalemate from the Northern Campaign further exhausted the already fatigued citizens of Great Britain. They felt that after six years battling in America, the war was taking an enormous toll on human life and on the British treasury. The patience of the British people had thinned. From their perspective, the time had come for a decisive battle that would bring the war to an end. Realizing the pressures and sentiment in England, Cornwallis moved his troops to the coastal community of Yorktown, Virginia. This maneuver proved to be a fatal move for the British army and for General Cornwallis.

Realizing that they had a competitive edge for the first time, the Continental Army decided that now was the time to proceed and fight a defensive war. They made plans to consolidate all of the troops in Virginia and took measures to secure and protect the southern command's military positions, and to move assets along the naval bases on the Chesapeake Bay. While Cornwallis was moving his men to Yorktown, Virginia, General Washington simultaneously moved all of his men, ammunition, and artillery southward to join General Greene and the other commanders of the Southern Campaign. Washington also believed that the time had come to end the war.

After six long years of battle, Washington was returning to his home of Virginia to bring the war to a close, one way or another. Private Samuel Cornwell from Connecticut, the loyal Patriot solider who had served with General George Washington at Valley Forge, marched with his Commander to the Battle of New York City, on to Trenton in New Jersey, on to Philadelphia, and now made the long march southward to Virginia. Some of the men marched to Virginia without shoes, after boiling the leather soles and eating their footwear to satiate their hunger pangs.

On September 5, 1781, the French Navy, an American ally, arrived in the Chesapeake Bay to confront the smaller British Navy secured in port. After a four-day battle at sea, the French succeeded in securing the waters around Yorktown, essentially providing a naval blockade.

Watching the events unfold, General Cornwallis must have sensed that the events of the war were about to radically change. As

Cornwallis received reconnaissance from the field, he learned of the massive number of men on foot arriving from the north, and of the French ships in the Chesapeake Bay with their gunnery aimed directly at him. Cornwallis was out-maneuvered. With a military force of more than 17,000 French and American men surrounding the British by land and sea, Cornwallis was trapped.

The combined American and French armies decided to conduct long-range cannon fire on the heavily fortified city, hoping that the trapped Cornwallis would surrender before reinforcements came to support the British general and his men. On the evening of October 14, 1781, the Continental Army proceeded to attack the outer batteries of Yorktown, Virginia. Only five days later, on October 19, 1781, Private Samuel Cornwell witnessed one of the most notable days in American history: the day when Lord General Charles Cornwallis surrendered and more than 7,000 British men laid down their arms to General George Washington.

Cornwallis' surrender at the Battle at Yorktown did not end the war. The British still had almost 20,000 men scattered throughout the colonies. However, the entire British military forces across the continent were now on the defensive. The British public could not understand why they were still fighting when Britain had the world's strongest army and a naval armada that was the envy of their fiercest competitors. The war in America was costly, a tremendous drain on the British treasury and it only prolonged a severe national recession that impacted every Englishman in one way or another. First the French and Indian War, and now a rebellious uprising: The colonies were supposed to generate money for England, not cost lives and deplete the treasury. Britain's citizens wanted an end to the war.

The various remaining British troops joined forces and retreated to the cities of Savannah, Georgia, and Charleston, South Carolina, where fierce fighting raged on for another twelve months. On November 30, 1782, after Parliament voted to end the war, the British put forth an initial treaty that conceded that their former thirteen colonies were to be forever known as the United States of America. In the spring of 1783, the British soldiers left America through the city of New York. On September 3, after eight long years, the British signed the Treaty of Paris, and the Revolutionary War was finally over.

2.7 Caesar Russell, Private in the 4th Massachusetts Regiment

Towards the end of the war, another African American patriot served the Continental Army. His name was Caesar Russell, from the town of Beverly, Massachusetts. On March 5, 1781, Caesar Russell enlisted in the Company Command of Captain Francis, who was assigned to the 7th Regiment of Colonel John Brooks.[126] Much of Private Russell's two-year military service was spent in the state of New York at West Point, under the command of Captain Jonathan Allen's 4th Massachusetts regiment. Private Russell, Harold Cornwall's 3rd generation great-grandfather, was selected to serve as a personal servant to Captain William North, who was an *aide-de-camp* to the Prussian General Baron von Steuben, the general who masterfully made his mark by improving the horrific conditions at Valley Forge, Pennsylvania, and designing the successful military maneuvers in New Jersey.

Six months after Caesar Russell enlisted, on October 19, 1781, British General Charles Cornwallis, after being trapped on a small peninsula in Yorktown, Virginia, finally surrendered to the American General George Washington. It took almost two years after Cornwallis' surrender for the Treaty of Paris to be signed. Although the war came to an end, General Washington, who knew only too well the psychological trickery of the British military, did not want to disband the Continental Army in the event that the British resume their attack. Washington wanted a transitional army, one that would shift from a wartime army to an army that would eventually protect the new nation's borders. General Washington entrusted General Baron von Steuben and his aides to establish a transitional military force.

Caesar Russell, as a personal servant to General North, witnessed firsthand the final days of the war and the formal demobilization of the Continental Army. As part of the Army's demobilization, General Washington asked Steuben and his aides to design the military defense plan for the new nation. These men scrutinized the role of the military versus the role of a centralized federal government, and the interface of the military with decentralized state governments.

As a civilian, George Washington went to Philadelphia and presided over the formation of the new United States government. The Continental Congress decided to move the new government from

Philadelphia to the swampy marshlands on the Potomac River between Baltimore, Maryland, and Richmond, Virginia. Another former aide to General Washington and General Steuben was the French-born Pierre L'Enfant, who served as an architect and engineer, and had helped design the military camp at Valley Forge. Following the end of the Revolutionary War, Pierre L'Enfant was asked to design the seal and insignia for the Cincinnati Society, a fraternal order for retired military officers.[127] L'Enfant later designed the nation's new capital city, named for General George Washington, in the area known as the District of Columbia.

At West Point, General Steuben and his aides worked long, laborious hours to figure out the most efficient centralized military command, as well as how to sustain life cycle management in order to move men and supplies rapidly. They put in place the organizational structure for the new nation's army and navy, ensuring the protection of the country on land and sea. They also established military discipline through effective training, and a leadership-training program that communicated new policies and procedures to the troops in the field through rigid training protocols.

While General North worked hard alongside General Steuben to establish the new American army, Caesar Russell managed his daily routine. Caesar ensured that North's uniform was befitting of a man in his military command, and that he was on time for meetings and social gatherings. Caesar would often schedule North's appointments with other commanders and military officers, and facilitated the distribution and receipt of military papers and attaches.

Although it is unclear if Caesar Russell attended any of the meetings, he was certainly privy to classified materials, discussions and activities. Though General Steuben helped establish the new government's military code, there is no evidence that they established a basis for today's concept of "secured personnel" or security clearances, a complex military system of protection important information and military activities. If such as system existed, Caesar Russell certainly would have had a high security clearance, for he was intimately knowledgeable of General North's daily habits and briefings, and he had access to North's papers. Caesar Russell was knowledgeable of

North's personal contacts, and was probably aware of any dalliances that the General may have encountered.

General Steuben, General North, and Captain Benjamin Walker, having worked long tireless hours together, and living in relatively close quarters, developed strong personal relationships with each other. Through the years, it has been widely speculated that the close relationship among the men was more than simply friendly. As a personal servant to General North, with his almost unlimited access, Caesar Russell must have known firsthand the many secrets about General William North, especially secrets about whether Generals Steuben and North had a "romantic relationship" as speculated at the time.[128]

If the allegations about Steuben and North's relationship were true, Private Caesar Russell must have been conflicted in his loyalties to his commanding officers. Throughout history, the "hired help" kept many secrets of the men and women for whom they worked. The need for secrecy increased in the midst of war, and the men on the battlefield had to trust the men for whom they served. Most commanding officers had enough challenges with troop morale without having to address questionable behavior amongst their men, let alone their officers. While each generation and military environment has looked at homosexual relationships differently, in the late 1700s, a relationship of this type was certainly one that would presumably have caused a scandal.

When General Steuben first arrived in America to meet with General Washington, he had only one credential - a military medal from the Prussian Army. General Washington was in such dire need of the expertise of a European military officer who could bring disciplined skills to battle that few, if any, questions were asked of Steuben. However, in recent years, scholars and historians have surmised that many of the rumors that followed Steuben across the Atlantic Ocean were not flattering - and although widely speculative in nature, were the reasons he was forced to leave the Prussian Army.

2.8   Patriotic War Veterans Return Home to Build America

Once the Revolutionary War finally come to an end, veterans returned home and attempted to resume and rebuild their former lives. These men had been permanently changed by the war. The former soldiers and their communities also had to make amends with the humiliated Loyalists who had supported the British monarchy. Then, they could finally begin the process of building a new nation. Although the Continental Congress guided the young nation through the turbulent times of war, much needed to be done to establish a fully integrated United States, both domestically and internationally. After the war, the young nation grappled with a multitude of complex issues, including the post-war economy, European immigration, the treatment and import of African slaves, and the issues of governance. Some of the main political and military characters that had fought together during the Revolutionary War took opposing political sides in the war's aftermath.

General George Washington, the Commander in Chief of the Continental Army, presided over the Continental Convention that drafted the United States Constitution. The convention dealt with the tangled problems of reconciling the right of a centralized federal government with the individual rights of each state in matters of taxation, slavery, and elected representation. After the Constitution, was ratified in 1788, General Washington was selected the first President of the United States, taking the oath of office in New York City, in 1789 and serving two terms.

Major General Alexander Hamilton, an *aide-de-camp* to General George Washington, became a primary champion and promoter of a strong federal government supported by an entrepreneurial society. Hamilton became the first Secretary of the United States Treasury, and established the financial banking system. His political views cost him many friends and he died in a duel with Vice President Aaron Burr. Diametrically opposed to Alexander Hamilton's opinions were those of Thomas Jefferson, who was in favor of a strong local agrarian society run by the individual states. Jefferson was the nation's third President.

After the war, the drillmaster of Valley Forge, General Baron von Steuben, became an American citizen in March 1784, and was discharged from the military with honor. For his military service, he was granted property that included a home and twenty acres of land. But upon his discharge, Steuben quickly lost almost all of his money and was close to being destitute. He died a bachelor ten years later, leaving his property to his former aides, whom he referred to as "adopted sons," William North and Benjamin Walker. General William North, commanding officer over Private Caesar Russell, inherited the remains of the estate of General von Steuben, and later served on the Erie Canal Commission.

Although not as well known as the men described as America's "founding fathers," there were many other heroes and legends that served in the Revolutionary War, each with a story and legacy that contributed to the birth of this great nation. The members of the Cornwall Murphy family, including Benjamin Brooker, Samuel Cornwell, Cuffe, Charles and Simeon Grandison, and Caesar Russell, clearly had an impact on their communities and the nation they would now help to build.

After the war, Private Samuel Cornwell profited from a post-wartime economy. Having served essentially the entire duration of the war, he learned many skills that would help him in life and in business. He became a shipping merchant and owned or had partial ownership of a number of schooners that transported goods between the United States and Canada. Samuel Cornwell operated out of Eastport, Maine, which was a small island community with easy access to New Brunswick, Canada. His businesses thrived, due to his strong military contacts, his tactical knowledge, and his understanding of the military supply chain management, along with his familiarity with the Canadian, New England and New York Harbors and their surrounding communities. He traded in lumber, potatoes, fish, animal furs and other products that could easily be sold in the New York and Boston Harbors. He provided textile products and refined sugar products processed in the Boston refineries to the Canadian and Maine markets.

Also after the war, Samuel Cornwell married Sarah Mansfield, and they had seven children. Their son, Mansfield, was their third child, named after his mother's maiden name. Mansfield Cornwell was Harold Cornwall's great-great grandfather.

Private Samuel Cornwell died on October 26, 1840, in New York City. His wife Sarah passed away on October 24, 1850, also in New York City.

After the war, the young drummer boy from New Haven, Connecticut, Benjamin Brooker continued to live in the area of Hull,

Massachusetts, where he had been stationed during the war. No longer a young black slave joining the military to escape from life's cruelties, Benjamin Brooker was now a free man in the state of Massachusetts, and embodied all that America was to become - a land of opportunity and freedom.

Benjamin Brooker became involved in political activism in Boston, and was connected to one of its greatest orators and civil rights activists of the time, Prince Hall, the founder of the city's first lodge of African American Masons. In 1791, Benjamin married Harriet Grandison, daughter to another Revolutionary War hero, Private Cuffe Grandison of Scituate, Massachusetts. Benjamin and Harriet had two known sons, Benjamin and Samuel, the latter of whom was named after his father's friend, Samuel Brooker.

Private Benjamin Brooker died January 22, 1822, in Boston. His wife Harriet Grandison Brooker passed away July 28, 1823 in Bridgewater, Massachusetts.

Brothers Charles and Simeon Grandison served in some of the most rugged, exhausting environments for battle in the country and had been mistreated as prisoners of war. After they were discharged from the military, they moved to the town of New Providence in the Berkshire Mountains of Massachusetts. Their brother Cuffe remained in the town of Scituate and permanently changed his last name from the name of his owners, Clapp, to his parents' surname, Grandison. Like many African American men, he did not want to continue to use the name of his former owners. Although the Clapp family treated his family well and gave them access to a house and farm, many northern slaves, upon emancipation, changed their last names to reflect their newly freed status. Very little information is known about Cuffe after the war, other than his marriage to Ruth Raif in 1744 resulted in the birth of three children: Abigail, Harriet, and Charles. His daughter Harriet married Benjamin Brooker.

Private Cuffe Grandison passed away on August 2, 1810 in Scituate, Massachusetts, months before the 1790 Census was taken. His wife Ruth Raif Grandison passed away in 1825, also in Scituate.

After his first stint in the Revolutionary War ended in June, 1779, North Carolina's Private Edward Going received a "discharge" for his services. According to his pension affidavit, he sold his military discharge for six dollars to "W. Jno (John) Hall."[129] Three months after returning home, on August 3, 1779, Going purchased 75 acres of land on Hyco Creek in the St. Luke's District in Caswell County.[130] Perhaps motivated to purchase more land, Going joined the Continental Army a second time. Once the war was over, according to the North Carolina Genealogical Society Journal, Edward Going and his brother Jenkins on April 27, 1791 sold their discharge pay for Revolutionary War service to John Hall of Hyco, Caswell County.[131] While plausible that the funds were used to pay off old debts, it is more likely he used the funds to purchase additional land.

In 1784, Goings owned 100 acres of land valued at the British monetary pound system's £133 and taxed on six shillings and eight pence.[132] By 1791, Edward Going owned 245 acres of land in that part of Caswell County that was now part of the newly incorporated Person County.[133] On October 31, 1807, Edward Going/Gowen, according to their marriage bond, married Rebecca Anderson, daughter of mulatto Lewis Anderson and Winifred "Winnie" Bass Anderson. According to the Granville County, North Carolina Marriages, 1753-1855 Index, her brother, George Anderson was their bondsman.[134]

In his research, Paul Heinegg wrote in his epic book on the *Free African Americans of North Carolina and Virginia,* "Rebecca Anderson was the great-great-granddaughter of Kate Anderson, a Negro slave whose manumission created a great stir in the Virginia House of Burgesses. Her owner, John Fulcher of Norfolk County directed in his will of October 12, 1712, that his 15 slaves be freed. He directed his executor, Lewis Conner to give "to my Negroes, men and women and children, their freedom. According to colonial Virginia's Henning's Statutes, Volume III, "Kate Anderson and 14 other members of her extended family were also bequeathed by the will 640 acres of land in Norfolk County to the consternation of the Virginia legislators and planters. The House quickly moved to squelch the idea of freeing slaves in Virginia. They wrote legislation to "provide by a law against such manumission of slaves, which may in time by their increase and correspondence with other slaves ... endanger the peace of this Colony".[135]

Despite their consternation, the Virginia legislators and planters "could not legally undo the damage that slave Master John Fulcher had done, but they felt they could discourage it from ever being repeated. Lewis Conner, Fulcher's executor, sought to minimize the problem for Virginia by exporting it to North Carolina. He swapped the 640 acres in Norfolk County for a section of land in Chowan County, North Carolina, just across the colony line. The Anderson family was reluctant to leave Virginia, so the executor "sweetened the deal" with an extra 300 acres of North Carolina land. Five years later the Andersons were still in Virginia, the deed to the promised North Carolina land not having materialized. The family filed suit against Conner in 1717 in York County and produced Fulcher's will in court in an effort to obtain title to the land. The Andersons won the case, the court declaring that the wishes of a dying man were inviolate. But Conner appealed to the superior court in Williamsburg, and the verdict was reversed. Edward "Ned" Anderson, one of the children freed by Fulcher was back in court in 1734 trying to get title to the North Carolina land. Twenty-two years after the date of Fulcher's will, the North Carolina land lay in Bath County. Shortly afterward, Bath County itself was dissolved, and the Anderson family apparently gave up on the effort to secure its inheritance.[136]

The Colony of Virginia was not victorious in the matter either. It could not long hold back manumission either by law or by delaying tactics such as was used on the Andersons and the Gowens. When President George Washington died in December 1799, he had already specified in his will that his slaves were to be given their freedom. Patrick Henry, Thomas Jefferson, John Adams, Alexander Hamilton and other statesmen took a stand against slavery. Rebecca Anderson Gowen's parents, Lewis Anderson and Winifred "Winnie" Bass Anderson died without ever inheriting any of the Fulcher land".[137]

In 1783, Private Caesar Russell, after being assigned to General North and General Baron Von Steuben, was honorably discharged from the military for his service to the Continental Army, in the state of New York at West Point, with the balance of his military service unexpired. The 4th Massachusetts Regiment, also known as 3rd Continental Regiment, was disbanded at West Point. After his war service, Private Caesar Russell married Sally Richardson of Wilmington, Massachusetts[138], and they had twelve children.[139] The Russell family, Free People of Color, lived in the community of Beverly, Massachusetts, about twenty miles northeast of Boston.

In 1796, the Ship *Mary* sailed under Captain Nicholas Thorndike of Beverly, Massachusetts, to the East Indies and other ports in the United States. According to the Beverly Massachusetts Historical Society, Caesar Russell served as cook on this ship and signed his own name - not a mark, as was expected for illiterate workers - to the roster.[140] In 1798, Caesar's daughter Philinda was born. In 1801, Caesar was once again listed on the crew of Ship *Mary* as a cook.[141]

Although small in stature, a diminutive five-feet, four inches, Caesar's experiences were larger than life. While African and Indian men were still taken against their will to the United States and the Caribbean island of Trinidad and sold into slavery or indentured servitude, Caesar Russell, though only a cook, was traveling to the same international port cities as a Free Person of Color. Serving in the Continental Army with General von Steuben and General North and sailing around the world as a Free Person of Color were both enormous accomplishments for a man of African descent.

Caesar Russell also was unique in another way: he appeared to be somewhat literate. His signature on the Ship *Mary's* register did not need someone else to notarize an "X," a common practice among those that could not read or write. It is unclear where or how Caesar learned to write his own name, especially given that even white soldiers were unable to sign their military pensions in 1810. Caesar's ability to write his own name was an amazing accomplishment because at that time, most Americans of African descent were never taught the fundamentals of reading and writing due to discriminatory laws that limited education for all People of Color.

Private Caesar Russell outlived many of his old friends and several of his children and grandchildren. When Caesar passed away on October 20, 1861, in Taunton, Massachusetts, there were several documents that contradicted the date and location of his birth. The 1801 roster of the Ship *Mary* perhaps helps to resolve, to some degree, the question as to the year of his birth. In the roster, he is described as 35 years of age, placing the year of his birth as 1766, which matches the date on his military record in the Continental Congress. However, the uncertainty surrounding the location of his birth remains. The Ship *Mary's* roster states that Caesar Russell was born in Middleton, Massachusetts, which contradicts the other vital records discovered during research.

Caesar Russell's certified Commonwealth of Massachusetts Death Certificate states that he was 105 years old, making 1756 his year of birth. This record also claims he was born in North Carolina. However, the City of Taunton's Registry of Deaths states that he was 110 at the time of his death, though this record also states that he was born in North Carolina. Caesar must have had a wonderful sense of humor - or perhaps he wanted to diminish the age difference between himself and his wife, who was in fact much younger than he was - because on his 1850 United States Census form he told the enumerator that he was born in North Carolina and that he was only 76 years old, making his birth year 1784.[142] That also would mean that he was 87 at the time of his death.

But whatever the correct year of his birth, Caesar Russell was a remarkable man, having survived military service in the Revolutionary War, worked as Free Person of Color, and lived to be 87, 105 or 110 years young - an impressive feat during a time when the average life expectancy was 35.

After the Revolutionary War, Massachusetts' African American community was a tight-knit group of farmers, artisans, merchants and seamen. Boston was the cultural epicenter for African American families in the United States, where the sons and daughters of Revolutionary War veterans came together to celebrate birthdays, holidays and marriages. Their fathers also gathered to share stories of the military battles they had fought in and how they handled the challenges of race on the battlefield. The men talked about the heroes that they met, and their military escapades that one day would become legends.

Although these families lived miles apart, these social events also served as opportunities for young men and women of color to meet one another and to begin proper courtships. Caesar and Sally Russell's daughter, Philinda Russell, met and subsequently married Samuel Brooker, who was the son of Revolutionary War patriot Benjamin Brooker and his wife, Harriet Grandison, the daughter of Cuffe and Ruth Raif Grandison of Scituate, Massachusetts.

2.9 First United States Census

In the aftermath of the Revolutionary War, the young nation changed in dramatic ways that most had not anticipated. Up to that point, Americans lived in rural communities and looked toward acquiring farms and growing their personal wealth. The newly formed United States had richly abundant natural resources. It was also home to a workforce equipped with the skills necessary to build the rapidly growing nation. It was now critical for the Federal government to gather demographic information, as well as for the state and local governments to raise taxes to offset the exorbitant cost of the Revolutionary War. In addition, the growing number of territories in the west needed increased populations in order to meet the initial statehood requirements for formal admission into the United States.

In response to the growing need for workers, more and more Europeans immigrated to the new nation, building large cities in the northeast. War veterans started moving west and south in search of land. The slave trade continued, bringing more and more African slaves into the south. With the nation's population constantly growing and changing, many wondered: Who lives in America, and where? As Americans became increasingly mobile, the United States government commissioned the first United States Census in 1790, the first official count of the nation's diverse population. It provided invaluable information to the federal government and to each of the newly established states in the Union. In some instances, however, it provided too much information. The first United States census was not without controversy.

By 1790, the United States had grown from the original thirteen colonies to sixteen American states. The census collected the name of the head of household for every family in the country, as well as counting the number of free white males ages 16 and older for taxation purposes and in order to assess the country's industrial and military potential. The census also counted the number of free white males under 16, the number of free white females, including heads of families, and the number of slaves and all other free persons.

The first United States Census counted 3,893,635 inhabitants. Approximately 18% (694,280) of the population were African slaves, living mostly in the South. Of that, approximately 9% (59,150) of the Americans of African descent were free. At the time of the 1790 Census, Massachusetts and Maine had emancipated their slaves. Therefore no slaves were counted in the census for those states, only Free People of Color.

The first census served as a baseline for future decennial censuses, and as a major benchmark for recording the country's rapid population growth.

Figure 27: The First United State Census - 1790[143]

State	Free white males 16 >	Free white males ≤ 16	Free white females, 16>	Other free persons	Slaves	Total
Connecticut	60,523	54,403	117,448	2,808	2,764	237,946
Delaware	11,783	12,143	22,384	3,899	8,887	59,094
Georgia	13,103	14,044	25,739	398	29,264	82,548
Kentucky	15,154	17,057	28,922	114	12,430	73,677
Maine	24,384	24,748	46,870	538	0	96,540
Maryland	55,915	51,339	101,395	8,043	103,036	319,728
Massachusetts	95,453	87,289	190,582	5,463	0	378,787
New Hampshire	36,086	34,851	70,160	630	158	141,885
New Jersey	45,251	41,416	83,287	2,762	11,423	184,139
New York	83,700	78,122	152,320	4,654	21,324	340,120
North Carolina	69,988	77,506	140,710	4,975	100,572	393,751
Pennsylvania	110,788	106,948	206,363	6,537	3,737	434,373
Rhode Island	16,019	15,799	32,652	3,407	948	68,825
South Carolina	35,576	37,722	66,880	1,801	107,094	249,073
Vermont	22,435	22,328	40,505	255	16	85,539
Virginia	110,936	116,135	215,046	12,866	292,627	747,610
Total	807,094	791,850	1,541,263	59,150	694,280	3,893,635

The increasing importance of slavery on the South's economy, the reliance of immigrant labor in the north, and incremental growth of westward expansion would set the stage for strong political and regional debates in the months and years to come. In 1790, more than a third of the South's population were People of Color, and of that, over 95% of the population were enslaved men, women and children. Between 1790 and 1800, the population in the United States increased by 36%, from 3,893,635 residents to 5,305,982. This tremendous population growth created enormous problems for the new nation. During the same period, almost 20% of the nation's population was of African or mixed race descent. In just ten years, with the second United States Census in 1800, the African American population exploded from 694,280 to more than a million.

Four years after the first Census was taken, the US Congress banned the import of slaves from foreign countries. However, the growth of Americans of African descent exploded as African Americans, free and slave, repopulated, particularly in the southern slave states.

Figure 28: 1790 Southern States Racial Breakdown[144]

State	Free white persons	Other free persons	Slaves	Total	% White	% Non-White
Georgia	52,886	398	29,264	82,548	64.07%	35.93%
Kentucky	61,133	114	12,430	73,677	82.97%	17.03%
Maryland	208,649	8,043	103,036	319,728	65.26%	34.74%
N. Carolina	288,204	4,975	100,572	393,751	73.19%	26.81%
S. Carolina	140,178	1,801	107,094	249,073	56.28%	43.72%
Virginia	442,117	12,866	292,627	747,610	59.14%	40.86%
Total	1,193,167	28,197	694,280	1,866,387	63.93%	36.07%

These southern states were beginning to realize the significance of the vast numbers of Europeans migrating to the growing cities in the north. Similarly, northern states began to realize the full effects of slavery on the southern economy. Those realizations, combined with the increasing migration into the expanding new territories in the west, made Americans more determined than ever to explore and occupy all of the lands to the Mississippi River and beyond, all the way to the Pacific Ocean.

The ancestors of the Cornwall Murphy family can easily be found in the first United States Census in 1790, and the communities in which they lived were indicative and significant to the complex issues facing the country.[145] Most of the family's patriotic ancestors who served in the Revolutionary War were still alive in 1790 and can be found in the census, which also included critical information about their personal lives and their communities. Despite the perception that all African Americans were bound to slavery, almost all of the Cornwall Murphy family members can be found in the 1790 Federal Census, and all were designated as Free People of Color.

2.10   Continued Seeds for Rebellion

With any burgeoning nation, the military and political elite take their place within the new government, and the years immediately after a revolution are usually periods of tremendous turmoil and uncertainly. People question the leadership, the rule of law is debated, and the role of the military and civilian authority is defined. The emerging United States was no different.

As thousands of men returned home from war, they and their communities were faced with many questions and many challenges. How would these communities integrate men who had seen the harsh, brutal realities of war back into their communities as civilized and productive citizens? How would these same communities, which had lost the productive labor of these men and critical financial resources, galvanize both the labor force and tax systems into moving forward for the new republic of the United States? Where would power reside at the local and state levels of government? A more abstract challenge was the idealistic theory that all men were created equal: How would that manifest in a society that still viewed People of Color as second-class citizens? In a period of three short years, the young nation would be confronted by each of these challenges, and more.

Figure 29: The Challenges for the Young Nation

> - National and state treasuries had little to no money.
> - Soldiers returning home hadn't been paid for their military service.
> - Loyalists were chastised for supporting the British in the war.
> - Native Americans who supported both sides of the war were on the verge of losing their tribal lands.
> - African Americans who supported the war still found themselves shackled in slavery.

These confrontations would result in another rebellion that once again had to do with taxes. As the debate over Great Britain raising taxes in Boston was a catalyst for the American Revolution, the debate over the collection of state taxes in Massachusetts ignited an armed rebellion in central and western Massachusetts, referred to as the Shays' Rebellion.

Many of the soldiers who returned from war were destitute. Many had received little to no pay for their war-time service and their farmlands were in ruin from lack of cultivation. Unfortunately, the local governments faced tremendous financial constraints caused by a major post-war economic recession, and had to collect back taxes on farms, many of which were owned by the war veterans.[146]

Figure 30: Mistreatment of American Patriot Soldiers

"I have been greatly abused, have been obliged to do more than my part in the war, been loaded with class rates, town rates, province rates, Continental rates and all rates ... been pulled and hauled by sheriffs, constables and collectors, and had my cattle sold for less than they were worth ... The great men are going to get all we have and I think it is time for us to rise and put a stop to it, and have no more courts, nor sheriffs, nor collectors nor lawyers."

Plough Jogger, former Patriotic solider and an aggrieved farmer

The leader of the insurgence was Captain Daniel Shays, a military leader who served under General Seth Warner in the 5th Massachusetts Regiment, the regiment of Charles and Simeon Grandison.[147] Captain Shays successfully led his men, including the Grandison brothers, at the Battle at Saratoga against General John Burgoyne, where the British suffered one of the first major defeats of the war at the Battle of Bennington. General Shays led the men of this tax rebellion with the same valor with which he had led men during the war.

On August 29, 1786, in the Berkshire Mountains of western Massachusetts, Captain Shays led between 2,000 and 4,000-armed men in an attempt to stop the foreclosure of several farms that owed delinquent taxes by closing down county and state courthouses.[148]

Figure 31: They Fought for Their Country - Now
They Fought against Their Own State

"The hard-pressed rural debtors of western Massachusetts posed a more formidable threat to law and order. They held impromptu conventions, refused to pay taxes and fees, prevented county courts from conducting business, and nearly 2,000 of them took to arms as they marched hither and yon seeking additional recruits, weapons, and redress of grievances."[149]

Don Higginbotham, *The War of American Independence,
Military Attitudes, Policies, and Practice, 1763 -1789*

For the next year, all across central and western Massachusetts, the protestors stormed into local courthouses to disrupt judicial proceedings in an attempt to halt tax and collection processes by any means possible. In order to stop the protestors and to keep the rebellion from spreading to other parts of the state, Massachusetts sent several militias to the affected areas.

One unlikely militia to come forward and offer its services to the state of Massachusetts was a group of former Revolutionary War veterans of African descent. They were led by former slave Prince Hall and the men of the Prince Hall Masonic Temple of Boston. One such man was Benjamin Brooker, no longer a drummer boy, but now 21-one years old and experienced beyond his years.

Prince Hall, a war veteran who served in General Washington's regiment at Valley Forge, is widely credited as being the first black Civil Rights activist in America. "He devoted his life to helping the African American community to understand how to get together in the defense of their social, political, and economic rights."[150] He was perhaps the first African American leader on a national stage to publicly advance the dialogue of education and economic empowerment for families of color. He also called upon the political leaders of government to address the inequities imposed on Boston's African American community.

While General Shays was supported by predominantly young, disenfranchised white veterans, Private Prince Hall was advocating for young African American men across the entire state to demand a changed America, one in which the rhetoric of liberty and equality applied to all Americans, not just white Americans. As the white veterans were fighting about taxation and holding on to their properties, black veterans were steadfast in their beliefs that they did not fight just for freedom from England but also for freedom from slavery and unequal treatment. Veterans of all races wanted a voice in the political discourse of America.

The men of Prince Hall's Masonic Temple were well-trained African Americans, many of whom were self-educated and believed in the doctrine of the Declaration of Independence - that all men are created equal. If they had to, these men were prepared to fight as much after the war as they did during the war for those freedoms. However, they understood that if they demonstrated any civil disobedience similar to that of General Shays and his men, they, as men of color, would be treated very differently. On January 4, 1787, seventy-three African American men presented to the General Court of the Commonwealth of Massachusetts a petition for the right to return to Africa if they could not be respected as veterans of war equal to white citizens.

While no action was taken by the state, it was clear that these articulate men were frustrated with Massachusetts about the condition of their lives and the lack of respect afforded to them.[151] African American men in Boston had expected that their lives and the lives of their families would change upon returning home from their noble service in the American War of Independence.

Figure 32: Petition of Blacks Seeking Justice

"That We, or our ancestors have been taken from all our dear connections and brought from Africa and put into a state of slavery in this country; from which unhappy situation we have been lately in some measure delivered by the new constitution which has been adopted by this state, or by a free act of our former masters. But we yet find ourselves in many respects in very disagreeable disadvantages circumstances; most of which must attend us so long as we and our children live in America. ..."

The Petition of Blacks, January 4, 1787. Massachusetts State Archives[152]

Benjamin Brooker, the 3rd generation great-grandfather of Harold Cornwall of Brockton, Massachusetts, was one of the men who signed "The Petition of Blacks." The words of Benjamin Brooker and the other signatories of the petition were powerful because they provided a clear insight into the thoughts and feelings of these progressive men who eventually paved the way for political discussions on race relations for generations to come.

Figure 33: The Formation of a Centralized Government

"Large and small states shared reasons for supporting the creation of a powerful central government. Both wanted commerce regulated; both feared upheavals like Shay's rebellion, which a national government might forestall or speedily suppress; both had a stake in sold public fiancé and the protection of creditors; both saw that a national government might stimulate the economy …"[153]

Robert Middlekauff
The Glorious Cause, the American Revolution, 1773-1789

Not only did the Governor of Massachusetts and the state legislature ignore the petition, they also ignored Prince Hall's offer of a state militia. The state feared that a militia of African Americans would further agitate the insurgents of Shays' Rebellion and ignite racial hostilities between the western and eastern parts of the state. Massachusetts, though a center of intellectual thinking, was also a political hotbed of frustration. But this state was only one example of the overall frustration across the nation. Once Shays' rebellion was subdued, it was clear that a centralized form of government was necessary to handle matters of civil disobedience that had implications across state lines.

Meanwhile, delegates from each state were attending a Constitutional Convention in Philadelphia, Pennsylvania The political upheaval in Massachusetts caused the members of the convention to address not only the issue of a centralized government, but also the matters that impacted each individual state. The delegates drafted a constitution that served as a balance of power to ensure that no one stakeholder would be able to exercise power over another, be it a large state versus a small state, a northerner versus a southerner or civilian versus military authority. However, the Constitution was an imperfect document that did not address the issue of slavery, despite the fact that African American men fought bravely throughout the Revolutionary War to ensure that all men should be free and equal. The reluctance to discuss slavery was due primarily to the southern states, which threatened to revolt and leave the convention and the newly created Union if slavery was addressed in the Constitution in a way that would adversely affect their economic vitality.

On June 21, 1788, after two-thirds of the states ratified the U.S. Constitution, the document became the law of the new nation and its people. General George Washington was sworn in as President of the United States of America on April 30, 1789 in New York City. During President Washington's two terms, the young nation became more racially, economically and regionally diverse. Northern states rapidly industrialized their local, regional and state economies, and the region was soon known as the "industrial north." Meanwhile, the southern states took advantage of the warmer climate to develop a more agriculturally based economy. And, people began to move west, developing the land rights of the vast wilderness.

The returning African American soldiers in the north immersed themselves into the industrialization of the growing cities. They expected freedom and all that it afforded to free citizens. They wanted to buy land, commercially trade their goods and services and live in safe communities with good education for their children. They wanted no more than every other American in this new nation - equality under the law, as promised by the Constitution.

The African American soldiers returning home to the south had served gallantly in the Revolutionary War, and were not content to be treated as second-class citizens. While at war, these men had heard from other black soldiers of the freedoms People of Color enjoyed in the north, leaving the southern black men returning home with certain expectations. However, life in the south became increasingly difficult as the racial divide became more pronounced. Many white landowners in rural areas feared that the countryside was disproportionately populated with slaves from Africa and the descendants of Americans of African descent. For nervous southerners, the fear of a slave revolt was sparked by the news of another rebellion on the Caribbean island of Saint-Domingue.

The French colonial island of Saint-Domingue, now known as Haiti, was one of the most profitable colonies in the world, and reportedly produced forty percent of the world's sugar. Its success was predicated on the worldwide need for sugarcane and its byproducts, including sugar and rum. The colonial powers benefited from the sugar profits, while their plantation owners amassed enormous personal wealth. This balance of economic prosperity and wealth, however, required continued import of African slaves. Eventually the white plantation owners of Saint-Domingue were outnumbered by the African slaves by a ratio of ten to one. As more and more African slaves were brought to the island, the plantation owners feared a potential slave rebellion.

As the United States was trying to establish itself after its rebellion against Great Britain, the seeds of rebellion that sprouted in Europe during the French Revolution began to grow in the French Saint-Domingue colony. During the civil unrest in France, an instrument of execution known as the guillotine was introduced. The guillotine was widely used in public town centers to cut the heads from the bodies of those seen as dissenters of the government. Once the guillotine was introduced in Saint-Domingue to control the rebellious white settlers, the African slaves feared it was only a matter of time before it would be used on them, as well. The African slaves felt that, spiritually, dismemberment of the body, particularly removal of the head, was one of the most horrific things that could be done to someone.

The public executions caused an uprising on the island. The African slaves revolted en masse, murdering every white person on the island. Then the slaves attempted to murder all persons of mixed race. From 1791 to 1804, the riots on the Caribbean island of Saint-Domingue became the most successful African slave rebellion in the Western Hemisphere. And, it sent shock waves throughout America's southern states, and was cause for concern for anyone reading national newspapers in northern states. The United States and European nations imposed naval blockages on Saint-Domingue in an attempt to prevent anyone from traveling to the island to support the Africans, and to keep news of the revolts from the ears, minds, and hearts of other African slaves.

In the United States, the close proximity of the violent riots frightened southern whites, causing white politicians, particularly in the south, to enact additional laws that further restricted the release of slaves. Southern politicians and the land gentry felt that the growing numbers of free Americans of African descent, as well as the growing numbers of freed slaves, was a recipe for a major catastrophe.

Southerners feared that if their slaves had access to guns and other weapons, the slaves would revolt against their masters, especially since on many of the plantations, and even several of the southern states, the slave and free black population outnumbered the white population.

When Prince Hall and the other signatories, including Benjamin Brooker, presented the Petition of Blacks to the Massachusetts State Legislature, requesting to be sent to Africa, many Free People of Color at the time saw this as a viable option if they were not going to be treated as equal American citizens. The Massachusetts legislature had not yet freed all of its African Americans from slavery, and many seemed to think that the petition was a realistic option. Also, some white southerners, although clearly in the minority, were also inspired by the political discourse in the North. They advocated for southern states to consider transporting what they perceived to be the troublesome free blacks and Free People of Color to Africa, in order to keep native-born Africans and African American slaves from outnumbering the white citizens.

As racial tensions escalated, the opportunity to move west was an appealing alternative for both blacks and whites. For Americans of African descent, moving west was a better option than moving back to Africa. Meanwhile, white Americans thought they might feel safer in the open frontier, where the area wasn't so densely populated with blacks. Both groups knew they would benefit from the opportunity to accumulate inexpensive, large tracts of land. As families grew, the yearning for land and national expansion began to take hold. The United States became a country of frontier men and women. After the war, American families of European descent, many of whom had been indentured servants, no longer wanted to be an underclass. That was not what the Revolutionary War was about, that was not why they came to America, and they did not fight in the War for Independence to be considered second-class citizens.

The possibility and opportunity to own land in the west was a major draw for these first- and second-generation Europeans in this new land. In Europe, the wealthy owned land, but the poor did not. The opportunity to own land and to become something more than lower-class was a magnetic draw that would eventually open the west to millions and millions of men and women who would follow the call of the western frontier. The American pioneering spirit had begun to emerge.

2.11   Creating a Perfect Union

In May 1787, the framers of the Constitution met in secret at the Constitutional Convention in Philadelphia. They originally intended to address the deficiencies in the new government's Articles of Confederation. However, under the direction of James Madison and Alexander Hamilton, a decision was made to create a new, more centralized and functional government, rather than try to fix the existing one. Their mission was to establish a unified government that took all of the competing interests and forged them into a single centralized system. The states sent a total of fifty-five delegates to attend the convention to establish a more perfect union.

But as would be expected, the fifty-five voices had strong, divergent opinions and objectives. James Madison, the architect of the initial constitutional outline, created a new outline known as the Virginia Plan, which reflected Madison's nationalist views. Madison's supporters argued that the recent Shays Rebellion in Massachusetts demonstrated that the current decentralized national government was disjointed, underfunded, and incapable of resolving and managing problems within and between the states. The first draft of the constitutional outline was based loosely on the Greek and British form of three-tier branches of government, with an executive, a two-house legislative, and a judicial branch, each serving as a check and balance for the other.

Within short order, most of the delegates' contentious issues were resolved. However, matters involving the protection of the institution of slavery, proportional representation, and methods for taxation were arduously debated. The fifty-five delegates had individual interests, politically and personally, and whenever the issue of slavery came up, the twenty-five delegates who owned slaves insisted the plantation society was the basis of their livelihoods and the foundation for their states' economic stability and they could not and would not compromise. The delegates from the northern states believed that the Revolutionary War was the beginning of the end of slavery. Several northern delegates came from states where their state constitutions had already emancipated their former slaves, or they came from states where their legislatures were in the slow process of guaranteeing freedom to every American citizen. Southern delegates, however, adamantly opposed this view, and refused to hear any suggestions that would get rid of slavery, threatening to not join the United States if slavery were abolished and sowing the seeds for another major conflict in less than one hundred years.

Figure 34: Conflicts within the Constitutional Convention

- Composition and election of the Senate
- How "proportional representation" was to be defined (whether to include slaves or other property)
- Executive power and the role of the president, term of office and reasons for impeachment
- Whether judges should be chosen by the legislative or executive branch of government
- Nature of a fugitive slave clause and whether to allow the abolition of the slave trade
- Rights belonging to the individual states
- National laws versus inconsistency of state law

Another contentious issue was the manner in which slaves would be counted towards proportionate representation in the Federal government. Delegates from the south suggested plans that primarily benefited their own states, as did delegates from the north. Southern states, ironically, wanted their slaves to be counted as a whole person for proportionate representation, but did not want them to be counted as property for tax purposes. This perhaps was the only time that the southern states, albeit selfishly, referred to African Americans and Free People of Color as individual, whole persons and not just chattel property.

But the southern delegates' plan did not go unnoticed, and northern states, argued that if slaves were to be were considered property, they should be taxed as such and not counted towards the population for proportionate representation. With the southern states threatening to secede from the fragile Union, the delegates agreed to the Three-Fifths Compromise, which eventually became Article One, Section Two of the final Constitution. This compromise counted three-fifths of the slave population towards the proportionate representation for Congress, which solidified the institution of slavery because it effectively counted each slave as three-fifths of a person - and officially characterized them as property, not people.

The issue of slavery and proportional representation would have a profound impact on the Cornwall Murphy family in both the north and the south. No matter how the delegates resolved this issue, the family would be in the crosshairs of the aftermath. On September 17, 1787, none of the delegates in Philadelphia had gotten exactly what they wanted, and by all accounts, none were totally happy with the final product. Still, most believed it was the best that could be done at the time.

The constitution consisted of six articles, each supported by independent sections. Nine months later, on June 21, 1788, two-thirds of the states ratified the Constitution of the United States, and it became the law of the land.

Each of the Articles of the Constitution had their own separate and distinct Sections within them. Article 1, Section 8, of the Constitution defined the powers of the Legislative Branch, how the government should regulate commerce with foreign nations and among the states, and how the government should protect itself domestically and internationally by collecting taxes, engaging in commerce and raising of an Army and Navy for the defense of the nation. With the ratification of the new Constitution, the United States of America was now positioned to conduct business as a unified nation, and to interact with world powers as a single voice.

Figure 35: Annotated United States Constitution

We the people of the United States, in order to form a more perfect union, establish justice, insure domestic tranquility, provide for the common defense, promote the general welfare, and secure the blessings of liberty to ourselves and our posterity, do ordain and establish this Constitution for the United States of America.

Article 1: All legislative powers herein granted shall be vested in a Congress of the United States, which shall consist of a Senate and House of Representatives

Article 2: The executive power shall be vested in a President of the United States of America

Article 3: The judicial power of the United States, shall be vested in one Supreme Court, and in such inferior courts as the Congress may from time to time ordain and establish.

Article 4: Full faith and credit shall be given in each state to the public acts, records, and judicial proceedings of every other state. And the Congress may by general laws prescribe the manner in which such acts, records, and proceedings shall be proved, and the effect thereof.

Article 5: The Congress, whenever two thirds of both houses shall deem it necessary, shall propose amendments to this Constitution, or, on the application of the legislatures of two thirds of the several states. ...

Article 6: The ratification of the conventions of nine states, shall be sufficient for the establishment of this Constitution between the states so ratifying the same.

However, the Constitution was not a perfect document, and its flaws would lead to a challenge against the nation's sovereignty in 1812.; divide the nation in 1860 over issues of race and slavery; and, with its finer points, be used to justify the legitimacy of the Jim Crow laws in the 1890s. Additionally, it would force the Cornwall Murphy family to constantly adapt to and sometimes challenge the effects of the Constitution's subsequent amendments and the conditions of the ever-changing nation.

2.12   Gabriel's Rebellion

When the framers of the Constitution left Philadelphia, the remaining contentious issues were, so to speak, "kicked on down the road" to be resolved for another day. This included the most contentious of all - the issue of slavery. As magnificent as the United States Constitution was written, it was intentionally silent on the issue of slavery, to the point that the word is never mentioned in the document. The Constitution's framers were likely well aware that the concept of slavery was diametrically opposite to the very values that they believed in, fought for in the American Revolution, and were now espousing as law.

However, in 1787, with the exception of the collected value of real estate, the institution of slavery was the most valuable single asset that the young United States government had. As an institution, slavery was certainly the most valuable asset that any one southern state had. The framers of the Constitution, with all of their competing interests and opposing values, didn't know how to resolve the social and moral issue on a national level while addressing the economic impact and realities at a regional level. After the United States Constitution was ratified and the signatories left Philadelphia, the issue of slavery and all of its ramifications lingered, and thirteen years later, its contentious presence reared up in Richmond, Virginia.

In August 1800, a group of slaves plotted to take control of the city of Richmond, the state's capital. These slaves planned to kidnap the governor and negotiate the release of the city's slaves. While the rebellion in 1800 was neither the first nor the last insurrection, it was one that had the most profound implications for the entire white population in the south. The slave rebellion dramatically changed the laws relative to the institution of slavery and the rights of Free People of Color. Although though no Cornwall Murphy family members were involved, it directly impacted the family and friends of James Melton and his son David, of Hertford County, North Carolina.

Gabriel's Rebellion was named after its leader, Gabriel Prosser, a slave born in Henrico County, Virginia, in 1776. Gabriel's physical and intellectual attributes made him a natural-born leader, particularly in the slave community. He had a striking appearance, standing at "six feet two or three inches" tall, and unlike most slaves, he was able to read and write.[154] As a twenty-four year old blacksmith, Gabriel traveled throughout the countryside as a "hired-out" slave by his master, and was able to meet, befriend and interact freely with other hired-out slaves, Free People of Color and poor white laborers who were also disenfranchised by the oppressive southern caste system.[155] A gifted young man, Gabriel was not interested in living the rest of his years as a slave he desired more from life. In ordinary circumstances, Gabriel would have simply run away and passed himself off as a Free Man of Color in another county or state. But, as a natural born leader, he wanted more for himself and for his people.

Gabriel Prosser was exactly the kind of leader that southern whites were fearful of, particularly in the aftermath of the Saint-Domingue Rebellion. Southern whites feared that such a rebellion could happen in their communities, especially if any of their slaves became aware of the horrific events that took place on the Caribbean island. It has been postulated that Gabriel was indeed aware of the events in Saint-Domingue, because of his reported friendship with several French expatriates, and that the island rebellion may have inspired him and his co-conspirators to plot a similar rebellion.[156] At the time of the rebellion, Richmond, Virginia was deeply divided between "Democratic-Republicans who controlled the countryside and the Federalist merchants who controlled the urban centers." This political division also caused a tremendous rift within the white community where urban white men were as disenfranchised as the black slaves. Because of this division, there had been rumors of some type of insurrection supported by whites and blacks.[157]

Since Gabriel, with military precision, "was able to make decisions, delegate responsibilities, and pursue routine tasks to their completion in order to avert the strong possibility of disaster, the rebellion came to be known as Gabriel's Rebellion."[158]

As the leader of the insurrection, Gabriel had hoped that the division and animosity in the white community, particularly amongst the poor white laborers, and the strong desire for freedom amongst the slave population would provide the necessary alliance to forge an aggressive attack on the city. Perhaps his relationship with a Frenchman by the name of "Charles Quersey...who was to be a commander in the rebellion" led Gabriel to believe that the conspirators would be supported by likeminded and disenfranchised white people such as Quersey.[159]

The tactical strategy for rebellion was set for the weekend of August 30, 1800, where it was projected that "over a 1,000 slaves were to march to Richmond" and enter the city simultaneously from three different access points catching the residents off-guard and causing complete havoc and chaos.[160]

Figure 36: Gabriel's Rebellion

"In its tactical dimensions his rebellion was a coup that would hopefully inspire an insurrection: a small guerrilla force of about two hundred men would enter Richmond at midnight, thoroughly terrorize the city by burning its warehouse district and (initially) killing indiscriminately, capturing stores of arms and taking the governor as hostage"

Gerald W. Mullin,
Flight and Rebellion: Slave Resistance in Eighteenth Century Virginia[161]

Unfortunately for the insurgents, a strong weather front came into the area, flooding roads and bridges, and limiting access to the city by the approaching slaves. Before the insurrectionists could regroup and execute its leaders' their plans, they were betrayed when several slaves came forward and told their owners of the planned rebellion.

The governor, James Monroe, a future President of the United States, dispatched the militia and captured all of the known conspirators. Once captured, the slaves were immediately sent to trial, and they were convicted and executed along with suspected Free Men of Color and white sympathizers, including several French expatriates. The fear of a slave uprising was exacerbated by fact that some of the rebellion's sympathizers were French, which bore strong similarities to the horrific Saint-Domingue Rebellion. The raw emotion of the African American slaves, their intellect, and their strong desire for freedom were demonstrated when one of the captured men shared his feelings at his trial, in the likelihood that he would be hanged for his actions.

Figure 37: An Insurrectionist Prepares to Give His Life for Liberty

"I have nothing more to offer than what General Washington would have had to offer, had he been taken by the British and put to trial by them. I have adventured my life in endeavoring to obtain the liberty of my countrymen, and am a willing sacrifice in their cause: and I beg, as a favor, that I may be immediately led to execution. I know that you have pre-determined to shed my blood, why then all this mockery of a trial?"

John H. Franklin and Alfred A. Moss,
From Slavery to Freedom: A History of African Americans[162]

The residents of Richmond, including members of the State General Assembly, were aghast at the rebellion but were thankful that it was thwarted before its execution and did not have the same dire consequences of the 1791 Saint-Domingue Revolution, in which thousands of lives were lost. Nonetheless, the white residents of Richmond and surrounding communities called for immediate steps to ensure that such a rebellion was never to be repeated. Until Gabriel's Rebellion, Virginia was considered one of the more tolerant states relative to the treatment of its slave population. This changed significantly in the aftermath of the rebellion. The Virginia State Assembly, along with other southern state legislatures, immediately enacted some the harshest laws restricting the movement and rights of Free People of Color, including their rights to education and assembly.

The Virginia General Assembly took formal steps to pass legislation making it unlawful to educate slaves, free blacks or mulattoes - including teaching them how to read or write. The newly enacted laws also severely restricted the rights to property ownership and freedom of movement for Free People of Color. The ownership of land in the south was vital to southern wealth, power and politics, and the basic necessities for survival. In 1806, the Virginia General Assembly passed a law to expel all free Americans of African descent from the state, and restrict all slaves, free blacks, or mulattoes from assembling in numbers greater than three. The law also prevented People of Color from holding religious meetings or worship without the presence of a white minister. The repercussions from Gabriel's rebellion were severe and punitive.

While these laws pleased southern white plantation owners, businessmen and politicians alike, they offended the sense of basic decency of southern blacks, many who had represented their states proudly as they fought on its behalf of freedom and liberty in the Revolutionary War.

The punitive measures imposed after the rebellion in Saint-Domingue and Gabriel's Rebellion had long-term effects and repercussions on southern blacks, particularly the slave population. These measures also had a profound effect on the Free People of Color throughout the south, including the Ballard, Chavis, Gowen, and Melton families, many who still lived and owned property in Virginia. The overly restrictive laws enacted after Gabriel's Rebellion were the catalyst that forced Free People of Color to leave the state of Virginia and to move to North Carolina, and the western trials on the other side of the Appalachian Mountains.

2.13   Migrating to the Western Passage

In the wake of Gabriel's Rebellion, as young families before them had done, members of Margaret Melton's family looked westward for land and opportunities. White families, fearful of another dreadful slave rebellion, left the urban and rural areas that were more susceptible to a revolt. Family members who were Free People of Color looked to move west to the Ohio Valley and the Northwest Passage. As each subsequent generation migrated further into the Northwest Passage, many Free People of Color married and remarried the offspring of the European settlers, and soon many identified less as Free People of Color and more as descendants of Europeans. These extended family members credited their "traces of color" to heritage from various Native American tribes "back east." While true in many cases, several of these family members were indeed of African American descent. However, anyone with mixed race coloring still had to be careful, particularly in the Northwest Passage, where Native American raids on the white settlers were commonplace. As the raids became more frequent and more violent, being Native American was not necessarily a good thing.

At the conclusion of the Revolutionary War, with the signing of the Treaty of Paris in 1783, the British had ceded to the United States the area known as the Northwest Territory, which included present day Ohio, Indiana, Illinois, Michigan, and Wisconsin. American frontier families poured into the area in order to obtain land permits. As the frontier land was being settled and turned into farmland, local Native American tribesmen began to retaliate by attacking the settlers for encroaching on their tribal lands.

The settlers who migrated into the Northwest Territory believed that the armed Native American raids were being supported by the British government. Many Americans suspected that the British supported the Native American tribes because they strategically wanted a neutral boundary between the United States and the British Canadian colonies to the north, and that a neutral territory would provide a clear boundary for the British from their archenemy the French and the French colonial port city of New Orleans to the south.

2.14   Samuel Cornwell Moves North to Disputed Territory

In the aftermath of the American Revolution, the destiny of North America had been changed forever. While the Revolutionary War resulted in the United States of America, the boundaries and borders between the young nation and its Canadian neighbor to the north were not yet defined. Many exiled American Loyalists moved north to the British Canadian territories and became the founders of two Canadian provinces, Ontario and New Brunswick.[163]

In 1783, "approximately 28,347 American Loyalists arrived at the mouth of the River St. John" - all from the state of New York - in what is now considered St. John, New Brunswick, Canada.[164] Prior to 1776, "the land east of the present day State of Maine, that portion of Nova Scotia, now known as St. John, was considered the fourteenth British American Colony."[165] Although the residents of St. John were not necessarily pro-British, they were required to take a "pledge of Alliance" to the British monarchy, or face losing their property. St. John's newly arrived transplants from New York took steps to build the area's infrastructure, creating a major transport hub between the newly formed United States, the European continent, and ports along the Canadian seacoast.

Figure 38: British Loyalist Move to Canada

> "Throughout the war, New York had been the principal rampart of British power in the thirteen colonies... Long Island, New York had temporarily become a Loyalist province, the resort of thousands who... had given defiance to the upstart authorities who acted in the name of the Continental Congress."
>
> - W. Stewart MacNutt,
> *New Brunswick, A History 1784 – 1867* [166]

During the Revolutionary War, commercial trade came to a virtual halt between the former British colonies. However, after the war, merchants on both sides of the border between Canada and the United States vigorously resumed commercial trading. Coastal port communities such as St. John became vital trading posts immediately after the war. "The shippers and traders of Massachusetts and Maine, which was part of Massachusetts at the time, were quick to break the bonds independence had imposed on them. Traders and merchants, whose true allegiance was dubious, swarmed into the prematurely developed seaport, attempting to make Saint John a base from which they could continue to enjoy the benefits" of inter-continental trade.[167]

As European port cities slowly opened to trade with the United States, sea captains and merchants would sail from the New England seacoast to St. John's ports, refuel, and stock up before crossing the Atlantic Ocean. With their heavy cargo ships, the captains were able to take more of their goods to sell if they could stop and refuel in St. John, though many of the New England shipmen didn't trust the former Loyalists who now lived in Canada and controlled most of St. John.

In order to support their business transactions and protect their investment in the dredging of the St. John port, financiers encouraged patriots as well Loyalists to move to New Brunswick and start businesses. Several patriots moved to St. John, New Brunswick, to help facilitate the expanding trans-Atlantic trade, including Samuel Cornwell, Harold Cornwall's 3rd generation great grandfather. Samuel eventually was able to acquire a number of schooners, and conducted business up and down the Atlantic seaboard, in the Caribbean, and to Europe. Merchants such as Samuel Cornwell were able to build their businesses as international trade expanded. At the same time, despite the fact that the US treasury was destitute, the nation moved forward in building a navy, in order to protect the nation's coastal cities from outside invasions, and to protect its commercial vessels from pirates and aggressive foreign vessels.

Samuel and his family were able to benefit from the newfound opportunities in a post-wartime economy, on both sides of the border. Aside from the family's success in the United States, Samuel and his son, Mansfield, established some level of prominence while in St. John. Based on court records obtained from Canada, it appears that Samuel was able to acquire a substantial amount of land. According to several wills, Samuel was mentioned as having sold land to various neighbors. For example, John Welling, from the Parish of Shediac, has a will stating that the family of Samuel Cornwell sold property to him[168]. In short order, the Cornwell family became intricately involved in the St. John's political, religious and business communities, as evidenced by business advertisements taken out in local newspapers and various political appointments that were revived. Mansfield Cornwell, on several occasions, served as a witness for probate transactions for several of his neighbors in Early Brunswick, Canada.[169]

Because of Samuel's active trading up and down the coastline, he was aware of political issues north and south of the Canadian border, and the growing unrest overseas. As a loyal and studious private under General George Washington, Samuel Cornwell was well aware of Washington's fear that the British would return and attack the young nation. As part of the Canadian campaign, Samuel was also aware of the underlying distrust between the Catholic French in Canada and their Protestant neighbors to the south in the United States.

As Samuel continued to build his business, he traveled in and out of East Coast port cities, and each voyage made him realize that while the ocean waters may have been calm, the political waters were not. The post-Revolutionary War years were a period of transformation for the United States. After the war, with all of the nation's emerging trade and military prowess, the United States and its political leaders were gradually arriving on the world stage. Former Loyalists, along with former Patriots and merchants such as Samuel Cornwell, served as a catalyst for the next major political and international controversy between England and its expatriates in United States: the War of 1812.

2.15   Events Abroad Caused International Strife

By 1790, the ancestral family of the Cornwall Murphy line now lived in five distinct clusters. The English Samuel Cornwell and his family had migrated to St. John, New Brunswick, Canada. The African American families of Caesar Russell and Benjamin Brooker lived in the coastal communities around the city of Boston, Massachusetts. The African American Gardiner and Jackson families lived in the coastal communities around Long Island, New York. The tri-racial families of the Ballards, Chavis, Gowens, Howells and the Meltons lived in and around Norfolk, Virginia and the developing counties in northeast North Carolina, and many of their extended family members were slowly migrating into the Ohio Valley and Northwest Territories. Though these families tried to settle down in the aftermath of the Revolutionary War, another conflict was brewing.

The Cornwall Murphy family would soon be directly affected by the kidnappings of merchant sailors along the Atlantic coast. They would see migrating settlers murdered and scalped, and watch villages get plundered on the western frontier. General Washington's fears of a British retaliation were well founded. In just a few short years following the Revolutionary War, the British military was back on the shores of the American Atlantic seacoast.

In 1793, when France declared war on England, the British Royal Navy benefited greatly from the common practice of "impressment" whereby British men of fighting age would be forced to serve as sailors and merchant mariners on British naval vessels. Initially, many young men with seafaring abilities were taken against their will from towns and villages all across England. However, when the British were unable to find enough men to fulfill the necessary quotas, rather than address the inhumane treatment of their own seamen, they looked across the high seas and kidnapped large numbers of men from Canadian communities such as Halifax, Quebec City and the port town of St. John, where Samuel Cornwell and his family had relocated and conducted business. The impressment problem became so bad that residents of St. John rioted and refused to allow their sons to enlist in or be impressed by the Royal Navy.

The war escalated in 1803, and when French Emperor Napoleon Bonaparte threatened to "defeat England on its own soil," the British Parliament believed that an invasion of Britain was inevitable.[170] Britain expanded its military, constructed new battleships, and fortified its national defenses in the event that the French Emperor kept to his word. In order to protect British waters and patrol the entire coastline under Napoleon's control, the British built more and more ships, and needed more and more sailors. As the war raged on in Europe, the French controlled the land, while England controlled the sea.[171]

However, the British Royal Navy lacked one key thing, available seamen. To compound England's manpower challenges, British seamen were deserting in sizable numbers as a direct result of the harsh working conditions in the Royal Navy. Many of English seamen were going to the United States for better working conditions, more money and the hope of acquiring land grants, something they would never be able to do in England.

The British Navy had only one way to increase its manpower: It resorted to kidnapping American men from captured merchant ships in the Atlantic Ocean.[172] With the growing need for qualified sailors for the British, and with large numbers of British sailors defecting to America, impressment of American men, as well as other mounting factors, strained the already fragile relationship between the United States and Britain.

Figure 39: Growing Conflict between England and the United States

- United States and its former British colonial ruler each had legacy issues resulting from the American Revolution.
- British impressment of American seamen resulting from British desertion in sizable numbers and going to the United States for better working conditions, more money and the hope of acquiring land grants.
- British loss in trade revenue caused by its declining influence in international trade as a result of the gradual prominence of the United States in the international marketplace.
- Conflicts in the Northwest territories over American expansionism
- United States continued relationship with France, Britain's archenemy.

While Europe was engulfed in war where its port cites were closed to one another, the United States, as a neutral nation, was able to expand its presence in the global marketplace and develop its international trade. Within only a few years after its independence from Britain, the growth of America's naval commercial trade was staggering, particularly considering that it was a young nation still struggling with challenges typical to any new nation. Despite its newness, "the United States captured most of the trade between Europe and the Caribbean, and re-imports (which constituted about half of America's export trade) soared from $2,000,000 in 1792 to $53,000,000 in 1805."[173] Most of the United States increases in trade dollars were trade dollars lost by Great Britain, which helped set the stage for another enormous conflict between the two nations.

Since the United States commercial and naval fleets were expanding, the new country also needed experienced seamen. Much to the dismay of the British, the United States began to actively recruit and hire seasoned British seamen. In short order, between "50,000 to 100,000 seamen employed on American ships were British" - which only served to create a complicated military and tactical problem for the British as they struggled to protect their nation from the aggressive French and the vast coastal waters around them.[174] They needed experienced seamen, too.

As the United States and Britain competed for available manpower, the situation became openly hostile out in the Atlantic Ocean, particularly when the Royal Navy boarded American commercial ships and kidnapped not only British navy men who had deserted to America, but American seamen as well, claiming that these sailors may have been born in England. From 1793 through 1812, it is estimated that between 6,000 to 9,000 Americans were illegally impressed by the British.[175] To combat the loss of kidnapped seamen, American captains began to recruit from an unlikely population of well-trained men, who were familiar with combat, discipline and the proper use of firearms: the Revolutionary War veterans.

African American war veterans, including Caesar Russell and Cuffe Grandison, Harold Cornwall's 3rd generation great-grandfathers and former soldiers in the Revolutionary War, eventually came to work on commercial maritime vessels. During the height of tension between England and the United States, war veteran Caesar Russell was found on the "Roll or List of the Crew" on the Ship *Mary* out of Beverly, Massachusetts and again on the List of the Crew as a cook in 1801 on the Ship *Mary*. As they proved themselves seaworthy, other African American men and men of color were recruited, including Margaret Melton Murphy's great-grandfather, James Melton of Northampton County, North Carolina, also was a seaman out of Norfolk, Virginia.

According to conservative estimates, more than fifteen percent of the seamen were African American, and much like their service in the Revolutionary War, their representation as seamen was greater than the representation of the general African American population. For African American men, being a seaman in 1800 was one of the most honorable professions available, where a man with extensive nautical experience could make as much as $30 to $35 a month in a time when the average monthly wage was only $18 to $21. Although it was usually a short career and primarily for younger men because of the physical work involved, being a seaman was one of the few professions where an African American man was rated as an equal to his white peers.[176] Once on the open seas, shipmates had to respect one another, because they had to rely on their individual and collective skills for survival. The value of a man was judged not by race, but by the ability to count on him in severe waters, treacherous storms, or in dangerous port cities around the world.

In 1807, tension was further escalated between the United States and England when the thirty-eight-gun *USS Chesapeake* was stopped by the fifty-gun British frigate *HMS Leopard*, three miles off the coast of Norfolk, Virginia, in international waters. The British captain "demanded the right to search the *Chesapeake* for possible deserters."[177] As the two captains yelled at each other across their ships' bows, it became apparent that the British captain was not going to be allowed to have his men board the *Chesapeake*. Thus, "the *HMS Leopard* fired a warning shot and broadsided the *USS Chesapeake* …resulting in three men from the *Chesapeake* being killed, eight others seriously wounded and the ship's captain, along with ten more, slightly being wounded."[178]

After the attack, the British finally boarded the *Chesapeake* and took with them four men that they believed to be British citizens. Of the four impressed seamen, three were black, and these men had actually deserted from His Majesty's frigate, the *Melampus*, when the vessel made a port call at Hampton Roads, Virginia, only to turnaround and reenlist for more money into the U.S. Navy. The fourth man, who was reportedly white, was hanged in Halifax, Nova Scotia.[179] The provocative actions of the *Leopard* against the *Chesapeake* struck a chord of nationalism all across the United States. Regional politicians from all over the country, seldom agreeing with each other, agreed that the actions of Britain were tantamount to an act of war.

As England upped the ante on the United States, it took steps to limit the nation's newfound prominence in the international trade marketplace. Great Britain instituted a series of trade restrictions that prohibited the United States from trading with any county on the European continent, targeting the specific trade between the United States and France. Once the British imposed these sanctions, France imposed a similar measure barring the United States from trading with England. No matter whom the Americans wanted to trade with, this was a war in which they would be the losers.[180]

In his last year of office, after serving as the nation's 3rd President from 1801 to 1809 Thomas Jefferson imposed a trade embargo on

England, hoping that "limiting or banning America's oceangoing trade would deliver British concessions without recourse to war."[181] The embargo had an adverse and devastating effect on American coastal communities, especially in the coastal towns of New England, where trade with Europe, particularly England, was the greatest. Seaport communities -such as Beverly, Massachusetts, where Caesar Russell lived with his family and Scituate, Massachusetts, where the families of Cuffe Grandison and Benjamin Brooker lived - were economically devastated by the embargo. The elected officials from New England and other communities along the Atlantic coastline strongly opposed the embargo on trade with England. Upon taking office, President James Madison let the Jefferson trade embargo expire.

While England was at war with France on the European continent, and was engaged in turmoil in the Atlantic by kidnapping American citizens, it was also watching its flank on United States soil. England had claim over a portion of territory in America, west of the Appalachian Mountains. The British feared that their archenemy, France, would attempt to amass a powerful claim to the remainder of the North American continent by linking the French territory of New Orleans with the French territory in Canada. That British concern did not lessen after President Jefferson and the French government in 1803 concluded the Louisiana Purchase, which gave the United States the land about which the British were concerned.

As Americans settlers moved westward to the rich farmlands of present-day Ohio, Indiana, Michigan, and Wisconsin, they were met with tremendous opposition by the British and their unexpected allies, several local Native American tribes. Dangerous tension was now mounting between the United States and Britain, thanks to a roiling concoction of kidnapping, trade conflicts, and concerns on the Western front.

2.16   Lion Gardiner of Long Island, New York

As large numbers of American frontiersmen in the west moved into the newly opened lands obtained in the Louisiana Purchase, Americans back east were becoming pioneers in their own right. Like Harold Cornwall's 7th generation great grandparents, Thomas and

Rebecca Cornell, the Gardiner family was another prominent family from England who settled in the area at the eastern end of New York's Long Island Sound. Lion Gardiner, the patriarch of the Gardiner family, was born in England in 1599 and was an engineer in the British Army. Lion Gardiner came to America in 1635 to build a city at the mouth of the Connecticut River.[182] He acquired the island known today as Gardiner Island, at the eastern end of Long Island Sound. The small island is widely associated with the infamous Captain William Kidd, the notorious pirate and profiteer known as "Billy the Kidd". Captain Kidd allegedly buried part of his treasure on Gardiner Island from time to time. Reportedly, some of his riches were dug up and transferred to the Massachusetts Bay Colony.[183]

The Gardiner family, with their large real estate holdings on Long Island, actively bought and participated in the African slave trade, like many of the other wealthy families on Long Island. For the Gardiner family, the early African slave population provided inexpensive and skilled labor, which was instrumental in building the agricultural and maritime economy on Long Island, contributing to the wealth of the European American gentry in the early days of New York.

Europe's working poor immigrated to New York to escape the tyranny of European monarchies and to seek their personal fame and fortune in America, but the institution of slavery conflicted with their interests. As extended Melton, Ballard and Rucker family members moved west, so did many of the newly arriving Europeans. However, many other European immigrants were too poor to migrate westward and so remained behind in New York City. Large apartment complexes were built to house the steady stream of European immigrants but New York's slaves lived predominantly in the outskirts of New York City and throughout the state in small, rural townships and farming communities.

Competition for work was fierce among European immigrants for low wage jobs. The immigrant population was predominantly against slavery, since the existence of free slave labor only increased the competition for paying jobs. By 1788, the political pressures from New York's abolitionist movement and the immigrant population caused the state to enact a law that provided for the freeing of slaves, but protected the elderly and the sick from being freed without adequate provision for their long-term care. By 1799, the New York state law required that all children born of slaves be registered with the town clerks and set free.[184] However, the owners could retain the child's service until age twenty-eight if male and twenty-five if a female.

John Lyon Gardiner, the 4th generation great-grandson of Lion Gardiner and then the owner of Gardiner Island and new Lord of the Manor,[185] had one of the largest holdings of slaves on Long Island. Having inherited his grandfather Lion Gardiner's estate, he employed some 22 hands to perform the many tasks of his large farming enterprise, where they worked side-by-side with freed men and women, as well as Montauk Indian workers[186]. John Gardiner was prolific in his writings and kept meticulous notes on all of his business transactions. For each of his slaves, John Gardiner personally applied for their release once he felt that they were capable of independently taking care of themselves, as seen in the application he filed in February 24, 1806.

Although some of New York's slaves purchased their own freedom, many earned their freedom after working for a specific period of time under an indenture arrangement. Some slave masters liberated their slaves directly or in their wills, but the majority of slaves were freed under New York's gradual emancipation laws. In 1797, the city of Albany became the new capital of New York because citizens feared the political influence of the state was shifting to the boroughs of New York City and the rapidly increasing immigrant population.

Figure 40: County Petition to Emancipate a Slave Man

"Whereas John Gardiner of the town of Huntington in the County of Suffolk and the State of New York hath (in pursuance of the provisions of the Statute of the State aforesaid in such cases made and provided) made application to us the undersigned Overseers of the Poor of the Town of Huntington aforesaid for the emancipation of a certain Negro man Slave named Cato. We have therefore examined into the state and Circumstances of Said Slave and find him to be under fifty years of age and in our judgment and Opinion of sufficient ability to provide for and maintain himself. We'd therefore hereby Certify that we approve of and consent to the Manumission of said slave."

John Gardiner of Suffolk County, New York, February 24, 1806[187]

Prior to and during the American Revolutionary War, New York City and the surrounding areas, including Long Island, were a haven for British Loyalists who felt comforted and protected by the British military occupation of the area. The Loyalist movement became a vocal minority in a country where the patriotic majority favored colonial revolution. During the war, when the British occupied New York City and Long Island, Loyalists were able to come and go as they pleased and felt a sense of security under the command of the British military.

One part of Long Island that was not controlled by the British Loyalists was the area of East Hampton, where the residents "had unanimously signed the Articles of Association, declaring their support for the American cause."[188] Under the advice of officials, the Gardiner family left the island until after the Revolutionary War. Once the family left the island, "the British anchored their ships in Gardiner's Bay"[189] and remained there until the events of the Revolutionary War favored the Continental Army, at which time the British Loyalists began to flee New York City and Long Island for England, Canada or British territories in the Caribbean. When the Gardiner family went into exile to Connecticut, they brought with them many of their slaves who joined the Continental Army and served in the regiments from Connecticut and Rhode Island. Found in the muster rolls of General Washington's Army are the names of David Gardiner of the Connecticut line, and from the Rhode Island First Regiment, Mintus Gardiner, Prince Gardiner, Priamus Gardiner, and Sharper Gardiner.

As the British navy sailed back and forth through the interior of the country and to Canada, they took many of the prominent Loyalists with them.[190] Once the war was over, the American Patriots, who strongly resented their treatment during the war, were less than generous to their former Loyalist neighbors. Since many of the colonists felt that the Loyalists had betrayed the American cause, they were openly antagonistic and hostile. Left with few options, Loyalists had to either declare their affiliation with the new government of the United States or permanently leave the country. Many of the Loyalists chose the latter and moved north to Canada.

After the Revolutionary War, the Gardiner family moved back to their island and began to rebuild their estate. "The peace on the island was once again disturbed between 1812 and 1815 during the Second War with England" when the British moved to blockade the Atlantic coastline, including Gardiner's Bay.[191] Not to be an ungracious host, John Lyon Gardiner, the seventh lord of the manor, was cordial to the

British as they once again anchored their ships off of the coast of his island. However, when Gardiner got word that the British were being sent to arrest him, he feigned an illness, hoping to escape capture.

Figure 41: Delicate Lord of the Manor Outsmarts the British Royal Navy

"Upon the arrival of the troops he went to bed in the green room, feigning sickness, and being a delicate man, the reflection of the green curtains of the bedstead and windows gave him a sickly look. A little round table was placed by his bedside with medicine, glasses and spoons. When the officers appeared and insisted upon seeing their victim, Mrs. Gardiner came forward, with tears in her eyes, asking them to make as little noise as possible admitted them to her husband's room. They were completely deceived, and not wishing to be encumbered with a sick man on board ship, turned away."

Sarah Diodati Gardiner
Early Memories of Gardiners Island: The Isle of Wight, New York[192]

While the island was surrounded by the British Royal Navy, John Lyon Gardiner was essentially under house arrest. In order to survive on the isolated island, Gardiner's former slaves, many with the family surname of Gardiner, would periodically row over to the island under the cover of darkness and bring food and other necessary items to the Gardiner family. John Lyon Gardiner, the Lord of Gardiner Island, was the former slave master of the grandparents of Lewis Gardiner, who fathered Keziah Gardiner of Huntington, New York, the maternal grandmother to Harold Cornwall of Brockton, Massachusetts.[193]

2.17   War with England: the Second War of Independence

As the political tension grew between the United States and Britain, tension also grew between the United States and Canada. With the British blockade along the United States coastline, mariners and merchants such as Samuel Cornwell found it harder and harder to travel in and out of the ports of St. John, New Brunswick. Samuel's fortune was all invested in his schooners, and this had become his only source of income. The escalating events between the United States, England and British Canada were now having a direct impact on the livelihood of Samuel Cornwell and similarly situated merchant mariners in Canada.

Prior to the second war with England, Samuel Cornwell "owned a schooner that he loaded with lumber at Eastport, Maine to be sent to New York, and in route the vessel and cargo were either lost at sea or stolen" in 1800.[194] It was extremely difficult for the owners of merchant ships to acquire insurance due to sailors being kidnapped and the rampant pirating of undermanned and vulnerable schooners. Many ship owners either sailed without insurance or were unable to acquire insurance because of the exorbitant costs. Due to the loss of his ship, cargo, and lack of insurance, Samuel was near financial ruins, and spent several years trying to recoup his financial losses at sea.

In Washington, DC, members of Congress were hearing more and more stories of merchant mariners who were losing cargo, ships and their fortunes to the pirates and to the British who were kidnapping sailors, leaving the United States' ships more vulnerable to pirate attacks. Samuel Cornwell was a poster child for what was going wrong on the Atlantic coastline: He was a loyal American who was a patriotic veteran who had served honorably with General Washington at the Battle of Quebec, suffered with the General at Valley Forge, marched with him to Trenton, and witnessed the British surrender at Yorktown. Now he had lost virtually everything to the thieving British.

The grievances against England were debated by the politicians in Washington included not just the individual stories of men like Samuel Cornwell. They also included Britain's general disrespect for American seamen, the growing loss of American revenue due to international trade restrictions and the perceived British support of overly aggressive Native American attacks on frontier families expanding into the Northwest Territories -which included Ohio, Indiana, Illinois, Michigan and Wisconsin, which in 1787 included part of present day Minnesota. Many Americans, particularly from the south and the western frontier states and territories, now clamored for war with England.

In Great Britain, the English saw the United States as a backward frontier country that served only as a major obstacle in England's ability to fight directly with France and win the war against Napoleon. Many in Parliament also feared that the United States would try to weaken Britain's colonial power by annexing their Canadian territories and, as they perceived, were aggressively stealing British sailors from the Royal Navy. The relationship between the two nations was fragile, as each country had endured huge losses during the American Revolution. Both countries faced severe economic recessions at home as a result of the long war. Many in the United States Congress felt that the time had come to declare war, but neither country was prepared.

However, on June 18, 1812, President James Madison declared war against the British, in what is now referred to as the "Second American Revolution" or "Madison's War." The thirty-two month war was fought on three separate theaters: along the Atlantic coast and port cities of the United States, along the Canadian frontier and in Great Lakes region, and in the American south and along the Gulf of Mexico. From the beginning, it was clear that the much of the war would be fought on the sea, pitting the enormous naval forces of Great Britain against the meager naval resources of a much-unprepared United States and an overly zealous Congress.

2.18   The First Theater of War: the Atlantic Coast

The United States had only 27 frigates to use against the British Royal Navy, which had the enormous capacity of more than a 1,000 warships, - of which more than 600 were continuously at sea.[195] It was a true David and Goliath scenario. The United States knew that the only way to win the war was to force England to continue to fight with France. With most of the British naval assets blockading the French on the European continent, this would distract the British navy long enough to help the underfunded United States until it was able to build its own naval force. As the United States slowly built its naval assets, it began to experience the same manpower challenges that rival England had experienced - a lack of trained sailors.

The continued impressment of American merchant sailors into the Royal Navy meant that the United States was unexpectedly forced to recruit and allow African American men to serve in the navy. These men served dutifully and, as was the case in the Revolutionary War, African Americans were unsung heroes and vital contributors to the United States in the War of 1812.

Figure 42: Blacks Serving in the U.S. Navy in 1812

"Large numbers of black sailors served in the U.S. Navy during the War of 1812 ...by one estimate, some 15 to 20% of the Navy's enlisted personnel were of African ancestry and on certain vessels that figure exceeded 50% ... crews manning the tiny, crowded naval vessels were integrated, and officers who compiled the ship and station muster rolls did not differentiate between black and white seamen".

Gerald T. Altoff,
Amongst My Best-Men, African Americans and The War of 1812[196]

Once the Americans declared war on England, the British navy took immediate steps to blockade the Atlantic coast of the United States. As was a common British naval tactic, they placed "one or two" frigates in each of the American "harbors, penning in the American warships while gathering up American merchant ships as they came crowding home once the war started."[197] While the American harbors were blockaded, frigates from the Royal Navy were dispatched to prowl for American merchant vessels trying to export goods to Europe or the Caribbean or for ships importing needed military supplies. One of the first naval confrontations of the war was between the HMS *Guerriere* and the USS *Constitution* that took place on August 19, 1812. As the *Guerriere* was returning to Halifax, Nova Scotia for minor retrofitting, it spotted the *Constitution* and decided to attack and take the vessel before returning to port. In a major and unexpected turn of events, after a thirty minute battle, the *Constitution* handily defeated the *Guerriere* and left it "a complete wreck, her masts gone, her hull shattered, seventy-nine officers and men killed or wounded, in comparison to only 14 casualties" on the USS *Constitution*.[198]

At the height of the war, in 1814, Samuel Cornwell was partial owner of a schooner this included owning half of its cargo of small fish and lobster. The other owner, Thelonius Stover, commanded the ship, which was bound for Boston from Eastport, Maine.[199] According to Samuel, his business partner either ran away with the vessel and its cargo, or was lost at sea - or it was a casualty of the War of 1812, as the British either confiscated the vessel or sunk it in open waters in the Atlantic.[200]

By 1814, the long-term effects of the first theater of the war had been severe for the mercantile class of farmers, sea captains, and merchants.

The general population along the Atlantic coast and port cites of the United States and Canada had experienced many hardships as well. During the early part of 1814, in America and Canada, the mercantile class, which included men like Samuel Cornwell, was now financially ruined as a result of the war. The war was also taking its toll on the British people, and they were tired of the recurring wars in America and the continuing war with France.

A thousand miles south of St. John, New Brunswick, Canada, where Samuel Cornwell and his family lived, the British positioned their large war ships on the Chesapeake Bay and the critical port cities along the bay, as part of its Atlantic coast campaign. At the southern end of the bay, in the general area of Newport News, Virginia Beach and Norfolk, Virginia, east of Southampton County, were the port cities of Hampton Roads, Norfolk and Chesapeake. Hampton Roads - the crossroads of one of the largest natural harbors, incorporating the mouths of the Elizabeth River, the James River, the Nansemond River and the York River- was the ancestral crossroads of Margaret Melton's family. Although by 1812, Margaret Melton's immediate family had just migrated over the Virginia border to North Carolina, extended family members still lived in Southampton County, Virginia, and the surrounding communities at the base of the Chesapeake Bay - including Norfolk and Hampton Roads, where descendants still live today.

With the blockade of the Bay, the local merchant marines knew when there was an immediate threat of danger. On the 18th and 19th of June in 1813, the informal communication channels began to work overtime. Something had stirred in the Bay and the British Royal Navy was making a move. With the threat of a possible British invasion, area families, including the Meltons, moved inland to safer grounds. On June 21, 1813, the British sent twenty ships of various capabilities and sizes to the Nansemond River in an area of the bay just west of Norfolk, Virginia, in search of the USS *Constellation*. In what is known as the Battle of Craney Island, the Americans fortified the mouth of the river "with cannons, and 150 sailors and 400 militiamen." On the morning of June 22nd as the tide was retreating, more than "2,500 British marines and infantry landed on the island's beach".[201] Once the British landed, the small American force waited until the British were in clear range on the wide-open beach and bombarded them with artillery. As the British retreated, their barges got stuck in the river's muddy low tide. The battle proved a crucial win for the Americans, in that it saved the vital shipbuilding port city of Norfolk, Virginia, and the surrounding communities from being pillaged by the British.

Angered by their loss on Craney Island, four days later, the British stormed the small coastal community of Hampton Roads, an area of only a thousand residents, and where many of Margaret Melton's ancestors lived.[202] The British burned the small village in retaliation for their devastating defeat. As Norfolk burned, members of Margaret Melton's family escaped to Southampton County to the west and North Carolina's Hertford County to the south. Other extended family members moved to Northampton County in Virginia, while others migrated to the Kentucky and Tennessee territories and onward to the rich farmlands of the Ohio Valley.

2.19   The Second Theater of War: The Great Lakes

The United States' second strategy in winning the War of 1812 was an offensive move into Canada, as the British had feared. While England and the United States battled at sea, the western frontier had changed dramatically in only a decade. When Americans spread westward, it forced the British to implement a defensive strategy that would protect their interest in Canada. American settlers, hungry for land, streamed into the Ohio Valley, and by 1800, Kentucky had a population over 221,000. By 1810, Ohio had a population that surpassed 231,000 inhabitants, and settlers were rapidly moving into Indiana and Illinois.[203]

The British knew that their attacks on United States merchant vessels in the Atlantic would only provoke an attack on the sparsely populated Canada, and their first instinct was to rely on the ground resources of the Canadian inhabitants, many of whom were former American Loyalists in exile from the United States. The British also needed a second line of defense while they continued their war in Europe. In the area around the Great Lakes and the Saint Lawrence River, the suspected area of a possible United States' attack, the British politically and militarily aligned themselves with the local Native Americans whose land was rapidly being overtaken by the settlers. Each ally believed they needed each other to defend from a possible attack by the United States.[204] During the early stages of the war, American political and military leaders foolishly believed that taking Canada would be an easy accomplishment. The United States conducted three invasions into Canada between June and November in 1812.

The debate as to why the Americans entered British Canada confounds many historians. These Americans' entry may have set the stage for a series of tactical errors that were costly military blunders. Some congressmen believed that the obvious difference in population would be an advantage to the United States in the event of an attack. With a population of 7,500,000 inhabitants in the United States versus a Canadian population of only 500,000, along with the fact that two-thirds who lived in what was referred to as Lower Canada were of French origin, it seemed that an attack on Canada would be simple and result in an early victory to the war, and settle the grievances between England and America.[205]

Figure 43: Invasion of Canada

"The idea of conquering Canada had been present since 1807… The conquest of Canada was primarily a means of waging war, not a reason for starting it. America in 1812 was acting essentially in reaction to British maritime policy. The British policy, though influenced by jealousy of American commercial growth, stemmed primarily from the necessity of waging war against France. Had there been no war with France … in all probability, there would not have been a War of 1812"

Reginald Horsman
The Causes of the War of 1812[206]

In 1812, early American military successes along the American and Canadian frontiers were severely hampered by the continued alliance between the British and their Native American allies north and south of the Canadian border. During the June-to-November American offensive into Canada, the Americans suffered the loss of Fort Mackinac in Michigan to the British in July. In August, Fort Dearborn, also in Michigan, was burned by the British after American soldiers and civilians were severely tortured by Native American warriors and the city of Detroit was captured and burned by the British. Finally, in October, along the Niagara frontier and at the Battle of

Queenstown Heights in present-day Ontario, U.S. Colonel Solomon Van Rensselaer and his men were defeated by the British and their Native American allies due to petty political infighting amongst the U.S. soldiers.[207]

The Canadian offensive was unsuccessful. As the war progressed in January 1813, the Americans continued to suffer the most treacherous and humiliating of defeats. American frontiersmen were particularly vocal of the tactics of scalping used by the Native Americans and the tacit approval of their British allies. The British were masters of psychological warfare and found an ally in the Native Americans who also believed in the art of intimidation in war. "Americans bitterly complained that the British failed to protect the prisoners taken by the Indians,"[208] and the Native Americans often were used by the British as the first line of defense because of their unconventional but successful intimidating tactics. The Native Americans argued that they were only using the same tactics of the American frontiersmen, particularly the frontiersmen from Kentucky that were used on other Native tribes.

Figure 44: American and Native American Atrocities

Captain Ballard of Kentucky "had two Indian scalps that he had taken at Frenchtown, and had concealed them in the waist band of his pantaloons while a prisoner. While in the fort ...he ripped opened his waistband, took out the scalps, fleshed then with his knife, salted them, and set then in hoops in true Indian style. He said he had twenty scalps at home, and...that he would raise fifty scalps before he would die."

Alan Taylor,
The Causes of the War of 1812[209]

At the Battle of Frenchtown, in the Michigan territory, on January 22, 1813, American, British and Native American troops engaged in a bloody battle, where there were atrocities on both sides. Reportedly, Captain Ballard of Kentucky, after being captured, hid several Native American scalps that he had acquired as trophies.[210] Although Margaret Melton's maternal family moved onto Kentucky, it is unclear if this Captain Ballard was directly or indirectly related to Margaret's mother, Sally Ballard, whose family was in Hertford County, North Carolina.

The next day, "at the dawn on January 23rd, the Kentuckians awoke" to a surprise attack by 1,200 men, a combination of British and Native Americans in what became a bloodbath on the banks of the River Raisin.[211] Soldiers and civilians alike were tortured or taken prisoner. This defining moment only solidified the resolve of the Congress in Washington, galvanized southerners in their fear that the British might free their slaves and encourage their rebellion, and strengthened the fortitude of frontiersmen who believed that the British would stop at nothing to see them all scalped.

On April 27, 1813, at the Battle of York - later to be known as Toronto - the United States, angered by the brutal atrocities at the Raisin River, easily took control over the capital city in Upper Canada. American soldiers went on a rampage and burned the city. "Little did they know that the British would seek revenge for their actions with a vengeance some sixteen months later" at the burning of Washington, D.C.[212] On May 27, 1813, at the Battle of Fort George, the Americans captured the strategically located fort on the Niagara River.[213] However, the Americans' good fortune came to an end on June 5, 1813, when the British forces defeated the Americans at the Battle of Stoney Creek in Canada and then at the Battle of Beaver Dams, where a large number of Americans were captured.[214]

This British gain was not reversed until the Battle at Lake Erie, which was one of the largest naval battles of the War of 1812, and became an important turning point for the Americans. It allowed the badly defeated United States to regain control over possession previously lost, and gave the Americans the opportunity to break the aggressive Native American attacks in the Ohio Valley.

"In March of 1813, Master Commandant Oliver Hazard Perry was assigned…to finalize construction and take command of the Lake Erie flotilla, based at Erie, Pennsylvania," but when the construction was done, Perry could only enlist 150 sailors, when 700 were needed. He requested additional men from his supervisors but was disappointed when he saw these men were "a motley set, blacks, Soldiers, and boys" and voiced his displeasure to his superiors.[215] Commandant Perry received an unexpected reply from his commanding officer, Commodore Isaac Chauncey.

Figure 45: African American Sailors in the War of 1812

"I regret that you are not pleased with the men sent you… for to my knowledge a part of them are not surpassed by any seamen we have on the fleet, and I have yet to learn that the Colour of the skin, or cut and trimmings of the coat, can effect a man's qualifications or usefulness. I have nearly 50 Blacks on board of this ship and many of them are amongst my best men…."

Gerald T., Altoff,
Amongst My Best-Men, African Americans and The War of 1812[216]

Perry believed that his commanders were keeping the best of the lot for themselves.[217] The men Perry received lacked the necessary physical skills and training necessary to command a ship at the height of a battle. With few options, it was a race against time, and Perry had no choice but to train the men as best he could to prepare them for battle.

Once his ships were seaworthy and his men trained, Perry and his sailors were ready to board their vessels. Master Commandant Oliver Hazard Perry prepared for battle on Lake Erie, and on September 10, 1813, set his overly enthusiastic sights on the British Navy in the area of the lake referred to Put-In-Bay. Perry's "motley set" of blacks, soldiers, and boys severely and resoundingly defeated the British Royal Navy. The battle of Lake Erie "was the most important balance of power in the west and enabled the United States to recover all that it had lost in 1812."[218]

The historical significance of African American sailors was noteworthy not only during the success at Lake Erie, but repeatedly, in battle after battle, on ship after ship. During the Revolutionary War, the British Commanders could not help but notice the bravery of African American men who served in the military on land, and now they witnessed the same determination, resolve and bravery of African Americans on the water.

On March 14, 1814, the long, exhausting British war against France came to end, and the British were now able to focus all of their attention and military resources on the war in America.[219] In short order, the British had sent virtually all of their war vessels and men to the United States, and extended their southern blockade to the entire Atlantic seacoast. The New England coastline was now included in the blockade, although until this point, the region had been relatively exempt from the harsh British southern blockage. England, tired of the American nuisance, wanted to bring the war to a speedy and successful conclusion. The British sent troops through Canada to enter New York from the north while utilizing British war vessels off the American coast to simultaneously attack American cities from the south.

By June 1814, after blockading the Chesapeake Bay for two years, the British were familiar with the Bay, its currents and tributaries. Britain understood how to quickly navigate the bay, and move up and down its rivers with ease. With a reinforcement of an additional 15,000 soldiers redeployed from France, the British Royal Navy was well positioned to attack the major port cities along the tributaries of Annapolis, Baltimore, or the capital city of Washington.[220]

Figure 46: A Proclamation

WHEREAS, it has been represented to me, that many Persons now resident in the UNITED STATES, have expressed a desire to withdraw there from, with a view of entering into His Majesty's Service, or of being received as Free Settlers into some of His Majesty's Colonies.

This is therefore to Give Notice,

That all those who may be disposed to emigrate from the UNITED STATES will, with their Families, be received on board His Majesty's Ships or Vessels of War, or at the Military Posts that may be established, upon or near the Coast of the UNITED STATES, when they will have their choice of either entering into His Majesty's Sea or Land Forces, or of being sent as FREE settlers to the British Possessions in North America or the West Indies, where they will meet with due encouragement.

Given under my Hand at Bermuda,
This 2nd day of April, 1814, ALEXANDER COCHRANE.
By Command of the Vice Admiral, WILLIAM BALHETCHET.
GOD SAVE THE KING[221].

In addition to traveling the coastline for the past two years, the British, masters of psychological warfare, knew that the best way to taunt the Americans, particularly southern Americans, was to arm former slaves. Partly as psychological warfare and partly an effort to add additional manpower to their ranks, the British took a page from their Revolutionary War playbook and disseminated a petition aimed at recruiting southern slaves into the Royal Navy or Army, aimed at causing havoc amongst the southern whites. The escaped slaves became part of a British unit referred to as the Corps of Colonial Marines.[222]

As the British entered the next phase of battle in the Chesapeake Bay, they knew that African Americans would play a pivotal role in their success, one way or another. After Gabriel's Rebellion, the British knew that white southerners felt that the mere presence "of any British warship off of a southern state's coast only serve to heighten anxiety that the enemy would incite a long-feared uprising."[223]

Figure 47: Slaves Were Encouraged to Desert and Take up Arms

> "The Slaves continue to come off by every opportunity and I have now upwards of 120 men, women and Children on board....Amongst the Slaves are several very intelligent fellows who are willing to act as local guides should their Services be required in that way, and if their assertions be true, there is no doubt but the Blacks of Virginia & Maryland would cheerfully take up Arms & join us against the Americans."
>
> Gerald T Altoff,
> *Amongst My Best-Men, African Americans and The War of 1812*[224]

The possibility that the slave population would take up arms against their white masters in Virginia and Maryland was welcome news to the British as they strategized on how to take the largest and most important cities along the Chesapeake Bay: Washington D.C., the capital city of the United States, and Baltimore, an important commercial hub.

On August 18, 1814, the British proceeded up the narrow Patuxent River as far as they could go, with the appearance that they were going to attack Baltimore to the north, but their direct aim was the city of Washington to the southwest. The British believed that the capture of the American capital city would destroy the seat of government, decimate American morale nationwide, and hopefully disorganize the American military.

As the British approached, a proclamation was issued "requiring every able-bodied person, including all free men of color, to help build defense works" around the city. On August 24th, after easily defeating the Americans at a small town eight miles outside of Washington, the British marched on to Washington and with virtually no opposition, burned most of the major government buildings including the White House and the United States Capitol.

The following day, the British set their sights on the port city of Baltimore, presuming that it too would be an easy target. While Washington was an important victory psychologically, Baltimore would be an important victory militarily, for it had one of the most active shipbuilding ports in the country, and it had warehouses filled with strategically important military arms and supplies needed for tactical maneuvers. It was also home to many of the privateers who constantly escaped through the British blockage of the Chesapeake Bay. However, the expected victory turned to failure when the British were challenge on land and sea by a very different American military force.

2.20   Third Theater of War: the American South and Gulf of Mexico

In the third theater of the war, on the American coastline and off the Gulf of Mexico, the British hoped to achieve another decisive victory in their southern campaign. The British amassed 10,000 men from the Caribbean island of Jamaica in preparation for their offensive attack on New Orleans, the port city that the United States had recently acquired in the Louisiana Purchase from the French.[225]

Since the British didn't have the necessary small boats to engage the city, they decided to attack the city through Lake Borgne, where they came upon twenty-four year old Lieutenant Thomas A.C. Jones. Although Lieutenant Jones was instructed to only block the passage of the British in the event they ever came through to the Lake, once they came, he believed that he had little option but to engage the British. In the early morning hours of December 14, 1814, Lieutenant Jones and a small flotilla of only five gunboats bravely battled an impressive fifty war ships with 7,800 soldiers on board.[226] Although the young Lieutenant did not prevail against the British - he was captured during the battle and sent to a British jail in Bermuda - he and his men's heroic effort delayed the British arrival in New Orleans.

Less than a month later, on January 8, 1815, in perhaps one of the most decisive victories of the war, the United States was successful in defeating the British invasion at the Battle of New Orleans. Once the British entered the city, they were confounded by the topography of the area surrounding New Orleans - including impassable canals and waterways, thick terrain, a low tide and adverse weather conditions. At the conclusion of the Battle, the "British had 291 killed, 1,262 wounded and 484 missing or prisoners of war. For the United States, the battle resulted in 13 killed, 39 wounded, and 19 missing." This was the final major battle of the war.[227]

The War of 1812 had taken its toll on both nations. The United States was virtually bankrupt and could no longer afford to pay its solders or creditors, and the British had gotten word that the peace accord in Europe was on the verge of collapse, resulting in a renewed war in Europe. The British doubted they could win a victory in America if war broke out again in Europe, and the Americans were certain that they could not win the war without paying their troops. The time had come for the war to end, and on February 17, 1815, with the ratification of the Treaty of Ghent, the war ended with both sides exchanging concessions and retreating from land they did not own prior to the war.[228]

While the war was hard on the financial coffers of the United States and Britain, the war also had taken its toll on many Americans and Canadians, particularly merchants and merchant mariners. In 1818, after serving under some of the most deplorable conditions in the Revolutionary War, veteran Samuel Cornwell and his wife Sarah had to succumb and ask for a veteran's pension, having lost all of their possessions due to his maritime business investments being lost, stolen or destroyed at sea as a direct result of the war. He lost all of his real estate and his personal property, and at the age of sixty-six, after having served his country heroically during two wars, his net worth was less than seven dollars.[229]

The War of 1812 was a defining moment for the United States. On the world stage, it demonstrated that the newly independent United States was a legitimate nation after having waged two wars with England, at the time the most powerful nation in the world. It tested the resolve of men of different political persuasions from all regions whose opinions differed widely, but in the end they came together as one nation. Many people on both sides of the issue of slavery were emboldened in their beliefs. The war established a clear need to move west.

2.21 David Melton and a Group of Sundry Persons of Color

Once the War of 1812 was over, the treaty between the United States and England brought to closure many of the international issues that were unresolved and left over from the earlier American Revolution. However, within the United States, the war and its aftermath only resurfaced many of the unresolved issues between the North and the South - issues concerning the new territories in the west, slavery, taxation, states' rights, and international commerce. The War of 1812 concluded with what was essentially a draw between the two nations, and now, the bitter internal animosities within the United States worsened between the northern and southern states - and between members of Congress - setting the stage for the next major event in American history: the Civil War. Unintentionally, the Cornwall Murphy family became inextricably involved with the regional and national political and social issues of the day.

As the United States was engulfed in the second war with England, the state of Virginia and other states in the south were systematically devising ways to restrict the rights of Free People of Color and ensuring that sympathetic whites, such as the Quakers, didn't free their slaves and add to the number of free blacks in the general population, for fear of a dreaded slave rebellion.

The white community was well aware that news in the black community always traveled fast. The communication network between the slave populations was interesting, and one that southern whites didn't quite understand, let alone trust. Whatever the mode, news always traveled quickly amongst the slaves, and the whites feared that it would someday be used against them as in the rebellion in Saint-Domingue and Gabriel's Rebellion in Richmond, along with increasing numbers of smaller insurrections all across the south. This fear was particularly fixated on the Free People of Color, because white felt that they had to be the instigators, facilitators or at least the co-conspirators of the rebellions and insurrections that had taken place, as slaves weren't assumed to be intelligent enough to execute tactical rebellions without the advice and direction of a free person.

Southern port cities along Chesapeake Bay needed the transactional business of interstate commerce if they were to buy the goods that they needed to survive, and if they were going to sell their products in the northern and European markets. Southerner accepted that northern captains and merchants were a necessary evil for southern livelihoods. The one big problem on these commercial vessels was that they would come into port with a significant number of African American sailors who were part of the crew.

The logical fear in southern port cities was that African American sailors would bring unwanted news to the local black population that could give the impression that slaves had rights not intended by the white population, or worse, incite them to rebellion, a constant fear in white southerners' minds.

When the Virginia legislature became concerned that its Free People of Color population was a threat to the welfare of the state, it took specific measures to force certain African Americans to leave the state. Families whose ancestors had helped found the earliest colonial settlements were forced to leave the state or be subjected to discriminatory laws and public humiliation. Free African Americans feared that additional laws would be enacted that would strip them of their rights to freedom. The Ballard, Chavis, Gowen, Howell, and Melton families moved from the southeastern counties of Virginia over the state line to the fertile tobacco lands of North Carolina, in Hertford, Granville, Guildford and Northampton counties. Though many of Margaret Melton's family members and friends remained in Southampton, Virginia, many ancestors and other extended family members moved to the fertile lands of North Carolina.

While the less affluent North Carolina had been more than happy to have wealthy investors come into the state, even if they were Free People of Color, once-friendly North Carolina was now less receptive to a large population of blacks. In short order, the General Assembly began to pass its own legislation. This time, the state's legislators wanted to keep tabs on the newly arriving Free People of Color. Moreover, they wanted to pit the slaves and Free People of Color against one another with the belief that a divided black community was an easier community to control.

The North Carolina legislature enacted a law that allowed slaves to testify against Free People of Color. On the surface, the law was designed to be a reasonable legislative action. However, it intended to encourage slaves to testify in court against a Free Person of Color, and also allowed disgruntled white plaintiffs to take legal action against Free People of Color and have their slaves support their allegations, whether factual or not. Its effect would allow neighboring white landowners to testify against their Free People of Color neighbors and attempt to wrestle their land from them by legitimate legal means. Free People of Color were worried that slave testimony could not be unbiased unless the slave owner wanted it to be unbiased.

In November 1822, more than 130 Free People of Color sent a petition to the North Carolina General Assembly requesting the repeal of an act of the legislature that declared that slaves were competent witnesses against Free People of Color. This remarkable petition, filed by the group "Sundry Persons of Colour of Hertford County", was a landmark legal request. Perhaps, if these men had not been veterans of both the Revolutionary War and the War of 1812, they would have been shot and killed when they brought the petition to the courthouse, or even worse, they and their families would have been killed at night while they slept.

Although the racial climate was not as harsh in Hertford County as it was in neighboring counties the aftermath of events in Saint-Domingue along with recent Native American retaliation on the western frontier created a hostile environment for all peoples of color. One of the courageous 130 men who risked his life and the safety of his family to sign the petition was David Melton, Margaret Melton's grandfather.

The Sundry Persons of Colour knew they were putting their lives at stake by demanding equality. David Melton, his family, his friends and his neighbors clearly understood the severe risks they were taking when they challenged a political system designed to disenfranchise these men for no other reason than the color of their skin.

Much like The Petition of Blacks Seeking Justice in Boston in 1787 that was submitted to the Massachusetts State Assembly by Prince Hall and endorsed by men like Benjamin Brooker, nothing came of the petition. But although not much was said about the petition, there was a slow and gradual storm brewing on the horizon of Hertford County, North Carolina.

Figure 48: Sundry Persons of Colour of Hertford County

To the Honorable General Assembly of the State of North Carolina

Your petitioners coloured persons citizens of this State would approach your Honorable Body with all the difference [deference] & respect due to the Character of Representatives of the People. They beg leave to state that some of them whose names are assigned to this petition bore and honorable part in the Seven Years War which established the Liberties of their Common Country: That during that eventful period they were taught to believe that all men are by nature free and equal, and that the enjoyment of life, liberty and property ought to be secured alike to every Citizen without exception and without distinction.

With these views they need not attempt to express to your Honorable Body the deep concern with which they learned of the passage of a Law at the last Session of the Legislature by which their lives and liberties are virtually placed at the mercy of the Slaves. They would ask of your Honorable Body whether their Situation even before the Revolution was not preferable to one in which their dearest rights are held by so slight a tenure as the favour of slaves and the will and caprice of their vindictive masters, for it cannot escape the notice of your Honorable Body that persons of this description are bound to a blind obedience, and know no Law, but the will of their masters. Your petitioners will not believe that Your Honorable Body will hesitate to lend a compassionate ear to their well-grounded complaints, and to redress a grievance so oppressive to them, and so wholly in congenial with the spirit of our republican government.

They therefore humbly pray your Honorable Body that the Act of the last Session of the Legislature making slaves competent witnesses against them in criminal cases may be repealed.

Signed by David Melton, as one of the 130 Sundry Persons of Colour of Hertford County, North Carolina, November 1822

2.22   Nat Turner and Southampton, Virginia Rebellion

Less than ten years after David Melton and the other Sundry Persons of Colour of Hertford County petitioned the North Carolina General Assembly with their grievances, another man just forty-five miles north over the county border in Virginia took action on his grievances as a result from a calling from God. In Southampton County, Virginia, where the Melton family originally came from, the most serious slave rebellion in United States history took place between August 21st and 22nd in 1831. For white southerners, it was reminiscent of the 1791 slave rebellion in Saint-Domingue. In just two days, the white southerners' greatest fears came true during the Nat Turner Slave Rebellion.

Nat Turner, an escaped slave, was reportedly inspired by a vision from God. Turner, who was a self-educated preacher and philosopher, often spoke of divine interventions. On one sunny afternoon, he interpreted an eclipse of the sun to be such a divine intervention, imploring him to take up arms against white southerners - and, like Moses, free his people from slavery. Initially, Turner only had a handful of insurgents, but within 72 hours he had recruited 70 slaves to be part of his rebellion. Turner and his insurgents killed approximately 60 whites, including men, women and children, before the rebellion was put down a few days later.[230]

Once the rebellion was suppressed, the farmers in the area retaliated and killed more than 200 slaves and free persons of color, including many who had absolutely no involvement with the insurrection. According to some reports, massacres followed, with a number of innocent blacks shot down.[231] Turner remained in hiding for several months after the insurrection, but was eventually captured, quickly tried, and subsequently hanged.

While not an isolated incident, since many free blacks migrated from Southampton County in Virginia to the neighboring Hertford Country in North Carolina where the David Melton and his family lived, a company of militia from Hertford County reportedly killed 40 innocent blacks in a one-day attack.[232] Reportedly, vocal Free People of Color who often spoke out and militant slaves in Hertford County suspected of participating in the rebellion were also beheaded by the militia, "and their severed heads were mounted on poles at crossroads as a grisly form of intimidation."[233]

For James Melton and his son David, one of the "Sundry Persons of Colour of Hertford County" that challenged the North Carolina General Assembly, there now was much with which to be concerned. The vigilante militias from Hertford were indiscriminate in their horrific assault on their black neighbors, slave or free. The single objective of the militia was clear - to strike the fear in the hearts of all People of Color in Hertford. This sent a strong message to the Hertford County slave population. Any more rebellious actions by slaves or Free People of Color would lead to a similar fate for them and their families.

White southerners were more convinced than ever that they needed stronger control over their slaves, and stronger laws to restrict the rights and privileges of "free" Americans of African descent. Many Free People of Color suspected that their neighbors were intentionally singled out by the white vigilantes not because they were suspected of any collusion with Nat Turner, but for their valuable land. Race relations were coming to a head. As southerners argued for stricter laws, many in the north argued that the only way to prevent further uprisings and bloodshed was through full emancipation of the African slaves. A change was in the air, and everyone could sense it. The stage was now being set for the Civil War, a bloody, internal struggle that would divide the nation and its people.

Early Map of Africa, highlighting the African territories as defined by European colonial jurisdictions. Kongo is highlighted in southwestern portion of the map.

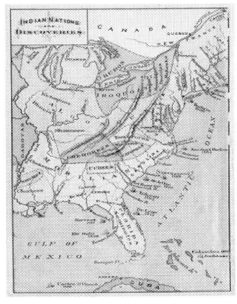

Colonial map highlights the Indian Nations along the eastern North American coastline.

Samuel Cornwell, eight dollars per month Revolutionary War Pension Record (right)

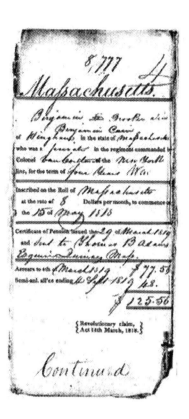

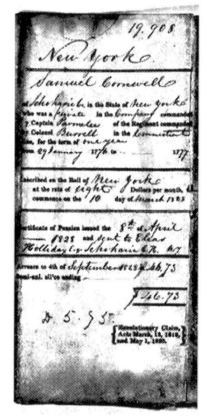

Benjamin (Cain) Brooker, eight dollars per month Revolutionary War Pension Record (left)

Valley Forge in Pennsylvania was the military encampment of the Continental Army during the winter of 1777-1778, where Private Samuel Cornwell and more

than 2,500 patriotic men almost lost their lives to the bitter cold and lack of warmth, food and shelter. Under the direction of Baron Friedrich Von Steubin, the men were taught military discipline, including culling the forest to build log huts for shelter. "As an encouragement to industry and art, the General promises to reward the party in each regiment, which finishes their hut in the quickest and most workmanlike manner with twelve dollars"- General Orders, December 18, 1777. The above picture are replica huts meeting the specifications of 14x16 feet for each hut with a door next to the street and a fireplace in the rear, enabling 12 men to be housed.

The Revolutionary War Battle of Guilford Court House was fought on March 15, 1781 in what is now county of Greensboro, North Carolina. Although the 2,100 British

force led by Lieutenant General Charles Cornwallis defeated Continental Army Major General Nathaniel Green's army of 4,500 men, the battle was a major turning point in the war. Picture was taken at the fields of a replica of Joseph Hoskin's farmhouse where the North Carolina militia, which included Edward Gowen, were drawn up behind the fence line ready to attack Cornwallis' men who were on the road just below the farmhouse.

William Lloyd Garrison, orator and abolitionist, best known as the founder and editor of the 1831 weekly abolitionist newspaper the Liberator.

Recruitment posters were used to encourage African Americans to join the Civil War effort. On July 17, 1862, Congress passed legislation allowing enlistment into the United States Colored Troops. Enrollment officially took place after the issuance of the Emancipation Proclamation the following January.

Frederick Douglas, former slave, abolitionist and African American statesman argued that the Civil War was being fought to end slavery and African American men should be allowed to fight for their country - and to fight for their freedom.

Sargent William Cornwell, son of Flushing and Harriet Cornwell, served in the 5th Massachusetts Colored Calvary. Photograph taken after the Civil War battle in Petersburg, Virginia, circa 1864, where William lost his thumb and index finger on the battlefield.

William Cornwell Civil War
Military record

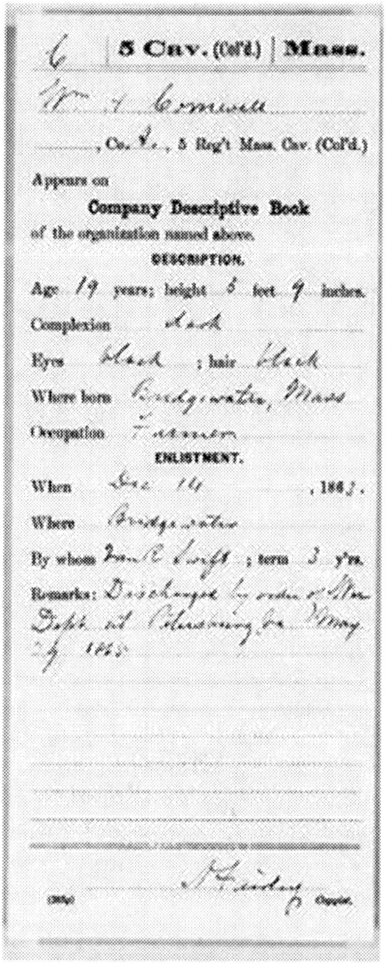

6 | 5 Cav. (Col'd.) | Mass.

Wm. [illegible] Cornwell

, Co. [illegible], 5 Reg't Mass. Cav. (Col'd.)

Appears on

Company Descriptive Book

of the organization named above.

DESCRIPTION.

Age 19 years; height 5 feet 9 inches.

Complexion dark

Eyes black ; hair black

Where born Bridgewater, Mass

Occupation Farmer

ENLISTMENT.

When Dec. 14, 1863.

Where Bridgewater

By whom Jno. R. Swift ; term 3 y'rs.

Remarks: Discharged by order of War Dept. at [illegible], Va. May 27, 1865

[illegible] Copyist.

Former slaves Private Othello Fraction and his brother Sargent Thomas Fraction ran away from the Solitude plantation and joined Nashville, Tennessee's 40th United States Colored Infantry, where they were responsible for Louisville and Nashville Railroad, and the Nashville and Northwestern Railroad, as pictured.

The plantation Solitude was owned by Confederate Colonel Robert T. Preston and was home to James, Othello and Thomas Fraction of Montgomery County, Virginia. This is the home where Colonel Preston summoned his slaves and threatened them if any man joined the United States Colored Troops.

Part 3: The American Civil War

We hold these truths to be self-evident, that all men are created equal...
The Declaration of Independence

3.1   The Transformation of the United States

With the rise of the nineteenth century, dramatic changes came to the United States. Immediately after the Revolutionary War, the interests of the northern states were similar to those of their southern compatriots. The United States transformed itself from a dependent colony of farmers and frontiersmen, reliant on colonial British rule, to a nation of growing urban centers of business, education, and international commerce in the North; and had tremendous capacity for agricultural production of cotton and tobacco in the South. Between 1820 and 1850, there were rapid changes, and with rapid change came regional stress and national tension.

The Brooker, Grandison and Russell families of Massachusetts saw increased urbanization in Boston and its surrounding communities. In Massachusetts communities such as Fall River and Northern Bridgewater (where the Brookers and Grandisons lived), and Lowell and Lawrence (near where the Russells lived), new industrial factories now dotted the landscape that was once occupied by small, family owned farms. Each of these factors contributed to a growing and thriving economy, which provided employment opportunities for the African Americans in the surrounding communities, and also resulted in the need for more and more workers.

Modern immigration in the United States began after the War of 1812 in America and the Napoleonic Wars in Europe, setting the stage for large-scale immigration from the 1850s through the early 1900s. European immigration helped to transform the United States from a "nation of colonists clinging to the eastern seaboard into a transcontinental country of immense power and potential."[234]

By 1815, thousands of working class Europeans came to America each year. Initially from Germany, Ireland, and Italy, these immigrants helped to transform northern cities such as Boston, New York and Philadelphia into urbanized communities, with ethnic enclaves sprouting up in sections of each city. Newly arriving immigrants sent word of the tremendous opportunities in America back to their family and friends in Europe. As travel costs between the United States and Europe became less expensive, Europeans found it easier to come to America and the possibility of setting up a business or owning land in the vast open spaces in the west was too alluring to pass up.

In order to support the arrival of new immigrant workers, a wage labor system developed and with it, a new and growing middle class. The labor system enabled the employer and the employee to trade hours worked for a predetermined wage. Between 1800 and 1850, the advent of the wage labor system played a large role in transforming the social fabric of America's northern cities, giving birth to America's first middle class. Comprised mostly of white-collar workers and skilled laborers, this growing middle class became the driving force behind a variety of reform movements. White-collar workers hired skilled laborers and artisans to build their lavish new homes and landscape their gardens, and financially compensated black and white domestic workers to help to maintain their households.

Figure 49: Becoming a Nation of Immigrants

Census Year	Total US population	# Immigrants	Foreign Born	% of population
1790	3,929,214	60,000		7.9%
1800	5,308,483	60,000		10.8%
1810	7,239,881	60,000		13.5%
1820	9,638,453	60,000		13.2%
1830	12,860,702	143,000	200,00	13.7%
1840	17,063,353	599,000	800,000	13.4%
1850	23,191,876	1,713,000	2,244,000	11.9%

By 1850, more than 1.7 million immigrants had come to America, transforming the United States in a way that had not been done before. In cities such as "New York, St. Louis, Cincinnati, Chicago, Cleveland, Detroit and San Francisco, over half of each city's population was foreign-born," according to the U.S. Census Bureau. Immigrants not only changed the demographics of urban centers, but they were also able to open up the western frontier, and dotted the western landscape with new settlements and outposts.

However, there was one region which most immigrants carefully avoided the South. With its antebellum societies and land barons controlling large swaths of land, immigrants "saw the slave societies and slave economies as unattractive and that there was little place in the South for immigrant labor."[235] While the North was expanding and urbanizing, the South remained predominantly a rural, agricultural society, where slavery and cash crops such as cotton and tobacco were staples of their economy. European immigrants were strongly opposed to the increase of slavery in the South, fearing that the growing slave labor would eventually pit immigrants in direct competition with slaves for jobs.

Figure 50: Distribution of Slaves in the United States[236]

Number of Slaves and Free Blacks by Census Count						
Census Year	# Slaves	# Free blacks	Total black	% free blacks	Total US population	% black of total
1790	697,681	59,527	757,208	7.9%	3,929,214	19%
1800	893,602	108,435	1,002,037	10.8%	5,308,483	19%
1810	1,191,362	186,446	1,377,808	13.5%	7,239,881	19%
1820	1,538,022	233,634	1,771,656	13.2%	9,638,453	18%
1830	2,009,043	319,599	2,328,642	13.7%	12,860,702	18%
1840	2,487,355	386,293	2,873,648	13.4%	17,063,353	17%
1850	3,204,313	434,495	3,638,808	11.9%	23,191,876	16%
1860	3,953,760	488,070	4,441,830	11.0%	31,443,321	14%
1870	0	4,880,009	4,880,009	100%	38,558,371	13%

By 1800, before the first big wave of Europeans immigration, more than 19 percent of the United States population was of African American descent. In some southern states and communities, the black population exceeded 60 percent. Prior to 1810, any increase in the slave population resulted primarily from the new arrivals from Africa and the Caribbean but from 1810 to 1830, the increase in the slave population was due primarily to a significantly higher birthrate among the slaves. Between 1800 and 1850, the slave population in the United States, particularly in the South, increased more than 250 percent. The population of Free People of Color grew more than 300 percent, despite laws that prevented interracial marriages and took specific steps to place a heavier tax burden on Free People of Color. This significant growth, for both free and slave populations, was almost entirely due to an increase of native-born Americans of African descent.

Slavery was extremely profitable in the South, where men, women, children and the elderly were forced to work long, strenuous hours in the tobacco and cotton fields. According to the 1850 United States census, most slaves lived on plantations or large family farms that had ten or more slaves. In the North, however, slavery was becoming less profitable, particularly as Europe's poor immigrated to northern cities and provided relatively skilled, cheap labor. As northern states gradually enacted manumission laws - the act of slave owners freeing their slaves - and emancipated their slaves, the northern economies became more diversified. Many of these newly freed indentured servants and slaves began to debate the merits of slavery in the South.

The state of Massachusetts was especially vocal in its rejection of slavery. Boston became the epicenter for a much larger and broader debate on the role of race, class and slavery in America - and members of the Cornwall Murphy family would once again be thrust into a national dialogue that would eventually lead the family with branches in the North and the South into the next war.

3.2   The Northern Abolitionist Movement

One of the first and largest groups in America to be against slavery was the religious order of the Quakers, who fundamentally believed that all men were created equal. After the Revolutionary War, all across the country, the Quakers released their own slaves and preached against the evils of slavery. When possible, the Quakers also helped slave families to freedom. Formed in 1816, the Quaker American Colonization Society's mission was to free the slaves and repatriate them back to Africa.[237] In 1821, the American Colonization Society settled the colony of Liberia in Africa as a new home for the repatriated slaves.

During the mid-1840s through the early 1860s, one of the most radical antislavery states in the union was Massachusetts, and one of the most outspoken and prolific abolitionists was William Lloyd Garrison of Boston. A former member of the American Colonization Society, Garrison founded the New England Anti-Slavery Society in

1832. As editor of the abolitionist newspaper *The Liberator*, Garrison was also one of the founders of the New York based American Anti-Slavery Society. His followers were often referred to as "Garrisonians ...who crusaded militantly for immediate, unconditional and universal emancipation."[238]

Garrison ultimately disagreed with the American Colonization Society's position on the repatriation of slaves to Africa, a land these slaves no longer had any connection to, and he felt that full emancipation was more important than removing slaves and free blacks from America. He used his own newspaper, *The Liberator*, to disseminate a single but clear message - he supported the liberation of slaves, with no reparations to their slave owners. Garrison's abolitionist message intrigued northern intellectuals, who openly discussed the wrongs of slavery. But it enraged southerners, who espoused the virtues of slavery.

Figure 51: Northern States Emancipate Their Slaves

1777	Vermont	State constitution abolished slavery from the beginning
1780	Pennsylvania	Emancipation
1783	New Hampshire	Gradual abolishment of slavery
1783	Massachusetts	Judicial decision abolished slavery
1783	Maine	Maine was originally part of Massachusetts ... Judicial decision abolished slavery
1784	Rhode Island	Political compromise for gradual emancipation ... 1840 gradually abolished
1784	Connecticut	Political compromise for gradual emancipation ... 1830 gradually abolished
1799	New York	Gradual abolishment of slavery ... 1827 full emancipation
1802	Ohio	State constitution abolished slavery from the beginning
1804	New Jersey	Gradual abolishment of slavery ... 1846 full emancipation
1847	Delaware	Never passed out of committee

The Garrisonians, were articulate, vocal, and influential. They shared their beliefs through a series of public speeches and well-written publications across the northeastern states. Through their growing influence, they were able to take control of the state's political system, enabling Massachusetts to have some of the most powerful abolitionists, including "two of the strongest antislavery senators in Congress, Charles Sumner and Henry Wilson.[239] The Garrisonians and other abolitionist societies all across Boston sponsored weekly debates on slavery at Faneuil Hall and the Tremont Temple, in Congregational Church basements, and at the African Meeting House on Boston's Beacon Hill. Sponsored events attracted noted abolitionists, including legends such as Harriet Tubman, Sojourner Truth, David Walker, and Frederick Douglass.

Much like the earlier African American civil rights leader and abolitionist Prince Hall of Boston, one of the more articulate abolitionist speakers was Frederick Douglass, a former runaway slave from the Eastern shore of Maryland. After he escaped from slavery, Douglass married his first wife, and relocated to New Bedford, Massachusetts, where he eventually met abolitionist William Lloyd Garrison. As the two men developed a friendship and perfected their strong abolitionist views, Douglass was encouraged to speak at anti-slavery rallies nationwide and all across Europe.

Douglass' oratory skills mesmerized crowds as he shared a deeply personal perspective on the cruelty of slavery and what it felt like to be treated as chattel property. Douglass spoke about the brutality of the whippings and beatings he endured as a young man, and how deeply the desire to be free burned within him. By the time the Civil War erupted, Frederick Douglass was one of the most eloquent speakers to address the plight of the black man in America. He profoundly believed that African Americans needed to be equal participants in the fight for their freedom and independence. Frederick Douglass, the fugitive ex-slave, was now the voice of all slaves who wanted freedom.

Abolitionist publications galvanized northern support while infuriating southern opponents. The abolitionists gained influence in the Republican Party, and leveraged that influence every way that they could. They spoke at state capitals in the North, and persuaded like-minded politicians to advance emancipation laws within their own states. As individual states in the North began to slowly emancipate their slaves, abolitionists set their sights on a national emancipation law.

3.3   Samuel Brooker of Boston, Massachusetts

The oratory skills of the northern Abolitionists, as well as the printed words of the New England Anti-Slavery Society, dramatically changed the public debate on the negative aspects of slavery and helped convince northern states to emancipate their slaves and helped to prevent the expansion of slavery in the western territories. William Lloyd Garrison and members of the Prince Hall Masonic Temple engaged the African American community on issues relative to slavery and the need for African American activism particularly in states such as Massachusetts.

Benjamin Brooker, a Revolutionary War veteran and one of Prince Hall's confidants, and his wife, Harriet Grandison, taught their sons Samuel and Benjamin, Jr. to be socially conscious and politically engaged. With a father, two uncles, and a grandfather all having served in the Revolutionary War, Samuel and his brother Benjamin probably both understood how lucky they were to be free black men, and to be able to raise their families in free state. Samuel Brooker, who was Harold Cornwall's 2nd generation great-grandfather, as well as most African Americans in Boston were well aware of the events surrounding the Nat Turner slave rebellion in Southampton, Virginia, and the subsequent brutal murders of innocent slaves and free blacks in Virginia and North Carolina. Samuel married Philinda Russell, who was the daughter of Revolutionary War veteran Caesar Russell and his wife Sally Richardson. Samuel's father-in-law often recounted how slaves were treated when he was a child in Massachusetts, and how much worse they were being treated all across the South.

When black seamen like Caesar Russell and Cuffe Grandison sailed south and saw how other African Americans in the South were treated, they were appalled, offended, and often times, too frightened to leave the ships, worried they would be captured and forced into slavery. The few times they dared to venture off the ships, they stayed in the waterfront area and sought out other blacks to engage them in conversation about their lives in the South.

Northern black sailors were always interested in learning about how life on southern plantations compared to their lives in the North. Meanwhile, southern blacks were hungry for any information from outside their community that would shed light on the possibility of emancipation. They often asked these northern sailors what people in the North were doing to abolish slavery, and the black people in the South wanted any information about how they might be treated in friendly communities in the North if they were able to get there.

Samuel and Philinda Brooker, along with his brother Benjamin and his family, initially made their homes in the same tenement building in Boston's racially integrated section of the North End.[240] Once Samuel and Philinda's four children were of age, the family moved twenty-five miles outside of the city and made their home in the farming community of Bridgewater, Massachusetts.

As Americans of African descent, it is likely that Samuel and Philinda were quite proud of their fathers having served in the Revolutionary War. The Brookers recognized the profound importance of their fathers' military service, and how it enabled their families to live as free blacks in the United States. They understood that their fathers fought not only for the independence of their country but also for the freedom of African Americans all across the northern states. The Brookers raised their children with a sense of pride in their family's contributions and heritage. Samuel and Philinda wanted to make sure that their children understood the significance of their freedom compared to the slavery that African Americans still endured in the South. In subsequent years, their daughter, Harriet Brooker, learned this message well, and instilled this same sense of pride into her own children and grandchildren many years later.

3.4   Flushing Cornwall of St. John, New Brunswick, Canada

After the Revolutionary War, veteran Samuel Cornwall and his wife Sarah Mansfield, who were originally from Flushing, New York, moved to Saint John Parish, New Brunswick, Canada, with their seven children. Their son Mansfield, who followed in his father's business, became a sea merchant and captain, sailing frequently to the busy ports of Boston and New York. At the age of 16, Mansfield Cornwall and a young Native American girl named Hannah had a son, born on Christmas Day in 1810. Mansfield named his interracial son Flushing after the township of Flushing, New York, where he was born. According to an obituary in the *Brockton Enterprise*,[241] Hannah was reportedly the daughter of a Chief of a Warren Springs Native American tribe. At the time, a child born to a white father and a Native American mother was commonly referred to, disrespectfully, as a "half-breed."[242]

According to elderly family members, Flushing's physical appearance was very similar to his father, he was muscular and stood at 5 foot 8. As he aged, his waist grew portly, which made him appear mature and distinguished. While his light-colored skin and stature favored his father, his facial features were those of his mother and her Native American ancestors. His oblong face had the tanned color of someone who spent a fair amount of time in the sun. His deeply set eyes accented his narrow nose and thin lips, and his smile made those who met him feel relaxed and secure. Although Samuel and Sarah now lived in Canada, the Cornwalls still had strong family ties in New England's coastal states, and profited from their contacts and knowledge of the city of Boston and its trading partners.

Boston was an exciting city and was becoming known for its international commerce, political and intellectual thinking, and mass appeal to people from around the world. As a teenager, Flushing would often accompany his father to the Massachusetts' port cities and fishing villages. According to his wife's cousin, Pearl Ashport Brooks, Flushing always felt uncomfortable as a "half-breed" of mixed European and Native American heritage, and never seemed to fit into the local scene in St. John's all-white community.[243] He looked forward to the trips away from home.

Boston, with its busy harbor full of ships from all over the world and its bustling tenement neighborhoods inhabited by people with different languages and skin colors, appealed to the multiracial Flushing, who always thought of himself as different from the community in which he grew up.

One can imagine the first time Flushing arrived in Boston, amazed by the beauty of the harbor and the city that lay beyond the masts of the tall ships anchored in the crowded port. The height of the masts on the wooden ships in the deep blue water was accentuated by the height of the buildings on land. Each time he entered the port on his father's schooner, Flushing marveled at the beautiful brick buildings that reached three or four stories into the sky, nestled in between shorter buildings that were painted green, yellow, and deep navy blue. From Flushing's perspective, the city of Boston was a world away and much more energetic than the stagnant St. John, where every house was white, and every person was of European ancestry. on And once Flushing went ashore, he was even more amazed by the energy of the city that would always seem to wait for him.

With Boston's tall skyscrapers, its wide streets and its racial diversity - each a major attraction to the young Flushing, he quickly decided he no longer wanted to go back to the serenity of Saint John's rugged coastline and rural pastureland. He was in awe of the perfectly aligned cobblestone streets, where the sound of horses' hoofs reverberated against the tall buildings as they pulled carriages down the street. Flushing enjoyed walking the streets around the newly renovated Faneuil Hall, seeing all of the pushcarts loaded with the bright colors of the various fruits and vegetables, and listening to the immigrant street vendors selling their wares in the many different languages. He looked forward to the smells of the baked breads and to buying himself an Irish sweet roll.

Flushing also was amazed that each street was even more beautiful than the last as he walked deeper into Boston, away from the waterfront. Smoke from chimneys seemed to dance and disappear into the sky. Everyone walked quickly, as though they all had somewhere important to go. The men wore clothes that reflected their occupations. Flushing assumed the men in dark suits were bankers or tradesmen with whom his father would meet; the men with rolled up sleeves, brown vests and darker brown pants, and weather-worn faces probably worked in the grain and feed shops found along the Boston streets. With each visit, Flushing noticed the pretty girls more and more. He was fascinated by the fullness of their skirts, the yards and yards of material that went into making those dresses. He had never seen so many women dressed in beautifully patterned dresses, carrying small hand baskets and stopping to chat with each other as they went about their daily routines.

The further Flushing walked away from the ship and deeper into Boston, the more he was convinced that he wanted to live in this historic and magnificent city. The cold days of St. John Parish in

New Brunswick, Canada were behind him. After one stop in Boston, with the help of his father, Mansfield, rather than sailing back to New Brunswick, Flushing found a job working in the North End neighborhood of Boston, around the piers and merchant ships, doing chores similar to the ones he had done back home.

In the early 1800s, prior to the annexation of several surrounding townships, the city of Boston was essentially divided into four sections. The four core sections had a unique character unto themselves: the ethnic neighborhoods of the North End, the diverse mercantile class of the West End, the growing middle class of the South End and the wealthy merchants of Beacon Hill and the African American tradesmen who supported them. Boston's West End/Waterfront area bordered Beacon Hill to its South, the North End on its northeastern boundaries, the Charles River to the west, and Boston Harbor/Waterfront to the southeast. Initially, the westernmost areas of Boston's West End consisted of large, newly constructed red brick mansions, while the eastern portion of the West End attracted young European immigrant families, and the young men who worked as stevedores. These neighborhoods were linguistically, culturally and racially diverse, and a young man such as Flushing, with his coloring and facial features, looked just like the young immigrant men who worked outside all day in the harsh sun or the newly arrived young men from Italy with their olive complexions.

For a young man who was more than four hundred miles away from his family - coming from the monocultural community of Saint John, New Brunswick - Boston was an extremely attractive community and Flushing felt very much at home in his new environment. As time passed, he began to venture out from the racially and ethnically diverse neighborhood of Boston's West End to Boston's Beacon Hill's North Slope, a community where a large number of Boston's African American tradesmen and the middle class community lived. On one such walk, Flushing met Miss Harriet Brooker of Bridgewater, Massachusetts, while she was visiting her paternal grandparents, Benjamin and Harriet Brooker, on Boston's Beacon Hill.

Harriet's parents, Samuel and Philinda Brooker, were skeptical of her association with Flushing, especially as he was not from a well-known Bostonian family, nor from one of Boston's surrounding

African American communities. In addition, Flushing was a good-looking foreigner, and this made the Brookers all the more suspicious of his intentions with their daughter. The usual parent-child conflict developed. Samuel and Philinda wanted their daughter to meet and marry a young man from a good African American family, with strong roots to the growing Boston middle-class community, not an unknown stranger whose past and reputation they knew nothing about.

However, Harriet was smitten by everything her parents dreaded about Flushing - she admired his foreign accent, his maturity and sophistication, and his strikingly good looks. In 1828, Samuel and Philinda Brooker's eldest daughter, Harriet married the young, dapper Flushing Cornwall from Saint John Parish, New Brunswick, Canada.[244]

After their marriage, Flushing and Harriet Cornwall moved to Bridgewater, Massachusetts, near where Harriet's maternal grandparents lived. With their marriage, the prominent and sometimes controversial European Cornell family line, hailing from London, England, had now developed into a non-European family. The children of Flushing and Harriet were now the first generation of Cornells to identify as non-white. Depending on individual physical appearance, some identified themselves as Native Americans while others identified themselves as African American. The family lived far from Boston and could thus insulate their children from topics such as slave rebellions and revolts, kidnapping of young blacks from the harbor docks, or discussions surrounding the growing Abolitionist movement in Boston. However, it was just a matter of time before the discussions caught up with them in their provincial town of Bridgewater.

With Flushing Cornwell's family originating from Europe, and he himself having been born and raised in Canada, his perspective on slavery was very different from his wife's, whose family members were former slaves. Harriet Cornwall, as the granddaughter of slaves, had her perspective molded by her grandparents' frightening recollections of the humiliation of servitude and bondage. Flushing, despite being born of mixed race parents and being taunted as a child because of his color and being a "half breed," never thought of himself as less than equal to any other man. Harriet, on the other hand, was more realistic in her view of race relations, and always feared that at any time somehow she could be captured and put into slavery.

Harriet was born in 1817, by which time all of the slaves within the state of Massachusetts had been emancipated for thirty-four years. But southern slave catchers were constantly patrolling the city of Boston and surrounding communities, looking for potential runways and the unique opportunity to kidnap a Free Person of Color and take them South. According to her niece, Harriet had strong abolitionist views and felt that the only way that her family would be totally safe, even in the free state of Massachusetts, was if the institution was eliminated nationwide, and all slaves were emancipated. [245]

3.5   Henry Utley from Fayetteville, North Carolina

What made Frederick Douglass' message so powerful at Abolitionist meetings was his firsthand account of growing up as a slave boy, his challenges as a young adult, and his journey to become self-educated. The story of Frederick Douglass spoke to the lives of African American men, women and children all across the country, particularly in the South. Robert Murphy's maternal great grandfather, Henry Utley, was born a slave in 1818 in a community called Cross Creek, part of the Fayetteville Township in Cumberland County, North Carolina.[246] Fayetteville was the first community in the United States to be named in honor of the French General Lafayette, who provided significant help to the American Continental Army during the Revolutionary War. The community of Cross Creek and its sister community, Campbellton, were separated by the famous Pee Dee River. Cross Creek was populated in the mid-1700s by poor whites, free blacks and Iroquois Native Americans who married and intermarried with each other.

In the mid to late 1700s, there were a number of devastating fires in Fayetteville that destroyed a series of government buildings, which has limited the ability to conduct extensive research on the Utley family prior to this period. During the late 1700s, there were a number of white Utley families documented, but no documentation appears to exist for any Utley families of African descent. This is perhaps, in part, a result of a number of local laws passed that provide a glimpse of the racial attitudes towards the African American community in Fayetteville during this time period.

Similar to what the European Jews endured in Nazi Germany during the 1930s and 1940s, Fayetteville Township passed a law in 1785 that "required all free blacks in Fayetteville to wear distinctive shoulder badges with the legend 'FREE,' and established restrictions on their mobility, choice of occupation and relationship with slaves."[247] According to the First United States Census in 1790, there were only 32 families who were listed as Free People of Color, but the family of Henry Utley was not listed as being Free People of Color.

3.6   William Fraction from Botetourt County, Virginia

With each day, the North and South were more and more divided in their opinions on slavery. Every debate put them further at odds, the two regions were becoming two very distinct parts of the country - culturally, socially, and economically. Another issue that drove the North and South apart was the rapid expansion into the western territories. In the wake of the War of 1812, many Americans believed that God intended for them to spread democracy and Protestantism across the entire continent. This idea of "manifest destiny" spurred more than a million Americans to leave their homes in the East and set out on a quest to acquire land, stake their claim, and strike it rich in the western frontier.

Politicians capitalized on the public's sentiments to acquire all land between the Atlantic and the Pacific Oceans. The United States acquired the territories of Florida and Oregon - and declared war on Mexico in 1846, seizing possession of Texas, California, and everything in between. Botetourt County, Virginia served as a transfer station for hardy and adventurous Americans and European immigrants going west to the dangerous Oregon, Mormon, Santa Fe, and California Trails.

In 1770, Botetourt County, Virginia, was created after Augusta County split into two separate counties. Augusta County was once considered the largest county in colonial Virginia, extending from its home state to the vast landscape westward of the Mississippi River. By 1772, as pioneer families and immigrants poured into Botetourt County to take advantage of the rich farms lands the county split again to form Fincastle County.

As a result of the Revolutionary War, Fincastle was abolished and formed into three new counties: Kentucky County, which later became its own separate state in 1792, and Montgomery and Washington Counties. "Upon its formation in 1776, Montgomery County contained 12,000 square miles and extended as far west as the Ohio River. From this single county sixty other counties were formed including twenty-six in western Virginia, twenty-five in the state of West Virginia and nine in Kentucky."[248]

As settlers moved westward through Botetourt and Montgomery Counties, many decided to take advantage of the Shenandoah Valley's rich soil and pastureland. The issue of westward expansion had a profound effect on American politics and society during the antebellum years, and for some of the early settlers of Botetourt and Montgomery Counties, the expansion made them very rich. One such family was that of James Patton Preston, Governor of Virginia from 1816 to 1819. Governor and Mrs. Nancy Ann Preston had four children. His eldest son, William Ballard Preston, initially was a United States Congressman and subsequently represented Virginia as its Senator to the Confederate States of America during the Civil War.[249]

Figure 52: William Preston, Senator of the United States of the Confederacy

▪ Virginia Representative to the United States Congress form 1847-1849
▪ Secretary of the U.S. Navy, under President Taylor from 1847-1850
▪ Member of the United States Commission to France
▪ Delegate to the Virginia Conventions, 1850 and 1860
▪ Virginia Senator of the Confederate States of America
Joanne Spiers Moche *Families of Grace through 1900, Remembering Radford,* [250]

Governor and Mrs. Preston's middle son, Robert Taylor Preston (1809 – 1881), was a successful businessman and owned a number of slaves, including William Fraction and his brothers, Thomas and Othello. William Fraction was the great-grandfather of Robert Murphy of Norfolk, Virginia. While the Preston family was, by all accounts, prosperous, they did not own a large number of slaves like the wealthy planters in the eastern part of the state where the land was flatter and better suited for farming. In the 1860 United States Census Slave Holder

Schedule, Robert T. Preston was listed as owning 33 slaves.[251] He was one of the largest slaveholders in the county. Unlike other Virginia counties, and certainly in comparison to other counties in the southern states where the slave population was equal to or much greater than the white population, the total population in Montgomery County was 10,617 inhabitants and the median size of the farms in the county was only between 50 and 99 acres.[252]

A priceless Slave Schedule was found on the Preston plantation, and on September 5th and 6th of 1860, John C. Wade, the assistant marshal for Montgomery County, enumerated the number of slaves on Robert T. Preston's plantation, and found that the Preston plantation had 33 slaves, with the oldest being a 100 year old woman and the youngest being only 2 months old. There is no documentation to indicate if each person on the plantation was related, nor who the actual person was. However, based on plantation customs and a preponderance of evidence, the slaves on the Preston plantation were related to one another.

Figure 53: Robert T. Preston's 1860 Slave Schedule

No.	Age	Sex	Color	No.	Age	Sex	Color	No.	Age	Sex	Color
1	100	F	B	1	26	M	B	1	7	M	B
1	71	M	B	1	23	M	B	1	7	M	B
1	56	M	B	1	21	F	B	1	5	M	B
1	40	F	B	1	21	M	B	1	4	F	B
1	34	F	B	1	20	M	B	1	2	M	B
1	33	M	B	1	19	F	B	1	2	F	B
1	34	M	B	1	18	M	B	1	2	F	B
1	33	M	B	1	16	F	B	1	1	F	B
1	30	F	B	1	14	M	B	1	¾	F	B
1	29	M	B	1	9	M	B	1	½	M	B
1	27	M	B	1	9	F	B	1	¼	M	B

Schedule 2. Slave Inhabitants in Montgomery County, Virginia. 1860 United States Federal Census[253]

Based on the ages of William Fraction's family in the United States Census of 1870, ten years later, similar family members by age and gender can be found on the Preston Slave Schedule. Based on the age of William's brothers, Thomas and Othello, similarly aged men can be identified on the 1860 Slave Schedule.

The power and the prestige of the Preston brothers can be judged by their worth as summarized on the 1860 Selected United States Federal Census, Non-Population Schedules, 1850-1880, Agriculture Schedule. The Preston brothers, James, Robert and William owned three adjoining plantations in Montgomery County. The combined land of the three adjacent properties was more than 4,100 acres of prime real estate. The assessed value of their land was more than $125,500, excluding the value of the improvements and buildings, which was a substantial amount in 1860. Of the acreage owned, more than 2,200 acres was improved for farming and raising cattle. By virtue of their shear wealth and political connections, the Prestons' were clearly an important and influential family in antebellum Montgomery County. Their wealth and connections helped them transition into the railroad industry, and they hired out their younger and stronger male slaves who eventually transitioned into the railroad industry as well.

In 1848, railroad executives, eager to move westward, realized that Montgomery County offered the best location for traveling to the western frontier by rail. While "mountains blocked a western pathway for the railroads in counties to the north and south of Montgomery County, the Allegheny Mountain ridge in the county posed the only obstacle separating the level valley of the Roanoke River from the chain of valleys leading along the New River and beyond to the Tennessee line."[254] In 1851, the Virginia and Tennessee Railroad chose Christiansburg, the county seat, as a depot stop on the rail line going west to southwestern Virginia and to Tennessee and points westward. Railroads were soon critically important to local economies by connecting local exports to markets back east. Railroads opened commercial trade in a manner never provided before and communities thrived when a railroad "came to town."

In 1853, "leading Montgomery County entrepreneurs, including William B. Preston and Robert T. Preston" invested in the New River Railroad Company. In the same year "William B. Preston invested in the Allegheny Railroad Company in order to penetrate the market and exports of the coalfields of Brush Mountain."[255] Montgomery County "land values exploded from an average of $5.84 an acre in 1850 to over $91.00 an acre in 1860." William Preston and his brother, Robert, were the beneficiaries of the emerging railroad industry and the increased property values.

As the Preston brothers became more interested in the railroad business and its financial rewards, they took their stronger and healthier young male slaves away from agricultural work on the plantations and instead had them work on the rail lines. This plan was a win-win situation for the Prestons, who were able to make extra money by hiring their slaves out. Their land values increased, and they increased the value of any stocks they owned in the railroads. The business of hiring out strong young men was so profitable that the Preston brothers left the farm work to be maintained by the slave women, older men, and young boys not ready to be hired out.

For William, Thomas and Othello Fraction, working the Preston family plantation and farmlands was hard work, but working the rail lines was even harder. The long hours and backbreaking work would eventually pit the power and prestige of the Preston family against the Fraction brothers — and one would almost die as a result.

3.7   Keziah Gardiner of Suffolk County New York

African American disenfranchisement was not limited to the South. Although the pains of slavery and racism were more severely felt in the South, the residual effects, whether it was in the North or in the South, differed little. Lewis Gardiner and his family on New York's Long Island Sound and were gained freedom as a result of the state's gradual Emancipation Law, saw little difference between being freed and being enslaved, other than they were on their own to fend for themselves.

As recently emancipated slaves, Lewis Gardiner and his family were still dependent on the Gardiner family, their former slave masters. Although technically emancipated and now free people by law, Lewis' family members were figuratively enslaved by the limited opportunities afforded them because of their race and limited education. They had no access to resources that would enable them to advance forward. Even though they did not live in the South, they lived a life similar to that of a southern sharecropper. In many respects, the institution of slavery differed little between the northern and southern states.

By 1822, the formal institution of slavery was illegal in the entire state of New York, but the privileged upper class still practiced the elements of slavery and servitude throughout the entire state until the mid-1860s. The prolonged process of freeing New York's enslaved men and women produced a society in early nineteenth century Long Island where slaves and freed people lived and worked side by side. Although the African American population in New York's Suffolk County declined from 2,236 in 1790 to 1,907 in 1845, African Americans remained a critical and vital part of the labor force.[256]

According to the 1860 U.S. Census from Huntington, New York, Mrs. Elizabeth Rodgers, a widowed landowner, whose property was valued at $6,000, had a 28-year-old "colored" female servant by the name of Rhonda Seidmore. Elizabeth's son, Robert Rodgers, lived with his wife and young daughter on the property adjacent to his mother's. Like his mother, Robert and his wife, Sophronia, engaged the domestic services of a colored servant, a nine-year-old girl by the name of Keziah Gardiner, who was the maternal great-grandmother of Harold Cornwall of Brockton, Massachusetts. The work Keziah Gardiner provided was similar to the domestic services provided by other little girls on slave plantations in the South. The only difference for little Keziah was that her work was done outside the formal institution of slavery. Even though Keziah was a biblical name, it had the remnants of a slave name. Unlike the young white girls her age, she never attended school, and there was never a plan for her to have a formal education. Although she was now free, Keziah was expected to be an uneducated black woman her entire life, with the role of a domestic servant being her only career opportunity.

As a servant girl, as listed in the 1860 United States Census, it is presumed that each morning, Keziah would get up and perform the daily ritual of household chores by taking care of the baby and cleaning the house. She would assist in the preparation of the daily meals, and accompanied the neighboring servant woman, Rhonda Seidmore, to the markets, buying food and other household supplies for the two Rodger families. At the age of nine, this was Keziah's apprenticeship where she learned how to be a marketable domestic so that future employers would want to hire her and to provide room and board. While working for the Rodgers family, Rhonda Seidmore and Keziah Gardiner received room and board, but no pay other than an occasional pence on special occasions, and performed the exact same manual tasks as the slave women in the South. When the daily household chores were completed, they were expected to assist with the outside farm chores and work next to the farmhands.

Rhonda Seidmore and Keziah Gardiner were from long-standing African American families on Long Island New York. For generations, the families had intermarried and were connected by history, tradition and circumstances. The Seidmores and Gardiners had taken their family surnames from their former slave owners, and their economic condition in life reflected their former lives as slave families. Their families had dreamed of emancipation, but once emancipated, under the pretense of being called a servant, they still continued to work long, backbreaking hours washing clothes by hand and scrubbing floors. They still went to bed at night utterly exhausted. Though they were no longer called slaves, Keziah and Rhonda, as well as countless others, were still essentially slaves, with little money and no hope for a better future.

In 1860, the institution of slavery was becoming a complicated issue for both the North and the South. Aside from whether or not emancipation meant these People of Color were truly free, logistical questions also arose - Where would the freed slaves live? Should slave owners be reimbursed for their investments? If they were to be reimbursed, who would cover the costs, the federal or state governments, or the slaves themselves?

3.8   James Melton from Halifax County North Carolina

In the aftermath of the Nat Turner Rebellion in 1831, and the slaughter of countless innocent People of Color, the community of Hertford County was shaken to its core. Families, white and black, slave and free, were terrified that any additional retaliation could be far worse than the original incident. Many of the Free People of Color lived on sizable tracts of land and were physically and geographically isolated from one another. With the enactment of legislation that forbids more than three persons of color meeting with one another, the free blacks surmised that they were constantly being watched and tested to see if they violated the law. For fear of reprisals and specifically designed antagonistic moves, free People of Color kept their wives and daughters close to home and were careful when they sent their sons to the marketplace. Rumors were rampant, only making a tense and dangerous situation worse.

For many families, the time had come to make a very difficult decision - should they stay in Hertford County and hope that things would improve or would they be better off relocating to friendlier territories? The more practical families and friends decided that People of Color had suffered enough over the past 100 years and the time had come to relocate to the friendlier communities of the Ohio Valley, where slavery was not allowed and they would be able to get larger tracts of land. Family members who had already migrated to the valley and westward assured them that it was the right thing to do, and that it would be a smooth transition.

More optimistic People of Color felt that the growing Abolitionist movement in northern cities such as Boston and Philadelphia would soon resolve the issue of slavery. Many of these families felt that it was a matter of time, and sensed that change was in the air. Because of circumstances, they felt that they couldn't afford to pick up and move to a new place if they weren't positive it would be much better. They worried that the issue of race would just follow them, just as the issue of race followed them from Virginia. It was a gut-wrenching decision that no family took lightly, and the ultimate decision to move or not to move would eventually break up families, friendships, and communities.

James Melton, David Melton's father, was born in North Carolina's rural Halifax County, just over the border from Hertford County. He farmed his own land but according to the 1850 US Census, the property that he owned was not assessed a value of worth. [257] Similar to modern day property assessments, the property values of land owned by African American's were assessed differently and substantially lower than similar properties owned by their white neighbors. The property owned by free People of Color was selectively being reduced in value. Formally named "red-lining" in the 1960s, this practice began as far back as the original 1790 census tracking. In communities where African American property was adjacent to their European American neighbors, their property values were intentionally devalued in comparison to their adjacent white neighbors. In some instances, this was a blessing in disguise because the taxes owed on similar properties were less than market value. However, when the time came to sell the property, its value was less, based on the county's assessment, which meant less of a return to the African American family.

James Melton was listed as a Free Person of Color in the 1850 Census where he was listed as 80 years old, placing his birth around 1770, and as having worked as a "sailor."[258] At this time, a man who was a fisherman or worked on the sea would have been listed as a "seaman" versus a man who served in the Navy who would have been listed as a "sailor." Most men at eighty years of age would have been listed as a "farmer" or a "laborer," but James was given the distinction of being known as a sailor. While he owned his own farm, the distinction of being listed as a sailor probably indicated that the community at large recognized and respected him by his trade during his youth, which may support the evidence that he was a sailor in the War of 1812, and assisted in the defense of Norfolk, Virginia.

James was part Native American, having descended from the Chickahominy tribe of colonial Virginia. According to family history, his wife was from the nearby Native America tribe. Their son David was born in 1795. David's death certificate as well as several Census reports lists him as "colored," indicating he was of mixed racial heritage. David Melton was one of the signatories of the Group of Sundry Persons of Color from Hertford County who in 1822 petitioned the North Carolina General Assembly.

David married Jane Adkins, who lived next door to his father and whose father also descended from the Chickahominy from Virginia.[259] According to her daughter-in-law, Sally Ballard Melton, Jane Adkin's maternal family was reportedly a large "wealthy" North Carolina family of Quakers. Miss Jane, as she was called, had three multi-racial children before her marriage to David Melton. Jane Adkins lived on the farm next door to James Melton's farm in 1850, and since the farms were adjacent, it was only a matter of time before she befriended her neighbor's son, David Melton, and subsequently married him.

Although it was illegal to teach slave or free People of Color to read and write, Jane Adkins-Melton passed her educational skills on to her children and grandchildren. Despite being rejected by her family, Jane was not going to have her children treated as second-class citizens. After David and Jane's marriage, they had an additional four children, adding to Jane's three children from her former marriage. David and Jane's youngest child, Abner, was born in Halifax County, North Carolina on July 15, 1861, and was the father of Margaret Melton Murphy.[260]

Four months prior to Abner's birth, the United States of America inaugurated its 16th president, a tall lanky man from Illinois named Abraham Lincoln. These were turbulent times for the United States and for the state of North Carolina. Two months after Lincoln's inauguration, South Carolina fired on the federal Fort Sumter in Charleston harbor, and ignited the Civil War.

3.9   A Nation Elects a President and Turns to War

From the period of 1820 to 1850, the United States changed rapidly, and there were four major trends that dominated America's economic, social, and political life during this period. In the North, industry and immigration transformed the northern states, which urbanized drastically during this era, changing from a land comprised almost entirely of farmers in agricultural communities, to millions of people moving to the cities and working in more urban industries. Northern cities built factories, produced textiles and farm equipment, and manufactured railroad tracks for the massive locomotives that brought raw materials from the west, and sent factory-made products back to the growing populations westward.

The North's shift toward industrialization, urbanization, social reform, and a growing middle class clashed with the deep-seated, almost feudal social hierarchies of the South. By 1819, there was an equal political balance of power between the anti-slavery northern industrial states and the pro-slavery southern agricultural states. However, with more and more Americans moving westward and establishing new political territories, they eventually petitioned Washington to be granted the rights of statehood. Southern politicians, fearing that the balance of power would shift out of their favor, wanted the new territories to only be admitted if they became slave states. An intense debate erupted with the Missouri Territory, which wanted to enter the Union as a slave-holding state. Northerners were fearful that future territories would request to be admitted as slave states as well. Congress, led by Senator Henry Clay from Kentucky, eventually reached an agreement, known as the Missouri Compromise, wherein each new territory added to the Union as a slave-holding state had to be matched by the addition of another territory as a non-slave-holding state.[261] The Missouri Compromise essentially prohibited slavery north of the parallel 36°30' compromise line.

The political climate in Washington was becoming more polarized over the issue of slavery, and every action or lack thereof only served to further separate the Congressional delegations from the opinions of the individual states. While most Americans felt that the Missouri Compromise was fair and balanced, certain senators argued that that the compromise was orchestrated by the abolitionists and their sympathizers. The South's political and economic power could only survive if they could get new territories to become slave-holding states. The southern senators felt that individual states should be able to decide whether or not they wanted to be a free or a slave state, without federal or northern intervention.

As northern states increased their populations, through a combination of steady immigration from Europe and the ever-growing repopulation of white residents, northern interests surrounding slavery had little to do with an actual desire to eliminate slavery, and more to do with northern whites getting jobs. In 1790, more than 19 percent of the United States population was of African descent. By 1850, this percentage had dropped to only 16 percent, a dramatic shift caused primarily by a significant increase in the number of European immigrants.

As the issue of slavery became more contentious, a second agreement, known as the Compromise of 1850, was enacted to address the admission of the newly annexed territory of Texas into the Union. Texas and surrounding territories had been acquired during the Mexican-American War of 1846. Northern states demanded the "complete exclusion of slavery from the Mexican Cession" of new territorial land. Southern states then threatened "secession from the Union" if Texas was not admitted as a slave-holding state.

Senator Clay once again was called upon to mediate and shape the Compromise of 1850 in order to avoid a catastrophic collision between northern and southern political and economic interests, and the potential secession of the South.[262] The Compromise of 1850 temporarily avoided the secession of the southern states by dividing the newly acquired territories from the Mexican-American War into slave and non-slave states.

Senator Stephen Douglas, from the state of Illinois, was a political opportunist with Presidential aspirations, and wanted to appease both the North and the South. In 1854, Douglas proposed the Kansas-Nebraska Act, which repealed the Missouri Compromise and opened Northern territories to slavery. Senator Douglas argued that it was not Congress' right to decide the issue of slavery, but instead the decision should be left to the local people of a state or territory, and it was their democratic right to determine their own political destiny.

Northern legislators and abolitionists were outraged. Political discussions were so intense in Washington that after Massachusetts' Charles Sumner concluded a speech against the Kansas-Nebraska Act, a South Carolina Congressman entered the Senate Chambers, took out his walking cane, and beat Sumner severely.

Figure 54: In Washington, Discussions on Slavery Were Dangerous.

"Preston Brooks, a young Congressman from South Carolina, bludgeoned Charles Sumner of Massachusetts almost to death in the Senate chamber. Sumner, an outspoken abolitionist, was working at his desk after the Senate adjourned …when Brooks entered the chamber and began to beat him on the head as hard as he could with a gold-headed guttapercha walking stick. Sumner blinded by blood and trapped at a desk, valiantly struggled to rise before collapsing to the floor. Brooks said he had merely intended to "whip" Sumner …according to the code of a Southern gentleman. The provocation for this attack was Sumner's speech …in which he accused the South of demanding that Kansas enter the Union as a slave state."

John Stauffer,
The Black Hearts of Men, Radical Abolitionists and the Transformation of Race[263]

With each successive debate on slavery and westward expansion, the regions were driven further apart, until finally, by the 1850s, the

North and the South were two distinctly different places, culturally, racially, socially, and economically. The very things that helped to make America a great nation, its industrial North, its agricultural South, and the opportunity for expansion in the west - all things that elevated the nation onto the world's stage - were also the very things that were now causing it to divide. In 1857, the United States Supreme Court entered the heated political fray with their Dred Scott decision.

Dred Scott, a former slave who had lived for several years with his master in Illinois, arrived in the Minnesota territory -where slavery was legally forbidden- and declared that he and his family were now free. The mostly southern Supreme Court Justices issued a "comprehensive ruling intend to bar Congress from prohibiting slavery in any territory...and declared that the Constitution gave African Americans no civil rights or legal protections" under the law.[264]

The Dred Scott decision only deepened the national divide as the court ruled that slaves did not have the rights and protections of white citizens. Southerner felt a sense of vindication on the issue, while Northerners feared that slaveholders would bring slaves into free states and territories in an attempt to eventually weaken or compromise northern slave laws. European immigrants were also upset: They worried that if slave owners brought slaves to free regions there would be more competition for jobs and lower wages.

Many legal scholars at the time believed that the Supreme Court had overreached its authority, and underestimated northern anti-slavery sentiment. With vast numbers of recent immigrants arriving by the boatload in the port cites of Boston and New York - anxious for work, land grants and political opportunities - the decision only strengthened the northern resolve: They were against slavery. Key stakeholders in each region became more and more resolute in their political opinions and in their political differences.

From the period of 1850 to 1861, America saw three Presidents, each with very different personal and political styles, and each attempted to address the realities of a rapidly dividing nation. While in the U.S. Senate, President Millard Fillmore oversaw the Compromise of 1850, which included a series of legislative bills intended to mitigate the expansion of slavery in the new territories in the west, and to keep a balance between the interests in the northern states with the interests of the southern states. With the election of President James Buchanan, slavery dominated local, regional and national politics. President Buchanan was widely criticized for his failure to understand the widening national divide over the political realities of slavery. His inaction not only fueled the national slavery debate, it also strengthened the North's and South's resolve over the issue, and realigned political parties.

Within Senator Stephen Douglas' own state of Illinois, there were politicians who strongly disagreed with his 1854 Kansas-Nebraska Act. When Congress approved the Act, it "finally persuaded a young ambitious lawyer named Abraham Lincoln to join the anti-slavery crusade".[265] In 1858, Illinois' Republican candidate for Senate, Abraham Lincoln, participated in seven debates against the incumbent Democratic candidate, Senator Stephen Douglas.

The explosive debates centered on one of the most pressing issues in the state and in the Ohio Valley - the issue of slavery. Using the parliamentary style format, the Lincoln-Douglas debates were based on providing a theatrical "sequence of speeches" that defined the personal and political viewpoints of the candidates, and was designed to be printed in the newspapers around the country.[266]

Figure 55: The Dred Scott Decision and Slavery Influence the Election

"Lincoln used the Dred Scott Supreme Court decision deftly in his unsuccessful bid for the United States Senate in 1858, suggesting to Illinois voters that the Supreme Court ...planned to allow slave labor throughout the western territories, and eventually into northern states as well. Two years later, northern voters decided to elect a Republican president who could gradually replace the pro-southern majority on the Supreme Court with antislavery justices".

William K. Klingaman,
Abraham Lincoln and the Road to Emancipation, 1861 – 1865, [267].

The national media took an interest in the election and the debates because Senator Douglas was known nationwide for his Kansas-Nebraska Act, which repealed the Missouri Compromise and further separated the political interests of northern and southern legislators, particularly over the issue of slavery. The senatorial debates also launched the national prominence of young political upstart Abraham Lincoln, which led to his subsequent and successful presidential bid against Democratic challenger John Breckinridge.

With the election of President Lincoln in 1860, southern states felt that their voice was finally lost in the national debate over the issue of slavery. They believed that the growing political and economic power of the northern states would subject them to political bondage, resulting in the unthinkable release of millions of slaves and the total collapse of their way of life. Southerners feared that new President-elect Lincoln favored northern abolitionist interests over the interests of the South and believed that Lincoln had clearly stated his "Northern sympathies" and was against the sovereign right of southern states to own slaves. The political elites in the southern states, as they had done the first time they met in Philadelphia at the Constitutional Convention in May of 1787, threatened to secede from the union if their rights to own slaves were compromised. Between the time Lincoln was elected President in 1860 and officially inaugurated in March of 1861, seven states had seceded from the Union and formed their own nation, the Confederate States of America.

Six days after South Carolina seceded from the union, violence erupted at Fort Sumter in South Carolina on December 26, 1860. For the remainder of December, the North made several unsuccessful attempts to supply the fort with badly needed food and supplies, while South Carolina demanded that Union forces abandon Fort Sumter, also without success. The secession of South Carolina and the hostile act of a southern state taking arms against a federal installation caused massive conflict within the federal government and across the nation, raising the questions: Should the southern states be allowed to leave the Union? Should the North allow them to leave without a fight?

During his conciliatory inaugural address, Lincoln attempted to bridge the national divide, but it had no effect on the South. Despite the president's attempt to reconcile differences, the southern states, led by South Carolina, began to commission an army to defend the Confederacy's rebellion.

After the attack on Fort Sumpter, events that eventually led to a Civil war happen in short order. On March 11, 1861, the Constitution of the Confederate States of America was signed in Montgomery, Alabama. The following month, on April 12, 1861 -the official start of the Civil War - the "newly constituted government of the Confederacy began battering the walls" of Fort Sumter.[268] On April 14, 1861, Union Troops were forced to evacuate the fort due to the lack of supplies. The Civil War now had begun in earnest.

One by one, each of the southern states seceded, and by May 1861, the last state, North Carolina, joined them. Realizing that this war would not be a short one, President Lincoln addressed Congress on July 4, 1861, and requested the formal enlistment of a Union Army. The United States Congress authorized 500,000 men for war. The Union took up arms and built a military. Generals were recruited from West Point, strategic maps drawn, soldiers trained, supplies commissioned, all to prepare the Union for battle - which would be a long and costly battle for both sides.

3.10   The Union Army Burns Hertford County

The ancestral home of Margaret Melton Murphy of Hertford, North Carolina, was a coastal community on the Atlantic Ocean, incorporated into the United States in 1759. During the early days of the Civil War, this inshore community was attacked. On February 19, 1862, in one of the first amphibious attacks in American history, the *U.S.S. Delaware* and the *U.S.S. Commodore Perry* were on a reconnaissance patrol of the Chowan River when they engaged a small battalion of Confederate troops[269]. The Union Army and Navy attacked the Confederate forces in the town of Winton, the government seat of Hertford County. Once the Confederate soldiers retreated, the Union Army burned all of the government buildings in the town. During the war, the burning and destruction of government buildings all across the south was a major military strategy for the North in an attempt to demonstrate major military superiority and to cause havoc by eliminating places for the southern elite, politicians and military commanders to meet and strategize. However, one hundred fifty years later, the total destruction of the government buildings - including court houses where critical records including land permits, wills and records of births, marriages and death certificates were destroyed- hampers present day historical and genealogical research.

Winton being the first town in North Carolina to be burned and destroyed, the townsfolk were devastated. Some speculated that Hertford County was specifically chosen because of the events that happened right after the Nat Turner Rebellion, and that the burning was in retaliation and a reminder of what the southern town's white inhabitants had done to the countless numbers of slaves and free People of Color in the aftermath of the events in Southampton. With the burning of the government buildings, tension in Hertford County escalated. Out of frustration and anger came the desire to blame someone for what the Union Army had done to the town of Winton. The Quakers in town were quickly blamed for their abolitionist views on slavery. The free black families were blamed for their "uppity" separatist ways, and the remaining blame fell to the Southampton Rebellion and the "damn Yankees" that had burned southern government buildings because of it.

Many whites felt that Hertford County's problems were a direct result of the large numbers of free People of Color who resided within the county and vowed that swift action should be quickly taken to finally resolve the growing and intolerable problems of the free People of Color and their northern abolitionist sympathizers. The county's white felt that they were being forced to endure undesirable conditions of war because of the free People of Color and northern abolitionists.

Many Americans thought the war would be short, both in the North and in the South. But the war lingered, and the South in particular suffered under the severe economic conditions. Anger, frustration, tension and finger pointing were commonplace. Margaret Melton Murphy's family suffered tremendously as the war progressed. Their property values were depressed, like many other properties in the area, but because they were free People of Color, their land depreciated even more. The family found it hard to sell their farm products to market, and struggled to earn financing to get from one growing season to the next. The war's recession was affecting everyone, but Margaret's paternal Melton family and her maternal Ballard family, along with all of the other free People of Color across the entire South, felt the effects of the recession even more so.

Their white suppliers would no longer buy products from the Melton and Ballard families, and would no longer sell them goods unless they paid cash. This was tantamount to a boycott. While effects of the war would eventually make this a common practice all across the South, the Melton and Ballard families experienced this indignity long before their white neighbors. However, though an unpleasant situation at the time, this suffering, in part, helped these families survive the Civil War.

The Melton and Ballard families, along with all of the other free People of Color across the entire South, were forced to become self-sufficient and self-reliant. For fear of harassment and/or intimidation, they intentionally segregated themselves within their own communities for shelter, protection and sustenance. They developed their own underground network of food supplies. They bartered amongst themselves. In the true pioneering spirit of their grandparents and great-grandparents, they built each other's houses, traded livestock and assisted one another in harvesting crops. If these men and women were going to survive, they had no other choice. It was clear they were fighting in two wars - supporting the North against the South and as free blacks while many whites and even slaves fought against them.

On January 20, 1863, the Navy once again landed at Hertford County. The *U.S.S. Commodore Perry,* in another joint expedition with the Union Army, destroyed several bridges over the Perquimans River, "ensuring that there would be no bridges remaining on the Perquimans, so that goods sent from Norfolk to the Confederate enemy on the south side of the Chowan [had] to be passed over a ford, and the roads leading from that ford [could] be guarded by the troops".[270] This only exacerbated the racial tensions within the county and fueled the recession.

3.11   The Dueling Presidential Proclamations

Upon his election and after his inauguration in March 1861, President Lincoln reached out to the secessionist southern states, but to no avail. On September 22nd, 1862, President Lincoln promised to issue through Executive Order, a proclamation emancipating all slaves residing in any rebellious and secessionist Confederate state that did not return to the union by January 1, 1863. When the New Year came and none of the Confederate states returned to the union, Lincoln followed through on his promise and issued the historic Emancipation Proclamation, which essentially freed all slaves in southern states.

In response to President Lincoln's Emancipation Proclamation, Jefferson Davis, president of the Confederate States, issued a stern response: If any free People of Color or northern blacks ventured south they would immediately be enslaved. He then issued his own Enslavement Proclamation, resolving the issue of the large numbers of free People of Color in the South once and for all.

Figure 56: Jefferson Davis Issues Vengeful Enslavement Proclamation

"On January 5, 1863, four days after Lincoln signed the Emancipation Proclamation, Jefferson Davis, issued an Enslavement Proclamation...declaring that 'all free Negroes in the Southern Confederacy shall be placed on the slave status, and deemed to be chattel property, they and their issue forever.' Any black Union soldiers captured in combat would be subject to enslavement and their white officers subject to execution as leaders of servile insurrection."

David Williams,
A People's History of the Civil War, Struggles for the Meaning of Freedom[271]

3.12   Free People of Color are redefined as Chattel Property

The first month of 1863 was bittersweet for the hundreds of thousands free People of Color all across the South. Families were joyous, and proud that President Lincoln kept his word and signed the Emancipation Proclamation. For 488,070 free People of Color, almost now evenly split between the north and the south at this point, and for the 3,953,760 slaves, mostly in the south, President Lincoln's action was meant to resolve the issue of slavery. Initially they believed that Lincoln's Emancipation Proclamation would enhance their lives and that all People of Color would now be set free.

However, the retaliatory actions of Confederate President Jefferson Davis and his Enslavement Proclamation now declared that "all free Negroes in the Southern Confederacy shall be placed on the slave status, and deemed to be chattel, they and their issue forever," and with a single action, now took away every single legal right of the hundreds of thousands of free People of Color and now made them chattel property of their state and local governments.

The Jefferson Davis Enslavement Proclamation, combined with the earlier United States Supreme Court Dred Scott decision, now allowed white southerners to assume that no African Americans had civil rights or legal protections under the law. Confederate Jefferson Davis' actions and the Supreme Court's Dred Scott decision now provided the necessary legal cover and protection for thugs, county managers and registrars to deliberately destroy government records, especially public records, land deeds and wills that could have protected the property rights of People of Color

In communities all across the South, the Free Black Registries, which were originally designed to protect them and to prove their free status, were now used to taunt and harass free People of Color. White vigilante groups kept a close watch on the local free blacks to ensure that no aid or comfort was provided to any runaway slaves, and that no sons or husbands escaped to the North to join the Yankee Army.

Legal actions between whites and free People of Color that were once decided in court relative to land or property disputes, no longer had to be taken there. Free People of Color no longer had any legal rights. In many communities, any legal rights that free People of Color thought they may have had or any rights to freedom and property ownership they might have been able to proclaim in the past were now resolved or challenged directly at the end of a double barrel shotgun.

Unmarried or widowed women of color who were heads of household and managed farms by themselves were often taken away in the middle of the night with their children. The overzealous white southerners aimed their harassment at the more isolated and vulnerable black families, particularly those that owned valuable land. While the white South was just beginning to feel the effects of an economic recession caused by the war, free People of Color were now in a legal jeopardy, and their economic and legal demise were the first real causalities of the war.

Figure 57: North Carolina's Free Black Populations over Seventy Years

1790	North Carolina's free black population					4,975
1800	"	"	"	"	"	7,043
1810	"	"	"	"	"	10,266
1820	"	"	"	"	"	14,612
1830	"	"	"	"	"	19,543
1840	"	"	"	"	"	22,732
1850	"	"	"	"	"	27,463
1860	"	"	"	"	"	30,463

Rosser Howard Taylor, *The Free Negro in North Carolina*[272]

Fortunately for the ancestors of the Cornwall Murphy family that lived in North Carolina, they resided in counties where there were large pockets of free African Americans, and there was some strength and protection in numbers. By 1860, the number of free People of Color in the counties of North Carolina alone had swelled to more than 30,400 inhabitants.

The counties of Halifax, Wake, Craven, Robeson, Granville and Pasquotank had the largest free black population. In those communities, there were fewer problems for free People of Color than in other areas. By the 1800s, the ancestral families of Margaret Melton Murphy were free People of Color. They resided in Gates, Guilford, Halifax, Hertford, and Northampton counties in North Carolina, each having sizable free black populations. During the same period, the ancestral families of Marie Howell Cornwall were also free People of Color from the North Carolina county of Granville.

Figure 58: 1860 North Carolina Counties with the Largest Free Black Populations

Halifax	2,452	Granville	1,123
Pasquitank	1,507	Hertford	1,112
Robeson	1,462	Wayne	737
Craven	1,332	Guilford	693
Wake	1,446	Northampton	659
		Rosser Howard Taylor, *The Free Negro in North Carolina*[273]	

3.13 Frederick Douglass Recruits African American Men for a Call to Service

With the election of President Lincoln, Abolitionist activist Frederick Douglass felt there was finally an opportunity for America's slave population to gain true emancipation. President Lincoln was on record as opposing slavery and the Supreme Court's decision on the Dred Scot case. Douglass and many other northern abolitionists believed that in Lincoln, they had a president who could gradually replace the pro-southern majority on the Supreme Court with antislavery justices. Abolitionists saw hope in the newly elected president, and where there was hope, there were opportunities to be seized.

Figure 59: If Lincoln's Election Angers the South, It's a Good Thing!

Abolitionist Frederick Douglass saw Lincoln's election for the black man as "a shift, a change, a potential opening, for people long accustomed to disappointment will be happy take…anything that incensed the South the way that the rise of Lincoln seemed to, must be a positive development"

Paul Kendrick and Stephen Kendrick
Douglass and Lincoln, How a Revolutionary Black Leader and a Reluctant Liberator Struggled to End Slavery and Save the Union[274]

As the war effort increased, the need for additional troops dashed any remaining hope that this fight would be a short one. The battles were more and more severe, with casualties rising dramatically with each battle. President Lincoln requested an increase of 300,000 additional soldiers, but few men came forward. Although initially concerned that the recruitment of black soldiers would cause Border States to secede, the desperate need for combatants made the North realize both politically and publicly, that African-American men were needed to augment the strength of the Union troops. At the urging of the President, Congress hesitantly passed The Second Confiscation and Militia Act on July 17, 1862, which allowed the president to recruit African-American soldiers. The Act also repealed a 1792 law that prohibited free and freed African Americans from serving in the military. With the issuance of the Emancipation Proclamation on January 1, 1863, President Lincoln authorized the use of African-American troops in combat. [275]

While the U.S. Constitution protected the institution of slavery, Lincoln believed that as president and Commander-and-Chief, he could abolish slavery if there was a military necessity to preserve and protect the Union. The president did not want Great Britain to interfere and try to take advantage of the internal struggles of the United States, nor did he want them to take the wrong side in the war. He knew that the British were strongly abolitionist, and an act of emancipation would discourage Britain from taking the Confederate side in this battle. He also believed that emancipation of slaves living in any rebellious state would be a valuable weapon in his strategic and psychological war against the Confederate rebellion.

Abolitionist Frederick Douglass strongly believed that African Americans had to be equal partners in aggressively fighting for the freedom of the black man and for their own personal freedoms. He tirelessly traveled around the country to encourage large numbers of men of African descent to enroll in the military. In one of his most profound speeches, in Rochester, New York, Douglass outlined the construct of why African-American men needed to join the Union Army. On March 21, 1863, Douglass published a manifesto entitled *Men of Color, To Arms,* in which he challenged free black men to enlist because it was "Now or Never". He believed that if the black man did not take up arms and the North lost, they would never get a chance again to advocate for the end of slavery. And, if the cause was won without their participation then they ran the risk that they may never be considered as equal citizens because they did nothing to earn it.

As a result of President Lincoln signing the historic Emancipation Proclamation and the inspiring speeches of Frederick Douglass and other northern abolitionists, African-American men from all across America began to answer the call to service in overwhelming numbers. While only one percent of the North's population was African American, almost ten percent of the Union Army consisted of African-Americans soldiers. Almost 400,000 American sons of African ancestry had enlisted in the war effort in 166 regiments.[276] Without question, African-American men were prepared, no matter what the cost, and were ready to take charge of their own destiny, the total abolition of slavery.

Figure 60: African American Respond to the Call to Service

"The Bureau of Colored Troops recruited and organized over 185,000 blacks into the U.S. Colored Troops. Blacks accounted for about 9 to 10 percent of the Union Army and one-quarter of enlistments in the Navy. When black volunteers in independent and state units are included, it is estimated that close to 390,000 black served in the Civil War".

Martin Binkin, Mark Eitelberg, Alvin Schexnider and Marvin Smith
Blacks and the Military[277]

3.14   Conscription Act and Riots in the Streets

As President Lincoln called for the enlistment of soldiers into the military, on March 3, 1863, Congress passed the Conscription Act, which required every male citizen and immigrant who filed for citizenship between the ages of twenty and forty-five to sign up for military service. From the very beginning, the Act was extremely controversial. It required each Congressional District in the country to provide a certain number of servicemen, while also containing a provision that wealthy men would not have to serve. The Act also exempted African American men from being draft since they did not have the rights of full citizenship.

Recent immigrants and poor working class white men who were required to sign up for the draft felt that they were being specifically targeted to fight in a war they wanted nothing to do with, while the very men who wanted the war - wealthy Abolitionists who could pay a substitute to replace them if they were drafted - were exempt. There was also tremendous animosity towards African Americans, as draftees believed them to be the cause of the war and yet also exempt from the draft. Conscription protests erupted in cities all across the north and along the border states of the south, especially in places like New York City, where union bosses and politicians had financial interests that were economically tied to southern commerce, and thus encouraged their supporters not to sign up for the draft.

On July 13, 1863, one of the largest Draft Riots broke out in New York City when a vigilante mob of Irish immigrants set a Draft office ablaze in the Ninth District. In one of the largest civil insurrections in United States history, what started as a draft protest erupted into an ugly race riot that lasted three days. Drunken rioters went from neighborhood to neighborhood, smashing into saloons and throwing alcohol onto their burning rage. Initially, the rioters targeted only the homes of known abolitionists and draft supporters, but their protest soon turned more ugly as they began to break into the homes of innocent African Americans, dragging residents into the streets and setting their houses on fire. The African Americans were beaten and some died by hanging as their homes burned. African Americans were pulled out of stores, streetcars and, in some instances, police stations - where they were also savagely beaten or killed.[278]

A fire was set at the Colored Orphan Asylum at Fifth Avenue and Forty-Third Street, just minutes after all 237 children under the age of 12 barely escaped with their lives after running to the local Police Station looking for sanctuary.[279] For three days, African Americans all across the city lived in fear. Churches and public buildings in the rioters' path were destroyed. New York City was in complete anarchy. In the midst of the summer heat, the City's African Americans tried to flee the city, as did the wealthy whites, but many were trapped in their homes and could not escape.

On the fourth day after the riot started, the city was finally brought under control with the support of federal troops. In the aftermath, "initial estimates of the number killed ranged up to 1,200, but recent research has scaled this down to about 120. It was the worst riot in American history".[280]

Immigrants in New York, who felt their interests were not being served by the war, rioted in order to avoid the draft and signal their refusal to serve their country. In sharp contrast, African-American men from all across the country, who were personally invested in the defeat of the South and slavery, patriotically enlisted in the military and served their country with valor.

3.15 William Cornwall, Sergeant, 5th Massachusetts Volunteer Colored Cavalry

The national debate on slavery was discussed in every city, village, and hamlet across the country. It seemed that everyone had an opinion, and whenever several Americans came together the discussion would inevitably turn to the topic of slavery, the long-term effects of President Lincoln's Emancipation Proclamation, and the retaliatory response from the President of the Southern Confederacy, Jefferson Davis' Enslavement Proclamation. In October 1861, the Cornwall family of Bridgewater, Massachusetts, came together and they too were soon embroiled in a passionate discussion about the preservation of the Union after the South seceded, and what could be done to stop the institution of slavery.

On October 20, 1861, Caesar Russell, the Revolutionary War hero from Beverly, Massachusetts, died in Taunton, Massachusetts. As sharing memories is common at memorial services, when the family gathered at Caesar's funeral, they likely reminisced about the life and stories of this remarkable former slave - the family's patriarch. They recounted his many tales of serving in the Continental Army during the War for Independence, and the heroic fight with England. They remembered how he and so many other Americans of African descent had rallied around the cry for liberty and the call for freedom.

No doubt their recollection of Caesar's life emphasized the importance in answering the call for public service, especially for black men fighting for their freedom and those of the enslaved kindred. The young men were engulfed in discussions on how little the lives of African Americans had changed over the 100 years since their patriotic ancestors - Caesar Russell, Benjamin Brooker and Cuffe Grandison - provided honorable and historic service to the military and to the nation. It was a discussion of young men, mixed with anger, disappointment. It reflected their frustration at their current predicament, but also their hopes and aspirations for not only for themselves, but for the countless numbers of men and women who lived in the South under some of the most horrendous conditions in the world.

They each seemed to know stories about acquaintances that were able to escape the tyrannous activities of southern-plantation society and arrive in Boston. They were fixated on the story about Anthony Burns, a fugitive slave from somewhere in Virginia who escaped and came to Boston. When his slave master found him, he was arrested. President Franklin Pierce interceded and sent federal troops to Boston to take him back to slavery.

Many Bostonians felt that Burns was disrespected by the Federal troops as they marched him through the streets of Boston to a waiting ship. The story reminded Caesar Russell's family of how he always talked about personal responsibility, and inspired them and other African-American Bostonians with the support of white Abolitionists to take up a collection which allowed African-American residents of Boston to actually purchase fugitive slave Antony Burns' freedom from his master.[281]

African-American Bostonians and members of the Caesar Russell and the Benjamin Brooker families talked about how Boston and New England was the original epicenter for the cause of personal freedoms. They shared stories about the slave revolt on the Amistad, a Spanish schooner in the Atlantic Ocean on which fifty-four Africans took over in an attempt to return to Africa.[282] Upon capture, the men were tried in the Rhode Island court system, and Massachusetts lawyer John Quincy Adams successfully obtained their freedom through the trial, after which the men were eventually returned to Africa. They believed that there was no other place other than New England where African men would be given a fair trial and be returned to Africa without fear of being handed over to slave traders. The Revolutionary War spirit ran deep in the veins of Caesar Russell and Benjamin Brooker's grandsons and great-grandsons. They wanted to enlist in the war effort and they knew it would only be a matter of time before men of African descent would be allowed to join in the effort to end slavery - once and for all.

Two years after Caesar Russell's death, the opportunity to enlist in the war presented itself and the Men of Color of Massachusetts were allowed to enlist in the war. With the signing of the Emancipation Proclamation and The Second Confiscation and Militia Act of July 17, 1862, the Governor of the Commonwealth of Massachusetts, a strong abolitionist named John A. Andrew, was authorized by the state legislature to form three Colored units to serve in the Civil War and represent the state.

The three state units included the 5th Massachusetts Volunteer Cavalry, the 54th Massachusetts Volunteer Infantry, and the 55th Massachusetts Volunteer Infantry. The soldiers were recruited across the state by prominent abolitionists, including Frederick Douglass and William Lloyd Garrison. Once the state commissioned the three units, the descendants and extended families of Benjamin Brooker, Cuffe Grandison and Caesar Russell enlisted in the war effort, including William Cornwell of Bridgewater, Massachusetts.

Once Frederick Douglass convinced President Lincoln to recruit African American men into the military, his sons Charles and Lewis joined the Massachusetts 54th Infantry in April 1863. His eighteen-year-old son Charles, upon receiving the assignment as Sergeant, transferred to the 5th Massachusetts Cavalry to become its first sergeant.[283] Lewis Douglass became a sergeant major of the 54th, and was wounded in the assault on Fort Wagner in South Carolina.[284]

The soldiers of the Massachusetts 54th and the 55th Regiments were recruited by Boston's wealthy abolitionist community. The units were organized at Camp Meigs, near Readville, Massachusetts. At the time of their recruitment, black soldiers were told they would be treated and paid exactly the same as their white counterparts. Once enlisted, the men found out that the Commonwealth of Massachusetts was paying them only $10 a month, with $3 being withheld for their uniforms, while their white counterparts were being paid $13 a month, with nothing withheld - a six-dollar monthly difference. The men of the 54th and the 55th immediately began a protest, and refused to accept any pay until the entire payroll matter was rectified. In 1864, Congress granted equal pay to the U.S. Colored troops, to be paid retroactively.

On July 11, 1863, as part of the operations against the Defenses of Charleston Campaign, the Union Army attempted to take the beachhead fortification on Morris Island, known as Fort Wagner, in South Carolina. In the first unsuccessful attempt, the Union lost more than 300- soldiers, while the Confederate Army defending the Fort lost only twelve men. On July 18, 1863, two days after the horrific New York City Race Riots were brought under control, the gallant African-American Massachusetts 54th attempted to overtake the strategic Fort Wagner that protected South Carolina's Charleston harbor.

While many whites questioned the skill, the tenacity, and commitment of African-American troops, the Massachusetts 54th proved them all wrong. As they approached Fort Wagner, they faced every obstacle imaginable.

Though this second assault was unsuccessful, these African-American soldiers were later were commended by their military superiors for their determination and for their valor. The unit suffered 272 causalities, including the death of its young Colonel, Robert Gould Shaw. "The courageous fighting of the 54th and its long casualty list made the regiment famous. Especially coming only days after white rioters had marched through New York City attacking African Americans - this example of black soldiers giving their lives for the Union could not have been more dramatic."[285]

Figure 61: Blacks Fight to Preserve the Union, But Whites Fight against It.

"One of the most famous black actions was the ill-fated assault by the 54th Massachusetts on Battery Wagner, outside Charleston, South Carolina, on July 8, 1863, in which the regiment lost 272 out of 650 men. The event reflected hard upon the participants of the New York draft riots, and led President Lincoln to ask publically who deserved better of the republic, the black men who fought to preserve it or the white men who rioted to destroy it?"

James L. Stokesbury, *A Short History of the Civil War*[286]

The heroic actions of the Massachusetts Regiments encouraged other African-American men to join the military. While in Massachusetts, Frederick Douglass crisscrossed the state, giving rousing speeches in an attempt to reach into communities with prominent African American families. One such speech took place in Abington, Massachusetts, down the road from where William Cornwell, son of Flushing and Harriet Cornwell, lived. According to Martha Cornwall Royster, this would be the third or fourth speech that William Cornwell had heard. The speeches of Frederick Douglass and other abolitionists struck a chord with William, and combined with the many stories he had heard from both his grandfathers of their experiences in the Revolutionary War, this young man was inspired to stand up for what he believed to be right. William was an idealistic young man, and had grown tired of all the political rhetoric and fireside discussions about what should be done to end slavery. He felt that it was time to take action and to make things happen. Now that President Lincoln was forming African America regiments, William made the decision to enlist in the service.

William, anxious for reform and social justice, decided to volunteer so that he could fight for those things that he believed in. If things were going to change, he wanted to be part of it. Flushing and Harriet understood the enormous risk their son was taking by joining the war effort. They understood his desire to serve his country and to fight for freedom and independence, but they were still his parents, and were petrified of the Enslavement Proclamation. They knew that William, as a Free Man of Color from Massachusetts, ran the risk of not only being killed in battle, but worse, if he were captured, he would be sold into slavery without any hope of freedom.

William's older brothers were more practical, and tried to convince him not to enlist, but William would not hear any of it. He was not interested in working on the family farm, nor was he interested in working in the construction business with his brothers. To William, the American Civil War was not simply a regional battle between the industrial northern states and the agricultural southern states. It was not just about the division of the North and South. It was about the survival and treatment of Black men in America.

As the direct descendants of Black patriot soldiers who had fought in the American Revolutionary War, Flushing and Harriet Cornwall had strong puritan values and were fiercely protective of their country. They understood William's passion. They could only imagine the strong patriotism that their son William felt as he yearned to serve his country during time of war. But it was hard to disregard the anguish that Flushing and Harriet must have felt as parents - and as all free People of Color must of felt - watching one of their sons decide to go to war and to fight in a region of the country where open hostility could result in physical torture at the hands of enemy combatants, or a lifetime of emotional torture as a slave, never to be heard from again. Despite his family's concern, William Cornwell enlisted into Company A of the 5th Massachusetts Colored Calvary.

The 5th Volunteer Colored Calvary was organized at Camp Meigs, near Readville, Massachusetts, in autumn of 1863, and was "mustered" on January 9, 1864. While it was a colored regiment of cavalrymen, all of its officers were white. At Camp Meigs, Private Cornwall came into contact with hundreds of men much like himself, African American's from across the country, free men who had never known the harsh realities of slavery but did not want any more People of Color to suffer. One such man was First Sergeant Charles Douglass, the son of the famous African-American abolitionist, Frederick Douglass. William Cornwall told Charles Douglas how honored he was to have the opportunity to meet him because of the many speeches William had heard the elder Douglass give. Because of those speeches, William felt that he had known Charles his entire life. As their friendship grew, Charles Douglass, out of respect for William, recommended for him for the position of Sergeant in the 5th Massachusetts Cavalry. According to Martha Cornwall Royster, the two men developed a lifelong friendship. During the Civil War, the military rank of Sergeant was used by both the Union and Confederate Armies, and was the highest enlisted rank for a non-commissioned officer (NCO). The two men, along with three other Sergeants, worked long hours and trained their men well.

When the three all-black volunteer regiments were first assembled, they were mocked by many who felt that a regiment of black men would surely fail and would be an embarrassment to the state and the foolhardy President who had endorsed them. However, when the press and spectators came to view the troops in practice, "many came away with changed opinions after witnessing this fine looking set of colored men marching, drilling and shooting with a skill and élan equal to that of most white regiments"[287].

As Massachusetts' African-American men began to fill the ranks of the three historic units, African-American men from other parts of New England, the Mid-Atlantic States, and even within the borders of the rebellious Confederacy rose to the challenge of Frederick Douglass and the Massachusetts abolitionists, and enlisted. From every corner of the Union, the sons, grandsons and great-grandsons of slaves and former slaves served as soldiers, served as statesmen, or preached in the Sunday pulpits to stop the tyranny of slavery and the bondage of African American families. But no African-American family was any prouder than the parents of the men who served the Massachusetts 5th Volunteer Colored Calvary, the Massachusetts 54th and the Massachusetts 55th Volunteer Infantry. The historic battles in which they fought laid testament to their bravery and sacrifice.

Many of the soldiers were former slaves, and carried with them personal experiences with slavery. They continued to witness its horrific effects during the war, and they clearly understood that the war was not about state's rights, but whether one man had the right to own another man. Some soldiers fought for the preservation of the Union, but these former slaves fought bravely for their freedom and the freedom of all People of Color. Every day, these soldiers faced risk of being captured and enslaved, but it was a risk they were willing to take. As Sergeant Cornwall and his men headed south of the Mason Dixon line ultimately headed toward Petersburg, Virginia, they witnessed firsthand the effect slavery was having on African-American men and women, the elderly and young children. The soldiers were more resolved than ever to absolutely eradicate slavery.

In the spring of 1864, Sergeant William Cornwall's Company A of the 5th Massachusetts Colored Calvary unit went south as part of General Sherman's southern strategy. The unit was assigned to the 3rd Division, 18th Corps, to help protect the city of Washington, D.C. Then it was ordered to City Point, Virginia, where it initially performed reconnaissance and picket duties along the James and Appomattox Rivers. On June 15, 1864, as part of the Petersburg campaign, the Massachusetts 5th Calvary advanced towards Petersburg, Virginia, and participated in one of its largest battles of the Civil War at Baylor's Farm, on Petersburg Road.

Petersburg was of tactical importance because it was twenty miles south from the Confederate capital city of Richmond, Virginia, and was also a railroad junction through which most Confederate supplies and troops transferred.

Sergeant William Cornwell's 5th Massachusetts Colored Calvary, while not as well known to history as its brother unit, the Massachusetts 54th Infantry, saw extensive and historic combat as part of the Richmond-Petersburg campaign, which ultimately resulted in the surrender of the Confederate General Robert E. Lee.

The capture of Petersburg was of critical importance to the Union as it destroyed the Confederacy's critical supply chain. This accomplishment would play a significant role in ending the war, and in the 5th Regiment's confidence as they advanced southward.

The Confederate Army, well aware of the tactical importance of Petersburg to the capitol city of Richmond and the overall supply chain, constructed a series of elaborate earthworks that consisted of extensive obstacles and trenches to deter a possible Union advancement or attack on the city. Before the city of Petersburg could be captured, Union General Ulysses S. Grant had to march southeastward towards Richmond.

Grant suffered tremendous causalities in his effort to reach the Confederate Capital. On May 5, 1864, after three days of fighting, "the Union had staggering casualties of 17,500 men while the Confederates lost only 9,000".[288] Two weeks later, the two armies met again in one of the fiercest and bloodiest battles of the entire war, "where the Union lost 32,000 more soldiers."[289] Despite the exorbitant causalities, Grant continued moving toward his target.

The first attempt by the Union forces to actually take the city of Petersburg on June 8, 1864, ended badly. The Union lost "7,000 men in less than twelve hours, forcing the Union's General Grant to end the slaughter" by conceding defeat.[290] The earthen levies that surrounded the city proved to be almost impregnable and prevented the Union Army from achieving their strategic objective. The second attempt on June 16, 1864, was far more successful, thanks to the strength and fortitude of the men from the 5th Massachusetts Colored Calvary.

Figure 62: The Brave 5th Massachusetts Colored Calvary

> "On the evening of June 16, 1864 ... the unit had drawn a difficult assignment, they left camp about two in the morning ... they ended their march five miles from Petersburg. Alongside other black regiments, they started down the hill and into a wheat field, driving the enemies into the woods. [The] colonel ordered ... the line to fix bayonets and take on the rebel defense that had turned back the first wave". The officer yelled "Come on, brave boys of the Fifth"
>
> Paul and Stephen Kendrick, *Douglass and Lincoln, How a Revolutionary Black Leader and a Reluctant Liberator Struggled to End Slavery and Save the Union*[291]

The historic battle with the Confederate forces resulted in three dead and nineteen wounded. Sergeant Cornwall was one of the soldiers injured. He was shot in both legs and in his left hand, losing part of the hand and index finger. The regiment took part in the seizure of Petersburg, and after the surrender, camped in the vicinity of City Point to restore and maintain order until the close of the Civil War.

The Civil War was a harsh war - one of every two men that died was killed by disease or unsanitary medical conditions. Many northern Union soldiers, unfamiliar with the red clay of Virginia's soil, proclaimed that Virginia's earth was stained from the blood of Union and Confederate soldiers. Men died on the battlefield from starvation, froze to death from the harsh winters, drank bad homemade liquor and wood alcohol, or simply became severely ill and lacked the antibiotics needed to fight infection from unsanitary and primitive surgeries.

Figure 63: The Black Troops Showed the Veterans How to Do It in Style

> "Once more, Hincks and his black troops showed the veterans how to do things in style. Swarming over the cleared ground and into the red after-glory of the sunset, they pursued the (confederate soldiers) skirmishers through the tangled abatis, across the ditch, and up and over the breastwork just beyond. Formidable as they had been eye to eye, the fortifications collapsed at a touch; no less than seven of the individual bastions fell within the hour, five of them to the black soldiers, who took twelve of the sixteen captured guns and better than half of the 300 prisoners."
>
> Shelby Foote, *The Civil War, A Narrative: Red River To Appomattox*[292]

Sergeants Charles Douglass and William Cornwell were both injured on the battlefield of Petersburg. For the first time in combat, during the Civil War, nurses played a vital role in the health and safety of the wounded and dying soldiers. Much of what is known today about sanitary conditions and operative procedures are directly related to the lessons learned from horrific carnage on the battlefields of the Civil War.

In a series of letters, Sergeant Charles Douglass expressed the tremendous pain and agony he suffered. As Frederick Douglass had two sons critically injured in war, he sent a private communiqué to President Lincoln asking him to visit his son and release him from military duty, appealing to the President as both a Commander-In-Chief and a father.

After the battle for Petersburg and the Union occupation of the Confederate-burned Richmond, President Lincoln, upon the invitation of General Ulysses S. Grant, went and stayed for ten days at City Point, where Sergeants William Cornwell and Charles Douglass were stationed in a segregated camp military hospital. When President Lincoln went to visit Sergeants Cornwell and Douglass, they and the other men of the Massachusetts' 5th Calvary were honored to see their Commander-in-Chief. The President ordered the two sergeants to be transported to the hospital in Richmond.

Lincoln remained in City Point, hoping that Confederate General Robert E. Lee would surrender. On April 4, 1865, he went to Richmond to view firsthand the charred remains of the capital city of the Confederate States of America. Many southern white families had either fled to escape the city's burning or because they had no love for Lincoln and no interest in seeing the man responsible for, in their eyes, destroying the South.

It was mostly newly freed slaves that greeted the American President. Lincoln was overwhelmed by their warm response, and as part of the tour of the city, visited wounded soldiers in the Richmond Military Hospital. As the Commander-in-Chief, Lincoln was a complex man whose initial views on slavery and the role of men of African descent in the military grew over time. However, after the heroic display of patriotism by the all-black Massachusetts 54th Calvary and the Massachusetts 5th Calvary, along with the services of hundreds of thousands of other African Americans who fought in the war, there was no question in his mind that it was the right decision.

According to his granddaughter, Martha Cornwall Royster, the day that Sergeant Cornwall was visited by President Lincoln, he and the other soldiers were placed in full military dress, and Sergeant Cornwall had his picture taken on the same day.[293] During the Civil War, the color of the stripes indicated which branch of the military the Sergeant was from. If a soldier's stripes were red, it would indicate that he was part of the artillery branch, and blue would indicate that he was in the infantry.

Based on Sergeant Cornwall's uniform and his yellow stripe, he continued his service in the Calvary until the time of his honorable discharge in 1865. Also, as can be seen in the picture, Sergeant Cornwall wore the typical cavalry shell jacket with the high collar. During the Civil War, soldiers had the rank of private, corporal, or sergeant. The role of sergeant was one of the most pivotal non-commissioned officer positions in the battlefield and had the greatest impact on the soldiers in the field.

3.16 Othello and Thomas Fraction, Privates, 40th United States Colored Infantry

In the spirit of Confederate President Jefferson Davis' Enslavement Proclamation, white plantation owners all across the South felt empowered to bring their slaves together for a "talk." In Montgomery County, Virginia, on the plantation of Robert T. Preston, all of the slaves on the plantation were brought together, including the children and the old folks. Whenever a slaveholder brought all of his slaves together for a talk, every slave on the plantation knew it was bad news, and without being told, they knew what Master Preston was going to tell them even before he spoke. The African-American communication channels were rampant with the same story being told on one plantation after another; they were prepared.

The Preston plantation was the home of Robert Murphy's maternal great grandfather William Fraction and his brothers Thomas and Othello. As his slaves stood before him, and his trusted armed body guards on the parameters in the event there were any problems, Master Preston made it very clear to everyone in the audience that if any of his male slaves left the plantation to join the Union Army, there would be consequences for him and for his entire family. Preston also made it clear that any man who left and dared to come back, he would never leave again - at least, not still alive. Preston also made sure that the female slaves understood that they needed to keep their men from leaving, and if their man did leave, he would hold the women personally accountable.

While the enslaved men could consider running away, the women had an even smaller chance at escape. Slave women were often also mothers, and had to prepare every day for the moment their child would be taken away in the middle of the night and sold, or disappear, never to be heard from again. Slave mothers had to stand still while their children were whipped, or worse. Many of these women went to bed at night with the heaviest of hearts, only to rise the next day to clean the house and till the field for the very people they feared the most.

While the women knew what was going to be said, hearing it out loud sent chills throughout them, for they knew what their love ones wanted and were going to do. As Robert Preston and slave masters all over the South warned their enslaved men about joining the Union army, on those same plantations, slave mothers braced themselves for the inevitable - their sons would leave. These women knew better than anyone that their sons had to do what they must, and that taking this risk could mean a better life for all of them.

The powerless enslaved woman, Ester Fraction would soon learn the fate of her two sons, Othello and Thomas. Ester knew firsthand how powerful the Preston family was within the community as much as she knew that her family could not compete against such power. But she also knew in her heart that her boys wanted to control their own destinies, and in spite of the unavoidable trouble that would occur to her and the rest of the family, in her heart she knew that eventually her sons would leave, and when the time came, she would not stop them, no matter what the cost would be.

Despite the stern warning from Master Preston, at least two of the three Fraction brothers began to develop a strategy for their escape. However, they needed to be careful and wait for the right moment as their mother was getting along in years and could not withstand the harsh and brutal treatment guarantee to be bestowed upon her by Preston or one of his goons.

As their mother's health began to fade, William Fraction's younger brothers Thomas and Othello decided that there was little that Preston could do to their mother and decided to escape the plantation and enlisted in the Union Army. William Fraction's younger brothers Thomas and Othello each enlisted into the 40th United States Colored Infantry in Nashville, Tennessee, despite the tremendous risks to their own lives and the lives of their family they left back home. But this was the sacrifice that they were willing to make if it would grant them and their family freedom.

The brothers made their way westward and joined the 40th United States Colored Infantry in Nashville, Tennessee, in the early winter of 1864. As with most Colored Infantry, the officers were white. Many of the African-American men who made up the infantry came from Kentucky, Ohio and Tennessee. Much like the Fraction brothers, many of the infantrymen were runaway slaves.

The 40th United States Colored Infantry was attached to the protection and defenses of the Louisville and Nashville Railroad, and the Nashville and Northwestern Railroad. The new and advanced transport of railroad technologies revolutionized how people and supplies moved from one place to another. The railroad industry became a major tactical tool in the war for each side by providing both armies with the necessary logistical support when needed.

The 40th United States Colored Infantry was a valuable asset to both the Union and the railroad owners because they served as defense for the Louisville and Nashville Railroad and of the Nashville and Northwestern Railroad against Confederate sabotage and enabled the Union to transport soldiers when needed on the western flank of the war. The railroad industry got its start in the late 1820s and was initially supported by individual state governments who provided the necessary right-of-way passages to connect major commercial cities and centers with each other. Soon the rapid rail transport spread across the country and revolutionized population centers and commercial commerce. During the Civil War, the Union Army was able to take the most advantage of the railroads, because in the Union's territories there were some 22,385 miles of track versus in the Confederacy, which had only 8,783 miles of track at the beginning of the war."[294] The North, being more urbanized and commercialized, looked at centralizing its railroads to further economic growth and development, whereas the South looked at its rail industry, which was only a few miles long at most junctions, to bring its primary crops to steamboat landings for exports.[295]

During Thomas Fraction's service, he was appointed as Sergeant within the 40th United States Colored Infantry. His experience as a slave-for-hire working in the railroad industry must have provided him tremendous skill and expertise compared to the other men in his battalion. After the war, Thomas and his brother Othello were granted a furlough in April 1866 and went back home to Montgomery County, Virginia, for reasons that are unclear. While on furlough, Preston got word that his two runaway slaves who were now in the Union Army were visiting their mother's slave cabin. As Preston was getting armed reinforcements, the Fraction brothers got word that Preston was on his way and that they better escape before a major confrontation erupted.

As they were escaping, Preston confronted the two brothers, took direct aim at them and tried to shoot - but the gun misfired. Thomas and his brother Othello quickly retreated, but they were pursued by Preston who shot Thomas in the rear of his leg. Once to the ground, Othello stopped to give aide to his brother, but the two were badly beaten by Preston and his accomplices. Instead of being taken to a hospital, the two men were thrown into jail. While he was recuperating from his injuries, from April to June, 1866, Thomas was confined to a jail cell in Salem, Virginia. Prison was a rather dangerous place for a black man to be, particularly for one who had run away from his master, joined the Union Army and now dared to come back home despite being warned his life would be in jeopardy. Based on the fact that Thomas was shot and beaten almost to death before his stint in prison, it is presumed that he was similarly mistreated while in prison by the guards.

Once the Union Army got wind of the Fraction brothers being confined in the jail, they sent Union troops to free the men. Robert Preston argued for the men to continue to be held in jail, for he alleged that he was threatened and feared for his life. However, both Fraction brothers were released from confinement after a hearing with the War Department of Virginia who determined that the brothers had been "confined in prison without cause."

Figure 64: Our Master Said He Would Kill Us If We Ever Came Back

> Thomas and I were brothers in Company H of the 40th U.S.C.T. ...my brother was wounded in his right leg while home on furlough in April 1866 ... when our former Master and several others got after my brother and I, and shot my brother in the leg. That's because my brother was a union solider...and, Robert Preston our Master said if any of his "niggers" went to the army and came back he would kill them and he tried hard to kill my brother."
>
> *United States Military Pension, October 21, 1895,*
> *Baltimore, Maryland,* Othello Fraction[296]

Thomas was ordered for discharge by the military for exercising poor judgment in knowingly returning home to a hostile and dangerous environment. Thomas Fraction was given a discharge on June 18, 1866, having been demoted to Private beforehand.[297] As part of a pension application for his brother Thomas' widow's military pension, Othello Fraction provided a clear description of the account in a deposition filled on October 21, 1895, at which time he testified to the challenges and racism that he and his brother faced while they were in the war, particularly while on furlough and how his brother was almost murdered at the hands of his former master.

3.17 Aaron Jackson, Corporal, 26th United States Colored Infantry

The turning point of the Civil War happened in a three-day battle in July 1863, at Gettysburg, Pennsylvania. Confederate General Robert E. Lee was defeated so badly, that for the remainder of the war, the Confederate Army would never have enough resources to be able to invade a northern state. The losses at the Battle of Gettysburg were so staggering, for the North and the South, that President Lincoln dedicated a cemetery there for those who lost their lives in the battle. At the dedication, President Lincoln delivered what would become his historic Gettysburg Address, summarizing the purpose and desired outcome of the war in only a few minutes. President Lincoln referenced the Revolutionary War from "four score and seven years ago," connecting that war's effort for freedom and independence with the Civil War's effort to accomplish equality and freedom for all citizens, black or white.

Figure 65: The Gettysburg Address

"Four score and seven years ago our fathers brought forth on this continent a new nation, conceived in liberty, and dedicated to the proposition that all men are created equal.

Now we are engaged in a great civil war, testing whether that nation, or any nation, so conceived and so dedicated, can long endure. We are met on a great battlefield of that war. We have come to dedicate a portion of that field, as a final resting place for those who here gave their lives that that nation might live. It is altogether fitting and proper that we should do this.

But, in a larger sense, we cannot dedicate, we cannot consecrate, we cannot hallow this ground. The brave men, living and dead, who struggled here, have consecrated it, far above our poor power to add or detract. The world will little note, nor long remember what we say here, but it can never forget what they did here. It is for us the living, rather, to be dedicated here to the unfinished work which they who fought here have thus far so nobly advanced. It is rather for us to be here dedicated to the great task remaining before us-that from these honored dead we take increased devotion to that cause for which they gave the last full measure of devotion-that we here highly resolve that these dead shall not have died in vain-that this nation, under God, shall have a new birth of freedom-and that government of the people, by the people, for the people, shall not perish from the earth".

Abraham Lincoln, November 19, 1863

As the war continued into 1863, the sheer number of Confederate soldiers lost in battle demoralized the South. Many solders deserted as they learned about deteriorating conditions back home. There was infighting amongst the Confederate leadership, there was an inability to raise money, and there was growing opposition to the war. All of this was beginning to wear down the Confederacy. As southern Confederate states suffered from the psychological effects of the war, they also suffered severely from the naval embargo imposed by the Union's blockages.

Northern profiteers who wanted to benefit from the war often sent small cargo ships up and down the Atlantic coastline in an attempt to enter unguarded southern ports with food, ammunition, clothes and other valuables needed in for war effort. One such merchant was Sam Scudder of Long Island, New York. Like the Gardiner family, the Scudders were prominent in the Long Island community, owning vast tracts of land. Additionally, they were former slave owners.

Harold Cornwall's maternal grandfather, Aaron Jackson, was born in 1843, in the village of Huntington, New York. Aaron lived with his parents, John and Julia (Jones) Jackson, until he was twelve years of age, at which point he went to live as a "servant boy" with Sam Scudder.[298] In 1858, at the age of fifteen, the young and adventurous Aaron took to the "seven seas" as a cook on one of Scudder's small vessels that sailed back and forth between New York and various ports in the Caribbean.

During coastal storms on these voyages, Aaron and his cohorts discovered all of the tributaries and small ports along the Atlantic seacoast. They took advantage of these safe harbors during rough weather, and also used them to bypass the Northern ships patrolling the Southern ports in search of profiteers. According to Aaron's granddaughter, Martha Cornwall Royster, as they transported smuggled rum and whiskey up and down the East Coast of America, they repeatedly ran through the Union blockages to reach the southern ports along the Atlantic Ocean coastline.[299]

Several Union war ships often spotted these smaller and more agile schooners, but because of their size, speed and maneuverability, these boats were able to outrun the heavier Union war ships. Prior to the war, Scudder's vessels would often anchor in the waters off of the river port city of Alexandria, Virginia, to trade before making its long voyage back to New York. Although he was African American, Aaron had a very fair complexion, with hazel colored eyes and blond curly, coarse hair. When his shipmates would go ashore, for his own safety, he was told to stay on-board. Even though he had a fair complexion, he still looked of mixed racial heritage, and they were concerned that he would be kidnapped and sold into slavery. Port cities like Alexandria were filled with slave catchers.

But shore leave was shore leave, and Aaron, like the other men, wanted more than anything to get off the ship and indulge in the things for which port cites were known. However, what he saw on his visits to the southern ports had a profound effect on Aaron, and the issue of race relations would last him a lifetime. Alexandria, Virginia, was a major slave capitol, and Duke Street had one of the country's most robust slave trading centers. The self-contained four-story building consisted of various slave pens, where men, women and children were chained and shackled before being traded to various parts of the country. On many occasions, and always at a very safe distance, Aaron saw men, women and children, all in chains, disembark slave ships and get into enclosed wagons to be taken to the slave pen on Duke Street for inspection and subsequent sale. These were usually slaves from port cities further down the Atlantic who were going to be sold to buyers that would take them to cities and plantations, traveling by land.

No matter what city, harbor, or port, the docks were no place for the weak at heart. At fifteen, Aaron was adventurous, but as he experienced these tough port cities, he began to realize the danger he was in as a young African-American boy. Once, while on shore leave, Aaron had a very close call. He was stopped and asked for his papers. Coming from New York, Aaron didn't have papers to identify him. He was detained for a short period until his shipmates arrived to save him from "capture into slavery."[300] This traumatic experience stayed with him for the rest of his life, as he realized how close he had been to suffering the brutality of white slave owners.

According to Martha Cornwall Royster, Aaron's granddaughter, the reason he went into the military during the Civil War is that a Union patrol ship stopped the ship that he was on and was captured. The captured men were told they had to enlist in the Union Army or face going to jail. The choice an easy one for Aaron, and he went off to war.

In February 1864, Aaron, having witnessed and experienced servitude in Huntington, New York, and seen the harsh realities of bondage and slavery in the eastern seaboard and the South, had no qualms about enlisting in the 26th Regiment of the United States Colored Infantry that was organized under Colonel William Silliman at New York Harbor's Riker's Island on February 27, 1864.[301]

The following month, President Lincoln appointed Ulysses S. Grant commander of the Union Army, who in turned appointed William T. Sherman to lead the military division along the Mississippi River. As Robert E. Lee retreated from Gettysburg, Pennsylvania, back into Virginia, General Grant's strategy was a two-pronged approach. First, he wanted to immobilize Confederate General Lee in Virginia, and second, he wanted Union General Sherman to attack from the south, through Georgia. As part of General Grant's southern strategy, and the deployment of mass resources, Aaron Jackson's 26th United

Colored Infantry was ordered to the Department of the South, in Beaufort, South Carolina, on April 13, 1864, and was posted there until November 27th.

While the southern strategy was in full force, Aaron Jackson became a non-commissioned officer and was appointed Corporal. Although Aaron had previously travel to the South several times on the schooners owned by Sam Scudder of New York and was familiar with the hot temperatures in the South from his time sailing the Atlantic's southern coastline, it was very different to serve in battle with heavy multi-layered woolen clothing, while carrying military equipment. In the spring of 1864, General Grant attacked the Confederate strong holds of Virginia's city of Fredericksburg and Spotsylvania County, and finally at Petersburg, Virginia, which remained under strong Union attack from the spring of 1864 to the spring of 1865.

By late March 1865, it was clear that the Confederacy was close to collapse. After heavy losses on both sides, the final death toll was a loss of 60,000 men in the Union Army and 32,000 were lost from the Confederacy. The Union losses were severe, but the North had resources that could easily be replaced, while the Southern losses only wore down the morale of the troops.

With the end of the war in sight, President Lincoln originally planned to wait in City Point, just outside of Richmond, for the surrender of the Confederate Army. However, on April 8, 1865, he decided to return to the White House. The following day, on April 9, 1865, in Appomattox, Virginia, Confederate Army General Robert E. Lee and Union Army General Ulysses S. Grant met to arrange a Confederate surrender.

The Civil War was over.

Part 4: Industrial and Social Changes

4.1 The Death of a President

From the very beginning and throughout his presidency, Abraham Lincoln was plagued with the effects of war. The Civil War was primarily caused by the debate over slavery, the resulting secession of the southern states. Whites in southern states believed that the states' rights doctrine written into the U.S. Constitution gave them the authority to ignore calls for the end of slavery and secede from the Union. As President, Lincoln advanced three strategic political actions that framed the issue of slaves and ultimately the abolishment of slavery, while also setting the foundation for the secessionists to return to the Union.

The first action taken by the President was the decree of the Emancipation Proclamation on January 1, 1863. Lincoln believed that his wartime powers allowed him to free only those slaves who lived in the eleven states that had seceded from the Union. The second action was taken on December 8, 1863, when President Lincoln issued the Proclamation of Amnesty and Reconstruction that outlined specific steps southern states could follow to rejoin the union. The third action occurred in 1865 when Lincoln persuaded the United States Congress to pass the Thirteenth Amendment, which he believed would address any constitutional issues surrounding the Emancipation Proclamation. Lincoln's main concern once the war was over whether or not the slaves would remain free.

Lincoln's Proclamation of Amnesty and Reconstruction, issued in December 1863, pardoned "those who participated in the rebellion if they [would] take an oath to the Union. In any seceded state, the state government would be recognized if at least one tenth of the voters so wished, provided an oath to the union was taken and slavery barred."[302]

As the war dragged on, it devastated the South's economy and morale. Lincoln hoped that realistic southern political leaders and businessmen would realize that the war was not in their best interests, and would slowly begin to take steps to reintegrate their states back into the Union. As President Lincoln had hoped, in 1864, the southern states of Arkansas, Louisiana and Tennessee began to establish "Unionist governments," due to the strong political and military influence that the President had in certain parts of each state. These states became known as "Lincoln States."

As the war began to turn more favorably toward the possibility of a Union victory Lincoln thought long and hard about how the rebellious southern states should be treated and how their decimated infrastructure would be reconstructed. He was concerned about how the Confederate states and its leaders should be treated after the war, and about how the newly freed slaves would be integrated into society. His political enemies on the left and right, from the north and the south, challenged his every move and questioned his personal motives as much as his political ones.

Figure 66: Returning to the Union

"Governments had been set up ... based upon the votes of ... ten percent of the electorate, professing loyalty and swearing allegiance. Of these voters, some were consistent and devoted Union men who waited only the opportunity given by passing portions of their states under the control of Union armies. Other were disgruntled Confederates, the intensity of whose zeal was likely to be in inverse proportion of the vigor of their former protestations. Others were simply opportunists or office seekers. But whatever their records or their motives, they formed a political people upon whom the organization of restored states might rest."

Robert Selph Henry, *The Story of Reconstruction*[303]

The fifty-six-year-old president had visibly aged beyond his years under the tremendous pressure of all of his careful deliberations on each and every matter of importance to the Union. In order to address any potential concerns over the legality of freeing slaves during wartime with the Emancipation Proclamation, Lincoln advanced the principles of the Thirteenth Amendment - which was the first of three amendments to the United States Constitution that addressed the complex issues of slavery, equality, citizenship and voting rights.

Many southerners and Confederate supporters in the Border States were vocal about their strong dislike for Lincoln and members of his cabinet. They felt that the President and his strong abolitionist policies needed to be stopped at any cost. Several Confederates hatched a series of plots to kidnap or assassinate the President, believing that if they were successful, they would affect the outcome of the war. The President was well aware of the threats against his life and the lives of members of his cabinet. "Lincoln had to begin acquiescing to demands that guards surround him, making kidnapping more difficult than murder."[304] One such kidnapping plot was hatched by a young actor named John Wilkes Booth and several of his co-conspirators. They believed that if they could "kidnap Lincoln, take him to Richmond, and then trade him for all of the southern prisoners of war" the South would have the necessary manpower to prevail.[305]

In April 1865, as the Confederate Army fled to Richmond and other nearby points in Virginia, the Union Army aggressively pursued them. On April 2, the Union Army, under the command of General Ulysses S. Grant, surrounded the Confederates, and on April 9, after a long and arduous and costly war, Confederate General Robert E. Lee officially surrendered to the Union Army.

Staunch Confederates, angered by the surrender, attempted to develop strategies that would prolong the war. Immediately after hearing that "General Lee had surrendered his pitiful 9,000 men to Grant's 100,000 on the fields surrounding the crossroads of Appomattox, Virginia," John Wilkes Booth and his band of co-conspirators planned to cause turmoil within the upper echelon of the federal government, which would allow the Confederate government the opportunity to recover its strength, reorganize, and continue the war.[306]

Booth began to stalk the President and on April 11, 1865, he stood in a crowd outside of the White House and heard the President, in an impromptu speech, say that he "recommended suffrage for blacks who were educated or had served in the Union army." This enraged Booth, who vowed "That was the last speech Lincoln would ever make," Coincidentally three days later, on April 14, Booth arrived at the Ford's Theater, where he worked as an actor, only to learn that President Lincoln would be attending a performance of *Our American Cousin* that evening.[307] Booth and his accomplices set forth a plan to assassinate the President. That evening, John Wilkes Booth shot

President Lincoln. The next morning, Abraham Lincoln, the sixteenth president, died. Later that day, on April 15, 1865, Vice President Andrew Johnson became the seventeenth President of the United States.

Dubbed by many as the "accidental President," Andrew Johnson "began his fortunes as a tailor in Tennessee and had great affection for struggling white men who were trying to succeed. In contrast, he did not trust wealthy white southerners or African Americans."[308] His political philosophy reflected his poor upbringing and his deep-seated belief that the southern aristocracy had dragged the South into war. As the nation mourned the assassination of President Lincoln, state legislators, in a temporary act of reconciliation and remembrance, moved to pass the last piece of major legislation on which President Lincoln worked. The Constitution's Thirteenth Amendment was ratified on December 6, 1865, and the institution of slavery was abolished in the United States.

Figure 67: Slavery nor Involuntary Servitude Shall Exist within the United States

Section 1.	Neither slavery nor involuntary servitude, except as a punishment for crime whereof the party shall have been duly convicted, or any place subject to their jurisdiction.
Section 2.	Congress shall have power to enforce this article by appropriate legislation.

Thirteenth Amendment to the *United States Constitution*,
adopted April 8, 1864, ratified by the states on December 6, 1865

4.2   War Veterans Return Home

When word spread through the military camps of the United States Colored Troops, that the Confederate General Robert E. Lee surrendered at Appomattox, Virginia, the men were euphoric. The United States Colored Troops consisted of African-American men who were former slaves or the sons and grandsons of former slaves. They were men who courageously fought on the battlefields and proved their bravery and commitment to even the most critical of skeptics. They were overwhelmed by raw emotion and cried uncontrollably with excitement and joy. These men had volunteered to serve their country to end, once and forever, the institution of slavery. Because of their and others' tireless efforts and sacrifices, the Union succeeded.

For the United States Colored Troops, every step in their journey as soldiers gave them a unique sense of pride in their service and who they were as Americans. These men were overwhelmed with pride in knowing that they were instrumental in ending the institution of slavery, something that each man hoped would happen one day. For a time, while these soldiers publicly supported each other in fighting to end slavery, privately each man felt that he would never see the day when they would become something more than just chattel property. But now, they basked in the glory of knowing that the sacrifices that they and their families endured were all worth it - and for many of them, the sacrifice was enormous. The men of the United States Colored Troops admired President Lincoln for including them in the war effort, and for taking the enormous political and personal risk by emancipating the slaves.

Figure 68: Incredible War Record of the United States Colored Troops

"African American soldiers compiled a distinguished record ...in relation to their numbers; they had fewer desertions than their white comrades – and many more casualties. More than a third of those enrolled were dead or missing by the war's end – nearly doubled the rate for the army as a whole, mostly from wounds and disease. Combat troops took part in 200 engagements, 39 of which was classified as major. Some of the latter were the bloodiest of the war ...the Virginia campaign ...brought 37 Congressional Medals of Honor to the troops -14 went to African American soldiers. By the end of the war, many Union commanders who had doubted the combat effectiveness of the United States Colored Troops were ready to agree with General Grant ... all that have been tried in combat have fought bravely. Unfortunately, the black war record was soon lost to view. For generations to come the myth persisted that African Americans lacked courage in warfare. As a result, many African Americans have little knowledge of the part their ancestors played in winning them freedom and liberating American democracy from the incubus of slavery."

Robert Cruden,
The Negro in Reconstruction[309]

Without question, the United States Colored Troops had unwavering loyalty and the utmost respect for their Commander in Chief, especially when he visited them on the battlefields. As the war came to a close, there was even talk that the President believed that "literate blacks and Union veterans" deserved the right to vote and that he would make it happen. Despite the men's overwhelming joy, around the campfires at night, discussion would always turn somber as they voiced a genuine concern for their Commander in Chief.

Even in the field, they had heard the rumors of assassination attempts on the President's life. They feared the President would be killed before he accomplished his goal of freeing all of the slaves. As former slaves, they knew how vicious their southern adversaries could be, and as professionally trained soldiers of the United States Colored Troops they were concerned that Confederate supporters would assassinate Lincoln not only for attempting to free the slaves, but also in what they believed to be his ruining of the southern economy and dismantling their aristocratic way of life.

Five days after the Confederate surrender in Appomattox, all joy of victory vanished - the soldiers' biggest fear had become reality. The President was dead, shot by John Wilkes Booth in Washington, D.C.'s Ford's Theater.

The nation was in tumult, and as citizens everywhere mourned the President's death, some Confederates applauded the assassination. African-American Civil War veterans were angry and fearful that Lincoln's assassination meant that all they had fought for would not be realized. Soldiers such as William Cornwell, physically and psychologically injured on the battlefield, felt that the bullet from a cowardly assassin would destroy all that they had been accomplished in their hard-fought battles.

Soldiers such as Thomas and Othello Fraction - who escaped slavery, were beaten within an inch of their lives, were shot at and thrown into prison - feared that nothing would change. Soldiers such as Aaron Jackson, seen as liberators and saviors by the former slaves in South Carolina, worried that in some small way, they had failed their fellow African Americans. Additionally, all Americans of African descent feared that their newly acquired freedoms would not be honored.

The men of the United States Colored Troops heard rumors about then-Vice President Andrew Johnson, and they didn't trust him. Perhaps they had good reason.

Figure 69: President Threatens to Remove Black Troops from the United States

"President Johnson told returning black troops that they must "prove" themselves "competent for the rights that the government has guaranteed them," expressed hope the two races could live harmoniously in an "experiment" in freedom, and warned that if the experiment failed, the solution might lie in removing African Americans from the United States. African Americans doubtless sensed the implicit threat in view of the fact that newspapers were already quoting the President as having said: "This is a country for white men, and by God, so long as I am President, it shall be a government for white men."

Robert Cruden,
The Negro in Reconstruction[310]

Andrew Johnson was a stark departure from President Lincoln in the eyes of the African-American soldiers. The high spirits of the men in the United States Colored Troops had deflated, and they now wanted to walk away from the war they fought so bravely in, and go home to take care of their families and their personal lives. They had lost friends - white and black - on the battlefield, and now the President expected them to "prove" themselves. At the beginning of the war, these men of color experienced unbelievable scorn and ridicule from their fellow soldiers, white men who wore the very same uniforms, but by the end of the war, they received unexpected accolades for their bravery and heroism. Despite their many accomplishments, President Johnson had burdened them with an "experiment to live harmoniously with one another," placing the entire responsibility of this harmonious life on the shoulders of men descended from slaves - men who had been beaten, shackled, and murdered.

The United States Colored Troops had paid the supreme sacrifice by giving their lives in the war to save the Union and to end slavery. "More than 38,000 black soldiers lost their lives during the Civil War - a mortality rate almost 40 percent higher than that of white troops."[311] The surviving members could not believe that President Johnson now threatened to ship them to Africa, as though their families hadn't been in America for centuries. The men had little to no respect for President Johnson. But rather than preoccupy themselves with the President's irrational idea, the veterans from the Cornwell Murphy family accepted their honorable discharges from the service and went back

214

home to marry and raise their families - and hoped that the state of the union would be become better as a result of their efforts.

In 1866, veteran William Cornwell married Miss Martha Hill of Cambridge, Massachusetts. They initially resided in Boston, where they raised their two children, Benjamin and Mary. After the war, William, like so many other Civil War Veterans continued to be plagued by his physical war injuries, and the painful effects of rheumatoid arthritis from the disfigurement of losing a good portion of his left hand. The medical care that soldiers received while on the Civil War battlefields was primitive in comparison to today's standards. William suffered not only from the physical effects of his injuries but also from the emotional effects of the war. Like many of the returning soldiers, William suffered what was commonly referred to at the time with "soldier's heart"- now referred to as Posttraumatic Stress Disorder, or PTSD. His emotional problems resulted from the trauma of witnessing the horrific events on the battlefields and was, as in many cases such as William's, exacerbated by the former soldier's personal pain from his physical injuries.

During the war, William knew that as an American of African descent, being captured by the enemy held the additional risk of being sold or offered into slavery. William was strongly committed to preserving the Union, but he was absolutely devoted to abolishing slavery. As Sergeant, William led the men of his segregated African-American troop into battle, and constantly reminded them that their mission was to free the millions of Americans of African descent born into slavery, just as he heard Frederick Douglass say.

Many of his men had joined the ranks of the Colored Troops after being inspired by the speeches of civil rights advocate, Frederick Douglass. His sons, Charles and Lewis Douglass, trained with the Massachusetts 54th Infantry and the 5th Massachusetts Cavalry, and many of their fellow recruits asked them to enlighten the troops about the purpose of the war and how important it was. On the battlefield, during periods of long rest, the black soldiers challenged each other in discussion and debate about race, American citizenship, and personal freedoms. Many, such as William Cornwell, were great-grandsons of Revolutionary War veterans and they challenged America's commitment to giving African Americans in a new south and throughout the country the entire rights, freedoms and citizenship for which they had fought. The soldiers wore their battle-torn blue uniforms with tremendous pride as they shared their personal experiences with the institution of slavery.

At the end of the war, New York's 26th United States Colored Troops, in which Corporal Aaron Jackson fought, were stationed in Beaufort, South Carolina, and assigned the task of ensuring the full emancipation of South Carolina's slave population. Of all of the missions that this regiment had, to the men of the 26th United States Colored Troop, this symbolically was the most important - personally and militarily. The honor of fully freeing each African-American man, woman, and child in the state that started the Civil War was nothing short of poetic justice.

Aaron Jackson, born a Free Man of Color in Huntington, New York, was not only a part of history, but a true history maker. He risked his life to serve in the Civil War, and for that service to culminate with permanently freeing slaves was an extremely emotional and satisfying experience. By the end of the war, Aaron had climbed the ranks from Private, to Corporal, to Sergeant - but his greatest accomplishment was the honor of being considered a liberator and protector of the newly freed slaves, and seeing the many faces of African-American men and women in South Carolina as his troops entered Charleston. As he told his grandchildren many years later, that was the greatest honor any man could ever have. Upon his honorable discharge, veteran Sergeant Aaron Jackson married Keziah Gardiner from Sunken Meadow, New York. They had nine children, including the sisters Cora and Grace.

Privates Othello and Thomas Fraction of the 40th United States Colored Infantry mustered out on April 25, 1866. By all accounts the brothers considered themselves to be most fortunate to have survived the war, in that they had not been slaughtered at the hands of the Confederate soldiers in battle and they weren't murdered at the end of a shotgun belonging to their former master, Confederate Colonel Preston, in the woods outside of their parents' home. Having run away from their home on the Robert T. Preston plantation in Montgomery County, Virginia, the brothers knew they would not have the luxury of easily settling back into their communities once they came home from the war. The Fraction brothers only hoped that now the war was over, they could go home and settle into the only community that they knew. They didn't want any problems but still wanted to stay in the area, so they decided they would not go near Preston's property and would try to avoid him as much as possible.[312]

After the conclusion of the Spanish American war in 1897, the residents of Massachusetts recognized the heroism of the three African-American regiments that bravely served in the Civil War by erecting a monument in honor of the Massachusetts 54th Volunteer Colored Infantry. The bronze memorial was sculpted by Augustus St. Gardens, and sits handsomely on one of the most expensive pieces of real estate in Boston, at the intersection of Beacon and Park Streets, on the picturesque Boston Common and directly across the street from the Massachusetts State House.

The expert craftsmanship of St. Gardens portrays each solider individually sculpted carrying his own canteen, backpack and Army-issued rife. Actual members of the regiment served as models in their uniforms so as to capture the real expressions of their African-American faces, hands and stature.[313]

At its dedication services on May 31, 1897, guest speakers included civil rights leader Booker T. Washington and veterans from the Massachusetts 54th and 55th Regiments and the 5th Massachusetts Calvary. For the veterans of the Colored Regiments in attendance, the moment was a long time coming. Much had taken place in their lives since they mustered out from the Civil War. Many were now grandparents, and to be able to share this moment with their wives, their children and their grandchildren must have been overwhelming for the men.

The veterans were quite moved to watch regiments of young white soldiers march by in their pressed uniforms and then salute the veterans in honor of all they had done and accomplished. Thirty-two years after the end of the war, men still bore the injuries and psychological wounds of not-forgotten battles, but participating in the statue's dedication and the parade commemorating their service brought many to tears. Many who had faded into the doldrums of everyday life were now elevated to their rightful place in history and would be remembered for generations.

The monument honoring the African American soldiers also depicts the regiment's Colonel Robert Gould Shaw, the young white officer who bravely led his men into battle at the assault on Fort Wagner, South Carolina, where sixty-two men were killed. After Shaw's brutal torture and death, the Confederate army, in an act of grave disrespect, buried his body at the bottom of a ditch and placed the bodies of the dead African-American soldiers on top. After hearing of this, Colonel Shaw's father reportedly said that this in fact was the way his son would have wanted to be buried - along with his soldiers.

This impressive statue and other tributes were not only for the veterans of the three Colored Regiments, but for all of the African-American men who served in the United States Colored Troops - who had fought and died for the preservation of the Union; helped to end slavery; and helped bring about the passage of the Thirteenth, Fourteenth and Fifteenth Amendments. Frederick Douglass was right - given the chance, these men could change their fate and the fate of their people.

Figure 70: African American Soldiers Deserved the Right to be Citizens

"Once let the black man get upon his person the brass letter, U.S., let him get an eagle on his button, and a musket on his shoulder and bullets in his pocket, there is no power on earth that can deny that he has earned the right to citizenship."

Frederick Douglass Speech

Should the Negro Enlist in the Union Army,
August, 1863[314]

4.3   Reconstructing a Nation and the Restoration of the South

When Lincoln was alive, he challenged himself and others with three basic questions: What was the North fighting for? How should the issue of slavery be resolved? And what should be done with the secessionist southern states after the war? As the war came to a close, Lincoln spent much time thinking and discussing how to address these pressing issues. Sadly, he was assassinated by John Wilkes Booth on April 15, 1865.

Vice President Johnson stepped into the role of President. However, unlike his predecessor, President Andrew Johnson did not have the reputation of being a deep thinker. He was immediately confronted with the awesome burden of reuniting an extremely polarized country, and had little time to consider the long-term impact of his decisions. For any President, Reconstruction would have been difficult, but for Andrew Johnson, the challenge would be even greater.

Johnson knew that Lincoln wanted to take all measures necessary to restore order nationally, and to restore full citizenship to the residents of the secessionist states as soon as possible, "so that peace, order, and freedom might be established."

On May 29, 1865, as a continuation of Lincoln's polices towards national reconciliation President Andrew Johnson issued his own form of amnesty, and declared that any former Confederate who hadn't taken advantage of the previous amnesty offered by President Lincoln in 1863 could now declare their allegiance and take an oath to the defend the Constitution of the United States.

Figure 71: An Absence of Trust during a Difficult Reconstruction

> "Neither the north nor the south could easily forgive and forget all the bitterness nor all of the distrust that had been generated between the sections for decades before it culminated in open war, or the blood and anguish that four years of fighting had entailed."
>
> Avery Craven,
> *Reconstruction: The Ending of the Civil War*[315]

The Johnson Amnesty Proclamation was intended to be a direct blow to his "hated planter aristocracy" and anyone of importance in the antebellum South, who he personally blamed for the war and wanted to force each person to seek a special pardon directly from the President himself.[316]

Figure 72: Secessionists Had to Request a Presidential Pardon

> Johnson's Amnesty Proclamation "pardoned all participants in the rebellion, restored their property (except slaves and that which had been or might be legally confiscated), and required them to take a loyalty oath. It excluded, however, fourteen categories of people from the general pardon. Mainly these were upper-echelon Confederate civilian and military officials and all persons possessing over $20,000 in taxable property. Such individuals would have to apply to the President for a restoration of their rights to vote and to hold office."
>
> Albert Castel,
> *The Presidency of Andrew Johnson*[317]

Many northern Republicans believed that Johnson was being too lenient on the southern states in offering another chance at amnesty. His critics believed that the South should pay a heavy penance for causing the war and acknowledge their defeat and the abolition of slavery. Johnson's overemphasis on oaths and pardons drew sharp criticisms from northern Congressmen and former abolitionists. Johnson's actions and his beliefs set in motion the initial retreat from the well thought out Lincoln Reconstruction policies.

Johnson believed and often stated that "there is no such thing as reconstruction and that the southern states had not seceded from the Union. He believed that it was the citizens who were the guilty ones … and that their oaths and his pardons constituted the basic steps for restoration."

At the time, many believed that Johnson's philosophy of "the oath and the pardon, as the only required evidence of repentance, were his undoing"[318] and perhaps the greatest travesty to the newly freed slaves and to his presidency.

On September 1, 1865, former Confederate Colonel and slave master of the Fraction family, Robert T. Preston, took his Loyalty Oath to support and defend the Constitution of the United States, and to uphold the emancipation of his slaves.

His letter, addressed to "His Excellency Andrew Johnson, President of the United States," attested that he was obligated to join the rebellion because his "allegiance was to his native state and that it was his duty to share her fate," and once the Governor of Virginia bestowed upon him the "office of Colonel" he continued to "provide service to his state for two years in the command of a Virginia Regiment, endeavoring to do his duty faithfully to his state."

Colonel Preston had to apply personally for amnesty because he was one of the individuals whose property in 1860 was valued more than the $20,000 threshold.

As a requirement of the Johnson Amnesty Proclamation, Preston's wealth required him to personally submit his amnesty request directly to the President.

Once the Letter of Request was written to President Johnson and the affidavit attested to, former slave owner Robert T. Preston then signed his Loyalty Oath to the Constitution of the United States, and sent the package to the Governor of Virginia to be forwarded on to the President of the United States. The letter signed to the President concludes with "I have the honor to be very respectfully your 'Old Friend,' Rob T. Preston."[319]

Figure 73: Confederate Solider Loyalty Oath

STATE OF WEST VIRGINIA:
MONROE COUNTY RECORDER OFFICE

September 1, 1865

I, Robert T. Preston do solemnly swear in the presence of the Almighty God; that I will henceforth faithfully defend the constitution of the United States and the Union of States thereunder; and that I will in like manner abide by and faithfully support all laws and proclamations which have been made during the existing rebellion with reference to the emancipation of slaves. So help me God.

Rob T. Preston

Subscribed and Sworn to before me in my office aforesaid this 1st day of September, 1865

JS Morningside, Deputy Recorder, M.C.[320]

All across the south, former Confederates were proclaiming their loyalty and oaths to the government, but in short order, their hallowed actions suggested an ulterior motive. "Toward the end of 1865, the newly-formed Southern legislatures of the so-called 'Johnson governments' began passing what were called the Black Codes. Their ostensible purpose was to assist the African American in his transition from slavery to citizenship".[321] However, it was soon clear that these codes were making it impossible for African Americans to accomplish anything but continued servitude and indebtedness.

The Black Codes, as designed by the former Confederate leadership and members of the southern gentry, were intentionally written to force the newly freed slaves back onto the plantations into long-term contracts with little to no opportunity for escape.

To many in the North, the codes seemed tantamount to restoring slavery. The codes clearly indicated the attitude of the southern legislators and those who supported them.

Figure 74: The Black Codes

- African Americans under eighteen years of age who were orphan or parents could not take care of them were to be apprenticed, preferably to their former owner

- African Americans who were vagrant, had no shelter, committed a crime, or preached without a license could be hired out to a white person if they could not pay a heavy fine

- An African American who left his white employer without permission could be arrested and if unable to pay a fine, be forced to work for free

- African Americans were not able to practice a skilled trade without a license, possess firearms or weapons or rent land outside an incorporated town

- African Americans who were stubborn or refractory were liable to a fifty-dollar fine, and if unpaid, could be forced to work for six months unremunerated.

Albert Castel,
The Presidency of Andrew Johnson[322]

Seven months after President Johnson put in place his Amnesty Proclamation, in December 1865 in the small town of Pulaski, Tennessee, six college men, former veterans of the Confederate Army, started to wear disguises in an attempt to harass and strike fear in the hearts of local African Americans. As the secret vigilante group grew in participants, its reign of terror began to spread all across the south. By 1867, the group to be known as the Ku Klux Klan, "had many former Confederate officers, including a number of generals, and drew from among the best citizens in the areas in which it rode."

Under the darkness of night, the secret organization targeted "troublesome" freed blacks and their sympathizers. During the light of day, the southern aristocracy and powerful political factions used the organization to primarily strategize how to "prepare for the coming political struggle for control of the South."[323]

One of the primary causes of unrest in the South was its economic plight due to the cost of the Civil War, which was staggering. The Confederacy's cost in the war totaled a billion dollars. The Confederate debt ran over $1.8 billion in 1864. The Confederate inflation rose to 7,000 percent.[324] The North was concerned with the economy as well. The Union's cost at the end of the war totaled $2.3 billion dollars and the costs increased the national debt from $65 million in 1860 to $2.7 billion in 1865. The Union's inflation peaked at 182 percent in 1864. Based on today's dollar, the cost of the war was approximately $17 billion for the Confederate succession government and $27 billion for the Union, for a combined cost of 44 billion dollars.[325] The aftermath of the Civil War presented enormous political and economic changes in both the Northern States and in the Southern former Confederate States.

Despite the Union's increase in debt, the economy in the North flourished as a direct result of the War, it spurred economic development and had a tremendous positive impact on the North's overall economy. In order to transport soldiers to the southern war front, the Federal government spent enormous monies to build a national railroad system.

Northern businessmen grew rich by selling war supplies to the Federal government and since so many men had been recruited into the military practically everyone who wanted to work was working. In the war's aftermath, northern businessmen had plenty of reserved capitol and the necessary funds to strengthen their businesses as well as expand into new lines of business. With the expansion of business capital came new employment and other economic opportunities for the returning soldiers and for their families. Despite the war debt, the north survived the effects of the war and was even expanding in a post-war economy.

In contrast, the South's economy was devastated by the impact of the war. The South's economy and its infrastructure were completely ruined. All across the South government buildings were destroyed, and vital railroad lines needed for the transport of goods and materials in order to generate revenue were demolished. But the most significant cost of the war was the after effect of the Emancipation Proclamation.

As former Confederate soldiers returned home, they expected to return to their former way of life and hoped to look for new opportunities. Instead, they found a South they didn't recognize, its pre-war agricultural dominance was now devastated by a lack of slave labor as thousands of acres lay dormant and unproductive.

Figure 75: Life As We Know It Will Never be the Same

"Life after the war was profoundly different from what it had been before, and would never be the same again. Aside from the horrible human cost, which left almost every Southern and Northern family in mourning, and the dismal impoverishment of the South, the centralization of the government that had happened during the war years changed the fabric of society. Until 1860, the only direct contact with the federal government the average citizen had was the postal service. Now, the War Department controlled state militias; many direct taxes were imposed, a Federal Bureau of Internal Revenue was in place, national banking system had been instituted and federal money had been printed."

Joe H. Kirchberger,
The Civil War and Reconstruction, An Eyewitness History[326]

The cost of the war didn't stop after 1865, "twenty years later, interest payments on the war debt plus veteran pensions accounted for almost two-thirds of the federal budget."[327] The human costs of the war were also staggering, and impacted every American family. More than 360,000 Union soldiers and 260,000 Confederates died, and another 275,000 Union soldiers and 225,000 Confederate soldiers were wounded.[328]

The North had an abundant population, and could absorb the loss of dead men as well as the loss in revenue. The South could not. It needed every able-bodied man to return the South to its economic base of agribusiness without the free labor of the slaves.

Over a three-year period, Congress passed a series of laws in an attempt to reconstruct the South, and to ensure certain protections for the newly freed slaves. On March 3, 1865, the United States Congress created the Bureau of Refugees, Freedmen and Abandoned Lands within the War Department, which became known as the Freedmen's Bureau.

The Bureau, modeled after the Army's "experience in the occupied South," was a critical agency in helping the newly freed slaves navigate the challenges they faced as newly recognized citizens in an overtly hostile region, that had only months ago treated them as chattel property.[329]

"The Republicans from the North reasoned that since they had taken the lead in seeing the successful conclusion of the war, they should take the lead in shaping the peace."[330]

Figure 76: Lofty Intentions of the Bill to Create the Freedmen's Bureau

"When the time came to establish the Freedmen's Bureau, the Republican Radicals saw an opportunity to realize the most ambitious of their dreams - their desire to impoverish the Southern planters by stripping them of their property. It could be done by writing two simple provisions into the bill setting up the agency. One provision entrusted the management of all abandoned and confiscated lands to the Bureau. The other authorized the Bureau to divide up the land into 40-acre parcels and then sell or rent these parcels to African Americans and white Unionists."

Milton Lomask,
Andrew Johnson, President on Trial[331]

The Freedmen's Bureau was set up to ensure that the rights of the newly freed men were going to be protected. Northern Republicans believed that the goals and objectives of the Freedmen's Bureau were consistent with the major outcome of the Civil War. "The war had not only preserved the Union - it had also created a nation," where all People of Color were free, and in which black suffrage had to be ensured.[332]

The members of the Freedmen's Bureau knew that once African Americans got the right to vote, they would favorably remember the Bureau and vote Republican for generations to come. Southern state legislatures and former Confederates were well aware of the political advantages this Bureau could gain, and because of this, the Freedmen's Bureau was reviled all across the South.

The well-intentioned Bureau, charged with protecting African Americans against the most blatant forms of exploitation and mistreatment, was met with challenges from the very beginning. The agency lacked the necessary funding to succeed, which in turn caused the agency to lack critical personnel. However, despite its organizational and bureaucratic limitations, the agency carved out invaluable services all across the South during a period in which they were badly needed. The Bureau distributed food and clothing to impoverished people of both races and assisted families with finding shelter.

The Bureau went into communities and "established hospitals, schools and colleges in collaboration with Northern charitable agencies".[333] The Bureau reported the enormous abuses against

African Americans all across the South, and gave the more radical Republicans the opportunity to enact legislation that could prevent the full implementation of the Black Codes.

Figure 77: Challenges of the Freedmen's Bureau

"The record of the Union government toward the freedman was a mixture of success and failure, humanitarianism and exploitation, kindness and cruelty. The government's policy often seemed confused and shortsighted; but the government was faced with an unprecedented situation. There was no tradition of government responsibility for a huge refugee population, no bureaucracy to administer a large welfare and employment program. The Union Army in the government was groping in the dark. They created the precedents. No other society in history had liberated so many slaves in so short a time; no other army had ever carried through such a social revolution. No other country had established a Freedman's Bureau to deal with the problems of emancipated slaves; no other society had poured so much effort and money into the education of the ex-slaves. Small as these efforts may have been they were revolutionary by the standards of the time."

James M. McPherson
Ordeal by Fire, The Civil War, Volume II [334]

Southern states once again tried to use the Dred Scot Supreme Court Decision as the narrow definition for African-American citizenship - or lack thereof. Southern states argued that since the court ruled that Americans of African descent could not be citizens of the United States, that they could not enjoy the benefits of citizenship, and that the newly enacted Black Codes were designed to protect the freed slaves since they did not have the full protection of citizenship.

In response to the failed southern argument and to address both the physical and administrative violence being perpetuated against the newly freed slaves all across the South, Congress passed the Fourteenth Amendment in 1866, which finally resolved the issue of citizenship and made "all persons born or naturalized in the United States, and subject to the jurisdiction thereof ... citizens of the United States and of the State wherein they reside."

The Fourteenth Amendment to the United States Constitution's Citizenship Clause overruled the Dred Scot Supreme Court decision, and provided a clear but broad definition of citizenship for all Americans, including citizens of color.

Figure 78: Fourteenth Amendment Provides Citizenship to Former Slaves

Section 1. All persons born or naturalized in the United States, and subject to the jurisdiction thereof, are citizens of the United States and of the State wherein they reside. No State shall make or enforce any law which shall abridge the privileges or immunities of citizens of the United States; nor shall any State deprive any person of life, liberty, or property, without due process of law; nor deny to any person within its jurisdiction the equal protection of the laws.

Section 2. Representatives shall be apportioned among the several States according to their respective numbers, counting the whole number of persons in each State, excluding Indians not taxed. But when the right to vote at any election for the choice of electors for President and Vice President of the United States, Representatives in Congress, the Executive and Judicial officers of a State, or the members of the Legislature thereof, is denied to any of the male inhabitants of such State, being twenty-one years of age, and citizens of the United States, or in any way abridged, except for participation in rebellion, or other crime, the basis of representation therein shall be reduced in the proportion which the number of such male citizens shall bear to the whole number of male citizens twenty-one years of age in such State.

Section 3. No person shall be a Senator or Representative in Congress, or elector of President and Vice President, or hold any office, civil or military, under the United States, or under any State, who, having previously taken an oath, as a member of Congress, or as an officer of the United States, or as a member of any State legislature, or as an executive or judicial officer of any State, to support the Constitution of the United States, shall have engaged in insurrection or rebellion against the same, or given aid or comfort to the enemies thereof. But Congress may, by a vote of two-thirds of each House, remove such disability.

Section 4. The validity of the public debt of the United States, authorized by law, including debts incurred for payment of pensions and bounties for services in suppressing insurrection or rebellion, shall not be questioned. But neither the United States nor any State shall assume or pay any debt or obligation incurred in aid of insurrection or rebellion against the United States, or any claim for the loss or emancipation of any slave; but all such debts, obligations and claims shall be held illegal and void.

Section 5. The Congress shall have power to enforce, by appropriate legislation, the provisions of this article.

> Fourteenth Amendment
> *United States Constitution,*
> adopted July 9, 1868

As former Confederates and southern state legislatures tried everything they could to disenfranchise the African-American population, the final Reconstruction Amendment to the United States Constitution, the Fifteenth Amendment, was enacted. The Fifteenth Amendment prohibited the federal or any state government from using race as a determinate for voting qualification.

The true purpose of the Fifteenth Amendment had little to do with providing African Americans with the right to vote - several northern states did not provide that right. Rather, this Amendment ensured that the Republican Party won the 1868 Presidential and congressional elections. By providing African Americans the right to vote in those close elections, the Republicans could gain a decisive victory. To ensure passage of the Amendment, "the Republicans required that the states of Virginia, Mississippi and Texas ratify the amendment first, as it was an added requirement to be added for re-admission into the Union."[335]

Figure 79: States Can Not Deny a Citizen the Right to Vote

Section 1. The right of citizens of the United States to vote shall not be denied or abridged by the United States or by any State on account of race, color, or previous condition of servitude.

Section 2. The Congress shall have power to enforce this article by appropriate legislation.

Fifteenth Amendment,
United States Constitution, ratified February 3, 1870

4.4   Othello and Thomas Fraction, and the Freedmen's Bureau

With the enactment of the Reconstruction Amendments, the South's hopes for a major source of cheap labor - the former slaves - disappeared. As the South attempted to rebuild its economy, its agricultural fields remained decaying and dormant, and many of its railroad lines continued to be destroyed by the effects of war. For southern farmers and businessmen, there was little to no money in the banks for borrowing to pay for repairs to farm equipment and fields. With the constitutional amendments, former slave masters were required to now negotiate with their former slaves to work under written contracts that ensured these freed men would be paid for the work that they did.

The former southern aristocratic way of life was gone. Many young southern families, devastated by the effects of the war, simply uprooted their families and took advantage of the fertile lands in the new west. They felt that there was nothing left for them in the devastated south and formed large caravans to explore the potential opportunities of the vast western frontier. As white Americans went west, black Americans began to go north to achieve personal freedom and economic independence. For many of the descendants of the "original" free families from Virginia and North Carolina, who had lived in the South since the colonial 1600s, the decision to move north was difficult. However, these families knew that cities such as Boston or Brooklyn afforded greater opportunities to provide for their families. Many of the recently freed slaves also began the slow migration north, turning their backs on the humiliation and degradation of years of generational slavery. They went to cities in the Midwest such as Chicago and St. Louis, hoping to find opportunities where they would be paid for their long hours of work.

While many families, white and black, left their ancestral homes behind after the war, other families decided to stay where they had grown up, and tried to carve out an existence in the war's aftermath.

After leaving military service, Thomas and Othello Fraction made a difficult, heart-wrenching decision, choosing to go back home to Montgomery County, Virginia. Despite having been shot, beaten, and jailed after defending themselves against their former Master, Robert T. Preston, the former slave brothers decided to return home because their families and intended wives lived there, and that was the only home they knew. Having just left military service, the bothers were physically fit and well nourished, unlike most men in the area. Robert T. Preston needed strong men to bring his plantation back to the lush production it had in the days before the war. Shortly after their arrival in the area, Thomas and Othello were approached by several of Preston's associates and told that they were to return to work for the Preston family. The passage of the Black Codes meant the brothers could be thrown back into jail if they refused - or worse. Thomas, the more outspoken of the two, instructed Preston's men to tell their boss that he was a former Union solider who had fought for his country, and he and his brother were now free men. The only people they were going to work for were themselves.

Once Preston got word of the exchange he was furious. As one of the leading members of the county, he perceived the Fraction brothers and their family to be nothing but problems. Instead of staying on the plantation and entering into extended employment contracts as Preston had expected, the Fraction family and other former slaves refused to stay on. The third brother, William Fraction, the grandfather to Robert Murphy, and his family had already left the area and moved to the neighboring county of Botetourt.

As the son of a former Virginia Governor, the brother to a former Senator, and as a former Confederate Colonel, Robert Preston was not going to have any former slave, let alone an entire family, disrespect him in public. Thomas Fraction had to be put in his place.

Preston was well aware of the activities of the Ku Klux Klan and other anti-black terrorist groups within the county, several had even suggested that they could take care of his problem. But Preston had his own ideas as to how to take care of his problem and restore his prestige within the community - which was necessary not only due to the Fraction debacle, but also because during the war, his Confederate officers had asked Preston to resign, "charging he was ignorant of anything military."[336]

Although his military career continued, Preston always believed his judgment was being questioned. Disciplining the Fraction family might give him the chance to redeem himself. Robert Preston had to wait. He had only just submitted to President Andrew Johnson's Loyalty Oath, and was still waiting for a favorable reply. He also knew the dreaded Freedmen's Bureau Chief was watching him and his men. If Fraction, a former Union soldier of color, ever showed up dead, the federal Freedmen's Bureau would automatically accuse him and he would not have his citizenship restored. The Fraction brothers could not be killed, at least not yet.

Upon of hearing of the confrontation, members of the black community and Fraction's family warned Thomas that Preston was a vengeful man. Thomas needed to protect himself because Preston's men would come back, and when they did, Thomas and the rest of his family were in danger. The black community was well aware of the escalating hate crimes in the area and throughout the south. Everyone had heard stories of the growing problems with night raids, when groups of white thugs would target certain families and entire communities, coming in at night to intimidate residents and burn the black shanty towns. Some had even heard about people who came in various disguises and took black men away in the middle of the night - those men were found the next day in the woods or along the river, dead, another victim of the KKK's terrorism.

However, Thomas and Othello were prepared for Preston's threats. The first time he threatened them, when they were captured and jailed, the brothers had assumed Preston's threats were simply the empty ranting's of an angry slave master. They underestimated his vitriol and desire for revenge. After their capture the first time, they vowed to each other that it would not happen again. Upon returning to their barracks of the 40th United States Colored Infantry, they took their military training much more seriously. Now the Fraction brothers and the other soldiers understood that they would not only have to defend themselves on the battlefield, but also when they got home. Now, back in Montgomery County, Virginia, the brothers were well aware that they were being followed and watched by Preston's men. Other blacks in the community were well aware that Preston still held a grudge and was waiting for the right opportunity to get back at the Fractions. But the brothers felt, based on their military training that they were prepared for anything Preston would try to do to them.

Meanwhile, once Colonel Preston received word that his American citizenship had been restored by President Johnson, he no longer needed to wait for his revenge. Preston needed to demonstrate to the white community at large that he was still a powerhouse in the community, and now was the time for him to punish the Fraction brothers and anyone else who crossed him.

Preston used his influence and told the sheriff to wait until the brothers were separated from each other, then instructed the sheriff to have them both arrested and jailed for violating the Black Codes of Virginia and for attempting to him. On February 6, 1867, while Thomas was working on his house and Othello was at work, the sheriff's men, in two separate incidents, surrounded and arrested each brother.

Despite their desperate attempts to resist arrest, the Fraction brothers were beaten severely and thrown into jail.

Friends and family notified the local Freedmen's Bureau, and the case was assigned to Bureau Agent C.S. Schaeffer, out of the Christiansburg, Virginia, office. For the protection and safety of the two brothers, Agent Schaeffer sought the assistance of his supervisor, the superintendent of the Freedmen's Bureau of the 8th District of Virginia.

Agent Schaeffer discovered, after interviewing a number of witnesses who had testified that Preston's harassment of these brothers originated before the end of the war. Schaeffer explained to the Bureau's superintendent that Robert T. Preston had threatened to shoot the brothers from enlisting in military service and leaving his plantation. Thomas had responded with a letter that stated "they would not quietly submit to being fired upon, but would be prepared to defend themselves - although they never thought that Preston would ever carry out the threat." And because the Fractions doubted Preston's initial threat, they made the mistake of trying to return home while on leave from battle. However, Preston held true to his word and attacked the brothers when they arrived back on his property. He shot them at close range, but the gun jammed, so they were only severely wounded. The brothers were thrown in jail until ordered to be released by Union General Alfred Howe Terry, Department of Virginia.[337]

Once again, the federal government came to the aide and rescue of Thomas and Othello Fraction, two black men whose only crime was to stand up for their civil rights. With the help of the superintendent of the Freedmen's Bureau of the 8th District of Virginia the brothers were released from jail the second time. However, much to their displeasure, they were told that if they valued their lives, it was in their best interests to permanently leave the area. The brothers were military men, and everything they had worked and sacrificed for - their service as Colored Union Soldiers, helping to free millions of African-American men, women, and children from the bonds of slavery - had culminated in having to leave behind the only home they had ever known. This advice did not sit well with them.

Figure 80: Justice Denied to Civil War Veterans

"Since their discharge from the Army, they have been living in the vicinity of Mr. Preston's but have never ventured upon his property or molested him anyway but try to avoid meeting him as much as possible. On Wednesday the sixth while working (one building a Log House for his family, the other in the field) they were arrested by the Sheriff of this county on a Bench warrant issued by Judge Fulton, some four months since, for the offence herein stated; and brought to Christiansburg for examination before a Magistrate. The case instead of being examined at once was postponed until the following Saturday - and they are still incarcerated in the county jail. On Saturday for some trivial cause it was postponed until Wednesday of the present week - on Wednesday postponed again until Saturday; and thus for three months may again elapse without a trial, while their families are suffering and their employers deprived of their labor. I would further state that one of the principal witnesses is somewhere Richmond - another is in Salem, but neither of these has been summoned to appear at the examination before the Magistrate, although their testimony goes to prove that the brothers simply acted in self-defense. Bail has also been offered by responsible parties, for their appearance at any time, but rejected by the Magistrate who appears to be afraid to take action in this case least he might offend Colonel Preston who is a prominent man of the county and also very anxious just have the brothers convicted and sent to the penitentiary."

Ira Berlin, *Freedom, A Documentary History of Emancipation, 1861-1867 Series II, The Black Military Experience*[338]

Though this was disheartening, the Fractions knew what was happening to them was happening to black veterans all over the country. The brothers came to understand, the next time they more than likely will not be sent to jail, but to the morgue.

What Thomas and Othello did not know was exactly how devious Preston had been by sending the brothers to prison. The South's strategy for keeping blacks in their place was contingent on the prison system. Once African American men were put into prison, they were transferred to the prison gangs all across the south - chain gangs that were essentially an extension of slavery, in perpetuity. This was a twisted interpretation of the newly enacted Thirteenth Amendment, which stated that "neither slavery nor involuntary servitude, except as a punishment for crime whereof the party shall have been duly convicted" would exist in the United States. While the Ku Klux Klan was terrorizing African Americans at night, during the day, the southern political elite were devising strategies to keep the African-

American labor force under their control. The political elite understood that if they could get a man into the prison system, they could get him back into slavery - legally.

Robert Preston, by placing the Fraction brothers into the prison system, hoped to accomplish two things. Montgomery County's railroad business was booming, and the work surrounding the industry's growth was extremely labor intensive. In supplying what was essentially slave labor by imprisoning the Fractions along with other former slave men, Preston believed he had ensured an increase in the value of his railroad venture and all of its residue effects. His second objective, much more personal and devious, was ensuring that the Fraction brothers would be imprisoned in chains for the rest of their lives and subjective to the new form of legal slavery.

Othello and Thomas Fraction understood with certainty that they could not remain in Montgomery County, not if they wanted to keep their freedom. In the hopes of getting away from Preston and his thugs, Othello and Thomas and their respective families moved northwestward to Salem, Virginia, located in the neighboring county of Botetourt, where they joined their brother, William, and his family.

Thirteen years after the brothers' second arrest and subsequent departure from Montgomery Country, the Fractions finally knew that their battle with Confederate Colonel Robert T. Preston had come to an end. They had outlived Preston, who died on June 20, 1880, and was buried at the Preston cemetery at the Smithfield plantation.[339]

During the war, the Roanoke Valley depot stations served as critical transfer stations for the Confederate Army, but after the war, several towns in the valley, nestled in between the Blue Ridge and Allegheny Mountains, were about to change dramatically as a result of the growing railroad industry. One such town was Salem, Virginia, the community to which the Fractions had moved, and the rival town of Big Lick Township. Big Lick was originally named for the salt deposits created by runoff from the mountains. The community became a vital part of the national route for Americans moving westward, due in large part to the controversial issue of division and distribution of Federal land in the west.

In 1862, Congress passed the Homestead Act, which offered 160 acres of free land to any head of household. Prior to the Civil War northern states were initially opposed to passage of a Homestead Act, fearing that if the west were opened and land was given away for free, factory workers would leave their undesirable situations behind for a chance to acquire wealth out west. Southern states were also concerned that if the government supported westward expansion, plantations would be put in direct competition with smaller farmers, or worse, African Americans would escape the plantations they were forced to live on and move west to start their own farms. Following the end of the Civil War, however, the Homestead Act was widely accepted. European immigration had changed the demographics of the industrial northeast corridor of the United States, and southern farmers were disenfranchised by hard farming conditions, particularly without the help of slave labor. The intrepid American spirit of expansion had come alive again, Americans were now on the move westward for open lands and new opportunities.

By the 1870's, the American landscape was changing rapidly in the post-war economy, and small railroad villages and towns such as Big Lick Township played a major role in transforming the country. Big Lick Township was incorporated into the city of Roanoke, which raised the necessary funds to bring the Shenandoah Valley Railroad to the newly created city.[340] As the city continued to grow, it became one of the major transport stations for northern and southern homesteaders headed west. A thriving railroad hub, Roanoke County, which consisted of the two cities of Roanoke and Salem, attracted all kinds of people-northerners and southerners, white and black. With the expansion of the railroad industry and the steady stream of transients arriving on their way westward, the new cities of Roanoke and Salem prospered. Despite the general prosperity, opportunities were limited for the recently freed slaves of Roanoke and the surrounding jurisdictions. Immediately after the Civil War, the new freedmen in the area had no jobs, no housing, limited employable skills, and few prospects. They were trained, generation after generation, to till the soil, tend to the crops, or conduct other manual or domestic skills generally associated with their slave labor. The burgeoning railroad industry was unfamiliar work for many African Americans. However, by the late 1870s, African American men were able to make the transition from farm work to industrial work, and gained meaningful employment on the railroad, as well as in tanneries, the brick plant, and other new businesses in the area that supported the railroad industry.[341]

As Roanoke developed, African American men such as William, Thomas and Othello Fraction began to make their own money, which allowed them to purchase new homes for their families and reinvest in their communities, buying land on which to build schools and churches. Within a fifteen to twenty year period, the Fraction brothers as, a result of being employed by the railroad industry in Roanoke, went from abject poverty as newly freed slaves, to home ownership. By 1884, Civil War veteran Othello Fraction purchased land for $75.00, other family members purchased land and had modest homes built for their families.

While the railroad industry provided Thomas with a good income to take care of his family, and to also buy a home for them, it ultimately caused his death. Thomas Fraction worked as a brakeman, side-by-side with the conductor, in one of the most important but also most dangerous jobs on the railroads. It was the brakeman's responsibility to manually stop or slow the train at the request of the conductor. The brakeman was also responsible for one the most dangerous tasks of all - physically coupling each railcar to one another. While working for the Northwest Railroad, Thomas was critically injured when his shoulder got caught as he was coupling a railcar. He became permanently disabled and died several years later as a result of his injury.

4.5   David Melton of Northampton County

The challenges that confronted Thomas and Othello Fraction were not unique to them, nor limited to the state of Virginia, but were prevalent throughout the former Confederate states and many of the Border States. For fifty years after the end of the Civil War, southern state and local governments took specific and deliberate measures to disenfranchise African Americans and control their everyday lives. The wounds from the Civil War were raw, and America was extremely polarized. During Reconstruction, wealthy Americans were very much removed from the struggles of the lower class that was severely impacted by the war's devastating aftermath.

For many southern whites, they were thrown into poverty after the war as a result of the total collapse of the southern economy. Southern whites, in general, didn't blame the aristocracy for getting them into the war and for their current economic conditions, but they did blame the Reconstruction measures created by the Republican Party in the North for all of their problems. They also blamed the hated Freedmen's Bureau, whose goal was created to improve the economic conditions for the newly freed African slaves and the free Americans of African descent, because southern whites believed that Black men would take away jobs that were meant for them. White southerners were also concerned with people coming from the north to expand their businesses during a time of economic distress for the devastated southern lower class. In many communities all across the south, it was believed the profiteers from the north were moving south to take advantage of potential business opportunities while exploiting poor southern whites.

The Republican Party consisted of three major constituencies: the northern farmers, the business class and wage earners, and Americans of African descent. After the Civil War, it was these three constituencies from which the Republican Party hoped it would derive its major political support and power.[342] Since the Republican Party was ostensibly synonymous with Reconstruction policies, which southerners deplored, southern whites moved in droves to the Democratic Party.

Immediately after the war, as southerners moved to the Democratic Party, the militancy of racial hate groups was growing in opposition to the federal government's reconstruction measures. While the family of David Melton had persevered during the war, they were not immune to the discord between northern and southern states. They were caught between supporting the northern objectives of abolishing slavery and even the North's desire to punish the South for secession, and being surrounded by communities that were devastated by the war and the abject poverty in the South. Although the Melton family did not live in an area of North Carolina where African Americans suffered racial discrimination and disparate treatment, they were still very much concerned about white supremacists harassing African Americans throughout the south. Members of the Melton family lived on remote farms and were isolated from their neighbors. If anyone was attacked or harassed in the middle of the night, they had to fend for themselves.

In North Carolina, where the Melton family lived, one particularly noteworthy militant white supremacist group was called the Constitutional Union Guard, formed in Lenoir Township in Caldwell County. Initially, the Constitutional Union Guard consisted of former Confederate Officers whose primary goal was to steal livestock and ruin farmlands, anything to prevent black farmers from harvesting profitable crops and succeeding in the marketplace. But as the Constitutional Union Guard's membership expanded, it included town officials such as the "deputy sheriff, a lawyer, and the county chief".[343] With that kind of local political power, the group became more violent, with no fear of reproach from the law. In short order, they maimed, tortured and killed those with whom they disagreed with and extended their reach by obtaining mutual support of local counties in an effort to stymie the Reconstruction efforts of the Republican Party.

Figure 81: White Supremacy Groups on the Rise in the South

"The Constitutional Union Guard moved to dispose of a neighboring Sheriff O. R. Colgrove, a northerner who had settled in Jones County with his brother after the war. The Colgroves and a few others constituted a new white Republican establishment in this largely black county, and by virtue of their African American following held most of the local political offices. Colgrove was therefore the object of the hatred among displaced conservative whites ... A purse was raised for any man who was willing to kill Cosgrove ... and on May 28, 1869, nine or ten men of the Constitutional Union Guard murdered Cosgrove along with an African American accomplice, at which time a big barbecue was held to celebrate the event. Colgrove's brother, a State Senator, called for state troops justifying his request "We cannot tell at night who will be living in the morning."

Allen W. Trelease,
White Terror, The Ku Klux Klan,
Conspiracy and Southern Reconstruction[344]

The North Carolina Constitutional Union Guard engaged in divisive politics, as did other white supremacy groups, to the point where they aggressively and physically attacked white Republicans, any Reconstruction sympathizers, and those who supported the advancement of African Americans. Republicans and African Americans were targeted for harassment, torture and murder all across the state and elsewhere across the south. The very institutions that should have protected them, such as local sheriff offices and the court systems, had been infiltrated and corrupted by white supremacists, and offered little to no support.

Although the Constitutional Union Guard's violence reached the eastern counties near where David Melton and his extended family lived, they were not impacted as much as the African American families who lived in the central and western counties. However, the Constitutional Union Guard and similar organizations, such as the Ku Klux Klan, terrorized citizens all across the south. For the Melton family and other African American families, particularly in Northampton and Hertford Counties, where people had been similarly terrorized after the Nat Turner Southampton rebellion in 1838, the long-term effects of this white hatred were all too familiar.

Although David Melton and his African-American and tri-racial contemporaries had been challenged by their white neighbors and the toxic racial politics at the local and state levels since the early 1700s, they had never experienced white hatred of this magnitude. In 1793, the state of Virginia passed legislation for the removal of Free People of Color from the state, and created a mandatory registry for free African Americans and mulattoes, requiring all of them to register with the Clerk of Court in their county of residence and subsequently carry their "free papers" with them at all times. But now, during a time when every person was supposed to be free and equal, when so many of them had in fact arrived in America before many of the white Europeans, the rampant vitriol now directed towards all African Americans was astonishing.

When the government first used the term "mulatto" in 1705, it applied to any person who was one-eighth (or more) of African descent or one-half Native American. By 1866, one-quarter African blood made a person "colored," whereas one-quarter Native-American blood made a person Native American. While the legal definition of mulatto changed over time, if the records survived over the years, the registrations of free African Americans would commonly appear in one or two places, namely in court documents or a separate register which lists registrants by their certificate number. With these records, white supremacists were able to go out of their way to harass anyone they believed had a drop of African- or Native-American blood, which further exacerbated the fear of all persons of color within communities all across the south.

After the dismal administration of Democratic President Andrew Johnson, African Americans all across the south hoped that the newly elected Republican President Ulysses S. Grant would begin to address many of the problems and challenges that his predecessor had been either unable or unwilling to do. After the Civil War, hoping for major political changes in the south, Melton family members and many other African-American families all over the country were ardent supporters of the Republican Party - the party of Lincoln. In the eyes of African Americans, General Grant, who had brought the Civil War to a successful conclusion, was an excellent choice for President, and they hoped Grant would restore order across the south and begin to build the southern infrastructure while fulfilling some of the many ambitious objectives of the proposed Reconstruction programs.

For the most part, David Melton wanted what most other African Americans wanted and that was to seek out a basic living for himself and to take care of his family. Despite what his white neighbors and the white supremacists seemed to think, David Melton did not receive any special privileges from the Republican Party, nor the Freedmen's Bureau. He was no longer an idealistic youth petitioning the North Carolina State Legislature. He was just a family man trying to work hard and make an honest living.

As African Americans tried to rebuild their lives after the war, white supremacist groups expanded there terrorist activities in the western counties of North Carolina. While these activities were not limited to North Carolina by any stretch of the imagination, the Governor of North Carolina set the stage for what was called the Kirk-Holden War of 1870. He released the state militia against the Ku Klux Klan after they murdered a Republican State Senator, then an African-American town commissioner in a nearby county, and another African-American legislator. Elected Republican officials and candidates fled the contentious counties fearing for their lives and the safety of their families.

Tired of the intimidation, African Americans began to retaliate in large numbers. Governor William W. Holden hired a former Union Colonel to end the insurrection, bring order to the western portion of the state, and to rid the state of the Ku Klux Klan. Colonel Kirk arrested the suspected murderers - including "several county sheriffs, young attorneys, and a former Congressman".[345] More than 100 men were arrested. After the arrests, as a result of a series of overzealous policing, the men were eventually released by the Chief Justice of the North Carolina Supreme Court. Governor Holden became the first governor in the country to be impeached, and Colonel Kirk was chased out of the state and went into hiding in Tennessee.

During his impeachment proceedings, the North Carolina Governor met with President Grant in the hopes that the federal government would take some responsibility for ridding the state of the militant, violent Constitutional Union Guard and the Ku Klux Klan, but there was no federal involvement.[346] Once the Klan members were released, they were more emboldened than shamed by their experience, and their harassment and abuse only increased. As Republican elected officials, both white and African American, as well as the newly freed men all across the south, were terrorized and murdered, pressure mounted on President Grant to do something.

Between 1872 and 1876, there was an influx of white southerners into the Democratic Party. To strengthen their influence nationally and regain control economically and politically, southerners aligned themselves politically with northern Democrats, in an attempt to regain full political power in the south, and in the process, slowly and methodically disenfranchised the emerging black political power in the south.[347]

The Democratic Party in the South was shaping up to be a political party reminiscent of the time before the Civil War, focusing on the interests of the southern aristocracy, the planter society, the secessionists and those that believed that African Americans still should be slaves. During the Presidential elections of 1868, in many communities all across the South, the southern Democratic Party, supported by white supremacists, used violence to keep African Americans from voting, and thus keep Republicans from getting elected. As tensions grew in the western counties of North Carolina and across the South, the President and Congress took action to curb the violence and the abuse of the Fifteenth Amendment. On May 31, 1870, the Enforcement Act was ordained. The Enforcement Act was clear in its command to ban "the use of force, bribery, or any intimidation that interfered with the right to vote because of race," but it was also intended to ensure that people arrested for disobedience did not get off on technicalities, as was the case with the arrests in North Carolina.

Figure 82: The Enforcement Act

The Enforcement Act was enacted which banned the use of force, bribery, or any intimidation that interfered with the right to vote because of race. This prohibition affected every local and state election and applied to any officials who might refuse to receive honest votes or who might be tempted to count dishonest ones. It prohibited disguised groups from going upon the public highways or upon private property with the intent to injure or intimate citizens. Federal courts would hear cases arising under the law, and federal officials and troops could supervise elections and make arrests.

William Gillette,
Retreat from Reconstruction, 1869-1879[348]

As white supremacy groups focused more on ruining the lives of men such as David Melton, African Americans realized that in order to combat the still rebellious southern whites who wanted to keep blacks out of political process, they had to become more involved. They surmised that if the white supremacists' groups spent that much time trying to keep African Americans from voting, that was all the more reason that they needed to participate. While there are no records of any of David Melton's family running for public office at the time, descendants recall that elderly relatives and family friends would often reminisce about how the Melton family supported early Republican African-American candidates for local elected positions.

In local communities where African Americans were in the majority population, African American candidates were elected, and most of the elected officials were Republicans. Despite acts of terrorism and violence designed to keep them powerless, African-American candidates were elected to office at the local and state levels - and much to the chagrin of many southern white Democrats, African Americans were also elected to national offices. As African Americans began to turn out the vote and elect their candidates in record numbers, white Democrats were openly hostile, which resulted in numerous violations and charges filed under the Enforcement Act of 1870. In just seven years, there were more than 3,320 Enforcement Act criminal charges brought in the southern states.

Figure 83: Enforcement Act Criminal Charges in Southern States 1870-1877

States	1870	1871	1872	1873	1874	1875	1876	1877	Total
Mississippi	n/a	n/a	490	268	120	187	4	6	1,075
N. Carolina	n/a	65	3	303	181	2	3	2	559
S. Carolina	n/a	112	96	554	555	9	1	58	1,385
Alabama	n/a	n/a	12	3	2	12	74	31	134
Florida	n/a	4	n/a	7	17	1	5	7	41
Virginia	n/a	8	n/a	4	2	2	3	n/a	19
Georgia	n/a	n/a	n/a	7	7	4	14	25	57
Louisiana	n/a	1	n/a	1	n/a	n/a	n/a	2	4
Texas	n/a	n/a	n/a	2	6	3	4	2	17
Arkansas	16	n/a	n/a	n/a	n/a	1	n/a	n/a	19

William Gillette,
Retreat from Reconstruction, 1869-1879[349]

As time wore on, the African-American community felt that the Republican Party was taking them for granted, and the politicians were not doing enough to promote African-American causes or eradicate the racism promoted by the Democratic Party. Even though African American candidates were elected to regional positions, they were elected posts with little to no influence on a broad scale. Despite their frustration, the African-American electorate was staunchly Republican, and felt that it was a political party that would have more of their interests at heart than the southern "Dixiecrats." Once their political power was restored and national allegiances solidified, southern white Democrats began to take steps to solidify their power locally, and to limit the political influence of the black voter.

Republican Representative Henry Cabot Lodge of Massachusetts introduced a bill referred to as the "Force Bill" in 1890, designed to protect the relatively newly acquired voting rights of the black voter. With the introduction of the bill, rich southerners convinced poor whites that it was in their political interests to oppose the bill because of the threat that black men would abuse any political power they gained, telling them that it was in their best interest to actively oppose the bill and any legislation that would give political power to the freedmen. The lower class southern whites were convinced that the large numbers of freedmen would align themselves with the large number of free black's families such as the Melton's and form political allegiances that would unseat candidates favorable to the white community.[350] The Force Bill did not pass, and its failure began a litany of actions meant to restrict the rights of the southern black voter. From 1890 to 1908, the white electorate across the south used specific tactics to eliminate all political and economic gains made by the freedmen.

After the Civil War and Reconstruction, the United States Supreme Court set the stage for the establishment of the Jim Crow laws, based on several of its decisions, including the Court's landmark decision in the case of *Plessey v. Ferguson,* which affirmed the doctrine of "separate but equal" - which was tantamount to saying a steak dinner was the same as a dinner of filet of rat. The Jim Crow laws essentially made the segregation of the races legal. The laws ensured that the black population would be racially segregated. It limited their access to educational opportunities and prevented employment opportunities for a large portion of the population. The Jim Crow laws made it legal to have separate water fountains for whites and blacks. It was legal to have signs posted outside of rest room facilities, reading "Whites Only" or "Blacks Only." Of course, the "Whites Only" restroom was cleaned every day, while the bathroom labeled "Blacks Only" were cleaned, at best, every other day but more often once a week.

During the late nineteenth and early twentieth century, these laws helped to instigate a large migration of southern blacks to northern, urban cities such as Boston, Chicago, Philadelphia, New York and Washington, D.C. - where there were jobs, improved housing, and the chance for their children to be educated. Members of the Cornwell Murphy family were some of the earliest of African-American migrants to move north.

4.6   Post-Civil War Industrial Changes, and the Cornwells

In the aftermath of the Civil War, the communities of Roanoke and Salem, Virginia, were not the only communities that changed dramatically. All across America, cities and towns were changing in the midst of a post-war economy. Although it started almost a century prior, the industrial revolution in the United States was just beginning. As with most wars, it was difficult for Civil War veterans to return home and seamlessly integrate themselves back into their communities. It was also hard for returning veterans to take advantage of the post-war time economy.

In the few short years immediately after the war, the United States was predominantly an agricultural nation. However, by 1870, only five short years after the end of the Civil War, the United States post-wartime economy presented tremendous opportunities for millions of Americans, thanks to the country's vast natural resources, federal government support, and the continued growth of its cities.

The discovery of iron ore in 1887 led to the massive production of steel, the metal used for building the railroads. The railroad barons needed thousands of miles of track crisscrossing the nation and they became the largest customers of the steel industry. But in short order, other uses were found for steel that dramatically improved the conditions of everyday Americans, particularly in the northern industrial centers. These improvements included the construction of the Brooklyn Bridge in 1883. The post-war economy was also a period of technological innovation. In 1880, Thomas Edison patented a system for producing and distributing electrical power. By 1890, electric power ran a number of machines that dramatically and rapidly improved industrial production.

The quality of everyday life was improving across the United States, and Americans were tired of the dirty and muddy streets that they grew up with and had to endure. They were tired of streets lined with potholes and horse manure, and all of the flies, rats and other vermin roaming the dirtier areas. Americans wanted paved roads and sidewalks. They wanted to harness the capacity for extended daylight hours, and they wanted the ability to put kerosene in lanterns to light their homes at night. Americans wanted convenient facilities when they went to the bathroom. The push was on to improve the technological, social, economic and cultural conditions of mid-nineteenth century America.

William Cornwell's parents, Flushing and Harriet, lived in the mostly rural town of Bridgewater, Massachusetts, and at this point most of their children were grown and had families of their own. Their children and their families -- including war veteran William, his wife Martha and their two, children Benjamin and Mary -- moved to the adjoining town of North Bridgewater. As North Bridgewater rapidly urbanized after the war, it became a totally different community than the much more rural southern part of the town. In 1874, the town of Bridgewater split and the northern portion incorporated into the City of Brockton, Massachusetts.

While the long-term effects of Posttraumatic Stress Disorder (PTSD), sometimes then called "Soldiers Heart," continued to challenge William after the war, the other sons of Flushing and Harriet Cornwell were active participants in the newly incorporated City of Brockton. They were part of the economic fabric that helped change and build the new community.

In 1878, William's brothers, Charles, Philip and Samuel, established one of the largest construction firms in the area. As highlighted in the 1886 Brockton City Directory, the entrepreneurial Cornwell brothers were expert concreters and asphalt pavers.[351] Having had 11 years of successful experience in the manufacturing and laying of concrete, they stated that they made every effort to procure the best material to make first class, durable work (see advertisement). They emphasized the use of the "Trinidad" asphalt pavement, which dried quickly and could be used as soon as it was laid. According to their ad, the type of pavement that they used had been used in the fashionable city of Paris, France, for more than thirty years, and was also used in Boston, Massachusetts, on Commonwealth Avenue and in the historic Court Square of downtown Boston. The Cornwell brothers' growing city of Brockton was becoming a model city nationwide and laid claim to several national and global "firsts."

On October 1, 1883, Brockton became the first place in the world to have a three-wire underground electrical system when Thomas Edison threw a switch to activate it. Brockton claims to be the home of the world's first theater to be tied into the three-wire electrical system when the City Theater opened its door on October 24, 1894. The city of Brockton took another place in history by opening the first electrically operated fire station in the United States on December 30, 1884. Aside from electricity, another notable first was that Santa Claus, the national mainstay of most department stores during the Christmas season worldwide, first appeared in Brockton in December 1890, when James Edgar, the owner of Edgar's Department Store on Main Street, suited up for role for the very first time.[352]

Brockton, often cited as a model city, was becoming an example of how to leverage a community's financial resources with economic development for its residents and its businesses. As prominent businessmen and contractors in the city, the Cornwell brothers installed the city's first asphalt roads. As the streets were being constructed for improved city services and infrastructure, the Cornwell brothers had the unique opportunity to meet and work with some of the eras greatest tycoons, including the great inventor Thomas Edison. They were part of Edison's team that developed the conduits for the underground electrical system, and they reconstructed the roads and paved them to new community standards.

After Philip Cornwell had the opportunity to work with Thomas Edison, he was inspired and reportedly was encouraged by Edison to pursue his passion for developing new technologies. He submitted two scientific patents designed to save energy and money by regulating the heat from coal burning stoves, steam boilers and hot air, water and steam furnaces, while shifting the ashes from the coals. For the next several years, while Phillip waited to see if he would ever receive his patent, the Cornwell family expanded. As each of Flushing and Harriet's sons married, the racial lineage of the family changed once again, much like it did for the Cornell family with the birth of the mixed race baby boy, Flushing Cornwell.

With the marriage of Flushing and Harriet's son, William, to African-American Martha Hill, their children and lineal family continued to be Americans of African descent. William's brother, Hanford, married Native-American Mary Peters from Massachusetts' Martha's Vineyard on September 20, 1885. The Peters family was an original Native-American family from the Martha's Vineyard's island town of Aquinnah, Massachusetts, also known as the town of Gay Head. Mary Peters was a full-blooded Native American from the Massachusetts Wampanoag tribe of the Algonquian nation.

The Peters family, even to this day, is one of the oldest and largest Native-American families in Massachusetts. The family owned most of the land in southeast Massachusetts, including the historic and scenic properties of Cape Cod, New Bedford and Fall River, as well as large portions of land on the islands of Nantucket and Martha's Vineyard.

Flushing Cornwell was ill for a period of time, and in the fall of 1888 he passed away. As devastating as the news of Flushing's death was, shortly after his passing, it became a bittersweet period for the family. Harriet was so proud to hear the news that her son, Philip Cornwell, a businessman and inventor, had his patent approved and registered

(#390,284) with the United States Patent Office, in Washington, D.C. on October 21, 1888. Phillip's patent was for the Draft Regulator, which was a "Safety Gas, Heat Controller and Draught, which was used for steam boilers, hot air and steam furnaces."[353]

At the time, portable gas stoves and heaters could easily be turned over, which often resulted in fires. Philip's design and invention saved countless lives and property, and was advertised in the local newspaper, the *Brockton Enterprise*. After the huge success of his first patent, Philip modified his invention and filed a second patent (#491,082) on February 7, 1893. One hundred years later, Philip Cornwell was posthumously recognized as one of the top 100 African-American inventors by the Association for the Study of African-American Life and History, in conjunction with the Association for the Study of Negro Life and History.[354]

On April 11, 1891, Philip's nephew, Benjamin Cornwell, married Cora Jackson, daughter of Aaron and Keziah (Gardiner) Jackson of Huntington, New York.[355] The marriage of Benjamin and Cora brought together the families of two Civil War Veterans - Sergeant William Cornwell and Corporal Aaron Jackson. The men reminisced about the war and their own personal conquests and struggles. They shared their thoughts on the treatment of the newly freed southern African Americans, the reconstruction of the South's economy, and the day-to-day struggles of being African American in the North. Each had his own story and each had their own unique perspective. The two war veterans had much to talk about.

Given the time period, each man was unique, being Free Men of Color before the war and coming from small towns in the northeast states of Massachusetts and New York. They had risked their lives while in the service of their country and had contributed to the freedom of millions of slaves nationwide. They shared a bond that few men dared to share, having survived the battlefield with the knowledge that one wrong move and anyone of them could have been captured by the enemy Confederate army and sold into the shackles of slavery, or worse, tortured and mutilated beyond recognition, if not killed outright.

Aaron Jackson and William Cornwell had the unique and distinguished opportunity of being non-commissioned officers who led their men successfully into battle and participated in some of the more important battles of the war. As non-commissioned officers, they observed firsthand the tactics of the white commissioned officers up and down the chain of command. Aaron and William learned strategic and tactical commands, and how to translate those commands to their men.

While on the battlefield, they experienced many things, including the racism of the white officers and soldiers. They also saw the strength and fragility of men on the battlefield. For the most part, their officers were magnanimous - they didn't have much choice, as they had to depend on the unity and support of their African-American troops to win battles and protect their lives. One of the most profound moments in Aaron Jackson's life was the experience he had as a soldier who happened to be black, and as a black man who helped to liberate the emancipated slaves in South Carolina - the state that led the secessionist movement. He would never forget the pride that he felt in seeing their faces and hearing their joyous voices as hundreds of slaves entered Charleston, South Carolina, to learn for the first time that they were free men and women.

When the families got together, the two men reminisced repeatedly of the reasons they went into war, the scenes on the battlefield and the horrors that they witnessed that were perpetrated against the former slaves as they marched south in battle. They did not want their children or grandchildren to forget the atrocities of slavery or the lives that it took. However, because Aaron's wife, Keziah, was a former servant girl in New York, he also recognized the struggles of the poverty-stricken European immigrants, as their conditions in tenement neighborhoods were not much different from some of the African-American neighborhoods in New York City or on Long Island. He saw very little difference in the treatment of the South's African American slaves and the treatment of New York's poor whites that were herded into the gritty tenement neighborhoods to work in the dangerous garment factories in the Bowery for what was tantamount to slave wages. Remembering the stories of the terrifying New York City Draft Riots, Aaron realized that the institution of slavery and servitude was an institution of the wealthy to force the poor to work for no or limited wages, regardless of their skin color.

William, who was three generations removed from the institution of slavery and lived in a more homogenized community, was much more offended by the institution of slavery and how terribly people were treated for no reasons other than the color of their skin. Although he did not go as far south as Aaron while in the service, what he saw during his military tour was that despite a similarity in living conditions, slavery was designed to protect the white southern aristocracy, and was a racial issue much more than it was a class issue. Poor whites suffered much, but People of Color suffered much more, in William's opinion. While in battle, William, much like Aaron, was surrounded by men who escaped from slavery and who wanted to fight against the institution and end it once and for all. William heard the soldiers' stories of how they were treated before the war, and could not understand how the three Reconstruction Amendments, each designed to protect the newly freed African-American men and women, could be so twisted and ignored that People of Color were being treated no differently now than they were before the war.

Having grown up in Bridgewater, Massachusetts' predominantly white community and having fought for his country and to end slavery, William was not uncomfortable sharing his strong views that more African Americans needed to speak up. He began to realize that emancipation was no guarantee of freedom, equality and respect, and believed strongly, as his mentor Frederick Douglass had done twenty-five or more years earlier, that African Americans needed to speak loudly and often.

With the complications of his war wounds and the ever-growing bitterness over the acceptance of slave-like conditions in the South, William sunk deeper and deeper into his "Soldiers Heart," and disagreed bitterly with most people he came into contact with over his political viewpoints. As his bitterness grew, so did his distance from his family. He could not understand why members of his own family weren't more vocal in their beliefs and anger over the adverse treatment of Americans of African descent and the growing prominence of racist white supremacist groups such as the Ku Klux Klan. William's brothers could not understand what it was like to have served on the bloodstained battlefields. They tried to be sensitive of their brother's horrific experiences and strong political views, but they found it difficult to understand William's passion, his bitterness and his vitriol regarding race relations. Although they understood the struggles of being African American in a tumultuous country, in order to also be sensitive to their wives, who were European and Native American, and their multi-racial children, they thought it best to distance themselves from the agitated brother.

William was an abolitionist to his core, and was very progressive in his political views on race relations. He was perhaps too early a pioneer on issues relating to the civil rights of African Americans, at least for his family. Although William's daughter, Mary Cornwell Yancy, continued to stay in touch with her father, her brother, Benjamin, and his wife, Cora (Jackson) Cornwell, who lived in the same closely-knit community, saw less and less of his father. As William aged, the pain from his injuries was more acute, his posttraumatic stress only worsened, and he grew more bitter and angry and ultimately became estranged from his entire family. In 1926, William died at the United States National Homes for Disabled Volunteer Soldiers.

In 1891, Benjamin and Cora had a son, Benjamin Cornwell, Jr. However, shortly after the child was born, Cora was stricken with the early stages of consumption (commonly known today as tuberculosis). Cora eventually became gravely ill and needed assistance with the raising of her son. Her younger sister Grace came from Huntington, New York, to care for her ailing sister and her son. Grace was a logical choice to tend to her sister, as she knew all about the care of ailing family members. She was the long-term caregiver for her mother, Keziah (Gardiner) Jackson, caring for her until she died in 1889. Although under the dutiful care of her sister, Grace, in 1900, Cora Cornwell, as so many other Americans at the time, died from the complications of her "consumption."

William's brother, Samuel Cornwell, was the last of Flushing and Harriet Cornwell's children to pass away, in July, 1953.[356] His obituary in the local newspaper, the *Brockton Enterprise* was slightly exaggerated and referred to him as the inventor of the heat draught regulator, though it was his brother Philip who actually invented it. However, Sam was certainly a colorful character. As the last child of Flushing and Harriet (Brooker) Cornwell, Sam Cornwell's life reflected the changing times and was indeed marked by great triumph and diversity. While he glorified the truth about being a descendant of Lord Cornwallis of England and a Native-American princess, his ancestry was indeed rich and colorful, reflecting the true spirit of being an American.

Three of his great-grandfathers fought in the Great War that brought independence to the United States of America, two of whom were men of African descent who served bravely and with distinction. He witnessed his older brother William going off to serve in the Civil War, at tremendous risk of being captured and sold into slavery, only to be scarred physically and emotionally by the most horrific war fought on American soil. His beloved wife, Ione Auten Cornwell, was struck and killed by a bolt of lightning only days after their last child was born. Samuel Cornwell had witnessed North Bridgewater transform itself from a rural town comprised of small farms and cow pastures, into the thriving commercial City of Brockton, Massachusetts.

4.7   John Chavis, Granville County's Preacher and Educator

In the immediate aftermath of the Civil War, all across the south, the original African Americans who were Free People of Color became, for the most part, leaders within the African American community. Many knew how to read and write, had some business management skills prior to the war and emancipation, and because of the extensive Free People of Color network, had experiences and exposure outside of the limited and constrained plantation society. Many of them understood the fundamentals of the Bible and were suited to be the pastoral leaders for many of the freedmen within their communities.

While many provided spiritual leadership, these pastors also provided academic leadership by teaching the newly freedmen on how to read and write. During Reconstruction, in most communities, religion and education were seen by most as the only vehicle of helping the black man go from slavery to freedom successfully. During that period, many of the original Free People of Color were the local conduits between the community and the northern churches that came south to establish freedmen's schools at the primary and secondary levels.

In practically every village and hamlet in the South, the African-American church became the institution of self-sufficiency for the freedmen; and the black preacher was the vehicle for social, educational and political advancement. Prior to the Civil War, there were few stories of a black preacher able to advance the conditions of members of the African-American community in which he lived, but one such preacher was John Chavis of Granville County, North Carolina.

John Chavis was born in 1763 in Granville, North Carolina. He was, by all accounts, an educated man. According to an interview with his biographer, Helen Chavis Othow, John Chavis taught white and black children, and was also a Presbyterian preacher and an American patriot.[357] During his early years, he served as a private in the Continental Army in the American Revolutionary War, as did many African-American men in Granville County's, 5th Virginia Regiment.[358] Immediately after the war, he was listed on the Mecklenburg, Virginia's tax list as a Free Person of Color.

According to Helen Chavis Othow, the mysterious circumstances surrounding John Chavis' death had been a topic of speculation over the years. Many hypothesize that his death was not from natural causes.[359] After the 1831 Nat Turner rebellion in Southampton, Virginia, white southerners argued that only an educated man could have plotted such a horrific rebellion, and began to move forward in strictly curtailing the activities of all Free People of Color across the South. As southern states moved forward with specific laws to block literacy for all free blacks and slaves, the activities of John Chavis were halted. He was informed that he could no longer teach his African-American students, free or slave, how to read or write, nor could he preach at the pulpit, nor could he meet with more than three other African-American men at any one given time, for each offense was punishable by law with a severe fine or imprisonment.

For seven years after being forced to stop preaching and teaching, Reverend John Chavis found ways to continue with his ministry and teachings. One such man who benefited from the teachings was John Howell, the son of Granville County's Freeman Howell and the father to Christopher Howell. John Howell's wife Jane Harris Howell was a second cousin to John Chavis and a third cousin to John Howell. As with so many other preachers throughout the south in the early 1800s, the gospel was important in keeping the communities together and uplifting spirits at a time when many had little else. Preachers had to provide pastoral counsel to support the need for self-sufficiency. In the 1830s, Reverend Chavis and his preaching were at the center of all black activities within Granville County. Chavis' monthly sermons had to be kept secret because of the imminent danger that he was in, but they served as the basis for social gatherings, holidays and special occasions.

As a former Revolutionary War hero, John Chavis may have felt that he was indispensable and that as a preacher no harm would come to him. Based on oral history and early 1931 publications, each time he taught or preached, the Reverend risked his life. In her book, *John Chavis, African American Patriot, Preacher, Teacher and Mentor* (1763 – 1838) and in an interview with her, John Chavis' biographer, Helen Chavis Othow, shared that John Chavis may have been beaten to death in his home by whites in the surrounding area who found out that he was teaching and preaching to the Granville County's African-American free and slave communities.

Some thirty to forty years after his pastoral work, the Reverend John Chavis' life work has been credited in helping the African-American community of Granville County, North Carolina, and Mecklenburg County, Virginia, transition through the two county's last days in the antebellum period, through the turbulence of the Civil War to the beginnings of the South's Jim Crow period.

4.8 Christopher Howell of Granville County, North Carolina

During the early 1880s there perhaps was no other community like Granville, North Carolina. This county had many different African-American families that were Free People of Color, descended from the original Angolans that arrived in Jamestown in 1619. While Granville County certainly had enslaved African Americans who worked on the vast tobacco farms, the county was rich with men and women who reflected more than 250 years of rich Afro-Euro-Native-American blended cultures. Granville County was unique because during the antebellum period, for the most part, African-American men and women were able to conduct their daily lives as free people. Based on state and county records that go back to the original formation of the county, African Americans owned substantial tracts of land from the very beginning of Granville's creation.

The county was formed in 1746 from Edgecombe County, and was named after the Second Earl Granville, John Carteret, who was the secretary of state to King George II of England. Earl Granville, heir to one of the eight original Lords Proprietors of the Province of Carolina, supplied land grants, and provided one to an African American, Gibrea Chavis, an ancestor of the Reverend John Chavis. The grant was for several thousand acres of land in Granville County.[360] Gibrea Chavis was also the 5th generation great-granduncle of Marie Howell Cornwell of Brockton, Massachusetts.

Marie Howell Cornwell's 5th generation great-granduncle, William Chavis, "owned thousands of acres of land in Granville County, which he inherited from his father, Bartholomew Chavis." According to the family's deed "the Earl of Granville granted him all of the land from Collins Creek and Tar River to the County line."[361]

Granville County, North Carolina, where Gibrea and William Chavis and other free African Americans received original land grants, was a community similar to many others throughout the early 1700s in south, where large numbers of free Americans of African descent migrated to as they left Virginia. They were descended from the early Angolans, and married each other, with Native Americans from the Saponi and other Siouan-speaking tribes of the area, and with European Americans. They developed and built sustainable frontier communities such as Fishing Creek and Oxford townships, and developed defenses to protect them against hostile forces.

As Granville County developed, its residents became more protective of their rural and agricultural community, fostering a strong sense of self-preservation. In remote communities across the thirteen colonies, European colonists formed local militia to defend and protect the public. During the Revolutionary War, the descendants of the original Jamestown Angolan families, the Chavis, Games, Gowen, Harris, Hatcher, Howell, Hunt, Jones, Pettiford and Simms families participated in the Continental Army with the North Carolina military units, as part of the 1778 Granville County militia.

Another of Marie Howell Cornwell's ancestors who resided in early Granville County was Freeman Howell. The Howell family descended from Elizabeth Owell, who was first found in colonial Virginia in York County in 1695, and is presumed to be a white indentured English woman. Much like the Chavis family, Elizabeth Owell's children, including her daughter Peggy Owell and her progeny, descended from the Angolans who came to America in 1619. Peggy Owell was taxable in Charlotte County on 2 free male tithes and a horse in 1793. Unable to pay her tax, on June 3, 1793, the Charlotte County court bound Peggy Owell's mulatto children Freeman, John, and Peggy Howell to William Flood. The court also ordered the church wardens to bind out Peggy Owell's grandsons Peter Toney and Edmund Booker, the children of her daughter Peggy Howell.

The following year in 1794, the grandsons of Peggy Owell and the sons of Peggy Howell both Free Children of Color were kidnapped and presumably sold into slavery.[362]

Freeman Howell, the 2nd generation great-grandfather to Marie Howell Cornwell, was born around 1780 in Charlotte County, Virginia, where, according to county records, he was taxable from 1794 to 1797. Several years later, according to the Mecklenburg County Tax Records in Virginia, he was taxable there from 1806 to 1820. In 1820, in Mecklenburg County, he was listed as the head of a household of eight Free Persons of Color.[363] Next door to Freeman lived his father, Matthew Howell, who was also listed on the 1820 Census as a head of a household of thirteen Free Persons of Color.[364]

Figure 84: Stolen at Night and Sold into Slavery

Peggy Howell, a "free mulatto of Charlotte County" on 16 July 1794 reported in the *Virginia Gazette and General Advertiser* that two of her children Peter Toney and Edmund Booker, both about four to five years old, had been kidnapped on June 20, 1794.

On 26 July 1794 the court examined Thomas Stewart of Person County, North Carolina, on the charge of stealing the children Peter Toney and Edmund Booker on the night of 20 June 1794. James Moore testified that he apprehended Thomas Stewart in Halifax County, Virginia, and that Stewart confessed that he and James Stewart went at night by horse to the house where the children lived and purchased them outside the house from a man named John Ravens with the intention of selling them.

Stewart was sent for further trial at the district court in Prince Edward County.

Paul Heinegg
*Free African Americans of
North Carolina, Virginia and South Carolina
from the Colonial Period to About 1820,*[365]

Freeman passed away in 1869, and died without a will. His property and real estate went into Probate Court, and was distributed by the Probate Judge on November 19, 1870 to his children and grandchildren. Freeman was predeceased by his son, John Howell.

John Howell[366] was born in 1801 and married Jane Harris in 1830,[367] in Tar River Township of Granville County, North Carolina. John's wife, Jane Harris Howell, was the great-granddaughter of William Chavis and Frances Gibson, both descended from other historic families who trace their ancestry to the original Angolans who arrived in colonial Jamestown, Virginia in 1619. William Chavis descended from Elizabeth Chavis, who was born around 1645. Elizabeth Chavis, on March 28, 1672, petitioned the General Court of Virginia to release her son Gibson (first name and last name are the same) from an unlawful indenture,[368] thereby making her the ancestor to both William Chavis and his wife, Frances Gibson, his fifth cousin.

John Howell and his wife, Jane Harris, had a large family and each of their children was listed on their grandfather Freeman Howell's probated will, which included his grandson Christopher Howell. John and Jane's children were dark in complexion and they needed to make sure that there was no confusion as to their Free People of Color status, so they gave each child a patriotic name to distinguish them in the event they were ever stopped and challenged on their free or slave status.

The patriotic John and Jane, in keeping with American history, named their darker skinned daughters Missouri and Indiana after newly formed American states - Missouri became a state in 1821 and Illinois in 1818 - and they named their son Christopher Columbus Howell after the explorer.[369]

Their son Christopher married Harriet Gowen, also of Fishing Creek Township, North Carolina, in 1875.[370] Harriet Gowen was the granddaughter of Edward Gowen and his wife, Rebecca Anderson, and she was the 6th generation granddaughter of John Gowen, who originally came from Angola and was brought to Jamestown in 1619. With the marriage of Christopher and Harriet, were now six distinct African-American families - the Anderson, Bass, Chavis, Gowen, Harris and Howell families - directly descending from the original historic Angolans brought to colonial Virginia in 1619.

Flushing Cornwell, son
of Mansfield and Hannah
Cornwell, and his wife,
Harriet Brooker, daughter
of Samuel Brooker and his
wife, Philinda Russell,
in Bridgewater,
Massachusetts, circa 1870

Flushing Cornwall's
Funeral Card circa 1888

Flushing Cornwall's Green
Card stating that he was
a British citizen because
he was born in Canada, a
British territory at the time.

Philip Cornwell, son of
Flushing and Harriet
Cornwell, in Brockton,
Massachusetts, circa 1890.

Brockton City Directory's
1898 advertisement of, Phillip
Cornwell's Patented Scientific
Invention old fashion "pot-
belly stove damper".

Hanford Cornwell (above), son of Flushing and Harriet Cornwell, in Brockton, Massachusetts, circa 1990.

Hanford Cornwell's family: wife Mary Peters, a Native American from the Massachusetts' Wampanoag tribe (center left), daughter Coral Cornwall (center), son Forrest Cornwall (far right) and an unidentified man far left.

Samuel Cornwell (left), son of Flushing and Harriet Cornwell and member of the City of Brockton, Massachusetts, Free Masons, circa 1900 (picture courtesy private collection-Connie Curts).

Brockton City Directory advertisement for the Cornwell
Brothers Concreters, circa 1886.

Christopher Howell, son of John Howell and Jane Harris, Oxford, North Carolina, circa 1915.

William Howell, son of Christopher and Harriet (Gowen) Howell, in Brockton Massachusetts, circa 1915.

William Howell and his wife, Matilda Watson, daughters Marie (Cornwall) and Lois; son William Jr. not yet born, in Brockton, Massachusetts, circa 1918.

Marie Howell Cornwall, daughter of William Howell and Matilda Watson, Brockton, Massachusetts, circa 1940.

Railroad Station, Boydton, Virginia, family home of Matilda Watson, circa 1915.

Lincoln Congregational Church, Brockton, Massachusetts, circa 1922. Matilda Watson Howell (first row left) seated in black dress, white hat.

Abner Melton, son of David Melton and Jane Adkins, and his wife, Sally Ballard, daughter of Edward Ballard and May Parks, in Ahoskie, North Carolina, circa 1904.

Margaret Melton Murphy, daughter Abner Melton and Sally Ballard, Boston, Massachusetts, circa 1925.

Julia Utley, daughter of Henry and Elizabeth (Murphy) Utley, in Norfolk, Virginia, circa 1905

Walter Fraction son of James and Julia (Utley) Fraction) and his wife Opal in St. Paul, Minnesota, circa 1950.

Elizabeth Fraction, daughter of James and Julia (Utley) Fraction, in Boston, Massachusetts, circa 1940

Viola Fraction, daughter of James and Julia (Utley) Fraction, in Boston, Massachusetts, circa 1930.

Robert Murphy, son of Viola Fraction in Boston, Massachusetts, circa 1925.

Robert Murphy and his wife Margaret Melton, in Boston, Massachusetts, circa 1965.

City of Brockton Massachusetts YMCA Young Men's Basketball Team, Harold Cornwall far left, second row, circa 1921.

Harold Cornwall and his wife, Marie Howell, in Brockton, Massachusetts, circa 1945.

Jack Cornwell, son of Harold and Marie (Howell) Cornwell, Private, Korean War, circa 1950 (courtesy private

Harold Cornwall, son of Benjamin Cornwall and Grace Jackson, in Brockton, Massachusetts, circa 1950.

December 1940 NAACP Crisis Magazine Cover article highlighting acts of racism in United States Air Force by showing U.S. Army training airplane in flight over Randolph Field, Texas, with the caption "FOR WHITES ONLY."

Lieutenant Colonel Leo Gray Jr, son of Leo W. Gray and Ralphia Mitchell, was a World War II Tuskegee Airman. He joined the 100th Fighter Squadron of the 332nd Fighter Group, and became known one of the Red Tail Pilots (picture courtesy of Avstop.com, Alan Murphy)

Admiral Lawrence Chambers. While Captain of USS Midway, directed the rescue of over 3,000 Americans and South Vietnamese during the fall of Saigon, circa 1975, (courtesy of the United States Archives).

USS Midway, aircraft carrier commanded by Captain Chambers during 1975 evacuation of Saigon.

Part 5: International Wars and Internal Conflicts

5.1   James and Julia Fraction of Roanoke, Virginia - Where Railroads Unite the States

According to the 1870 United States' Census, William Fraction, brother to Othello and Thomas, moved his family to the community then known as Big Lick Township, nestled in the foothills of the Virginia Blue Hill Mountains. William and his wife, Jane Lampkin, moved to a segregated community of former slaves and free People of Color. Their son, James Fraction, provided a wealth of information about his life in an application for his World War I military pension, filed in October 1918.[371] It also documented the lives of his immediate and extended family in Big Lick Township. In his sworn deposition, James stated that as a child, he lived at home with his widowed mother, Jane Lampkin Fraction, and with his sister and two brothers. James also indicated that he lived in the same household as his grandmother, Lucy Rucker Lampkin, and his mother's brothers, Alexander Rucker and Stephen Lampkin.[372]

The community of Big Lick Township, where James grew up, was later renamed Roanoke, Virginia. Roanoke became the crossroads for many Americans and European immigrants on their journey going west, inspired by the chance at free land and other opportunities. By the mid-1870s, the railroads were taking people westward in large numbers and at rapid speeds, a significant change from going west in slow wagon convoys. Having grown up in Roanoke, James Fraction knew all about the railroad industry, the trains that traveled on the tracks, and where each train would take its cargo and passengers. James often wondered what it would be like to be one of those passengers, and travel west.

Prior to the wide-scale use of rail passenger services, in the early to mid-1800s, the steamboat was the primary method for traveling north and south on the east coast. Maryland and Virginia were separated by the shelter of the Chesapeake Bay, which was also "pierced by long deep rivers reaching almost 100 miles inland from the bay."[373] James Fraction's first known job was as a porter with the Baltimore Steam

Packet Company, an overnight steamboat service that operated from 1840 to 1962, providing efficient luxury service on the Chesapeake Bay from the port city of Baltimore, Maryland, to the port city of Norfolk, Virginia, and various seaports in between. The steamship company, also known as the Old Bay Line, was famous for its high-end service, and the "magical blending of the best in the North and the South, made possible by the Company's unique role in bridging the two sections. The North contributed its tradition of mechanical proficiency, making the ships so reliable, while the South contributed its gracious ease."[374]

For a young African-American man in the 1880s, the opportunity to work any of the steamboats was a very good chance to have, especially because it allowed these young men to meet a variety of people. One such individual whom James met was Miss Julia Utley, whose family had recently relocated to Norfolk, Virginia, from Fayetteville, North Carolina. The first known member of Julia's family was Henry Utley and his wife, Elizabeth Murphy, from the Fayetteville community of Cross Creek in Cumberland County, North Carolina. James W. Fraction and Julia B. Utley married on October 7, 1891.

In an effort to leave the racial tension caused by the segregationist Jim Crow laws, James and Julia Fraction decided to move to the more tranquil and progressive St. Paul, Minnesota. Both of them had noticed that many African Americans were leaving the South and moving north and west. Then, Julia decided that she wanted to be near her brother William and his family in St. Paul, a move that made perfect sense. [375]

James' and Julia's decision to migrate was, in part, assisted by the fact that the transportation industry was gradually unionizing, and southern state legislators were enacting laws that kept men of African descent from working better, higher-paying jobs. This was particularly true in the railroad industry, but had also affected the steamboat industry. However, once in St. Paul, James was able to get a position as a cook on the private car of railroad icon William T. Tyler, the First Superintendent of the Eastern Division of the Great Northern Railroad.[376]

In the fall of 1893, James Fraction was hired as one of the first employees in a new division of the famous Great Northern Railway, headquartered in Breckenridge, Minnesota. According to the Great

Northern Railway Historical Society, this railroad "was created in September 1889 from several predecessor railroads in Minnesota, on a system 8,316 miles in length, with trains carrying freight, passengers, mail and express in the area between the Chicago rail yards, the Great Lakes and the Pacific Ocean."[377] The Breckenridge Division was considered one of the company's most important and profitable divisions.

In a pension application deposition written for Fraction, William T. Tyler, the Senior Assistant Director and Division Operator of the U.S. Railroad Administration, stated that "while he was the Breckenridge Superintendent, James Fraction was employed in his service as his private cook."[378] As the railroad consolidated the various railroads that had preceded it, Tyler moved to Havre, Montana, as Superintendent of the Montana Division, and took the Fraction family with him - including James' infant daughters, Viola Geneva and Elizabeth.

Havre, Montana, was incorporated in 1893, and became the central rail outpost between Seattle, Washington, and St. Paul, Minnesota. Havre was a major distribution point for the Great Northern Railway between the Midwest and cites on the west coast. The railroad transported not only people but also commercial products between all points on its route from east to west.

In 1895, when Julia became pregnant with her third child, the township of Havre had fewer than a thousand residents. Having just moved to Montana, Julia was concerned about the lack of medical facilities, and did not want to give birth around strangers, so she went back east to live with her parents in Fayetteville, North Carolina, until their son Walter was born.[379]

The trip back to North Carolina was exciting for Julia because she got to experience something with her daughters Viola and Elizabeth that none of them had ever seen before. As their train rolled over its tracks in the tall, lush grasslands of the American prairies, they witnessed one of the most magnificent views in the world. Julia and her daughters were glued to the windows of the train as they watched the wild American buffalo on the open prairies. These impressive animals were not native to North Carolina, so Julia was absolutely amazed by the animals' enormous size and graceful beauty as they roamed the open prairies. The train's engineer, always fearful that the herds would cross the tracks in front of the train and cause a collision, slowed down, making the experience more beautiful for those enjoying the scenery for the train.

As the wife of a railroad man, Julia had often heard her husband and other railroad men complain about the challenges of the buffalo herds when they crossed the railroad tracks. The free-range buffalo herds could do serious damage to the locomotives. However, this time, the animals were a good distance from the train, so Julia felt safe enough as she sat back and admired the majestic beauty of the animals. Many years later, Julia's daughter, Elizabeth Fraction Chapman, would reminisce about their arrival in North Carolina, excitedly talking about the huge beasts that seemed to run along with the trains.[380]

When Walter was three or four months old, James went back east to meet up with his family, and together, they returned to Montana. Because the family was departing from North Carolina, where the Jim Crow laws were in full effect, they were forced to sit in the segregated part of the train. But they could still look out the windows, and Julia expected to once again see the beautiful and powerful buffalo herds grazing in the lush fields - instead, a horrific sight greeted her. Julia lowered the blinds, and would not let her daughters look out the window. While the girls played on the floor and kept asking when they could see the roaming buffalo, Julia held her infant son close to her and glared at her husband, blaming him and the other railroad workers for the awful images that were now forever burned into her mind.

Julia had heard stories of the buffalo extermination, but nothing had prepared her to witness it firsthand. As the train neared Montana, one of the last areas in which the wild buffalo still existed in sizable numbers, Julia caught a glimpse of hundreds of dead buffalo, and vile turkey buzzards feasting on their carcasses. According to Elizabeth Fraction Chapman, her mother Julia was terribly upset by this incident. But what traumatized Julia even more was that she believed that the massacre of the calm, gentle giants she saw just months ago was not only for the sake of building railroads, or even for the thrill of the hunt - it was a vindictive act meant to destroy a significant resource that Native-American people of the prairies relied so heavily on for sustenance, and other things necessary for their survival.

As the animals lay dead outside her window, Julia - a woman of color with Native-American Lumbee ancestry - was angry with her husband, the railroad industry, and all the men who had contributed to the buffalo extermination.

Upon Julia's return to Montana, the initial adventure of living in the Wild West was gone. Being the mother of three small children was difficult enough, but being the wife of a railroad man who traveled for weeks at a time on that "engine of death" bothered Julia. While she had just left Fayetteville, she was already missing North Carolina. A cowgirl she was not, and she was not interested in becoming one.

Living in Havre, Montana, in the late 1890s was challenging for everyone, but for an African-American woman with children in this rough railroad outpost, it was especially tough - more difficult than anything Julia had seen in the South. This life was not something she wanted for her children. The few respectable women of the town were well aware of the hard-drinking, tough-talking men who came into town on the trains. The women had heard stories about bar fights at the saloons, the abundance of drinking, the rise in prostitution and the gambling in most parts of the town that made live dangerous for women.

Western frontier life was one to which Julia could not adapt. She encouraged James to seek a transfer back east or anywhere other than Havre, Montana. She explained to him that she felt terribly isolated, and she could not erase the images of slaughtered buffalo from her mind. She felt especially unsafe as an African-American woman. She found the men of town to be barbaric, and she did not want them around her children. Deep down inside, she knew that the company her husband worked for was the very instrument that made all of this happen, and she hated it. According to her son-in-law, on many occasions, Julia threatened to take the children back east unless the entire family relocated back to Virginia.[381]

The only thing that Julia enjoyed while in Montana was teaching. Because her mother, Elizabeth Murphy Utley, was Irish Catholic, she encouraged Julia to learn how to read from the Bible at an early age. Having grown up in the segregated South, Elizabeth Utley felt it was important that Julia and her brother, William, attend the religious schools sponsored by the northern Catholic missionaries. Julia enjoyed reading, and the missionaries also taught her the fine art of writing. At some point in her life, Julia was given a metal crucifix, which she then gave to her grandson, Robert Murphy. Julia Utley Fraction's crucifix is still in the Cornwall Murphy family's possession.

While she was in Montana, Julia began to teach Bible lessons at the local Catholic missionary, using the various lessons she had learned from the missionary schools back in Fayetteville, North Carolina. Julia knew from her experience in the racially divided South that being able to read and write was an important determinate between race and class. After witnessing newly freed men and women still being treated like second-class citizens because they could not read, Julia wanted to make sure that her own children did not grow up illiterate, so she began to teach them the fundamentals of reading.

At the request of some of the neighboring women, Julia began to teach the children of other African-American railroad families, as well as the children from some of the Native-American families from the nearby villages. While this helped to distract her from the mundane, rural living, it also made her realize how much she missed being part of a stronger, more stabilized community. However, her commitment and love of teaching made it difficult for her to go back home to North Carolina, even when she became pregnant with her fourth child. She didn't want to take that wretched train ride until the entire family was ready to permanently move back, so she did not go back east to birth this child as she had did with Walter.

James and Julia's fourth child, Mary Medora, was born in May 1899. From the time that Mary was born, she was sickly. The following year, Mary caught the seasonal flu and died in the spring. Julia was heartbroken over her youngest daughter's death. She was convinced that the dusty back roads of Montana, the rough and tumble lifestyle of the railroad workers, and the immoral cowhands who worked the local farms and ranches all had somehow factored into her daughter's death. She also blamed her daughter's death on the transient poor southerners - white and black - who came through town, hungry and sick, on their way further west. More than ever, Julia wanted to move back east to be with her family and raise her surviving children.

Julia also blamed herself. She felt that by not going back east to have her baby, she had denied Mary Medora the opportunity to be born in comfortable and healthy surroundings. Seeing the internal pain that Julia was going through, James couldn't help but realize the tremendous toll living in Havre was taking on his wife. Moreover, the community was rapidly changing with each new transient arrival, particularly with the arrival of more and more southern whites.

Havre's once-welcoming environment had shifted, and bitter men and women, who suffered from the aftermath of the Civil War and Reconstruction, carried hostile and racist attitudes with them as they moved west. Originally, James had intended to move west to follow the railroad jobs and earn a good income for his family. He also wanted to remove his family from the racial turmoil in the South, only to find that it had now followed. But his beloved Julia was right: Living in Havre, Montana, wasn't worth the pain and bitterness his wife was going through. James and Julia Fraction, once again, made the decision to move - this time, back to Norfolk, Virginia.

5.2   Birth of the Civil Rights Movement

The Fraction family's return to Virginia was bittersweet. The West was a hard place for Julia to live in, and although she had faced less segregation and overt racism there, she was ready to come home. However, with each stop of the railcar, she was reminded of the separatist polices of the South, and became more aware of the ill effects of a recent Supreme Court decision known as *Plessey v. Ferguson*. As a railroad man, James had already heard talk amongst white passengers and black railroad workers about the Louisiana law known as the Separate Car Law, which prohibited African Americans from riding in the same passenger cars as whites.

Although the North had won the Civil War and freed the slaves, in the war's aftermath, the South did everything that it could to prevent African Americans from achieving true equality, including passing a series of stringent laws that kept the races apart in every aspect of daily living. These codified laws "came to be known as Jim Crow laws, after a common stereotype of black people based on a buffoonish minstrel show character by that name." African Americans and white sympathizers challenged these laws all across the South, believing that they violated the Thirteenth, Fourteenth and Fifteenth Amendments to the United States Constitution. One such case evolved around the "thirty-four-year-old Homer Adolph Plessey, who took a seat in the white first-class car of an East Louisiana Railway train ...Plessey had one black great-grandparent, (which made him an octoroon – having one-sixteenth African blood), which classified him as black under Louisiana law" and thus required him to sit in the segregated "Colored Car."[382]

Homer Plessey' refusal led to his removal from the train, his arrest, and being charged with a fine - setting in motion a series of lawsuits challenging Louisiana's law. Upon appeal, the case went to the United State Supreme Court on the basis that the Louisiana "law clashed with the United States Constitution," and that Homer Plessey's rights as an American had been undermined "by forcing him to sit in a segregated 'Colored Car' particularly since he did not look 'colored.'"[383]

The U.S. Supreme Court, in a seven to one decision, rejected the premise of Plessey's arguments on the narrow grounds that the state of Louisiana's statue did not violate the Fourteenth Amendment's Equal Protection Clause, and that separate but equal railroad cars were not discriminatory. The conservative and activist Supreme Court ignored the intent of the Fourteenth Amendment's Equal Protection Clause which required each state to provide equal protection under the law to all people within its jurisdiction.

Figure 85: United States Supreme Court decision, *Plessey v. Ferguson*

"Intensifying the deprived status of the African American was the system of legal segregation that gradually emerged throughout the South after the 1896 *Plessey vs. Ferguson* Supreme Court decision legalizing separate railroad accommodations. Legal segregation aborted the trend to recognize the citizenship rights of African Americans that had begun thirty-one years earlier with the Emancipation Proclamation and continued with the passage of the thirteenth, fourteenth and fifteenth Amendments."

Alferdteen Harrison,
Black Exodus, The Great Migration From the American South[384]

The U.S. Supreme Court decision on *Plessey v. Ferguson* remained in effect until 1954, when the Supreme Court reversed itself and ruled that "separate but equal" was not equal. However, in 1896, the Supreme Court's decision was a major blow to the progressive Reconstruction measures enacted after the Civil War. The fateful decision established the legal foundation all across the South for permanent legal segregation of public facilities and other accommodations for whites and for blacks. The decision, although limited to public accommodations, served as the basis for Jim Crow laws that expanded into every aspect of American life in the South. For most southern African Americans, the decision in *Plessey v. Ferguson* "simply underscored what they already knew from personal experience: that the quality of their lives and freedoms depended on the whims, will, and toleration of a majority of whites in their locality or state."[385] The ill effects of the court's decision were not limited just to the South. As African Americans migrated, the effects of *Plessey v. Ferguson* eventually crept north and west, and for the next fifty years, race relations and segregation affected everything from accommodations in hotels and restaurants to public schools and facilities.

Figure 86: A New Social Order Had Been Legitimized

"From the perspective of most white Americans, the new racial order had been affirmed formally and informally at the highest levels of society. The U.S. Supreme Court ruling in *Plessey v. Ferguson*, sanctioning "separate but equal" public facilities for blacks and whites, sanctified the wave of new legislation and business practices requiring disparate treatment of blacks and whites. The ruling's effects went far beyond the courts and legislative chambers. The open willingness of the highest court to base its seminal ruling on claims that were so clearly false – that train cars designated for blacks were no different from those of whites – sent a profound message to all Americans. So long as whites performed at least the bare rituals of due process and cloaked their actions behind claims of equality, the crudest abuses of blacks and violations of their due protections under law would rarely ever be challenged".

Douglas A. Blackmon,
Slavery by Another Name,
The Re-Enslavement of Black Americans
from the Civil War to World War II[386]

African Americans in all the southern states were humiliated in "daily encounters throughout the South - when they traveled, when they went shopping in stores, or when they tried to find restaurants that would serve them. They found discrimination at their place of work, if they were able to find work. When they sought higher education for their children and looked for schools or universities to send their children, they were constrained by sending their offspring to historically black colleges and universities. African Americans were barred from housing in districts under restrictive covenants."[387]

African Americans, no matter what their stations in life, also lived under the fear of the growing numbers of unjustified lynchings and murders. The "wave of lynchings and mob killings claimed over a hundred victims a year by the 1870s, and reached a high of 235 annually in 1892."[388]

As the African Americans' civil rights were being whittled away, state by state; as African Americans were increasingly being lynched and tortured across the nation; as the United States and State Supreme Courts ruled against them; and as thousands of African Americans were manipulated back into slavery via a corrupt criminal justice systems, the American Civil Rights movement was born. In communities all across the United States, but particularly in the South, leaders emerged to discuss and channel the debate on the rights of African Americans. Many of these leaders emerged from African-American churches.

Figure 87: The Black Church Was a Sanctuary for Education

"Forbidden by antebellum laws and customs from learning to read or write, enslaved black men and women sensed the importance of these skills by the very vehemence with which whites enforced the prohibition, the extraordinary measures whites adopted to criminalize black literacy and to insulate blacks from intellectual contamination."

Leon F. Litwack,
Trouble in Mind, Black Southerners in the Age of Jim Crow[389]

Throughout the history of African Americans, churches have been pivotal in navigating the challenges faced by congregants in communities all across the country. The black minister was charged with providing spiritual counseling, and he was often the educational leader of the community. He was also charged with community development and charitable giving, and even provided political guidance. In most southern communities, black churches only held services once or twice a month, but in the interim periods, the churches were a sanctuary for educating people of all ages, promoting knowledge as the vehicle for true equality and empowerment.

African Americans intuitively understood the importance of education for their self-reliance and survival in a system that did everything it could to put them down, while their ministers did everything they could to build community literacy and self-esteem amongst their congregants. They built classrooms on church property, they assisted gifted children in getting into historically African-American colleges, and they helped neighbors get jobs. Local black ministers also networked with other ministers in forming formal and informal organizations that carefully addressed the civil rights of African Americans all across the South.

5.3   The Spanish American War and the Birth of a New Century

In the few short years since James and Julia Fraction had first left Norfolk, Virginia, the city and the surrounding areas had changed dramatically. By the time the Fractions returned to the city from Montana, it had become a world-class shipbuilding center. Between 1883 and 1890, the United States, noticing that other world powers were building their naval fleets as they were becoming more industrialized, built nine steel-hulled naval vessels including the U.S.S. *Maine* and the U.S.S. *Oregon*. Within this short period of time, the United States became the world's third largest naval power, and Norfolk became a major ship building port. As the United States expanded its strength on the open waters, many Americans felt the need to become more involved in international affairs.

However, an entrance into international affairs meant the possibility of animosity between nations, but by the end of the nineteenth century, the United States became embroiled in the internal struggles on the Caribbean Island of Cuba, some ninety miles off of the United States coast, and a colony ruled by Spain. Once the most powerful colonial power, Spain now possessed only the Philippine islands, Guam, Puerto Rico, and Cuba. As the Cuban island revolted against Spain, many Americans were sympathetic to the Cuban people.

As tensions continued to build in Cuba, President William McKinley ordered the *U.S.S. Maine* to rescue the United States citizens on the island, bring them home and protect American interests on the island. On February 15, 1898, the *U.S.S. Maine*, while docked in Cuba's

Havana Harbor, was destroyed in an explosion that killed more than 260 Americans, mostly men of African descent.

It was widely reported and speculated that the Spanish government had blown up the ship, creating a means for the United States to declare war against Spain. Upon hearing of the explosion, Americans were outraged, and wanted revenge. The national newspapers were filled with the rallying cry, "Remember the Maine." It was a rallying cry for vengeance and war. The American response was quick and resolute. On April 22, 1898, the U. S. Navy blockaded Santiago Harbor and, declared war on Spain two days later. Once again, large numbers of African-American men enlisted for military service, dedicated patriots ready to serve and fight for their country.

The United States Congress activated ten regiments of all Black Troops: the 6th, 7th, 8th, 9th, 10th, 3rd Alabama, 3rd North Carolina, 23rd, 24th, and 25th. Only the 9th, 10th, 24th, and 25th Regiments saw actual combat in this short-lived war. As with the Revolutionary and Civil wars, recognition, honor, and leadership were some of the prime reasons African Americans wanted to serve in the U. S. Military.

Civil War hero Sergeant William Carney of the 54th Colored Infantry - the brother unit to the Massachusetts 5th Calvary, in which Massachusetts' William Cornwall served - was the first African American to receive the U. S. Military's highest decoration, the Medal of Honor. Sergeant Carney's recognition and popularity as a U. S. military man led other African-American men to emulate him and seek this type of national embrace and acceptance, particularly since many of the men who died on the battleship U.S.S. *Maine* were Navy men of African descent.

The Spanish American War was short, and after eight months, ended on December 10, 1898, with the signing of the Treaty of Paris. Despite its brevity, the actual war was costly for the once mighty Spain, leading to a devastating loss of control over the remains of its entire overseas empire - including its prized islands of Cuba and Puerto Rico in the Atlantic, and the Philippines and Guam in the Pacific. After the war, the United States established itself as a world naval power, and the port city of Norfolk was quickly becoming a major international seaport and a major shipbuilding port city.

Figure 88: Spanish American African American Recruits

The initial recruitment to fulfill the necessary regiments into the Spanish American War initially consisted of only white recruits. African American organizations initially protested at the under-representation of African American soldiers in the volunteer army. It was believed as it had been during the Civil War that honorable military service would win for African Americans greater respect in society as a whole and would assist in their struggle for equality. In response to mass meetings and agitating petitions over the exclusion of African Americans sent to the White House and Congress, President McKinley accepted African American recruits

Ivan Musciant, *Empire by Default, The Spanish-American War and the Dawn of the American Century*[390]

James Fraction had extremely marketable skills and he was able to go back to work at his old employer, the Baltimore Steam Packet Company, where he worked on the *Steamboat Alabama*. During this period the *Alabama*, which was launched in 1893, was considered one of the world's state-of-the-art modern commercial steel-hulled vessels, with modern electric lighting and private staterooms with bath facilities.[391]

The United States now had a strong military presence on the island of Cuba and in its port cities. As commercial American vessels docked in Cuban ports and provided humanitarian aid after the war, many Cuban men got jobs as translators, both in port and on the American ships. As Cubans became familiar with American customs and business practices, some of the Cuban workers and other foreign immigrants ultimately began to travel to American port cities such as Miami, Florida, and Norfolk, Virginia, where they worked on the American docks as longshoremen.

In February of 1903, tragedy struck and shook the Fraction family to its core. A Cuban longshoreman of Irish ancestry sexually assaulted Viola Fraction, resulting in a pregnancy. The young Viola went to live with her grandmother while she was pregnant. After her son Robert was born, she left him with his Irish maternal grandmother, Elizabeth Murphy Utley, Robert was given his grandmother's maiden name, Murphy, as his surname.

James Fraction was enraged by the news of the attack on his daughter. He physically confronted the perpetrator and got into trouble with the law. While sympathetic to the reasons for the confrontation, and since Norfolk was a rapidly growing naval community, it was strongly suggested that James enlist in the Navy to avoid potential legal troubles.[392] Two years after moving back to Norfolk, in February 1903, James enlisted into the service of the United States Navy and began active duty as a cook for the Commander in Chief. From 1903 until 1918, James served his nation honorably, including service during World War I.

Born a slave, James considered himself most fortunate to have seen the true beauty of the United States. Having been raised in Montgomery, Virginia; having worked in Norfolk, Virginia, and Baltimore, Maryland; and having traveled west to live in Montana and Minnesota, he got to see parts of America of which most men only dreamed. However, those experiences were eclipsed by the opportunity to serve in the Navy - which was beyond his wildest expectations. Working on the majestic ships became his passion, and visiting exciting new countries and ports became one of his greatest loves. As America invested heavily in its naval infrastructure, Seaman James Fraction had assignments on what was then some of the Navy's most prestigious and nationally recognized battleships.

Figure 89: Seaman Walter Fraction's Battleships Served

U.S.S *Franklin* (1906)	U.S.S. *North Dakota* (1910)
U.S.S. *Newark* (1906)	U.S.S. *Virginia* (1911)
U.S.S. *Tennessee* (1907)	Recognition Ship, Boston (1912)
U.S.S. *Constellation* (1907)	U.S.S. *Utah* (1916)
U.S.S. *Rhode Island* (1908)	U.S.S. *Wyoming* (1916)
U.S.S. *Georgia* (1910)	U.S.S. *Pennsylvania* (1917)
U.S.S. *Wabash* (1910)	

While at sea in 1909, James learned that his beloved wife Julia had passed away after a prolonged illness. Upon her passing, the three Fraction children went to live with her sister-in-law, Mary Emma (Fraction) Hunt, James' older sister and the wife of Reverend Dow Hunt, a prominent religious leader and community activist. Reverend Hunt, a Baptist minister, was an early activist clergyman, who helped to organize schools for free children and was one of the original founders of Salem's and Roanoke's early civil rights movement. James' grandson, Robert Murphy, went to live with his wife's brother in St. Paul, Minnesota. Once his children were settled in with his sister, and his grandson was settled in Minnesota, James went back to sea.

While James was in the Navy, turmoil and conflict spread across the European continent, and the Balkan Peninsula became the center of European interests. Russia wanted access to the Mediterranean Sea though the Balkan Peninsula and Germany wanted rail access to the Ottoman Empire in Turkey. When Archduke Franz Ferdinand, heir to the Austrian empire, was assassinated in Bosnia by a Serbian national, Austria-Hungry declared war against Serbia. This had a domino effect on European nations as each was pulled into the conflict, one by one. While the Napoleonic Wars of the early 1800s were primarily fought on European soil, and as the United States was drawn in the European conflict during the War of 1812 with England, it paled in comparison to the scale of Europe's new war.

After the Spanish American War, the United States was thrust on the world stage as a global power with exceptional naval strength. Some Americans felt that with the strength of its military came the responsibility to be involved in international affairs, while isolationist Americans wanted to stay out of the growing European conflict. However, many Americans had family ties in Europe, so it was difficult to remain neutral. But factors beyond America's control made neutrality impossible.

As Germany became more aggressive against its European neighbors, Americans became more engaged in the conflicts in Europe. With the sinking of several British and French ocean liners - including the *Lusitania* in the Atlantic by German submarine vessels, costing thousands of lives, hundreds of which were American - the neutral stance of the U.S. population rapidly shifted.

After the 1916 re-election of President Woodrow Wilson, neutrality was declared. However, Germany believed it could conquer England and continued to provoke the British superpower, convincing Wilson that America had no choice but to enter the European war and protect American interests worldwide.

When the United States entered the war, only 200,000 men were in the service, and very few had combat experience. In order to support the war effort overseas, the American government implemented the Selective Services Act, which required every able-bodied man to register for military service. As with every American battle before this, African-American men joined the war cry and enlisted in the service. Of the 3 million men who enlisted, approximately 400,000 were African Americans. As with previous wars, World War I provided tremendous social changes that transformed the lives of African Americans during, and after, the war.

The war stopped European immigration to America, an inconvenience at a time when American factories needed workers in the steel mills, munitions plants, and stockyards. It was a period in which northern industrial plants openly recruited African Americans to move north to work in the factories. African American newspapers wrote articles about the oppressive Jim Crow practices in the South and juxtaposed those struggles with the prosperity of African Americans in the North.

In 1914, Henry Ford was the first of the industrialists to offer employment to African Americans, putting them to work on the assembly lines in his auto plant. For Americans of African descent, the prospect of employment in the automobile and defense industries provided the right incentive to encourage them to move north, resulting in hundreds of thousands of southern blacks moving to northern cities such as Chicago, Detroit, New York, St. Louis and Philadelphia for job opportunities that were available to them for the first time. Also for the first time, large numbers of American blacks were becoming urbanized and transforming the basic social conditions within these cities.

Europe's landscape and population were devastated in the wake of World War I, leaving many with the belief that this had been "the war to end all wars." But unfortunately, the events of this war only set the stage for the next, larger World War. After World War I, the United States was slowly transforming to a stronger centralized Federal government and military, and it was making some incremental strides in the area of social reforms for African Americans and for women.

Americans also wanted some form of normalcy after the war. After seeing the bright lights of Paris, the bustling cities of England, and the sophistication of Rome, young soldiers returning from war longed for the excitement of America's growing cities. Many families on farms in the Midwest and the South asked the same, basic question about their newly returned sons, fathers, and husbands: "How do you keep them down on the farm after they have seen 'Paree?'" - the name of a popular song written in the wake of America's entry into World War I.[393] The song reflected the returning soldiers' desire for adventure, and was the accompaniment of a mass shift in the populace as young families moved from small towns and rural communities to larger metropolitan cities across America - particularly New York, Chicago and Philadelphia.

For the small town migrants, the big cities were places of opportunity, as well as competition, political change and intellectual challenges. America changed dramatically in the years before 1920, as was revealed by the 1920 United States Census. According to figures that year, 51.2 percent of Americans lived in communities with populations of 2,500 to more than a million. Between 1922 and 1929, migration to the cities accelerated, with more than 2 million people leaving rural farms and towns each year. For young small-town raised Americans, the energy and vibrancy of the cities were the place to be, and to seek their fortunes.

According to his military pension, while stationed in Havana Harbor in Cuba, James Fraction began to notice that he was having problems with blurred and double vision. Because of this, he was transferred to the Chelsea Naval Hospital near Boston, Massachusetts.[394] As he met with his doctors at the hospital in attempt to find out what was wrong with him and to, hopefully, garner his military pension, his daughters, Viola and Elizabeth, moved to Boston to take care of their ailing father. The sisters moved to the section of the city known as the South End, Boston's racially integrated neighborhood.

In 1918, Seaman Fraction received an honorable discharge from the hospital in Chelsea, Massachusetts, due to partial blindness in both eyes. James permanently relocated to Boston, where two of his three children rejoined him and his new wife, Mary S. Beams, in Boston's growing black community of South End. His son, James Jr., moved back to St. Paul and lived with his maternal uncle, Walter Utley, who had raised his nephew, Robbie Murphy. Many of the descendants of James and his wife Opal Fraction still live in the Twin City area of St. Paul and Minneapolis.

5.4   Abner Melton and Sally Ballard of Ahoskie, North Carolina

Prior to 1890, the community of Ahoskie, North Carolina, was officially unknown. This town was where Abner Melton raised his family, and it wasn't until 1894 that Ahoskie was officially recognized. After the Civil War, small rural and agricultural communities all across the South lived and died by their proximity to the railroad. The railroad was the major transporter of commercial products, and in the rural South, it literally became the engine that powered a local economy out of the post-war recession. In 1885, the area around present day Ahoskie, North Carolina, provided trees for timber. A log-train carried timber trees from the forests of Hertford and Bertie counties to the "sawmills that dotted the underdeveloped areas."

Through a series of mergers and acquisitions between 1885 and 1890, the timberline was reconstructed with an improved and straightened right-of-way, which eventually was converted to an all-purpose rail line. "The first passenger train to pass over the completed Norfolk and Carolina Railroad tracks was on April 1, 1890."[395]

When railroads arrived in small towns, there was usually a celebration, with the arrival was treated as a holiday because it meant that the community was officially connected to the outside world. Officials from across the region joined Ahoskie residents to welcome the train, excited for everything the new railroad promised to the community and its residents. The first whistle from the large main engine signaled to all who lived in the area that Ahoskie, North Carolina, would now become the Hertford County's center of trade, commerce, and transportation. But before that could happen, Ahoskie would have to establish a "Post Office Department in Washington, DC and establish itself in the law books of North Carolina."[396] By 1893, the federal government established an official post office and the state incorporated the community into the town of Ahoskie.

With the arrival of the trains and the intercommunity and interstate commerce that followed, it seemed that everyone in Hertford County, particularly the residents in the township of Ahoskie, benefited. The railroad served as a catalyst for new businesses and entrepreneurs in Ahoskie, and provided many opportunities to its residents. However, with the arrival of the railroad came many challenges, including rising property values and taxes. While the railroad helped to take local products to the outside world, it would eventually take away the next generation of young Ahoskie families, luring them to communities hundreds of miles from their families in Hertford County.

Several months before the first passenger train passed over the newly constructed Norfolk and Carolina Railroad tracks in Ahoskie, in the neighboring community of Rich Square in Northampton County, twenty-two-year-old Abner Melton married Miss Sally Ballard on January 9, 1890. [397] Abner and Sally followed the pacifist beliefs of the Quaker community of Rich Square, where they were both raised. "The settling of the community Rich Square began in 1750. By 1753, the Quaker community, a Protestant religious order, began their worship."[398] For the multiracial Melton and Ballard families, this was an inviting community, so they migrated away from the racially intolerant laws of Virginia. The Quakers openly welcomed People of Color and valued their contributions in the community.

Because Ahoskie was improving so quickly after the arrival of the new railroad, Abner and Sally Melton decided that they would temporarily move their family there. However, due to the railroad industry and the growing number of new businesses, land was becoming more and more expensive. At the close of the nineteenth century, Abner and Sally decided to move to Norfolk, Virginia, so that Abner could work in the industrial shipyards and earn the money necessary to buy valuable Ahoskie property. Living in Norfolk was easy enough, and a practical decision for the Meltons, since Ahoskie, North Carolina, and their extended family would only be forty-five miles southwest. The financial opportunities of Norfolk enabled Abner, Sally, and their six children to return to their Hertford County countryside in short order.

For Abner and Sally, living in Norfolk was an interesting experience. They were familiar with the surrounding communities of Norfolk, as they had often visited extended family and friends there for most of their lives. However, it was one thing to visit a community, and quite another to live there. While there were plenty of jobs and opportunities, there were also new challenges to face. In North Carolina's Northampton and Hertford counties, the single issue of race was always prevalent. However, in the metropolitan area of Norfolk, race relations also intermingled with the issue of a rapidly growing immigrant population competing for the same jobs. In addition, Abner and Sally had never had to contend with foreign languages and customs.

By the late 1890s, economic conditions had worsened in Eastern Europe while major portions of the United States enjoyed a period of relative economic prosperity, particularly in railroad and coastal shipbuilding communities such as Norfolk. Millions of Europeans were confronted with economic depression and famine as well as political and religious turmoil. Coming to America offered hope and opportunities not found in their native countries. Just as Abner and Sally Melton looked across the state line into Norfolk, Virginia, for opportunities that would enable them to buy land and live comfortably, millions of other families in Europe looked across the ocean to America for the same opportunities. While metropolitan Norfolk did not become the hub of European immigration to the same extent as large coastal cities - such as Boston, New York, Philadelphia and Baltimore - the small-scaled city still experienced a significant shift in cultural dynamics, as witnessed by Abner and Sally.

As the nineteenth century came to an end, the United States closed the doors on a tumultuous period that included a bloody Civil War and the abolition of 400 hundred years of slavery. The century ended with: the immigration of millions of disenfranchised European poor; the assassination of the sixteenth president, William McKinley; increased tensions over the long-term costs for the reconstruction of the south; and the marginalization of millions of African-American freedmen in the South. However, the ending of the century was not all bad. It also ended with major technological advancements that changed the daily lives of millions of Americans nationwide. Post-Civil War families, such as Abner and Sally Melton's, benefited from many of these advancements - the dramatic improvements resulting from the railroad industry to the highly sophisticated ships being built in Norfolk, Virginia, and the jobs and economic opportunities they provided for young families.

For Abner and Sally Melton, living in Norfolk, Virginia was like sitting at the window of the world. It seemed that every week, a different United States steel-hulled warship would dock at the Norfolk Ship Yard.[399] Occasionally, an international ship would visit the port for repairs. During these weeks, the port city would be filled with foreign sailors, dressed in their nation's uniforms and sporting their nation's accents. After a short period of time, Abner's hard work enabled him to save the necessary money to buy the perfect tract of land and a large two-story home back in Ahoskie, near the Winton town line, so that he could farm the land and raise his family. While in Norfolk, they didn't experience the dramatic effects of the 1896 landmark United States Supreme Court decision of *Plessey v. Ferguson*, where the court upheld the concept that separate but equal public facilities was constitutional.[400] However, while the family was away in Norfolk, they were unaware of the mounting racial tension back in Northampton and Hertford counties.

Although the state of Virginia and other southern states had implemented laws based on the Supreme Court decision, the area surrounding Norfolk had not practiced the wide-scale separate accommodations found in other parts of the state - or at least, not in the community in which the Meltons lived. Now back in North Carolina, as Ahoskie was expanding as a result of the new railroad line, new country stores and hardware shops had opened. When Abner and Sally went shopping, they were required to always walk into the store through the door with the words "COLORED" over the archway. Abner and Sally were raised to believe that they were nothing less than equal to their white neighbors, many of whom they grew up with. To be suddenly treated as second-class citizen was incredibly insulting to them.

Living in the South, this generation of the Meltons had always been aware of racial tensions, but had never before been subjected to it in such a personal way. The political climate caused by the expanding Jim Crow laws made their community hostile to all African Americans. Struggling against the profound racism consumed them and impacted their everyday lives. For many of the extended Melton family, the issue of race was becoming increasingly problematic and very personal. After generations of interracial marriages, the Melton family members' physical appearance came from many different shades of the human rainbow. Brothers and sisters would have blond, brown, red or black hair. Their eyes were blue, brown, hazel or green, complemented by skin tones that ranged from a pale white to a caramel brown. In light of the Supreme Court *Plessey v. Ferguson* decision, no matter what they looked like, none of them could not escape the increasing effects of Jim Crow.

Although the Civil War was long over, white southerners tried desperately to replicate the pre-Civil War way of life, politically and economically, and with the election of southern Democrats to political office came the legal promulgation of the Jim Crow laws. Immediately after the war, the balance of power in the South's economy was turned on its head. Farmers, plantation owners, and the mercantile class could no longer presume that they could succeed utilizing free slave labor. The Jim Crow laws were intentionally designed to systematically limit the educational, political and economic opportunities of the South's African American population.

Southern white farmers and plantation owners still needed cheap labor to work their fields, or else the fields would be ruined. Farmers designed convoluted sharecropper arrangements that enticed freedmen to live on the same land where they were previously enslaved, and then share with the landowners a portion of the crops and the profits that they raised with their laborious work. Despite the sales pitch, these sharecropper arrangements were never designed to benefit the black sharecropper.

Many of the newly freed men, as a result of denied education and an inability to read and write, had limited employment opportunities and little choice but to enter into harsh sharecropper agreements and abide by the restrictive Jim Crow laws. For African-American families, such as Abner and Sally Melton, this was a period of tremendous personal conflict. As their family had enjoyed certain social and economic freedoms for generations, many of the Melton and Ballard family members, including Abner and Sally Melton and their parents, were concerned about what they referred to as the "changing face of the South." This was a polite way of describing the growing racism in the South towards all Americans of African descent, regardless of one's social and financial status. The Melton and Ballard families were not used to this overtly racist attitude, particularly directed at them.

For the previous 400 years and numerous generations, the original families, who were Free People of Color, walked the streets of their communities as somewhat equal citizens to their white neighbors.

They had endured the murderous lynch mobs after the Nat Turner rebellion in Virginia; they suffered through the incremental chipping away of their civil rights by the states for 200 years; and they huddled away from their windows in the dark of night, fearing harassment or worse from members of terrorist groups. Now they had to face daily the open hostility of neighbors they once called friends. The families feared this was indicative of things to come. These African Americans were members of proud families and descendants of Free People of Color who owned and sold property. They worked their own fields and sold their own crops without fear, reprisals, or retaliation for being productive citizens in their own communities.

They strongly believed that their proud racial lineage, a mosaic of European, African and Native-American blood, resulting in a pedigree of people who were equal to whites, and even, in their personal opinions, better than the poor white hoodlums going around the countryside humiliating and harassing the "old colored" families. It insulted these old families to be treated no differently than the recently freed slaves, and to be disrespected like the poor whites across town. They distinguished themselves from the poor whites and the recently freed men, as they were able to read and write – in many cases, better than their white neighbors. They were able to conduct commerce, had the ability to independently work their own land, understood how improve their property, and lived off of the fruits of their own labors. They resented to the new terminology of the young white hoodlums referring them to being "uppity" for no reason other than their walking with the air of confidence that any man or woman would have who worked hard and asked for nothing in return.

They were not the sons and daughters of former slaves who had to depend on their white masters and overseers for food and shelter. Nor were they like the uneducated white former plantation owners who could barely read or write, who had limited communication skills, and no longer owned land or property, and by the chain of events were now dependent on the hard work of their former slaves for their mere existence.

Families such as the Meltons and the Ballards were a hybrid. They reflected the best of the South's European, African and Native-American cultures. From the earliest colonial periods, these were a people who understood that the ownership of land was a sign of economic prosperity and social status. These descendants of the original Free People of Color felt that their land ownership set them apart from their now very loud and boisterous white neighbors who were intimidating black families all across the South. As original families of the south, they knew that the ownership of land was vested in only a few white families, but also in many of the original African American families who were pioneers in these same communities.

These proud families now saw their white neighbors, once marginalized and angered by the wealth of the pre-Civil War white land barons, now attacking the wrong enemy, going to extreme measures to disenfranchise another group of people who had once been poor themselves. Now they were blaming their economic situations on the newly freed slaves, and taking their anger out on them. The Melton and Ballard families knew the loud and foul-mouthed hoodlums by name and face these people were commonly referred to as "poor white trash" who now felt that they were entitled to something from the government to take care of them because of their abject poverty caused by the war that they themselves believed in and participated in.

Because of the strong racial hostilities after the Civil War, the South, as these free families of color had once known and loved, was rapidly changing, and not for the better. The Melton and Ballard families were, for the first time, being treated as second-class citizens. The prominent white gentry's families were having major financial challenges after the war, and many were losing farms that their families held for generations. These families were also being treated as second-class citizens for the first time. Carpetbaggers[401] from the North were coming in and buying family farms and plantations right from under these once prominent families, at bargain basement prices.

The carpetbaggers treated the former southern white gentry no differently than they treated the loudmouth poor whites, and they treated both of them only a step above the freed slaves. This infuriated everyone, especially the southern elite. As the carpetbaggers purchased more property, the cost of land prices slowly began to increase in Ahoskie and the more fertile the land, the more it cost. Abner Melton knew the low cost of land would not last much longer, and as an astute businessman, wanted to buy some of the land that the old white farmers could no longer afford to maintain. He just needed the cash to invest in prime real estate.

5.5   William Howell and Matilda Watson of Boydton, Virginia

From the early 1700s to the mid-1800s, Granville County, North Carolina, was a relatively tolerant community for African Americans. For generations, the descendants of Revolutionary War patriots, white and black, coexisted without any major racial strife. However, as with almost every community across the South, after the Civil War, things changed rapidly. While some tension built between the free African Americans, who had owned their homes and land for generations, and the newly freed African-American slaves, the real tension developed from forces outside of Granville County. No county in North Carolina was spared from the paramilitary activities of white supremacist groups, such as the Constitutional Union Guard and its sister organization the Ku Klux Klan. The violent activities of these groups, along with the Jim Crow laws, changed the once tranquil Granville County, forcing it to succumb to the racial pressures from surrounding communities.

Christopher and Harriet Howell's son, William,[402] along with his other brothers, cousins and farmhands, would travel by wagon and bring their tobacco to the town of Boydton, located in the neighboring Mecklenburg County in Virginia. Although they could get more money for their crop by going south to Durham or Raleigh, North Carolina, the journey to Mecklenburg was far safer, and they were treated better by the auctioneers than they would be in the larger tobacco auction houses downstate. All of the farmers harvested their crops at about the same time, and the money they received depended on the quality of the tobacco crop and the overall growing season. The competition was fierce in Raleigh, and the Howell men were wise enough to know that the auctioneers weren't as friendly to African-American tobacco farmers, which meant they received considerably less money than the white tobacco farmers for the same quality of crops. Going to Durham or Raleigh was too much of a financial gamble for African-American farmers.

For the Howell men, selling their tobacco was a better bet over in Boydton where the tobacco auctioneers knew them, and they were treated as fairly as possible for black men. It also enabled Howell men to meet with their extended family and friends once a year. This gave them an opportunity to catch up on politics, family and business. Many times, they would take their entire family and visit their friend's homes for an extended stay. It was also a good opportunity to introduce their marriageable-aged children to children from other "good" families. On one of his many visits to Boydton, William Howell was smitten by the prettiest girl in the two counties, a young woman by the name of Matilda Watson.

Matilda was thin and had a very fair complexion, with long straight black hair. She was the daughter of Benjamin Watson and Amanda Hunt from Boydton, Virginia. Matilda Watson's family background was somewhat similar to William's as she also came from a free African-American family whose ancestry dated back to the 1780s.

Mitchell and Matilda Hunt of Boydton, Virginia, were the parents of Matilda's mother, Amanda Hunt. They were descendants of the original 19 Angolans, and they had seven children. Reportedly, Matilda's father was white and from a prominent family in the town of Boydton, who also fathered Matilda's two brothers. Unlike many of the other African American families in Boydton, the Watson family lived in a large home that was a short walk from the center of town. As William Howell courted Matilda, he became more cognizant of the rapidly changing segregationist views of his hometown in North Carolina. As he crossed the river in North Carolina to visit Matilda just over the state line in Virginia, he noticed these changing attitudes more and more.

William also began to notice the differences between the rural, underdeveloped tobacco growing community that he grew up in Oxford's Fishing Creek Township, and Matilda's community of Boydton, where tobacco was being sold, then shipped off to Petersburg and Richmond for sale and distribution to the North and overseas. Boydton, Virginia, prospered after the Civil War, with palatial homes built on the main streets, and the construction of a new county building, as well as other government and commercial buildings. Boydton had even built a rail depot station for travelers to the town. William liked the more progressive community and wanted to live where he felt the vitality of an urban center, where he could buy and own property without fear of racist segregation.

Prior to the Civil War many of the free Americans of African descent lived in communities where the general white population knew them and knew of their free status. These African Americans moved fairly easily throughout society and may have felt a false sense of security much like the Melton and Ballard families, thinking themselves removed from outside influences and politics. However, after the Civil War and its devastation on the South's economy, the fragile coexistence that once stood between southern whites and their black neighbors was rapidly deteriorating into open hostilities. After the war, the civility and kindness between Granville County's southern white and black families deteriorated as the economy continued to sour. Jobs once considered "black jobs" were now begrudgingly being taken over by poor whites.

The rise of Jim Crow laws angered members of the Howell family who had owned, cleared and farmed their land since the mid-1700s. Young men such as William resented the intimidation tactics of the roving gangs of white thugs that patrolled the major pikes as he went back and forth between North Carolina and Virginia. He had heard too many stories of young black men being accosted at night by the Ku Klux Klan runners. White children that William had grown up with were pressured to segregate themselves from their black childhood friends. He saw his community become socially and economically challenging for not only his family, but all black families.

William Howell and Matilda Watson, though in love and wanting to be married, decided that their future was no longer tied to the southern communities in which they were raised, even though their families had lived in these places for generations. North Carolina was not where they wanted to live or to raise a family. As part of the original Great Migration, they would leave North Carolina and Virginia, and migrate north, along with millions of other Americans of African descent, where they hoped that their standard of living would be substantially better. They hoped their children would get a better education and that they could excel economically without the racial overtones, tensions and restrictions of their southern communities.

William went north before marrying Matilda, and worked as a sales clerk on Brockton, Massachusetts' fashionable Main Street. As soon as he was able to afford a decent apartment, he went back to Boydton and married Matilda. Matilda would return to Virginia to visit her mother often, but, like so many other American men of African descent, William seldom went south to go back home to visit family and friends. Although William and Matilda had left the South, it was difficult for the South to leave them.

African American men knew that they could not frequently go back home for fear of being singled out by the Klan and other hostile whites. Often, men of African descent would be singled out on the train and harassed. They would be harassed for wearing business suits and for looking "uppity." They were embarrassed in front of their families and other travelers on the train as a reminder that while in the South, African Americans were only second-class citizens. Whites also harassed these men of color because they resented losing former slaves and wanted to quell any thoughts of further challenging the status quo. African American men and their families were forced to sit in the segregated portion of the train, as a constant reminder that they were coming back to the Jim Crow South.

As a proud American of African descent, William was not going to sneak in and out of the South just to visit his family. Traveling African American men were often taken from the trains in the middle of the night and arrested on falsified criminal charges so that they could not go back north with their families. William would not allow that to happen to his family. While his heart always belonged to the red clay and good tasting catfish of Fishing Creek, North Carolina, he knew that his life now belonged to the industrial opportunities and the rich black soil of Brockton, Massachusetts.

5.6 The Great Exodus from the American South

By 1877, Radical Reconstruction officially ended in the South. The subsequent period gave rise to the deliberate intimidation and discrimination of African Americans all across the South. Because the South had become such an undesirable place for People of Color, many of them decided to relocate to communities where there were better opportunities. From 1877 to 1900, a small number of African Americans, such as the Howells, made the exodus from the agricultural South to the urban communities in the North and in the Mid-West. Once relocated, these early urban pioneers sent word back home of the plentiful opportunities to be found in the North.

From the period between the end of the Civil War and the beginning of World War I, the United States Census data demonstrate that African Americans remained, for the most part, in the South. But the period between 1900 and the 1930s is generally considered to be the years that define the "Great Migration." While initially it was suspected that the migration of African Americans from the South was directly attributed to the racial attitudes of the South - and that was absolutely a factor for many - "the exodus of blacks from the South was primarily the result of individuals deciding to leave a relatively stagnant economy for one which offered more opportunity for security and upward mobility."[403] The Great Migration of between five million to six million African Americans from the rural South to points in the North, Midwest, and West happened in many mini-migrations in three primary stages.

Figure 90: The Civil War Set Them Free - Migration Gave Them Freedom

"The Great Migration reflected collective sensibilities, social networks, organizational activism, and circuits of communication and deliberation. From the outset African Americans widely imagined their moves as family and community strategies and even when departing as individuals, they laid out links in a developing chain of kin, neighbors and friends that would guide and support those who followed. By the mid-1910s they had built substantial bases across the South, and had established beachheads in the urban North. Back and forth along the chains flowed people, resources and information about living conditions, job prospects, and the civil and political atmosphere. Letters, reverse migrations and visitations alike told rural folk what they might expect and who might help" them in the North.

Steven Hahn, *A Nation Under Our Feet, Black Political Struggles in the Rural South from Slavery to the Great Migration*[404]

The first phase of migration happened between 1880 and 1900, when the initial wave of rural migrants moved to the more urban communities within the South, and to the urban centers in the North. They realized the tremendous prospects and opportunities to be had, and sent word back home in an effort to recruit family and friends to join them. After 1900, the migration accelerated.

When World War I erupted in 1914, many African Americans benefited from an increase in job opportunities. For the first time, African Americans were provided with "industrial employment" in the North. "World War I and the economic boom that accompanied it created the conditions that made possible the entrance of black migrants into northern industries."[405]

Figure 91: World War I Provide Northern Industrial Employment

"By 1916, increasing orders from both abroad and from a domestic market stimulated by military preparedness raised prospects for spectacular profits in most industries. Confronted with the loss of their traditional source of additional labor, northern employers looked to previously unacceptable alternatives they opened the factory gates to white women and black southerners."

James R. Grossman,
Land of Hope: Chicago, Black Southerners and the Great Migration[406]

Prior to the war, European immigrants were arriving in unprecedented numbers, fulfilling the growing needs of the industrial base in the North. With the outbreak of the war, immigration slowed to a trickle, which only increased the need for industrial workers.

As African Americans continued to move north after the war, the Harlem Renaissance was born, a period of a new African-American identity that included literature, music, dance and a strong sense of social consciousness. As poor and mostly illiterate African Americans moved north to the large urban enclaves of the big cities, their talents slowly were being recognized by the greater European-American middle and upper classes, thanks to the growing number of blues and jazz music venues. African-American music became more popular to white audiences as it began to become more mainstream. African-American literature began to influence a public dialogue on race relations and social conditions in the North and in the South. African-America newspapers - such as the Baltimore *Afro-American*, the *Chicago Defender*, the *Amsterdam News* in New York, the *Pittsburgh Courier* and the *St. Louis Sentinel* - provided information to southern African Americans about the expanding economic opportunities in the North, as well as giving a black perspective on the multitude of challenges that confronted African Americans in the South.

As African Americans moved north, the workforce in some of the larger cities in the South dwindled. This angered southern employers who were losing profit as blacks migrated to northern industrial cities. Several states, including North Carolina, formed Divisions of Negro Economics, the primary mission of which was to study the Great Migration's causes and impact to the state's economy. As a result of skilled and educated African Americans leaving the South in relatively large numbers, the U.S. Department of Labor established a Federal Division of Negro Economics to write about African Americans leaving the South and their migration to other parts of the country in 1916-1917.[407]

Figure 92: Black Population Changes in Selected Southern and Northern States

Region	1900-1910	1910-1920	1920-1930
Cotton South			
South Carolina	-72,000	-74,500	-204,300
Georgia	-16,200	-74,700	-260,000
Alabama	-22,000	-70,800	-80,000
Mississippi	-30,900	-129,600	-68,800
Industrial North			
New York	35,800	63,100	172,800
Pennsylvania	32,900	82,500	101,700
Michigan	1,900	38,700	86,100
Illinois	23,500	69,800	119,300

Alferdteen Harrison
Black Exodus, The Great Migration From the American South [408]

The second wave of migration occurred after the Stock Market crashed in October, 1929, when the flow of money from Wall Street slowed to a trickle, impacting the purchase of products from the South, further causing African Americans to seek employment in the North. The third and largest of the migrations happened between 1940 and 1970, when an estimated five million African Americans left the South, particularly from those states defined as the Deep South - such as Alabama, Mississippi and Louisiana. However, members of the Cornwall Murphy family that had migrated from the South during the first migration around the turn of the century were already well established in Massachusetts before this wave occurred.

5.7   Margaret Melton from Ahoskie, North Carolina

The first family member to go north as part of the Great Migration was Junious Melton, Abner and Sally's oldest son and older brother to Margaret Melton Murphy. He was part of the recruitment drive of the George Pullman Company, looking for handsome and exotic looking young men to serve as porters on the Pullman Railcar. In "1867, George Pullman introduced the first Pullman railroad car, called the President, a sleeper railcar with an attached kitchen, wine cellar and scullery." It was considered a luxury hotel on the railways,[409] designed to offer the wealthy rider the opportunity to travel in the same upper-class style they were accustomed to in the most expensive first class hotel anywhere in the country. The Pullman Porter, as they were called, was specially trained to provide personal attention to every need of the traveling public. George Pullman knew that his discerning passengers were not only interested in luxury accommodations, but also wanted the personal services to match their accommodations.

Two years later, William Melton followed his brother Junious and also became a Pullman Porter. The Melton brothers moved to Boston to become Pullman porters during the most glamorous years in the industry for young men of color, particularly for young men who desired to go north and escape the racism of the Jim Crow South. By time Junious and William Melton became Pullman porters in the early 1920s, the position was recognized as one of the major avenues for an African-American man and his family to become part of the black middle class. The Pullman Porter concept of a strikingly handsome young African-American men waiting on white patrons was based on the southern slave concept. Many of the Pullman Porters had been educated and trained to be doctors, engineers, lawyers and schoolteachers, but who couldn't find work in those fields because of their race and the discriminatory actions of potential employers all across the nation.[410]

The Pullman Porters toured the big cities that their neighbors only dreamed of visiting. They wore white shirts, jackets and ties. They were mostly Republicans and owned their own homes. They were men whose jobs took them from the East Coast to the West Coast, and gave the appearance of being "well-traveled" and learned in the ways that world travelers seem to have. These men were highly respected in their communities, and married the prettiest girls in town. The men traveled in small social circles and their wives sat down each Sunday to enjoy high tea and to play bridge, while their husbands talked sports, talked about the cities they toured, and in hushed tones bragged about the girlfriends they had in other small towns along their train routes.

Having grown up on their father's farm in North Carolina, hard work came easy to the Melton boys. Like many of the Pullman Porters, they were soon able to purchase homes. Junious and William purchased homes in Boston's Sugar Hill neighborhood, a rising black middle class community in upper Roxbury. Junious purchased a large, single family, Victorian-style house with fifteen rooms on Hazelton Street that remains in the Melton family today.

While Junious and William moved north, Abner and Sally wanted to make sure that the remaining children were isolated from the constant nighttime harassment of the Klansmen, and that their children would be well-educated and be able to compete in the urban communities up north. The Melton's were not financially independent, but they were able to send their children to private boarding schools.[411] Twentieth century southern boarding schools were often affiliated with northern churches such as the Congregational, Episcopal and Methodist Churches, or with northern philanthropic organizations concerned about the education of southern blacks.

During this period in North Carolina, most children did not go to school, white or black. Education was left to Sunday school or to a young woman who completed some form of schooling and taught children of all ages the basics of reading, writing, and arithmetic in a one-room schoolhouse.

Abner and Sally Melton sent most of their children, including their daughter Margaret, to boarding school.[412] The school Margaret attended was similar to finishing schools for women in the North. These were schools of higher learning where young women of color learned the fine art of entertaining, socializing, and the proper way to take care of a family and manage a household.

At boarding school, Margaret met the daughters of other middle- and upper-class black families, many of whom were the daughters of extended relatives or families with whom the Meltons had good business and personal relationships. While at boarding school, Margaret, or Maggie, as her friends called her, met a young girl her own age named Estelle Jones. Estelle, who was two years older than Maggie, would become her lifelong friend, as the two of them would eventually leave North Carolina and make the long journey to Boston, Massachusetts. After boarding school, Estelle moved to Boston to live with her aunt, and soon after, she met and married Alfred Dupree from Boston. She and Margaret became pen pals, writing to each other constantly. Each of their letters expressed the same wish. Estelle missed her dear friend Maggie, and wished that she would move to Boston. Margaret would write back and the friendship letters were pretty much the same, she missed Estelle, and desperately wanted to move to Boston, particularly since her older brothers already lived there, and her sister Odie was in the process of also moving there.

Estelle, who initially worked in a restaurant and would eventually open her own restaurant in Boston's South End, would write about the wonders of the big city and its very active social scene, and would always end her letters with "Maggie, I wish you were here." Maggie would always write back about how boring it was in Rich Square, North Carolina, and would quickly change the subject to questions about Estelle's fashion, friends and lifestyle instead. The exchange of letters was therapeutic for Estelle Dupree, because life in Boston was not as glamorous as she portrayed in her letters. The restaurant was not as glamorous as she would profess, the work was hard, and the hours were long. When she became a manger, she found the staff difficult to manage and she needed help. Estelle had a solution: She asked Maggie to move to Boston and work at one of the city's fastest growing and renowned southern-style restaurants.

Margaret wanted to explore the life of a big city, and a move to Boston was logical choice since her older brothers lived there. Her brothers, William and Junious, were exceptionally handsome, tall and lean with straight black hair. Their fair skin coloring allowed them to easily fit into the "mocha café society" of Boston. Because of their appearance, they were often asked what their nationality was and went so far as to say that they were Ethiopian, as to add an exotic flair to their cultural heritage and their prestige.[413]

Each Melton brother had bought a car before anyone else in the neighborhood could afford one. They both belonged to Boston's St. Mark's Congregational Church on Boston's Sugar Hill. Across the street from the church was where Junious purchased his large, fifteen-room Victorian home. Although they were recent transplants to a community that typically didn't take to newcomers, they quickly became pinnacles of Boston's black society and black Republican Party. Their sister Addie, who now called herself Odie, was also living in Boston with her new husband Joseph Rocha, a pharmacist in Boston's South End. Odie also encouraged her younger sister, Margaret, to make the move to Boston, and soothed their parents' concern about an unmarried woman living in the North by allowing Maggie to live with her and Joseph, rather than suggesting Maggie live with her playboy brothers.

In 1924, at the age of 21, the move to Boston was everything Maggie had imagined. The skyscrapers were certainly more impressive than anything she had seen in North Carolina. The elevated train system, which was the first to be built in the nation, enabled her to go from her brother's house in Roxbury, to work in the South End, or to the find stores in downtown Boston. When she took the bus, she could sit anywhere, even next to a white person. To Maggie, this was an important milestone in her life.

Maggie and her sister Odie would save their money and take the aboveground trolley once a month to have sandwiches at the lunch counter at the restaurant in the renowned S.S. Pierce and Company store on Coolidge Corner in Brookline, Massachusetts. S.S. Pierce and Company was founded in Boston, Massachusetts, and known internationally for its gourmet and specialty foods that were shipped around the world. Until her death, Margaret would always buy her jellies and jams from the local S.S. Pierce store as a sentimental reminder of her youth. She would always say that there was no better jam in the world than S.S. Pierce - unless, of course, they were the homemade jams made by her mother, Sally.

5.8   Robert Murphy of St. Paul, Minnesota

Approximately a year after she moved to Boston, Margaret Melton met a flirtatious young man attending the prestigious Massachusetts Institute for Technology, in Cambridge, Massachusetts. Maggie initially didn't like the arrogant young Robert Murphy, who was shorter and browner than the boys she usually dated.[414] While she would joke that he wasn't hard to look at, he didn't possess the debonair good looks of her previous boyfriends. Robbie, as she would eventually call him, thought he was smarter and more-worldly than everyone else because he had lived out west in Minnesota, he lived for a short period of time in North Carolina and Virginia, and he graduated from Boston public schools.

Many years later, Maggie would often joke that Robert was cocky and "full of himself." However, they did have a lot in common. Their family roots were grounded in North Carolina and Virginia, and they both were born in Norfolk, Virginia, in 1903. While it took a while for Maggie to fancy herself on Robbie, he had many of the qualities that she was looking for in a potential husband. But there was one other major issue keeping the two of them apart. Robbie was an only child and was very close to his mother, who "was one of the most difficult women" that Maggie had ever met.

Of course, as with any young couple, this was the perfect ingredient in a courtship recipe that would eventually lead to marriage between the couple, but friction and years of estrangement between Maggie Melton and Viola Fraction Warner, Robbie's mother. Viola Fraction Warner's initial reluctance to be overly friendly towards Maggie was out of her concern that while dating, the two of them would eventually decide that he should drop out of school to get married - and that is exactly what he did.

Viola had very definite plans for her son, who was a successful athlete in one of the most competitive schools in the world. Marriage was not one of Viola's plans for Robbie, particularly a marriage to a young woman who thought she was of a social station above Robbie and his family. Robbie's stepfather, John Warner, was born in Barbados, West Indies. He was a stern, rigid and unforgiving man, who believed strongly in education. Warner had very little patience for foolery and for anyone who subscribed to it, including his stepson.

John and Viola Warner lived in the gritty blue-collar section of Boston's first and second-generation immigrant South End. They didn't like anything about the people who lived up on Boston's Sugar Hill, whom they believed pretended to be better than everyone else. The Warners lived amongst the hard-working European immigrants and had no admiration for the so-called "colored Bourgeoisie" that fancied themselves as upper-crust people in Boston's "mocha café society".

John Warner was grounded in hard work and felt that his stepson was too "footloose and fancy free." As much as Robbie loved his mother, he despised his stepfather. The feelings were mutual; the two men did not get along well. Having been bounced around to family members as a young child, Robbie was not used to the discipline of a man like John Warner. Robbie felt that his stepfather was a miserable human being and he wanted to make everyone else's life miserable, especially Robbie's.

Warner constantly reminded his wife, Viola, that her son Robbie received an excellent foundation by attending private Catholic schools in St. Paul, Minnesota, and the public schools in Boston. In Barbados, only the children of wealthy families were afforded such an education. Warner knew his stepson could have a very promising future, if only he applied himself. Warner felt that Robbie needed discipline and direction, and that his goal should be college, not hanging out with his buddies and flirting with girls.

While Viola was sympathetic to her son's frustrations with his stepfather, she was also sensitive to what her husband was saying. She also grew up in an education-focused household. She wanted her son to go on to college. They were living in changing times and in the City of Boston, where some of the world's best colleges and universities could be found. John Warner was right - Viola's son had to get an education. Upon graduation from high school, Robbie had the unique opportunity to attend Massachusetts Institute of Technology. His family was very proud, because this was a unique opportunity for any man, let alone a black man - and they knew it. However, once college started, Robbie's studies took a back seat to his socializing. He never really had a stable environment or long-term friendships at home. But now in Boston, he could not get enough of his new companions.

In Boston's South End, Robbie met young men from all over the world. He met men whose experiences in North Carolina and Virginia he could relate to, and he met men from Germany, Russia, and Poland that gave him a new, global perspective on life. Robbie hated eating at home with his mother and stepfather, so when a friend extended an invitation to him, he always accepted. He loved to eat German, Polish, or Russian food, because the meals reminded him of what he ate while visiting friends and their family-owned eateries in Minnesota. He felt at home in their kitchens and with his European friends.

Robbie loved his newly adopted home. He loved everything about Boston, including flirting with the girls - until he met Margaret Melton of Ahoskie, North Carolina. Maggie Melton was cute and petite, and was dating Robbie's archrival, Moe Robinson. The two men were very similar in many ways. They both were young, brash, arrogant, and were both young African-American Republicans.

After Maggie broke off her courtship with Moe, Robbie asked her out on a date. She wasn't interested in Robbie Murphy, because she didn't want to date another boy like Moe Robinson. However, Robbie persisted and soon they were dating. With this, Viola and John Warner's fears materialized. Robbie decided that he wasn't interested in college, and instead solicited the help of Maggie's brothers to get a job as a Pullman Porter. After all, Robbie would rationalize, many of the Pullman Porters were college-educated men why spend the time and money to go to college when he could get the same job at the same pay rate as the college boys. Robbie and Maggie got married, and initially he did not go back to school.

This did not sit well with Robbie's parents. Viola blamed Maggie for her son not going back to college, and John Warner blamed the fast life of the South End's music scene and the pretentious life of Maggie's family and friends up on Boston's Sugar Hill. This was a recipe for a family disaster. Robbie's decision to leave school caused a permanent division between his young wife and the steel will of his mother that lasted a lifetime. Viola was a strong woman, and she decided that as long Robbie and Maggie were together, she was going to make Maggie's life miserable.

As Robbie and Maggie planned their life, Robbie thought he had it all worked out. In order to support a young family, Robbie decided to take a job as a "Red Cap," a nickname for a Pullman Porter, at Boston's Back Bay Train Station. Maggie's brother, Junious, used his connections to help Robbie get a job at the station. After World War I, between 1924 and 1925, the job market was especially competitive for young black men. Being a Red Cap was considered a very prestigious job for a young African-American man to have, particularly one who wanted to leave the grit of Boston's South End and move uptown to the large single-family homes in the neighborhoods of Roxbury's section of Humboldt Avenue. However, due to the financial conditions of the country and the traveling industry, the men were asked to work long hours and to be away from home for long periods of time.

After his first two children were born, Robbie realized, as did most young men, that the glamour of being a Red Cap was not all that it was cracked up to be. Having the responsibility to a wife and family, with a third child on the way, he went back to college part-time and attended night classes at the Wentworth Institute of Technology, in Boston's Fenway section of the city. This pleased his mother, Viola. Then, in 1929, the United States suffered from one of the worst economic downturns in history as result of the Stock Market Crash, followed by the worldwide Great Depression.

The Great Depression affected working conditions everywhere. Men who had jobs had to endure the rapidly deteriorating working conditions in all employment industries - after all, as they were constantly reminded by the press, by their friends, and by their family, they were the lucky ones. At least they had jobs.

The conditions for the Red Caps rapidly deteriorated as the railroad industry cut costs in order to remain solvent during the Great Depression. The Red Caps worked longer, backbreaking hours, with very little pay and even fewer tips. As the industry continued with various cost-cutting measures, the men were forced to cover work assignments that they were not hired for and to work double shifts. Men like Robbie, who were hired to be Red Caps and worked inside the trains, were often asked to fill in and load heavy cargo in the cargo compartments at the rear of the train, often in the middle of the night during Boston's cold, frigid winters. Jobs were cut and families were thrown into personal economic calamity.

Many of the young men became attracted to the growing talk of the union stewards. As his wife Maggie would often comment, Robbie loved to talk and was a good orator. His likeable demeanor, his worldliness and his education made him a likely candidate for becoming a political activist and a union steward. Robbie became a member of the Carmen's Union and served on the Boston Chapter's Leadership Team. While Robbie argued passionately for the rights of the Red Caps and porters, Maggie was always fearful that Robbie would lose his job, and his outspoken mother Viola was concerned that Robbie would not complete his education and have a true career, not just a job to make ends meet.

Although they were very close, Viola became more vocal with her son and advised him that if the working conditions were as deplorable as he professed, then the railroad industry was no place for a man of color to work. She constantly reminded him of the hard conditions that her father endured in the latter part of his railroad career, and the toll that it took on his family, particularly her mother. As the Great Depression and families' personal finances worsened, more and more college boys dropped out because their families could no longer afford the cost. Once again, Viola's hopes for her son's education were dashed, as Robbie soon could no longer afford to take care of his family and pay for night school at the same time.

Viola did not really place any blame on her son. After all, the economy was challenging for everyone and Robbie had a family to support. However, she continued to openly blame Maggie for her son dropping out of school and for not encouraging him to complete his education. To complicate the matter, Robbie's stepfather constantly reminded him of his failures as a provider for his family because he didn't heed his advice and pursue his education. The tension in Robbie's mother and stepfather's home escalated to the point where Maggie was not welcomed. While she allowed her children to visit their grandmother, the hostility between the two women was palpable.

Viola was soon stricken with cancer, and advised her only child that his family should be his priority, and not the Carmen's Union. She shared with him the stories of her own mother in remote Montana, and the challenges and heartbreaks she endured as the wife of a railroad man. As much as she didn't like Maggie, Viola didn't want that lifestyle for her grandchildren. In 1933, Viola succumbed to her illness. Upon her death, during the height of the Great Depression, Robbie left the Carmen's Union and started work with the Federal government as an engineer in the City of Boston's Charlestown Naval Shipyard, the same shipyard that his grandfather James Fraction once came to, while commissioned in the U.S. Navy, seeking medical assistance.

Although his mother attended the Columbus Avenue AME Church in Boston's South End, Robbie and Maggie attended the prestigious St. Mark's Congregational Church in Boston's North Dorchester neighborhood. Boston was considered to be the "hub of the universe," with its large number of top-rated academic institutions, some of the world's finest medical facilities, and rich social history. At the time, St. Marks Congregational Church was considered to be the hub of Boston's black political and social community. Robbie and Maggie were pillars of Boston's St. Mark Church.

St. Mark's Church, originally named the William Lloyd Garrison Memorial Church in honor of the famous abolitionist stalwart, and started out as a struggling church with fewer than 50 members. The church first started out in the expanding black community in Boston's South End, with locations on Washington Street and Tremont Street. As Boston's African Americans left Beacon Hill's North Slope and moved into the South End, they began to build a strong multi-cultural community with recent Irish and Jewish immigrants. In 1919, the deacons followed their congregants from the multi-ethnic, multi-unit apartment dwellings in Boston's South End to the larger and more fashionable homes in upper Roxbury, and purchased a stately church from The Massachusetts Quaker Fellowship. Located at the corner of upper Roxbury's Humboldt Avenue and Townsend Street, the church became home to a continuum of locally and nationally known political, social and religious leaders.

During the early days of the Great Depression, under the leadership of the young and impressive Reverend Samuel Leroy Laviscount, St. Mark Church experienced a spiritual, social and economic awakening. While other congregations across the country fell on financial hard times during the 1930s, under Reverend Laviscount's direction, St.

Mark Church contributed to the development of upper Roxbury and North Dorchester's social services and started a settlement house. The church provided food and clothing for those who fell on hard times because of the economic depression. The church leveraged its contacts in the South and served as a feeder for many of the southern black colleges and universities with gifted young African-American men and women graduating from Boston's high schools who wanted to go onto college. It helped its congregants find jobs at a time when jobs were hard to come by, and helped to facilitate economic development in the community.

Reverend Laviscount encouraged his membership to be actively involved in other unions across the city and in Boston's rough and tumble political scene. His intellectually inspiring Sunday morning sermons always integrated politics, individual empowerment and community activism. He always struck the right chord with his congregants, particularly with the ambitious men who were thankful for having jobs during a tight recession.

Reverend Laviscount was one of the first black clergymen to befriend the infamous James Michael Curly, who was born in the tough Irish neighborhood on Roxbury's Mission Hill, about two miles from St. Mark's. Curley, the four-term Democratic Mayor of Boston, the twice-serving state representative of Boston, and the one term Governor of the Commonwealth of Massachusetts, had tremendous respect for Reverend Laviscount and his congregants. The politically astute Reverend Laviscount could deliver votes from his predominately-black Republican membership and from the adjacent Irish, Jewish and upper middle-class Roxbury Ward 12 neighborhoods. The tough Irish politician understood the power of getting out the votes when he needed them, and Laviscount would always drive a hard bargain in return for his congregants, but he would always deliver.

The smooth and polished Laviscount preached from the pulpit about the value of watching Curley manage the tough Irish political machine in Boston and how he constantly and successfully succeeded in his rough and tumble battles with the openly hostile Protestant Massachusetts State Legislature. As Boston's premier political boss, Curley delivered for St Mark's Church. During his term as Mayor, neighborhood schools such as the prestigious David A. Ellis School were built, he found city and state jobs for Laviscount's congregants, always attended church socials, and would often be seen at the funerals of his "good friends."

This relationship came at a price. Laviscount had to constantly encourage the men in his congregation to become more and more politically active, and this separated his congregants from the social interactions of the other black churches, particularly in the South End and in lower Roxbury. St. Mark's acquired the reputation of an elitist church where only certain light-skinned blacks were accepted. Robbie and Maggie's involvement in the church only confirmed what Robbie's family had believed about the uppity, pretentious People of Color like Maggie, her family, and her circle of friends and colleagues.

For the first time in its history, as more and more southerners migrated north, Boston's strong black community was becoming divided along the lines of skin color, economics, religion and geography. Many of the social hierarchies of the old southern plantation society, along the lines of color and social status, were now becoming part of Boston's black community's social and political life. Each summer, as Robbie became actively involved in various political campaigns at the federal, state and, city levels, he worked in conjunction with the church in helping to get out the vote. He was instrumental in helping to get fellow church members to actively run for the staggered state representative seats from the District in the fall primaries. Maggie would take her children, Peggy, Bob, and Jackie, to visit her mother and father, Sally and Abner, in Ahoskie, North Carolina.

The most efficient mode of transportation was to take the Baltimore-Washington Railways, which stopped in Union Station in Washington, D.C., and then to switch trains to catch the Carolina-Virginia Railways. As a young woman, Maggie couldn't wait to leave Ahoskie, North Carolina, and move to Boston. But as an adult and the mother of three small children, Maggie missed the serenity of "down home," and each year looked forward to her annual pilgrimage to see her extended family, and the sights and smells of "Nor" Carolina. While she had little control over Robbie taking the children to see his mother and his Aunt Elizabeth, or even his stepfather, John Warner - whom Maggie despised and felt was "just plain creepy" - she knew that during the summer the children were with her and that Robbie's family would not have access to them.

Each time she returned home, Maggie was reminded of how much had changed in her life since she left Ahoskie. In Boston, she lived in a neighborhood that was predominantly white. She was able to go into any grocery store to buy food. She and her older sister, Odie, were able to take the trolley to sit and eat at the S.S. Pierce and Company's lunch counter, where they were served sandwiches and soda by a white sales girl. Back home, she would have to sit at a segregated lunch counter in the black section of the store. Perhaps the most important thing for Maggie, who as a girl was sent off to boarding school to avoid the segregated Jim Crow South, was that in Boston, her children went to public schools with white and black children in the same classroom. How different her life and the life of her children might have been had she remained in North Carolina.

The train ride from Boston to North Carolina was long, hot and often times uncomfortable, particularly if you had to sit in the less desirable "For Black Only" passenger cars at the end of the train. Once Maggie switched passenger trains in Washington, D.C., from the Baltimore-Washington to the Carolina-Virginia Railways, she was forced to switch from her socially and racially integrated life up north to the repressive and segregated Jim Crow ways of the South. As much as Maggie missed home and the family, she didn't miss this aspect of southern living, and didn't want her children to know the negative aspects of life in the segregated South.

Maggie had a fair complexion and would often times try to sit in the more comfortable passenger cars designated for "whites only." She would pass herself off as Italian, and if questioned, would inform people that she was an Italian Catholic married to an Irish Catholic from Boston. With the name Murphy and with a boarding pass from Boston's Back Bay Station, sometimes she could actually pull this masquerade off. Other northern white train conductors joined her protest, albeit silently, by letting her sit in the "White Only Cars" as long as she was quiet, though this was more challenging with young children. When Maggie or her siblings traveled south, they absolutely hated sitting in the railroad cars designated as "For Colored Only." The passenger cars were older with worn seats and were overcrowded.

Since the passengers could not visit or eat in the "White Only" dining cars, they had to bring their own food. The segregated passenger cars often smelled of fried chicken, boiled eggs, and an especially pungent southern delicacy known as "wrinkled steak" - during the summer months the stench worsened in the heat and humidity.

Going south for Maggie was bittersweet. It provided her with an opportunity to see family and friends, and get away from the bustle of the city. But the fresh air of the countryside served another purpose - her second child, Bob, had contracted rheumatic fever and it was important he get away from the grit and grime of the city and breathe some clean air. Rheumatic fever is an inflammation of the heart, joints and central nervous system, particularly in young children. Rheumatic fever usually follows a severe cold and strep throat. During the early 1930s, rheumatic fever was prevalent and affected scores of children worldwide. Robbie and Maggie's son, Bob, had one of the more severe cases of the illness and was placed in a sanatorium for eighteen months. Robert and Maggie were devastated when the doctors informed them that their son's heart had been permanently scarred and damaged, and he now had a life expectancy of no more than thirteen or fourteen years.

Once Bob was released from the hospital and given permission to go south for the summer, Maggie took him there as quickly as possible. She was relieved that her son would be getting fresh air and would be spoiled and pampered by her family. As her son became stronger each day from running in the fields of tall grass and breathing in the open air Maggie wondered if the urban life of Boston was truly the best place for her son and other children.

The family packed up their belongings and moved to the then-rural town of Framingham, Massachusetts, a soon-to-be suburban community some fifteen miles west of Boston. As the family settled into their new surroundings, World War II loomed on the European horizon, and America's involvement was just beginning. After World War I, most Americans wanted nothing to do with the escalating tensions in Europe. World War I was expensive for the Americans and they still were dealing with the economic crisis from the Great Depression.

But war was in the air.

5.9   Harold Cornwall of Brockton, Massachusetts

During World War I, the city of Brockton, Massachusetts, continued its tradition of benefiting from a wartime economy. During the Civil War, the city became one of the most important manufacturing cities in the country. Its importance on the world stage was a direct result of the manufacturing of hand-sewn shoes. Almost every able body in the city was directly involved with the manufacturing and support of the city's shoe industry. As young soldiers went south to fight in the Civil War, they needed shoes and boots to wear, and the City of Brockton was the largest producer of shoes and leather products in America. During the First World War, the soldiers who were now fighting overseas continued to need shoes and other leather products.

The city of Brockton established itself as the shoe capital of the world, and its residents were deeply proud of being part of history and part of the shoe industry. The importance of shoe manufacturing enabled the city to grow its infrastructure, develop support industries, and rapidly increase its population. As the shoe industry grew, the need for labor attracted skilled workers from around the country, and brought to the city immigrant labor from Western Europe. Benjamin Cornwall, Harold Cornwall's father, and other members of the Cornwall family's lives were intertwined with the growth of the shoe industry.

In March 1891, Benjamin and Cora Cornwall had a son, Benjamin Junior. After Benjamin Jr., the couple had another son in 1892, but he lived less than three months. After giving birth the second time, Cora began to have health problems and eventually became stricken with consumption. Consumption, known today as tuberculosis, consumed the entire body in a slow, painful manner. Caused by a highly contagious bacterial infection, in the past, consumption killed almost eighty percent of its victims. At the turn of the twentieth century, it was believed if patients were sent to a sanatorium and had access to fresh air, that they would be able to overcome the effects of the disease.

The family of Boston's famous Civil War abolitionist, William Lloyd Garrison, opened their summer home in Boston's Fort Hill section of the city to women and children who were victims of consumption. The medical care, good nutrition, and the fresh air helped many, but advanced medicines had not yet been developed to turn the tide of the disease. As Cora Cornwall became gravely ill, she needed assistance with the raising of her sons, Benjamin Junior and Walter, as well as needing someone to take care of her. Cora's younger sister, Grace, who was born in 1878, came from Huntington, New York to care for her ailing sister and infant son. Grace was a logical choice to tend to her sister, as she knew all about caring for ailing family members. She was the long-term caregiver for her mother, Keziah (Gardiner) Jackson whom she cared for prior to her death in 1889. Under the care of her sister, Grace Jackson, in 1900, Cora Cornwall, as so many other Americans at the time, succumbed after a very long and painful illness, from the complications of the consumption. Later that year, Cora's sister, Grace, and Benjamin Cornwall married and the following year had a son named Harold.

Benjamin Cornwall, like so many in Brockton, worked in the city's shoe industry. Familiar with the management and handling of horses, Benjamin's first job as a teenager was as a wagoner, where he transported shoes ready for market to the Crescent Street railroad depot. The shoe industry had a number of different positions of importance, and the dyeing of shoes was one of the most important positions that a manufacturer could have. At the turn of the twentieth century, American families prospered with the growth of the U.S. economy - and women adorned themselves with fancy fashions from Europe. Rather than wear the traditional black female boot shoes that were commonplace at the time, they wanted shoes that matched the colors of their dresses. The commercialization of women's shoes in different colors made the shoe industry realize the importance of the dyes that they used, which added the vibrancy of the colors to the shoes they sold. Shoe manufactures in Brockton began to manufacture shoes in different colors, and the brilliance of the colors enhanced the product's mass sales appeal.

As a young man, it was easy work as a wagoner, but with a wife and infant son, not much money could be made driving the wagons back-and-forth to the train depot. Benjamin switched jobs and became a dye foreman in the shoe factories. As foreman, Benjamin and his staff were instrumental in ensuring that the leather vats were properly flushed at the end of each day, and that they were primed each morning with the appropriate colors for dying. Each day of the week a different color was assigned for coloring the shoes. The dyes were strong and the men suspected that they were quite toxic. However, the money was better than working the machines that stitched the shoes.

Benjamin developed a rough cough. He initially feared that he had contracted consumption, the debilitating disease that had killed his first wife, Cora. Having watched her suffer, he was all too familiar with the effects of the disease. Over time, as his cough progressed, he began to wonder if it was consumption or might it be something else. No matter what it was, his body was being overtaken by it. His coworkers noticed that as the workday progressed his coughs got worse and he would often break out in cold sweats. When they brought it to his attention, he initially noticed that his coughs were not as bad when at home, particularly on his days off, so he knew from his wife's dreaded disease that it was not the consumption that was making him ill. He suspected that it might be the chemicals from the dyes that were causing his cough. But slowly he noticed that he was not as strong as before and became concerned that it might be something more serious.

Initially, his doctors also suspected that he may have been exposed to his wife's consumption and although he was strong and healthy during his wife's debilitating illness; his lungs had been exposed to the disease and was causing his shortness of breath and the steady decline in his health. His body was not consumed as it normally would if he had consumption, so they theorized that it might be a slow growing cancer in his lungs, perhaps from direct exposure to the dyes that he came in contact with at work.

As Benjamin's health continued to deteriorate, World War I was slowly coming to an end. Benjamin was no longer able to work, but the need for wartime shoes for the soldiers overseas also began to slow down as well. A weakened Benjamin and other citizens of Brockton proudly welcomed the veterans back home from the war in Europe.

In the fall of 1918, as the city rolled out the welcome mat, as was being done in countless cities and towns across the country, a very unsuspecting public was about to learn about the squalor that the soldiers had to endure while in Europe - and the dreaded effects of a new cold strain that was sweeping the nation. But this was not just any every day common cold that Americans were coming down with; it was, in fact, the start of a viral influenza pandemic that lasted from 1918 to 1919. The influenza virus that flu season, now known as the Spanish Flu, killed between 20 million and 40 million people worldwide. The 1918 Spanish Flu was a global disaster that affected ever corner of the planet, including the city of Brockton, Massachusetts. In 1918, Benjamin contracted the Spanish Flu and died, leaving behind his oldest son, Benjamin Jr.; his other children, Harold, Carlton, Martha and Cora; and his second wife, Grace Jackson Cornwall.

His son, Harold, had deep roots in Brockton and knew all of the city's old families. His uncles paved many of the city's streets, and the family was well known throughout this shoe city. A popular young man, Harold was a good friend with some of the sons of the influential families of the city. These boys enjoyed baseball, basketball, boxing and swimming. Harold would joke that as young boys, he and his friends knew what day of the week it was by going swimming. The dyes from the shoe factories were released into the streams adjacent to each of the shoe factories, so when the boys finished swimming, they were often the same color of the shoes that were dyed that day. Harold's favorite day was Thursday, the day he would come out of the water the color blue. These were the very same dyes and chemicals that had made his father ill, but the temptation was too much for a bunch of teenage boys looking for fun.

As a young man, Harold took up several sports. At one point, he saw himself becoming a professional athlete, even a pro-basketball player. He was captain of the Brockton basketball team, which won many state trophies. In addition, he won many awards for his outstanding swimming ability. Harold Cornwall loved his home, his family and the "City of Champions" in which he lived and raised his family. Because of different interracial marriages, he lived to see the family split into three racial groups - white, black and Native American -each family segment thriving successfully and in harmony, within the confines of his beloved city.

Every Friday night, Harold and his friends would go to the old boxing gym on Green Street in Brockton, where the boys would watch some of the amateur "ethnic" boxers fight. Harold remembered Brockton as a wonderful city and a melting pot of cultures. Tough Irish street kids who would fight one another, and enjoyed fighting the tough Polish kids. The Italian kids mastered the boxing ring, while the more laid-back Swedish boys thought it was smarter to hold back their punches and conserve energy, but they always seemed to lose.

As the boys got older and had a few beers on their nights out, they would dare one another to try their hand at competing against some of the boxers who were trying to qualify for tournaments. Harold, on several occasions, had been recognized for his skill as an amateur lightweight boxer. There are several pictures of Harold Cornwall in his boxing shorts and gloves. He always said that he looked pretty good in the "before" pictures, but was glad that there weren't any "after" pictures. Although a respectable amateur, Harold Cornwall never boxed professionally. According to the city's Centennial Publication, Sidney A. Davidson, Secretary Spoils Committee reported that there were eight bouts fought in the Armory, and in the 125-Pound Class semifinals, Harold Cornwall of Brockton beat Gerald Webster of North Easton in one round. In the final bout, Win Anderson beat Harold Cornwall in three rounds.[415]

Throughout all of Harold's life, there were three things that he would always say about his much beloved city of Brockton, Massachusetts. It was the best city in the world to live in, it was the "shoe capitol of the world" and it was known as the "City of Champions" because of the successes of several of its "native sons." These "native sons" were world-class boxers who trained in some of the same gyms where Harold had trained in during his amateur years. One such champion was Rocco Francis Marchegiano, a local Brockton kid, who became known as Rocky Marciano, who the undefeated World Heavyweight Champion from 1952 to 1956. Whenever Rocky Marciano was in town to fight an exhibition match or whenever he had a fight on the television, Harold Cornwall and his friends were there to watch. A second favorite boxer of Harold was Marvelous Marvin Hagler, who was the World Middleweight Champion from 1980 to 1987.

As busy as Harold was with sports, his friends, and work, he still managed to find time for dating. He met and married Miss Marie Howell, who he described as, "the prettiest girl in Brockton. They were married for 67 years.

5.10   Marie Howell of Brockton, Massachusetts

Unlike the Cornwall family, who had family roots in the Bridgewater and Brockton communities in Massachusetts, dating back to the mid- to late 1700s, the Howell family of Oxford, North Carolina, was a family new to Brockton. Marie Howell is eleven generations removed from John Gowen, the Angolan brought to Jamestown, Virginia, in 1619. While Marie and her sister, Lois, and her brother, William (also known as Badger), were each born in Brockton, they initially were considered first generation Brocktonians. But as the years passed, Marie Cornwall quickly became known as "old Brockton."

In most African-American communities in the North, the Congregational Church was the bedrock church of the black middle class. Founded by the early British settlers, the Pilgrims and the Puritans, the church represented the New England protestant work ethic. Marie's parents, William and Matilda (Watson) Howell, were among the original and active members of the Lincoln Congregational Church, one of the two original African-American churches in the city of Brockton. Lincoln Congregational Church was purchased in 1896, and served as a meetinghouse for Brockton's small but growing middle class black community, where congregants met to discuss and exchange views on education, religion, and politics.

Most of the founding members of the church originated from Virginia and North Carolina, and came north to escape the growing intolerance of their former homes in the South. Many traveled north together and now worshiped together in a city that they believed provided tremendous economic opportunities for them and their children. Many of Brockton's prominent African-American citizens - the Bakers, the Hillards, the Howells, the Mapps, the Russells and the Torrences - were the sons and daughters of Virginia and North Carolina's original Free People of Color. And through the generations were all interrelated somehow, many of the new arrivals knew each other long before they migrated to Massachusetts.

Coming from small southern agricultural towns, these families were a tremendous support system to each other in a new city in the North that was rapidly becoming more industrialized as it met the growing needs of its shoe industry. Working hard was not a concept foreign to these families. They were the descendants from the original pioneers and frontiersmen and women who worked long, backbreaking hours in colonial Virginia and North Carolina. These were hard-working men and women, with strong social ties to the community, a strong sense of religion and a determined desire to see that their children receive a good education and an improved quality of life.

Matilda Howell considered herself to be the epitome of style and fashion. Each Easter, she would dress her family in the latest fashions that were sold on Main Street in Brockton. Although her husband William was tight fisted with his money, Matilda, under the guise of needing Easter finery, would use the occasion to buy a new wardrobe for herself and her children. In fact, she used Christmas, Mother's Day, birthdays or any other occasion to buy something new.

As much as William would protest about his wife's spending - and according to his grandchildren, he did protest - he was still very proud of his wife and the constant compliments that he received because of her beauty and style. Once he became positioned in his new city, William Howell was able to establish himself as a prosperous businessman. He owned more than ten multifamily homes across the city, in the rapidly growing Montello and Campello sections of Brockton, which was quite an accomplishment since many of the units were in white neighborhoods. This was a feat he would never have been able to accomplish in the South.

William Howell also owned substantial land, which he farmed. He then sold the produce to market. Being an astute businessman, William knew the value of every penny that he had and would not give any of his produce or farm animals away. Many years later, his granddaughters would joke about the fact that he would give his wife a weekly allowance, and with that allowance she would have to buy the family food and poultry from him. While Matilda Howell hated to admit it, she did adopt some of her husband's more frugal tendencies, and trained her daughters to save their household money for more important things.

But William also gave Matilda an allowance because he knew she loved going to the movies on Friday evenings with the ladies from church. Because of the tight economy during the depression, the movie companies that were competing for business would give out free carnival glasses and other enticements to get the consumer to come to the movies. Matilda, in her own frugal way, would not spend the money to go to a movie show unless she got something free in return. It might not be the movie she really wanted to see, but if they offered something for free, she went. If a ticket to a movie she really wanted to see didn't also come with a free gift, Matilda did not spend the money to see it.

Matilda also liked to sit in front of her classic RCA radio and listen to the live Soap Opera broadcasts of her favorite radio show "The Guiding Light." The live broadcasts were called soap operas because during the commercial breaks they would sell airtime to the soap manufacturers, and since the laundry detergent was sold on her "show," Matilda only bought Tide to wash her clothes. Although her husband stressed frugality in the household, no matter what the price was in the grocery store, the Tide laundry detergent would always be a staple in her household. She was loyal to her soap operas for their terrific and compelling story lines, and loyal to the commercial brands that these soap operas marketed to their viewers.

Matilda's daughter, Marie, was very much her mother's daughter. Marie was current with the latest styles in the national fashion magazines, including her favorite women's magazines - McCall's and the Ladies Home Journal. Whenever she walked into her favorite high-end stores on Brockton's Main Street, the proprietors would always greet her with, "Good morning Mrs. Cornwall. I have an outfit that will fit you perfectly." They knew if they could get her to put on the right dress, it was a sale that they could rely on. Much like her mother, Marie's children and grandchildren knew not to call her during the week between the hours of 2:00 p.m. and 3:00 p.m. She would be glued to her television set watching her favorite soap opera, "One Life to Live." While she would often tell family members that she only watched the show because she wanted to see the latest fashions that the women were wearing and how they furnished their homes, they knew that she was really interested in the personal lives and daily challenges of the characters on the screen. She had grown up listening to the original radio shows with her mother - the men and women of "One Life to Live" were Marie's second family.

As a young girl, Marie lived with her sister, Lois, their brother, William, and her cousin, Ralphia Mitchell. Ralphia's mother was Anne (Howell) Mitchell, who was sister to Marie's father, William Howell - and the grandmother of Lieutenant Colonel Leo Gray, a noteworthy Tuskegee Airman helped make history during World War II.

Marie and Lois, and their cousin, Ralphia, were raised more as sisters than cousins. Each summer, the trio would take the train from Brockton, Massachusetts, to visit their grandmother, Amanda Watson, in Boydton, Virginia. William and Matilda Howell did not like the Jim Crow conditions of the South, however they loved the African-American community that they had grown up in and wanted their children to fully appreciate that part of the South, and the close relationships of family and friends that went back for generations. As first generation Brocktonians, they knew the importance of being connected to family and they wanted their children to have that same sense of family.

While the girls enjoyed the long train ride to visit their grandmother, they didn't particularly enjoy their stay. The summers were too hot and steamy for them. The town wasn't as developed as the City of Brockton, and the girls didn't understand why they couldn't play with the neighboring little white girls. In the South, black parents were protective of their children and made sure they understood how to stay in their place due to their segregation. This was a stark change for Marie, Lois and Ralphia, who were raised in the North by middle class black families that didn't want their children to feel that they were second class citizens and allowed them to go out and play games with white children. After all, it was expected that those were the same children that they would be competing against in life and in society.

Marie Howell Cornwall's grandmother, Amanda, lived in a large white Victorian-style house with a wrapped around porch - and all of her neighbors were white. But even though Amanda's neighbors were white, segregation was rampant, and the young northern girls were confused. They didn't understand why they could not go out and play with the white girls their age in the neighborhood, and why they couldn't go into the other girls' houses. Marie, Lois, and Ralphia simply thought that their grandmother had too many rules including: don't drink out of this particular water fountain, or don't go to that candy store. They couldn't play in the park down the street. Each year, there seemed to be more things that they couldn't do. The girls felt that they couldn't do anything and they weren't quite sure why their parents wanted them to come down here each summer if they couldn't have any fun.

Every Sunday, Marie's grandmother would make the girls go to the local Methodist church. But these northern girls weren't interested in the more laidback Methodist services, and instead snuck over to peek at the services of the local black Baptist church. To the girls, the songs of gospel hymnals sounded like fun, and they thought that this is what church should be all about. But Boydton, Virginia, was a very small community and it was not long before their grandmother would find out that the girls had not gone to church. As punishment, they would have to stay on the porch for the remainder of the afternoon. The girls felt it was unfair to be punished for not going to their grandmothers church - after all, they did go to church, just not hers. To avoid being "squealed on" again, the girls avoided talking to other people in town. Perhaps then, no one would notice them and tell their grandmother what they had been up to.

Marie Howell Cornwall fondly remembered an elderly black woman saying "Good Mawnig" to the girls. The girls were so amused by the woman's southern accent that they started to laugh at her. As Marie Howell Cornwall recalled their poor behavior and manners, she said that at the time, they had never heard anyone with such a strong southern accent and vernacular. The woman was aghast at the young girls' unruly behavior. She proceeded to ask them "whose chillins are you?" This was just too much for the northern girls to handle, and they ran back towards home laughing. But being mischievous little girls, they got sidetracked by the candy store in town that they weren't supposed to go into.

When the white storekeeper asked them if they knew they weren't supposed to go in to his store, they innocently replied that their grandmother told them not to go in there, but she wasn't around, and they were not going to tell her. The storekeeper allowed them to buy the candy. When the girls returned to their grandmother's house, they were surprised to see the elderly woman they had laughed at earlier sitting on the porch with her dear friend, their grandmother, Amanda.

The elderly woman was more than happy to tell Amanda everything that had happened that afternoon, including about the girls having the nerve of going into the "Whites Only" grocery store. The girls were sent packing, and that was the last time Marie Howell went to visit her grandmother's house.

William and Matilda Howell's daughter, Marie, married Harold Cornwall, from one of the most prestigious black families in Brockton. It was a marriage of true love that endured for more than 67 years. Harold and Marie Cornwall brought to their beloved city of Brockton, style, family values and a strong work ethic. It also brought together two of the oldest African American families in the country. It brought together the lineage of the South's oldest African-American family (consisting of the family lines of America's first African slave, John Gowen of Angola, and the family lines of Chavis, Harris and Howell of Granville, North Carolina) with the lineage of one of the North's oldest African-American family lines (the Cornwells, Brookers and Grandisons of Plymouth County, Massachusetts, and the Jacksons of Gardiner Island on New York's Long, Island.

Almost seventy years after her final visit with her grandmother, Marie Howell Cornwall went back to Amanda's hometown of Boydton, Virginia. Once there, she was pleasantly surprised by the beauty of the town, and its stately, symmetrical antebellum homes with their professionally manicured lawns, wooden swings on expansive porches accented by multiple flower boxes. Boydton was a typical southern town, with its immaculately maintained tree-lined streets and with young kids riding their bikes, followed by their mothers walking down the sidewalks pushing baby carriages. During Marie's visit, she attempted to find more familiar places that she remembered in her youth.

She spotted a beautifully landscaped cemetery, hidden behind a majestic stonewalls. Marie was certain that her grandmother and other family members were buried at this particular cemetery. She drove around the cemetery, but nothing looked familiar to her. As she left the cemetery, she noticed a sign on the stone columns holding the wrought iron gates. She got out of the car to read the sign, and returned with a scowl. The cemetery she believed her family was buried in was dedicated by the "Daughters of the Confederate Soldiers," and it was unlikely that her African-American family was buried there.

Realizing that there must have been two separate cemeteries, Marie then found the black cemetery where her grandmother was presumably buried. Marie was angry and disappointed with the deplorable condition of the African-American cemetery, particularly compared to the impeccable grounds of the Confederate soldiers and their descendants' cemetery. Marie was astounded by how disrespectfully the black cemetery's grounds were maintained and how many of the burial plots had been sunken in due to years of neglect. Many years later, this visit haunted her and made her remorseful to the way she acted with her grandmother, to her friends and the manner in which these decent people were treated in life and how they were being disrespected after their passing.

5.11   The Cornwall Murphy Families in World War II

The Great Depression of 1929 to 1940 impacted families across America differently. It kept Robert Murphy from completing his college education and it took the family from Boston to the fresh air of Framingham, Massachusetts, so that his son, Bob, could get the fresh air he needed to fully recuperate from the effects of his rheumatic fever. It delayed the Cornwall family's effort to buy their family home and forced Harold to work longer hours to support the family. But more than anything else, it instilled a sense of hard work to another generation.

After the U.S. naval fleet at Pearl Harbor was bombed by the Japanese on December 7, 1941, an attack which killed more than 2,400 Americans and wounded another 1,200, the nation entered into the Second World War. American factories were forced into massive production to support the war effort by President Franklin Roosevelt. Men from all walks of life were drafted into the war effort or voluntarily enlisted. Women were recruited to join the workforce and to work in the factories, and some enlisted in the various branches of the military that accepted women.

As the war began, Harold Cornwall went to work at the Fore River Shipyard in Quincy, Massachusetts, and Robert Murphy continued to work at the Charlestown Naval Shipyard in Boston. While the two men did not know each other at the time, they both contributed significantly to the war effort as civilians, and they committed themselves to the defense of the country much as their grandfathers before them had done. Their children and extended family members also committed themselves to the war effort but in many different ways. For example, the daughters of both men, who were in their mid-teens, took up collections for the wounded soldiers.

Black soldiers served in segregated troops during the war. Robert's daughter Peggy supported her high school boyfriend and soon-to-be husband, William W. Wright, who was in the 366th Infantry Regiment, a unit of the segregated 92nd Colored Infantry Division, 5th Army as part of the Eastern Defense Command. One of William's commanding officers was a recent college graduate from Howard University, a young Lieutenant Edward W. Brooke, who subsequently became the first black man elected to the United States Senate since Reconstruction. While in the service, William saw combat in Northern Africa and in the liberation of Rome, just days before the Normandy Invasion in France. Harold Cornwall's daughters, Janice and Joan, took up various collections and volunteered with church social events that supported the efforts of their famous cousin, a Tuskegee Airman named Leo Gray.

5.12   Lieutenant Colonel Leo Gray, a Tuskegee Airman

During World War II, members of the Cornwall Murphy family once again participated in combat as it had done with every previous conflict in American history. One such family member was Lieutenant Colonel Leo R. Gray of Boston, Massachusetts, who was the only child of Leo W. Gray and his wife, Ralphia Mitchell.[416] Prior to World War II, Gray served in the federal government's Junior Reserve Officers' Training Corps (JROTC) program at English High School in Boston, Massachusetts.

Lieutenant Colonel Gray graduated from high school in 1942, at a time when all able-bodied young men were drafted into the military and subsequently sent off to serve in the war effort overseas. While waiting to be drafted into the service, Leo volunteered for the aviation cadet-training program at the Tuskegee Army Airfield, in Tuskegee, Alabama. Upon passing the competitive exam and rigorous physicals, he was enrolled in the United States Army Air Corps training program at Tuskegee Institute, a private historically black land-grant associated college founded in the aftermath of Reconstruction by the renowned African-American educator and freedman, Booker T. Washington in 1881.

The U.S. Army Air Corps training program at Tuskegee Institute was formed in 1941. It was a follow up to the Civilian Pilot Training Program (CPTP) that was started in 1939. The CPTP was started in six black colleges and the Coffey School of Aeronautics in Chicago after tremendous pressure was exerted on Congress and Democratic President Franklin Delano Roosevelt from the black media, the Pullman Porters Union and Civil Rights organizations, including the National Association for the Advancement of Colored People (NAACP) and the Urban League. They were lobbying to address the issue of a more equitable inclusion of Blacks in the Armed Forces. They were lobbying to end the practice of a segregated Jim Crow military that had existed before and after World War I. They sought a more equitable inclusion of Black in all branches of the United States Armed Forces.

American society was predicated on the assumption that the white race was superior and the black race was inferior - and the United States military was a mirror reflecting these beliefs. Despite the need for African-American men in the military, a series of reports were published supporting ill-conceived notions that African Americans "lacked courage and the mental capacity" to serve as soldiers. However, these claims were not supported by the facts (the valor of black soldiers in every previous American war) or any scientific test results.[417] In fact, once test results were made public, they showed a very different result. African Americans in the North actually scored significantly higher than their white counterparts from the South, raising many issues as to why and how this could conceivably be possible.

Throughout World War I and early into World War II, as African Americans were recruited, they mostly served the most menial of tasks. During World War I, African American men served only as a cooks and laborers, and although many African American men wanted to be pilots, they were rejected by the United States Air Service Group. In 1917, Eugene Bullard, the first of only two black pilots in World War I, left the United States and volunteered with the French army during the war, because his own country didn't value his service.

Figure 93: Test Results of Black and White Soldiers, Army Results, 1918

Southern Whites		Northern Blacks	
Mississippi	41.25	Pennsylvania	42.00
Kentucky	41.50	New York	45.00
Arkansas	41.55	Illinois	47.35
Georgia	42.12	Ohio	49.50
		R. M. Yerkes, "Psychological Examining in the U.S. Army," National Academy of Sciences, Vol. 15 (1921)[418]	

Prior to World War II, "only 102 black civilians held pilot licenses."[419] As African-American political, business and religious leaders all across the country continued to address the racial injustices of the Jim Crow laws, they knew that the military was just yet another battlefield to overcome before they could achieve racial equality.

In the late 1920s, African-American aviation clubs appeared and by 1936 "some thirty-seven African-American flying clubs had been organized."[420] As African Americans became more interested in aviation, and as civil rights organizations became more interested in the role of African Americans in the military, it was inevitable that the two would merge into a coordinated voice advocating for the integration of the United States Armed Forces, particularly the Army Air Corps. From its inception, the Army Air Corps was considered the most elite branch of the United States military. As the military's "most aristocratic unit" it depicted strikingly handsome airmen with a "trailing white silk scarf draped around the neck, highly polished boots, and the long-stemmed Prince Albert pipe. The Air Corps stood out as the ultimate branch of the Army."[421]

In 1939, as German Chancellor Adolph Hitler marched across Europe and invaded the Czechoslovakian capital city of Prague. He also declared war against one of the strongest allies of the United States, Great Britain. Although the United States had declared neutrality in

Europe's affairs, it prepared its military apparatus as a precaution. As the war in Europe escalated, in the same year, the United States Congress under pressure from civil rights groups established the CPTP at six black colleges - including Delaware State College, Hampton Institute, Howard College, North Carolina A&T College, Tuskegee Institute, West Virginia State College and the private Coffey School of Aeronautics in Chicago.

The CPTP at black colleges was started six months after it began at white colleges. If not for the political pressures from the black media and Civil Rights organizations, the CPTP might not have been available to African Americans at all. But if successful, this would become "an important breakthrough in allowing African Americans to participate in federally funded flight training programs."[422] However, despite the effort of Congress, the Army delayed the program.

The 1940 "presidential election created a heated context in which to demand the end of racism in the American military, and President Roosevelt, seeking an unprecedented third term, needed the black vote."[423] While the "civilians and military leadership of the army" were publically indicating that they were moving forward with the admittance of "black aviation mechanics" there was very little movement, if any, on the admittance of African Americans to the Army Air Corps. Walter White, executive Secretary of the NAACP, prevailed on Mrs. Eleanor Roosevelt to arrange a meeting for him; A. Phillip Randolph, President of the Brotherhood of Sleeping Car Porters; and T. Arnold Hill, acting head of the National Urban League meet with President Roosevelt. The meeting occurred on September 27, 1940.[424]

Figure 94: Civil Rights Groups Request President Roosevelt to Make Reforms

- Reform government contracts related to industry and racial policies in the military.
- With the boom in defense industries, institute fair and equal employment practices
- The formal end to racial exclusion in the Army Air Corps.

Von Hardesty,
Black Wings, Courageous Stores of African Americans in Aviation and Space History [425]

After the meeting, the President came forward with a number of mandates signaling that African-American pilots and mechanics would be used in the war effort. On October 24, 1940, the "Air Corps was directed to abandon its long-standing refusal to admit blacks and was obliged to develop a detailed plan for the establishment of the unit that would be ultimately known as the 99th Pursuit Squadron."[426] Despite the President's best efforts, the military was not moving fast enough. "The agitation over the Army Air Corps participation reached fever pitch in December 1940, when the NAACP's monthly magazine *Crisis* showed an U.S. Army training airplane in flight over Randolph Field, Texas, with the caption "FOR WHITES ONLY."[427]

As Civil Rights groups continued to protest the lack of progress by the military in admitting African Americas, they also discussed the insurmountable unemployment of African Americans as a result of the nation's great economic depression. The groups pressed the President for reforms in the hiring process, particularly since the defense industry had expanded tremendously as a result of the growing wartime economy. The federal government supported the economic growth by hiring millions of Americans - very few, if any, being African Americans.

In March 1941, ground support personnel training began for blacks at Chanute Field in Rantoul, Illinois. On June 25, 1941, President Franklin D. Roosevelt issued "Executive Order 8802," ending racial discrimination in the hiring practices of the defense industries and the War Department - and mandating that blacks were to be admitted to training in the Army Air Corps."[428] After many promises, and a long delay, in July 1941 the U.S. Army Air Corps training program for African American pilots was formed. On March 7, 1942, five graduates completed the advanced pilot program at the Tuskegee Army Airfield Flying School. Those pilots comprised the Class of 42 C, the first African Americans to graduate from the program.

On Sunday, December 7, 1941, the government of Japan attacked the United States Pacific Naval Fleet by bombing the naval base at Pearl Harbor in Hawaii. The United States government was now at war. Much of the United States naval fleet in the Pacific had been destroyed by the Japanese bombing. The American defense industry went into expanded wartime production and built a number amphibious assault ships, cruisers, destroyers, submarines, transport docks, and aircraft carriers to transport military personnel and impedimentals, including fighter planes and bombers. As the United States defense industry went about its work, it developed a series of new generation aviation fighters and bombers.

When the United States entered the war, the training for the cadets at the Tuskegee Army Airfield Flying School was already underway. The original 99th Fighter Squadron was sent overseas in 1943. The 332nd Fighter Group, that initially only included three squadrons - the 100th, the 301st and the 302nd - was deployed overseas in 1944.

In November of 1942, eighteen-year-old Leo Gray of Boston, Massachusetts, took the rigorous U.S. Army Air Corps' Psychological Research Unit's standardized test that reportedly measured prospective candidate's dexterity, intelligence and potential leadership qualities.[429] According to Lieutenant Colonel Gray, although the tests were administered to all of the prospective candidates - white and black - the Army Air Corps used the tests as an instrument to ensure that only the "most skilled and intelligent young men would be allowed into the program." Before Gray was activated in May 1943, the 99th Fighter Squadron already was deployed to Africa. Gray initially was sent to Kessler Field in Biloxi, Mississippi, as a private for Basic Training. Then he was sent to Tuskegee Institute as an aviation student in the Army College Training Program. In October, 1943, Gray was sent to Tuskegee Army Air Force Base as an Aviation Cadet.

Upon graduation from the flight-training program, Leo Gray became an Army Air Corp Aviator and was commissioned as a Second Lieutenant. He became a naval flight aviator and was one of only 932 men who graduated from the advanced pilot training program at the Tuskegee Army Airfield. Those 920 graduates were the first African American military aviators in the United States. They flew in high performance military fighter planes on combat missions. In order to distinguish themselves from other fighter groups, the 332nd Fighter

Group painted the tails of their P-51 Mustang airplanes bright red. This enabled the pilots of the U.S. bombers to know that they were being accompanied by the fighters of the Tuskegee Institute training program and were in trusted hands. Because of their bravery and despite all of the challenges that they went through, the 332nd was respectfully known - by white and black Americans - as the Red Tail Pilots.

Once he received his "wings" on August 4, 1944, Boston's Leo Gray was sent to combat training at Walterboro Army Airfield in South Carolina for combat training and later to Ramitelli, Italy where he joined the 100th Fighter Squadron of the 332nd Fighter Group, becoming a Red Tail Pilot. During his combat tour, Lt. Col. Leo Gray flew 15 combat missions in the P-51 Mustangs. The P-51 was a single engine, long-range single-seat-fighter aircraft that was used during World War II to escort bombers in air raids over Germany. Prior to going overseas Gray flew the Curtiss P-40 Warhawk and the Republic P-47 Thunderbolt fighters in combat training. After returning to the United States, Gray also had flight time flying the C-47 transport, the B-25 medium bombers and the B-47 thunderbolts. Including his 15 combat missions in the P-51s, Lt. Col Gray accumulated more than 750 hours flying time while in the service.

On one of his missions he had a close encounter with two highly sophisticated German-engineered Messerschmitt ME62s Schwalbes, which were the world's first operational jet-powered fighter aircraft. While on a routine mission escorting a damaged Lockheed P-38 bomber, Gray, in his single engine P-51 When they were attacked by the two much faster ME62s. However the jets broke off their attack when three approaching P-51s from the squadron dropped their wing tanks, indicating that they were ready for combat and enabling Gray to successfully escort the bomber back to the home airfield. The incident showed that the Red Tail Pilots, who had an impressive military record, also were respected, however grudgingly, by an enemy that had faster and more sophisticated aircrafts.

Figure 95: Military Accomplishments of the Tuskegee Airmen

- 930 pilots were trained for high performance combat pilots from 1941 to 1946
- 355 were deployed overseas and 80 lost their lives
- 1579 combat missions were flown by the 99th Squadron and the 339 Fighter Group
- 179 bomber escort missions,
- 129 reconnaissance escorts
- of the 312 combat mission with an excellent record of protection with only a loss of 26 bombers
- 409 enemy aircraft destroyed or damaged
- 112 enemy aircraft destroyed in air-to-air combat with only 12 Red Tail pilots were shot down (10 -to-1 ratio)
- 950 rail cars, trucks and other motor vehicles destroyed
- One destroyer put out of action
- 40 boats and barges destroyed

The Tuskegee Airman endured racial discrimination throughout most of their training by the civilian and military members of the United States Armed Forces in the United States and while serving their country overseas. Despite the initial perception that the Tuskegee Airmen were not qualified to serve and did not fit the white Anglo-Saxon perception of what the U.S. Army Corps' pilot should look like, their military record as pilots was distinguished. The Red Tail pilots were awarded some of our nation's highest military honors.

Despite their heroism on the battlefield and in the air, and the respect that they earned by their white peers and their military commanders, once the war was over and the legendary Red Tail Pilots returned stateside, the racism didn't end just because the war did. However, throughout the nation when the war was over, communities now had Red Tail ambassadors who sought racial and social justice for African Americans in the United States after staring down the pilots of their mighty adversary who flew in their sleek and sophisticated aircraft. They now were prepared to tackle the residual effects of Jim Crow back home.

Figure 96: National Recognition and Awards of the Tuskegee Airmen

- Three Distinguished Unit Citations
  - 99th Pursuit Squadron: 30 May–11 June 1943 for actions over Sicily
  - 99th Fighter Squadron: 12–14 May 1944: for successful air strikes against Monte Cassino, Italy
  - 33d Fighter Group (and its 99th, 100th, 301st and 302nd Fighter Squadrons): 24 March 1945: for a bomber escort mission to Berlin, during which it destroyed 3 M262 enemy jets, probably destroyed two others and a M163 Rocket Plane, and damaged 3 jets.
- At least one Silver Star
- 96 Distinguished Flying Crosses
- 14 Bronze Stars
- 744 Air Medals
- 8 Purple Hearts

Lieutenant Colonel Leo R. Gray had become a different man while in the service. He left his hometown of Boston, Massachusetts, as a young man and came back stateside with the confidence of a Red Tail Pilot, who had seen much of the world in a very compressed period of time. He witnessed and participated in the destruction of the German war machine and its capital, Berlin. He lived amongst the war-torn people of Italy. He and his fellow Red Tail Pilots had risked their lives for their country on the battlefields and in the air in the European and Pacific Military Campaigns. They were an integral part in the successful war effort in liberating Europe and now they wanted to be part of liberating their communities back home. And because of their war-time successes and sacrifices, he and many other returning African-American soldiers and pilots had very little patience for segregationist polices.

Stateside and waiting to be discharged from the military, Lieutenant Gray was in New Orleans, Louisiana, in March, 1946. As was still the custom, African Americans had to board the bus from the rear. Several stops after he was seated a white couple boarded the bus and the man told him to get up from his seat and go back to the rear of the bus so that they could sit down. Words were exchanged, and he was called one of "Roosevelt's Boys," a derogatory phrase in reference to President Roosevelt's acceptance of supposedly unqualified African Americans for the war effort. He got off the bus at the next stop and walked to his destination. This single incident remained with him for the rest of his life. Lieutenant Colonel Gray left active duty in 1946, but remained in the U. S. Air Force Reserves until 1984. During Grays' forty-one years of military service, he earned a coveted Air Medal with one Oak Leaf cluster and a Presidential Unit Citation.

After entering the Army Air Force reserve, he returned to Boston and enrolled in the agricultural program at the University of Massachusetts at the Fort Deven's campus in June 1947, to study Agricultural Economics. Upon his completion of his Bachelor of Science degree, he continued his education and received his Master of Arts degree from the University of Nebraska. At the completion of his studies, he was offered an Agricultural Statistician position with the United States Department of Agriculture in their Boston office. After meeting the Officer in Charge and his future co-workers and told where his desk was, he was told to report to work on November 1, 1952. Before he was able to start work, the Division Director of the Agricultural Crop Reporting Service came to Boston and told the manager in charge that the honorably discharged Lieutenant Colonel Gray could not have the position because he was black. He then received a letter from Washington, D.C., informing him that he was overqualified for the job. The offer was rescinded.

Angry and insulted, Gray shared the story with a fellow alumnus from the University of Massachusetts, which resulted in the Chairman of the Department of Agricultural Economics, Dr. Adrian Lindsey, offering him a position as a Technical Assistant in Farm Management with the University of Massachusetts Agricultural Extension program. By 1954, the U.S. Department of Agriculture's reduction in force (RIF) had eased and the racial climate had begun to change in Washington, D.C., particularly after the desegregation of the federal workforce by Executive Order 9980 and Executive Order 9981, which integrated the United States Armed Services, as promulgated and signed by President Harry S. Truman on June 26, 1948.

In 1954, Leo once again applied for a position with the United States Department of Agriculture, this time in its Washington offices. Leo was quickly hired on the impressive merit of his qualifications as an Agricultural Economist with the Economic Research Service. In 1965, when he had achieved the rank of Lieutenant Colonel in the United States Army Corps, he also served as an economist and Director of Planning with the Animal and Plant Health Inspection Service in California. He retired with distinction after thirty years, during which he became the Director of Planning and Evaluation for the U.S. Department of Agriculture's Office of the Food Safety and Quality Service.

5.13 Two Brothers Served in the Korean War at Pusan and Seoul

When President Franklin D. Roosevelt died of a cerebral hemorrhage on April 12, 1945, and Harry S. Truman became the President of the United States, one of his first orders of business was overseeing, with England's Winston Churchill and the Soviet Union's Joseph Stalin, the May 8th 1945 Allied victory in Europe. When the Japanese Emperor refused to surrender, in an attempt to bring the war to an end, President Truman made one of the most difficult decisions of the war and dropped two atomic bombs on the island of Japan. The first atomic bomb was dropped over the Japanese city of Hiroshima and three days later the second atomic bomb was dropped over the city of Nagasaki. On August 15, 1945, the Second World War came to an end with the surrender of the Japanese government.

In the war's aftermath, the United States changed drastically. Soldiers returned home to a post war economy that exploded and swelled the ranks of the middle class. The nation, having endured two long and costly World Wars, wanted a world at peace and became a founding member of the United Nations. African Americans, having gained new freedoms and economic opportunity during and after the war, wanted parity in all aspects of American living. What the nation and its new President did not realize was that in a few short years, the desire for peace and prosperity did not go hand in hand.

Figure 97: Formation of the United Nations

In the aftermath of World War II, on October 24, 1945, an international body to be known as the United Nations was formed to maintaining international peace and security, developing friendly relations among nations and promoting social progress, better living standards and human rights.

United Nations

After World War II, civil rights groups pushed even harder towards full equality for African Americans across the country. As the nation grasped the full impact of the racial genocide and atrocities perpetrated against the Jews, the gypsies and homosexuals in Europe during the war, many found the nation's attitude towards its African-American citizens hypocritical. As African-American veterans returned home only to be discriminated against, beaten and maimed it impacted many Americans, including President Harry S. Truman.

Figure 98: President Truman Deplored the Treatment
of African American Veterans

President Truman himself was stricken in conscience. "My stomach turned,' he told a friend shortly after the war, 'when I learned that African American soldiers just back from overseas were being beaten.' Refereeing to an incident in which a returning solider ...had lost his sight, Truman continued: When a mayor and a city marshal can take an African American sergeant off a bus in South Carolina, beat him up and put out one of his eyes, and nothing is done by the state authorities, something is radically wrong with the system."

William T. Bowers,

*Black Solider, White Army:
the 24th Infantry Regiment in Korea*[430]

On July 26, 1948, President Truman promulgated Executive Order 9981, which was intended to officially end racial discrimination in all aspects of the United States armed services -, including housing and training. From the time of the Revolutionary War, when the ancestors of the present day Cornwall Murphy family enlisted into the Continental Army, to the War of 1812, to World War I and World War II, the sons and extended family members of the Cornwall Murphy family patriotically served their county. With the signing of the Executive Order, for the first time in modern history, African Americans joined the military in the hopes of career advancement in an integrated military.

As scores of young African-American men enlisted in the military hoping to see the world in an era of peace and prosperity, Jack Cornwall of Brockton, Massachusetts, the eldest son of Harold and Marie Cornwall enlisted in the summer of 1948, upon graduation from high school. Initially the media hyped the effects of President Truman's Executive Order 9981 as an immediate integration of all vestiges of the segregated armed forces. However, as Jack and other young African-American men were to soon learn, the integration of the armed services was a gradual process over several years. Upon enlistment, Jack was assigned to a segregated stateside unit.

For an African-American young man from the north, who had always lived in a predominantly white community and attended predominantly -white public schools, living in a totally segregated environment was a culture shock. It was even more shocking to go below the "Jim Crow Line" for training, and to experience the effects of the South's restrictive discriminatory practices. Jack had never been told that he could only shower in the dilapidated "colored showers" or that he could only drink out of the "colored water fountain" out back. Jack, who used to hang out with his buddies and go to Woolworth's department store and sit at the lunch counter while waiting for a soda after school was bemused at being forced to sit in the colored section of the mess hall to eat his meals.

As President Truman was addressing the issues of the military's discriminatory practices, he was also attempting to contain communism from stretching across the Sea of Japan to the Korean peninsula. After the war, Germany lost approximately twenty-five percent of its prewar territories and Japan lost its possession of the Korean peninsula. At the end of World War II, the two most powerful allies in the war, United States and the Soviet Union began to differ with one another as to how best to address the rebuilding and reunification of Germany and the control over the Korean peninsula. The political and philosophical differences between the two nations initially set the stage for major disagreements over how to realign the war torn European territories and the Korean peninsula in the Sea of Japan.

In 1894, after the Sino-Japanese War, China was removed as "overlord and protector of the peninsula nation of Korea" located between the Yellow Sea and the Sea of Japan. After a war with Russia, the victorious Japan annexed the Korean peninsula from China.[431] The Japanese ruled Korea until the conclusion of World War II, when the Japanese nation lost to the Allied Forces, who divided the Korean peninsula nation into two sections at the 38th parallel in 1945, with the Soviet Union military forces establishing a Communist style government in the north and the United States and Great Britain military forces establishing a pro-Western style nation in the south.

In 1946, the Soviet Union established the Provisional People's Committee who held elections under the direction of Kim Il Sung.

Under Kim Il Sung, the Provisional People's Committee established a new Stalinist style communist government known as the People's Assembly. Under the "new quasi-government" Kim Il Sung began to consolidate power under the direction of the Soviet Union.[432] By 1948 as Kim Il Sung consolidated power, over 2 million refugees fled North Korea to the south creating a fear that the peninsula was on the verge of a Civil War.

The Korean War was the United Nation's first war. The international body's founding members consisted of the five allied partners in World War II -France, the Republic of China, the Soviet Union, the United Kingdom and the United States. In an attempt to unify the split peninsula, the United Nations moved for a national vote to determine the form of government that the Korean people wanted to live under as a unified nation. On May 10, 1948 under the auspices of the United Nations, North Korea held its elections forming the Republic of Korea, with its capitol city in Seoul, ending the United States occupation of the southern portion of the peninsula. The Soviet Union led government refused to allow the people residing in the North to participate in free elections, and on September 9, 1948 formed the Democratic People's Republic of Korea, ending the occupation of the Soviet Union in the northern portion of the peninsula.[433] After the formation of the now two new governments, border clashes erupted and tensions grew between the two new nations.

Kim Il Sung with the support of Soviet Union's Joseph Stalin, in an attempt to unify all of Korea under the communist rule of the North's Democratic People's Republic of Korea, on June 25, 1950, invaded South Korea. The North's invasion caught the South's Republic of Korea government off-guard and totally demoralized the South's army and sent its President fleeing to the port city of Pusan (also spelled Busan).

Pusan, the second largest city in South Korea, is on the southeastern most point of the peninsula nation. As its nation was under attack, the Republic of Korea's President Syngman Rhee escaped to the "defensive perimeter of the city" of Pusan as his nation's capital city of Seoul and most of his nation fell to the invading forces of the North's Democratic People's Republic of Korea.[434] The free world feared that the communist invasion was a tactical maneuver aimed at controlling the entire peninsula - but more important, was the first step toward a greater Asian conflict which would eventually engulf Japan.[435] Under the vote of the United Nation's Security Council, the United Nations and the United States immediately came to the defense of South Korea.

The United States' entrance into the Korean conflict was consistent with President Truman's Doctrine as delivered before a joint session of Congress on March 12, 1947. The President believed that governments, such as the Soviet Union, were entering weaker nations and imposing their communistic will on the free people of those nations - and by so doing, was creating an threat to international peace and a specific threat to the national security of the United States.

Figure 99: South Korea's Army collapsed immediately after the invasion

"The quick and virtually complete collapse of resistance in the South's Republic of Korea Army energized the United States to enter the war in force ... which soon committed American air and ground forces to the fight"

Bruce Cumings,
The Korean War, A History,[436]

The Truman Doctrine, later to be known as the "Containment Policy," was designed to contain the expansion of communism worldwide and avoid a possible domino effect with one country after another falling under the Soviet Union's sphere of influence.

Figure 100: Truman Doctrine

With the Truman Doctrine, President Harry S. Truman established that the United States would provide political, military and economic assistance to all democratic nations under threat from external or internal authoritarian forces. The Truman Doctrine effectively reoriented U.S. foreign policy, away from its usual stance of withdrawal from regional conflicts not directly involving the United States, to one of possible intervention in faraway conflicts. Truman argued that the United States could no longer stand by and allow the forcible expansion of Soviet totalitarianism into free, independent nations, because American national security now depended upon more than just the physical security of American territory. Rather, in a sharp break with its traditional avoidance of extensive foreign commitments beyond the Western Hemisphere during peacetime, the Truman Doctrine committed the United States to actively offering assistance to preserve the political integrity of democratic nations when such an offer was deemed to be in the best interest of the United States.

U.S. Department of State, Office of the Historian[437]

As the United States amassed its war machinery to be sent to the war zone in support of the Republic of Korea, the heavy tanks used in World War II were not as capable of navigating the dense and mountainous terrain. The "air war in Korea was a juxtaposition of the old and the new." The single-engine propeller aircraft, popularly used in World War II and flown by pilots like Lt. Colonel Leo Gray - primarily the Corsairs, Firefly, Mustang and Republic aircraft "that once shot up German trucks and bunkers" were now being decommissioned. Newer, sleeker, and faster jet-propelled fighters were being introduced into the Air Force and Navy as they conducted reconnaissance maneuvers, aerial photography behind enemy lines, and clashed along the Yalu River on the border between North Korea and its northern neighbor, China.[438]

As Jack Cornwall's two-year military enlistment was about to come to an end, his service was extended and he was sent to the Air Force 932nd Engineer Aviation Group for training so that he could be deployed to the front lines in Korea. One of the first groups of soldiers deployed to Korea was the United States Army Corp of Engineers, who played a critical role during the war.

Figure 101: The U.S. Army Corps of Engineers during the Korean War

> "In 1950 the Korean Peninsula was an inhospitable place to wage war. Steep mountain ranges, narrow valleys, and numerous rivers divided its landmass. The summers were oppressively hot, the winters bitterly cold, and the monsoon season turned what few roads there were into muddy quagmires and transformed meandering streams into raging torrents. In short, Korea's arduous terrain and climate, coupled with a poor transportation network, made it a very difficult environment for the United States and its United Nations (UN) allies to fight."
>
> Army Corps of Engineers[439]

The Army Corp of Engineers was pivotal for the South Korean government during the opening days of the war. It also was important for the United States and the United Nations Special Forces. The engineers were able to stall the offensive North Korean armies from going southward by destroying critical bridges and "other vital facilities in their advance."

Figure 102: The Importance of Army Corps of Engineers

"In conjunction with the difficult terrain, North Korea's surprise attack also placed a premium on U.S. Army engineer operations. In the opening weeks of the war, engineers bought the UN forces valuable time; they destroyed bridges and other vital facilities to impede the enemy's advance, and after the UN forces withdrew to Pusan, engineers helped build a defensive line that enabled the beleaguered defenders to hang on. Also, during those chaotic early months of the war, engineer units frequently fought as infantry."

Army Corps of Engineers[440]

In the early days of the war, the engineers often found themselves fighting as infantrymen, and many of the segregated African-American soldiers were disadvantaged by their poor basic training. On July 12, 1950, the "all-black 24th Infantry Regiment in the 25th Infantry Division whose three battalions represented the first complete US regiment to see service in Korea," arrived in Pusan, South Korea. [441] It would be a long and humiliating hot summer for the American newcomers.

Figure 103: United States Army initially suffered
in the early stages of the Korean War

"In the summer of 1950, the Korean People's Army pushed southward with dramatic success, with one humiliating defeat after another for American forces. The United States Army that had bested Germany and Japan found its back pressed to the wall by what it thought was a hastily assembled peasant military, ill-equipped and, worse, said to be doing the bidding of a foreign imperial power."

Bruce Cumings,
The Korean War, A History[442]

To exacerbate the problem, the Chinese government supported the North Koreans, and was engaged in psychological warfare against the Special Forces of the United Nations, in an attempt to cause disruption amongst the coalition of participating countries in the United Nations effort. The Chinese would fly over coalition forces and drop propaganda materials specifically designed to cause dissension on the ground. Their initial propaganda and leaflets targeted the British soldiers, and they attempted to cause rancor between the white and African-American soldiers from the United States. When the three initial divisions of the United States 25th Infantry Division arrived in

Pusan, within weeks it came under heavy fire from the Democratic People's Republic of Korea's Army. At the beginning of the war, Pusan was one of the last large cities not under initial North Korean control, and strategically needed by the North Koreans if they were to control all of South Korea. As the city was under attack, the 24th Infantry retreated.

However, the Chinese propaganda strategy directed at U.S. troops backfired. President Truman's Executive Order 9981 was already in the process of desegregating the military and as troops rotated in and out of Korea, African-American servicemen were integrated into white units. Jack Cornwall was one of the first African American soldiers to help integrate the services when he was transferred from the stateside 932nd Engineer Aviation Group to the Company B of the 808th Engineer Aviation Battalion, in Korea. The specific unit that Jack was assigned to was the Special Category Army Personnel with Air Force troops, better known as SCARWAF.

Figure 104: The 24th Infantry was punished and
36 black soldiers faced court-martial

"Most black private soldiers broke and ran, abandoning a great deal of equipment. The 24th was clearly ill trained and prone to "bugging out" when under fire – a situation, of course, that was not unique to the 24th Infantry. However, because of the desperate shortage of infantry soldiers the 24th was returned to action. However the 24th Infantry was punished and 36 black soldiers faced court martial for misbehavior in the face of the enemy. Black reaction in the United States was intense and the Chinese propagandists capitalized on this by accusing the Americans of "Jim Crow" persecution of black soldiers in Korea. The Chinese leaflets urged black soldiers to abandon the war and fight "Big Business" in order to transform America into a world where all races would be equal."

Brian, Catchpole,
The Korean War, 1950-53 [443]

As the Army Corp of Engineers delayed the progression of the North Koreans by blowing up bridges, roads and other strategically important infrastructure, they also provided a vital window in which the SCARWAF could get in to modernize the Kunsan Air Base. The unit built the long, wide runways necessary to accommodate the newer F-86 jet fighters and large four-engine cargo aircrafts such as C-54s. At the beginning of the war, the old World War II Japanese built base was under the control of the North Koreans. However, on July 13, 1950, the base was under American control and served as a strategic asset during the length of the war. The 808th Engineer Aviation Battalion's SCARWAF unit, in which Jack was assigned, constructed a 5,000-foot runway for the larger aircrafts.

Upon his discharge from the military, Jack R. Cornwall was the last member of the Cornwall Murphy family to have served in the segregated United States Armed Forces. Shortly after his enlistment, Jack's younger brother, Harold, also enlisted in the military and was sent directly to an integrated unit to serve in the Korean War.

Harold and Marie Cornwall's second son, Harold, also served in the Korean War. A year after the war started, Harold Cornwall enlisted in the United States Air Force in May of 1951, where he was sent to Ithaca, New York, for basic training. Private Cornwall was one of the first African-American men to serve in the Armed Forces' "new" integrated military. Having taken a series of test, Private Cornwall was transferred to the United States Air Force Specialty School in Wyoming and St. Louis where he learned cryptography. He was then stationed to the United States Air Force Headquarters in Seoul, Korea, where he was initially part of the 15th Radio Squadron Mobile Communications Unit, and then transferred to the Headquarters' 16th Communications Squadron.

The Communication Unit was assigned to the Office of Strategic Services (OSS) a wartime intelligence agency and the predecessor of the Central Intelligence Agency. During the Korean War the OSS, as it was called, also used espionage, subversion and its own form of propaganda - dropping leaflets behind enemy lines to the North Korean people, trying to change their opinion about the war. As a cryptographist, Private Cornwall was responsible for staying in communications with American assets behind enemy lines.

The Korean War ended on July 27, 1953, with a truce signed by North Korea and its supporter, China, and the United Nations. South Korea did not sign the agreement, which left the peninsula divided - with a communist government to the north and a non-communist government in the south, separated by a demilitarized zone at the 38th parallel.

The truce was a viable solution for the North Koreans who were supported by the Chinese and the Russians, who had wanted to expand communism over the entire peninsula. The South Koreans, supported by the United Nations and the United States, were able to maintain an open government, therefore thwarting the communists from total control over the peninsula.

5.14 Rear Admiral Lawrence Chambers and Operation Frequent Wind

In 1950, as tensions were escalating on the Korean peninsula, the French were engulfed in a Revolutionary War with dissidents in their colonial governments on the Indochinese Peninsula. The Indochinese Peninsula is a region in Southeast Asia bordering the Gulf of Thailand and the South China Sea. After World War II, the peninsula was divided into four nations, - Cambodia, Laos, Thailand and Vietnam, an area on the eastern portion of the peninsula bordered by the South China Sea. The French colonized Vietnam in 1887, but lost possession during World War II when the Germans invaded France. At that time, the French colony was heavily influenced by the nearby Japanese, who invaded and held portions of the country until the end of the war.

After World War II, a weakened France attempted to reclaim the colony only to be confronted by militant Vietnamese who wanted independence from their former colonial power and were now supported by communist powers of China and Russia. In 1945, under the direction of revolutionary leader Ho Chi Minh, the militants declared an independent Democratic Republic of Vietnam. The French, not prepared to relinquish control, fought to regain their colonial power. By 1949, the communist powers of China and Russia were providing aid to Ho Chi Minh and his militants. As part of President Truman's Doctrine of Containment, and to once again avoid a possible domino effect of one Far East country after another falling under the political influence of the Soviet Union and now China, the United States provided support to the French.

Figure 105: Communist Super Powers Recognize the Rebel Vietnamese

"On June 25, 1950, North Korean forces surged across the thirty-eight parallel and four days later captured Seoul, South Korea's capital. Six months earlier, Chinese Communist legions had reached the frontiers of Vietnam after conquering all of mainland China. The Soviet Union and China both recognized the Ho Chi Minh regime, the Democratic Republic of Vietnam."

- Stanley Karnow,
Vietnam A History, the First Complete Account of Vietnam at War[444]

The Vietnamese resistance against the French was strong and fierce. The rebels knew the rugged and mountainous terrain better than the French, and had access to communist-supplied weapons. As the war lingered, the Chinese provided valuable supplies to support the emboldened revolutionaries, who safely hid in the mountains, against the undersupplied and undermanned French, who were constantly in "static positions." By March, 1954, little by little, the revolutionaries chipped away at the French defensive positions until they were trapped for three months in the Battle of Dien Bien Phu. After a "fifty-five day siege" the French positions were overrun, and defeated. They decided to pull out of Vietnam.[445]

At the 1954 Geneva Conference, Vietnam was to be temporarily divided at the 17th parallel with elections to be held by 1956 to establish a stable single unifying government. During the transition period of 1954-1956, the communist North and a non-communist South slowly began to sharply differ on regional issues of religion, economics and politics. In 1956, elections took place only in South Vietnam, as dissidents in both regions began to mobile against each other's form of government.

Figure 106: Vietnam Splits at the 17th Parallel

"A conference sponsored and attended by the United States, the Soviet Union, France and Brittan had already convened on April 26, 1954 in Geneva, Switzerland, to discuss the problem of the two Koreas and also find way to end the war in Vietnam. After seventy-four days of negotiations, a cease-fire agreement was signed on July 20. The principal clause of the Geneva agreements provided for the temporary partition of Vietnam at the Seventh Parallel, with the forces of the (communist) Democratic Republic of Vietnam in the north and those of the (nationalist) French Union in the south."

Bui Cong Minh,
A Distant Cause, A History and the Vindication of the Viet Nam War[446]

As the South Vietnam military was handling its dissidents, it accused the North Vietnamese of interfering and providing aide and support to the southern dissidents. North Vietnam wanted to unify the country under the communist government and South Vietnam, supported by the United States, attempted to prevent the spread of communism southward. In an attempt to deter an escalation of hostilities between the North and the South, in the late 1950s and the early 1960s, American aircraft carriers maintained a presence in the South China Sea. In the fall of 1964, the United States became embroiled in the Indochina peninsula's civil war when North Vietnamese torpedo boats attacked United States vessels in the Gulf of Tonkin. A second attack on the U.S. naval assets prompted President Lyndon Johnson to sign the Tonkin Gulf Resolution, declaring war on North Vietnam.

The eleven-year war was costly for America. It stirred resentment in African-American communities across the country, as young black men were disproportionately drafted and sent to war. The escalated presence of the United States in Vietnam caused riots on college campuses as America's youth marched in protest against U.S. involvement in the war. It was a tremendous drain on the American treasury, and was the cause of tremendous psychological trauma to the American public and the U.S. soldiers, who suffered from physical injuries, post-traumatic stress and drug addiction.

A 2011 Congressional Research Service Report estimated that the cost of the Vietnam War between 1965 and 1975 was $111 billion, and 2.3% of the gross domestic production at the peak of the war. At the time the report was commissioned, the $111 billion would have been equivalent to 738 billion dollars.[447]

After eleven expensive, draining years, the United States and North Vietnam agreed to a cease-fire on January 23, 1973.

A major participant in the closing days of the Vietnam Theater was Rear Admiral Lawrence C. Chambers, who served in the United States Navy from 1948 to 1984. While serving as Naval Captain, he was the commanding officer of the aircraft carrier *U.S.S. Midway* during Operation Frequent Wind, which involved the evacuation of American civilians and "at risk" Vietnamese from Saigon, South Vietnam, during the last days of the Vietnam War in 1975.

Rear Admiral Chambers was born in Lynchburg, Virginia, to Lawrence and Charlotte Chambers, the third of five children. He grew up in the African-American neighborhood of Shaw in Washington, D.C., after his father passed away and his mother went to work at the United States War Department.

Larry and his younger brother Andrew "enrolled in the ROTC program at the prestigious but segregated African American Dunbar High School in Washington, DC. After his graduation approached, Larry heeded the advice from several mentors [and] decided to attend the United States Naval Academy. There, he could be educated at no expense to his widowed mother. Larry passed the qualifying examination and on June 30, 1948, entered the naval academy in Annapolis, Maryland, as a midshipman. On June 6, 1952, he became the academy's second black graduate".[448]

Even as a young man, Larry had strong political ideals and communication skills. In an interview on the day of his graduation from the academy, he was pressed to talk about his experiences there. He responded, "My four years at the Naval Academy have been among the most satisfying of my life. I will always remember these years with appreciation of the fair, kindly and impartial treatment received from the Superintendent, Officers, Instructors, Midshipman and enlisted personnel stationed there."[449] However, in another interview more than twenty years later, Chambers candidly expressed a very different sentiment of his experiences at the Naval Academy by explaining that it had been more than two decades since he had set foot in Annapolis and although he "had some good memories, [he] also had some tough memories."[450]

While Larry was stationed on the West Coast attending to his studies, his brother, Andrew, attended Howard University, the historic African-American institution, in Washington, D.C. While there, Andrew met his girlfriend's friend, Janet Murphy, from Boston, Massachusetts, the third daughter of Robert and Margaret Melton Murphy. Although Andrew lived in the college dorms, he lived only six blocks from the black middle-class neighborhood of Shaw, where the Chambers family lived. Whenever Andrew went home on the weekends, he went in tow with his girlfriend and their best friend, Janet Murphy.

Whenever Andrew or his mother Charlotte communicated with Larry on the West Coast, they insisted that he meet Janet because she would be the perfect bride for him. They knew that she was a strong young woman who was bright, secure and would not be intimidated by Larry's brash, youthful ways. When Larry received the letters from his family, he initially had little interest in meeting Janet.

While furloughs were hard to come by for young officers, Larry did manage to return home every now and then. On two initial furloughs, when he returned home, he missed the opportunity to meet Janet, who was back in Boston visiting her family for the holidays. However, when he was temporarily stationed in Annapolis, his brother, girlfriend and Janet went to visit Larry.

According to family sources, it was love at first sight, and after a short courtship, the two became engaged. They held off marriage until Janet received her college degree from Howard University. The couple then moved to San Diego, California, where Larry Chambers, a young, bright and talented naval officer, ascended rapidly in the ranks. Soon after their marriage and the birth of their daughter, Janet passed away. Larry continued with his military career - and an impressive career it became.

Larry's career was intrinsically linked with the events in Vietnam. As the war escalated, the U.S. Naval Academy graduate rose through the ranks and was able to take advantage of opportunities not previously afforded to the countless numbers of African-American men who served in the U.S. military before him.

The signing of the January 1973 cease-fire did not bring an immediate end to combat. American airstrikes in the neighboring countries of Cambodia and Laos continued until August. As the United States slowly removed their assets from Vietnam, the northern communists strategically waited until they had the competitive edge over South Vietnam, before they struck with precision. Without the support of the United States, the South Vietnamese government was no match for the Soviet Union backed North Vietnamese. The intent of the North Vietnamese was clear - deceive the United States by ignoring the negotiated cease-fire. In fear that all of the Vietnamese peninsula would be overrun by the communist-backed North Vietnamese within days, President Gerald L. Ford launched Operation Frequent Wind.

Figure 107: Young Naval Officer Ascends to the Highest Ranks of the Navy

From 1968 through 1971, Chambers participated in the Vietnam War as a fighter pilot, flying missions from the aircraft carriers USS *Ranger* and USS *Oriskany*. He was promoted to captain on July 1, 1972, and placed in command of the USS *White Plains*. From January 1975 through December 1976, Chambers was in command of the USS *Midway*, which evacuated more than 3,000 U.S. personnel and South Vietnamese citizens following the fall of Saigon in April 1975. When a single-seat Cesena airplane carrying fleeing South Vietnamese major Buing Ly and his family had no place to land, Captain Chambers made a controversial decision and ordered helicopters valued at $10 million dumped into the South China Sea to create landing space on deck ad save the lives of those aboard the plane.

Catherine Reef,
African Americans in the Military[451]

Operation Frequent Wind was initiated and within days of the communist takeover, the American embassy in Saigon was evacuated on April 12, 1975. The USS *Enterprise* and the USS *Midway* which was commanded by Captain Larry Chambers had been redeployed to the South China Sea to oversee the operations. The *Midway* had ten Air Force planes and support helicopters on board to escort and pickup Americans and South Vietnamese civilians who wanted to escape. More than "40 sorties were made, bringing over 2,000 people back to the *Midway*." As United States assets were stationed offshore, almost "8,000 people were evacuated from South Vietnam as communist forces overran the country, including prominent South Vietnamese officials".[452]

Captain Chambers directed the rescue of more than 3,000 Americans and South Vietnamese on the USS Midway, including making the controversial call to clear the ship's deck of expensive assets so that South Vietnamese Major Buing Ly and his family could safely land. After Saigon fell to the communists, Captain Chambers was heralded for saving the life of a trusted and courageous South Vietnamese Air Force pilot and his family.

After the Vietnam War, Captain Chambers continued to serve his country with distinction. In 1977, he was appointed Rear Admiral in the United States Navy by President Jimmy Carter. In August 1979, Chambers was assigned commander of Carrier Group 3 in the Indian Ocean. His command consisted of six ships, including two destroyers, a guided missile cruiser, several frigates, more than 6,000 personnel and 85 planes.[453] The following month, on September 29, 1979, Vice President Walter Mondale was escorted across the flight deck of the USS *Midway* by Admiral Chambers. [454]

Less than two months later, on November 4, 1979, an angry mob of Islamic revolutionaries stormed the United States Embassy in Tehran, Iran and held more than 50 American hostages for 444 days. Because of his unique experience and knowledge of the waters of the China Sea, the Indian Ocean and the Persian Gulf, Admiral Chambers was tasked by President Jimmy Carter to be one of the "major naval leaders in the faceoff with the Russians over the Persian Gulf". As commander of the USS Coral Sea, Admiral Chambers spent more than 100 days in Middle Eastern waters, supervising air operations and maintaining a military presence near Iran, while the Americans were being held hostage. According to a magazine article, "never before in modern U.S. history has a Black officer ever been assigned such a critical military role, and in position where the slightest decision could affect the future of mankind."[455]

On March 1, 1984, after serving his final naval assignment, with the Naval Air Systems Command in Arlington, Virginia, Rear Admiral Chambers retired after a long a distinguished military career. His career was further distinguished by being awarded the Bronze Star, the Meritorious Service Medal, the China Service Medal, and the Vietnam Service Medal with three Bronze Stars.[456]

Admiral Chamber's younger brother, Andrew, retired from the United States Army as a Lieutenant General, with major military awards, including "the Distinguished Service Medal with oak leaf cluster, Defense Superior Service Medal, Legion of Merit, Soldier's Medal, Bronze Star with "V" Devise, Meritorious Service Medal with oak leaf cluster, Air Medal with three oak leaf clusters, Army Commendation Medal with two oak leaf clusters, Combat Infantryman Badge, Master Parachutist Badge and Army General Staff Identification Badge."[457]

5.15   The March on Washington

African-American soldiers fought bravely for their country in World War II and the Korean War, only to return home to segregationist polices in the South and discriminatory practices in the North. They began to question the geo-political communities in which they lived, and the government for which they had fought.

When the African-American veterans of World War II and the Korean War came home from war, they felt much like the African American veterans who came home after the Revolutionary War, poor, destitute, and ignored or rejected by the their government and country they had defended. The Revolutionary War veterans silently feared that they may not be given their freedom from slavery after serving valiantly for their country, as promised. They had fought for the right to be treated as equal citizens and to have a voice in the political discourse of America, similarly the war veterans from World War II and Korea had fought for the same rights.

Just as in 1783, when Revolutionary War veteran turned abolitionist Prince Hall advocated for young African-American men to demand a change in America, similar voices began to ring out across the country in the mid-1950s. As Frederick Douglass had advocated in 1863, African Americans had to become equal partners in aggressively fighting for the freedom of the black man and for their own personal freedoms. Almost a century later, young men and women all across the South, particularly on the campuses of the historically Black colleges and universities, called for similar action.

Despite the fact that the United States military had long been segregated and reluctant to make changes, during and immediately after the Korean War it had finally made significant and notable progress.

Figure 108: United States Military became the most
Integrated Institution in the Country

"In its February 22, 1954, edition, *Time* magazine reported that the military was the most integrated institution in the United States. After commenting on the history of integrating the armed forces and lauding recent advances, the article concluded: 'But there is a problem: the civilian world now lags far behind the military. Said an army brigadier general, 'What worries me is that a military career for a negro is about the top he can get.' A Negro G.I. said it in a different way: 'The Negro begins to see fellows getting along in the army and begins to say to himself, it would be so goddamn nice if it could be like that all over.'"

Lt. Col (Ret) Michael Lee Lanning,
The African American Solider, from Crispus Attucks to Colin Powell[58]

In 1958, Edward Murphy, the son of Robert and Margaret Murphy, left Boston, to attend Fisk University, a historically black university located in Nashville, Tennessee. The prestigious university was founded in 1866 in the aftermath of the Civil War by Clinton B. Fisk a white Union Civil War General, and a recently appointed senior officer of the Bureau of Refugees, Freedmen and Abandoned Lands. Fisk University, like many of the other historically black colleges, began a huge recruitment drive and accepted unprecedented numbers of African-American students from the North and the South.

Six years before Ed Murphy went south to college; a young man by the name of Martin Luther King traveled a different road and went north to Boston to go to college. In 1952, King enrolled in divinity school at Boston University and subsequently received his Doctorate of Philosophy degree. It has been suggested by many that his life in Boston was where Dr. King experienced the successes of an integrated society, and upon his return to the South advocated for the abolition of Jim Crow practices and segregation.

As thousands of young men and women from the North went south to attend school, they were dismayed by the segregationist rules that they were expected to obey. Many of these young men and women were away from home for the first time, and wanted to enjoy the freedom of being away at college, instead of feeling like second-class citizens.

While Ed Murphy was not a leader in any student advocacy movement, between 1958 and 1960, Fisk University became one of the epicenters for a number of activities that would soon engage the country on issues of race and segregation. As Ed and other young black students taking buses south to attend college, another group was also traveling south. These were the Freedom Riders, white and black civil rights activists who went south on interstate buses to fight against the federal government's non-enforcement of the Interstate Commerce ruling that challenged the U.S. Supreme Court ruling on *Plessy v. Ferguson.*

The Freedom Riders wanted the federal government to force southern states to allow African Americans to be able to use the restaurants and restrooms on interstate highways. In 1961, the interracial Freedom Riders would ride the buses and provoke local law enforcement by integrating the restrooms, lunch counters and the waiting rooms. As more and more Freedom Riders went south, local violence against them increased, and the nation's attention was now captured by the television screen as these non-violent protesters were often met with violent reactions.

As the Freedom Riders went further south on their rides into especially racist states such as Alabama, Georgia and Mississippi, they were often brutally beaten and thrown into jail. America watched each night on the evening news as buses were burned, dogs put on the passengers - and more than three hundred years of racial discrimination and hostility played out on the television screen.

As the Civil Rights Movement spread across the nation, African-American families engaged in heated discussion. Many Americans - white, black and Native American; rich and poor; Christian and non-Christian - felt the need to do something to overturn more than three hundred years of oppression.

On August 30, 1963, two buses and a dozen cars stood idling outside of St. Mark's Congregational Church in Boston in preparation for the eight hour drive to Washington, D.C. The congregation had made plans for weeks to attend the first of its kind march on the nation's capital. A good friend of the church and an organizer of the march, A. Philip Randolph, had asked that the congregation to support him. He shared with them that the Reverend Dr. Martin Luther King, the young man who once attended Twelfth Baptist Church down the street, was now galvanizing black congregations all across the south to non-violently protest segregation policies.

Robert Murphy and his son, Edward, left St. Mark's Church and began the long drive down to Washington D.C. with several other friends. It was a typically hot August day, with temperatures forecasted in the nineties for the next two days. Neither Robert nor his son Ed really knew what to expect once they got to the nation's capital. Whatever they had anticipated, it was dwarfed by the tremendous events they came upon when they and the other members of St. Mark's Church arrived the next morning.

Once a young theology student in Boston, the now famous Reverend Dr. Martin Luther King, Jr. gave a speech that was heard around the world. He spoke of a dream, one that reached back to the dreams of every African-American man, woman and child since that fateful day in 1619 when more than 4,000 Angolans were herded like cattle onto a boxcar and thirty-six ships waited to take them to America. Perhaps John Gowen, as the first African slave to walk off the Ship *Treasurer* and onto American soil, had imagined that one day, he and his descendants would be valued as equal, respected citizens.

Nearly 350 years later, Robert Murphy and his youngest son Edward were now active participants in the historic March on Washington, and like so many members of the Cornwall Murphy family before them - had now become a part of history with many more chapters and generations to come.

Epilogue

On June 25th, 2013, the United States Supreme Court "nullified a core provision of the Voting Rights Act in an ideologically divided ruling that eroded a landmark of the Civil Rights era and threw the issue into the lap of a gridlocked Congress." In the Shelby County, Alabama decision, the court held that it was unconstitutional that the nine states previously required to obtain Federal approval of any voting laws "now can immediately implement changes in their election procedures without first obtaining clearance from the [U.S.] Justice Department."[459] On behalf of the court's conservative majority, Chief Justice John Roberts stated that the Jim Crow era discrimination of the past no longer justified preventing mostly southern states from changing their elections practices in the future.

Ostensibly, the Supreme Court decided to change the 1965 Voting Rights Act in order to accommodate a time when African Americans are presumed to have achieved full equality and should not have to worry about being turned away from the polls for arbitrary and capricious reasons. However, at the time this was written, a post-racial America had yet to be achieved, and many feared these changes to the Voting Rights Act were an effort to prevent People of Color - as well as elderly, working-class and poor Americans - from voting.

After Barack Obama, a brown-skinned man of mixed (white and black) racial heritage, was elected in 2008, becoming the first black President of the United States, some states, mostly in the South, enacted laws restricting hours to vote. Mail-in ballots we limited, the hours polling stations were open for voting decreased and pre-election-day voting was cut back.

As widely reported, in the 2012 presidential election, elderly African Americans - some at least 100 year-old - stood in line at several locations across the South for four hours or more to help re-elect President Obama.

The Supreme Court decision more than seven months later sanctified the voting restricts used in the 2012 presidential election and provided state and local governments the political cover to enact more restrictions on voting. This campaign to restrict voting rights was reminiscent of the 1870's Black Codes, predecessor to the widely accepted Jim Crow Laws of the South. The road to freedom for our nation's African Americans has been, and continued to be at the time this was written, paved with many obstacles along the way.

From when African John Gowen hesitantly walked down the plank from the Ship *Treasure* in 1619 to be the first African sold in America, to three hundred eighty-nine years later, when Barrack Obama, a man of partial African descent walked down the red carpet to be sworn in as the 44th President of the United States, many African-American men and women have walked their own personal and long arduous road to freedom.

While the sons and daughters of many American families have served the military for generations, few families have distinguish themselves as did the patriotic men Benjamin Brooker, Caesar Russell, Cuffe Grandison, Edward Gowen and Samuel Cornwell, as they fought courageously against British tyranny during the Revolutionary War. As they fought on the bloodstained battlefields of New York to Valley Forge, to Guilford Courthouse to Yorktown, they fought for independence, for freedom and for civil rights for themselves and their fellow countrymen, culminating in a new form of government, as quoted by President Abraham Lincoln, a "government of the people, by the people, for the people."

A government where Aaron Jackson, William Cornwell, and Othello and Thomas Fraction bore arms during the Civil War to defend the United States Constitution and the right for all men to be free and to be set free. Where men like David Melton and Benjamin Brooker risked their personal safety and the lives of their families to set pen to paper and challenged their state governments to treat them as men and not chattel property. Where a man like James Fraction was treated less than a full citizen stateside under the laws of the Jim Crow South, but was expected to and did serve and defend his country while serving on a naval vessel overseas.

For more than three hundred and fifty years, the true spirit and grit of the Cornwall Murphy family is endemic to the countless number of African-American families all across the United States who have persevered through the multitude of challenges before them. Freedom

Road is not the end of a journey into one family's history, but the beginning of the next chapter for the generations to come.

One hundred years from today, the extended Cornwall Murphy family will look at the current United States Supreme Court nullification of a core provision of the Voting Rights Act as nothing more than what it truly was, an ideologically divided ruling that will temporarily erode one piece of the landmark Civil Rights Act of 1964. In the long run, the Court's decision will not deter African-American men and women for fighting for the end of discrimination based on race, color, religion or national origin, the basic principles for which the ancestors of the present day members of the Cornwall Murphy family and countless number of African-American families across the United States have fought and died.

We now leave the next chapter and the next fight to the generations to come, as they too will at some point walk down their own Freedom Road and have their own stories to share.

Critical Dates and Milestones

1483 Portugal establishes relations with Angola

1492 Christopher Columbus attempts to sails to India

1575 Portugal colony of Angola is founded

1577 William Conrad Rucker (b) Rothenberg, Bayern, Germany

1579 Catherine Margaret (b) Germany

1580 Basil Fielding (b) Rutland, England

1585 Elizabeth Ashton (b) Texhall, Staffordshire, England

1660s - 1610

1604 Rogers Fielding (b) Neunhan Pardox, Worcester, England

1606 England's King James I granted the Virginia Company Charter, to establish a settlement in the Chesapeake region of North America.

1607 Johann Georg Rucker (b) Rothenberg, Bayern, Germany

1607 Virginia Company explorers landed on Jamestown Island to establish English colony

1608 Elizabeth Neale (b) Neunhan Pardox, Worcester, England

1610 Isabella Rucker (b) Germany

1611 John Rolfe imports tobacco seeds from Trinidad

1613 Pocahontas captured and brought to Jamestown

1614 John Rolfe and Pocahontas married in Jamestown

1614 John Rolfe makes first shipment of Virginia West Indian tobacco grown to England

1619 First Africans arrive in Virginia

1619 John Gowen sold as headright in Jamestown

1620 Plymouth Colony founded

1629 Massachusetts was the first slave-holding colony in the "New World"

1630 Massachusetts Bay Colony founded

1637 Anne Hutchinson expelled from Massachusetts Bay

1637 Pequot War

1640 Ambrose Levi Rucker (b) Bayern, Germany

1642 Elizabeth A Beauchamp (b) France

1646 Elizabeth M Polteney (b) Bristol, England

1650s - 1690s

1660 Elizabeth Fielding, (b) Bristol, Gloucestershire, England

1661 Peter Rucker (b) Bayern, Germany

1670 Massachusetts law states the status of the mother determines if their child is free or enslaved

1680 Hester Paine (b)

1680 John Rucker, (b) St Marks Parish, Orange, Virginia

1691 Virginia law bans interracial marriages

1691 Virginia law prohibits whites from freeing blacks or mulattoes without paying to have them removed from the colony

1698 Jacob Cornwell (b)

1700s – 1760s

1700 US slave population reaches 28,000

1702 Daniel Cornwell (b) Flushing, New York

1708 Slaves on Long Island, New York, kill seven whites

1720 Cuffe Grandison Sr. (b)

1727 Edward Gowen (b) Brunswick, VA

1740 William Ballard (b) Virginia

1742 George Bowers (b) Boston, Massachusetts

1742 Joshia Milton (b) Southampton, Virginia

1743 Cuffe Grandison (Clapp) Jr. (b) Situate, Massachusetts

1745 Edward Gowen (b) Brunswick, Virginia

1750 US African population reaches 236,400

1752 Matthew Howell (b) Amelia County, Virginia

1752 Samuel Cornwall (b) New York, New York.

1755 Peggy Howell (b) Charlotte County, Virginia

1755 Ruth Raif (b) Situate, Massachusetts

1755 Susan Howell (b) Charlotte County, Virginia

1756 Caesar Russell (b) North Carolina

1756 Sally Richardson (b)

1759 Sarah Mansfield (b)

1760 Freeman Howell (b) Charlotte County, Virginia

1760 US African population reaches 325,806

1765 Sons of Liberty formed

1765 Stamp Act

1766 Benjamin Brooker (Cain) (b) New Haven Connecticut

1770s - 1790s

1770 Crispus Attucks runaway slave killed at Boston Massacre

1773 Virginia prohibits free People of Color from bearing arms

1774 Continental Congress in Philadelphia, Pennsylvania

1775 ▪ Battle of Lexington and Concord/ Start of Revolutionary War
   ▪ Battle of Bunker Hill

▪ Battle Ticonderoga

▪ George Washington and Continental Congress prohibits Blacks from serving in the Army

1776 United States Declares Independence

1770 Harriet Grandison (b) Situate, Massachusetts

1770 James Melton (b) in Southampton, Virginia

1777 ▪ Battle of Brandywine
   ▪ British seize Philadelphia
   ▪ Battle of Germantown

1780 Massachusetts new constitution "all men are born free and equal" including black slaves

1780 Sarah Townsend (b)

1781 Cornwallis surrenders at Yorktown

1784 Mansfield Cornwall (b) St. Johns Parish, New Brunswick, Canada

1789 George Washington, 1st US President

1790 US black population reaches 757,200 (59,557 or 19.3% free)

1791 First ten amendments to the Constitution, known as the Bill of Rights ratified

1792 France declares War on England

1794 US Congress bans slave trade with foreign countries

1795 David Melton (b) in Rich Square, Northampton, North Carolina

1795 Samuel Brooker (b) Boston, Massachusetts

1799 Philinda Russell (b) Beverly, Massachusetts

1800s - 1830s

1800 Gabriel's Rebellion, Richmond, Virginia

1800 Milly Hunt Brook, Boydton, Virginia

1800 US black population reaches 1,002,000

1801 John Howell (b) Granville County, North Carolina

1803 England begins to impress American

sailors

1803 James Edmond Ballard (b) Gates, North Carolina

1803 Runaway slaves and Native Americans of the Five Nations, move into Indian Territory

1805 African Society of Boston draws parallel between slavery and Revolutionary War

1805 Virginia passes law to expel all free blacks

1806 John Jackson (b) Huntington, New York

1807 Battle of USS Chesapeake and HMS Leopard

1807 Nancy James (b) Halifax, North Carolina

1808 Julia Jones (b) Huntington, New York

1810 Flushing Cornwall (b) St. John's Parish, New Brunswick, Canada

1810 Stephen Lampkin Big Lick Township Roanoke, Virginia

1811 Jane Harris (b) Granville County, North Carolina

1812 America declares War on England - War of 1812

1814 England burns Washington, DC

1814 Jane Adkins (b) in Rich Square, Northampton, North Carolina

1815 Henry Gowen (b) unknown, Granville County, North Carolina

1815 Lucy Rucker (b) Big Lick Township Roanoke, Virginia

1815 War 1812 ends

1817 Harriet Brooker (b) Bridgewater, Massachusetts

1817 New York Stock Exchange founded

1818 Henry Utley (b) Fayetteville, Cumberland, North Carolina

1822 Mitchell Hunt (b) Boydton, Mecklenburg County, Virginia

1825 Lewis Gardiner (b) Huntington, New York

1830 Baltimore & Ohio 1st American Railroad

1830 William Fraction (b) Roanoke Virginia

1831 Cherokee Nation v. Georgia

1831 Margaret Gilchrist (b) Suffolk County, New York

1831 Nat Turner's Southampton Insurrection

1831 William Lloyd Garrison begins publishing "The Liberator"

1838 Mary Ann Parks (b) Guilford, North Carolina

1838 Matilda Hunt (b) Boydton, Mecklenburg County, **Virginia**

1840s - 1860s

1851 Keziah Gardiner (b) Huntington, New York

1855 Amanda Hunt (b) Boydton, Virginia

1855 Harriet Gowen (b) Fishing Creek Township, North Carolina

1857 United States Supreme Court *Dred Scott Decision*, opens federal territories to slavery

November 6, 1860, Abraham Lincoln elected President of the United States

1860 Crittenden Compromise fails, South Carolina secedes from the Union

1862 Homestead Act

1863 Abner Melton (b) in Rich Square, Northampton, North Carolina

1863 New York City Draft Riots

1863 President Abraham Lincoln issues the Emancipation Proclamation which freed slaves in the Confederate states

1863 Proclamation of Amnesty and Reconstruction

1864 Battle of Petersburg

1864 President Lincoln re-elected

1865 Lee surrenders at Appomattox Court House

1865 Thirteenth Amendment/ Abolishment of Slavery

1865 13th Amendment passed which abolished slavery

1865 Freedmen's Bureau established

1865 President Lincoln assassinated

1866 Fourteenth Amendment/ Civil Rights Act

1866 James Fraction (b) in Roanoke, Virginia

1867 Reconstruction Acts divides former Confederate South into separate military zones

1868 Fourteenth Amendment

1868 Julia Utley (b) Fayetteville, North Carolina

1869 Benjamin Cornwall (b) Boston, Massachusetts

1870 Fifteenth Amendment/ Voting Rights

1872 Sallie Ann Ballard (b) Rich Square, North Carolina

1877 Reconstruction officially ends

1878 Grace Jackson (b) Huntington, New York

1879 William Howell (b) Oxford, North Carolina

1884 Matilda Watson (b) Boydton, Virginia

1890 Louisiana passes *Separate Car Law* (segregated Jim Crow trains)

1892 Viola Geneva Fraction (b) in Roanoke, Virginia

1896 United States Supreme Court *Plessey v. Ferguson Decision*

1899 U.S. entered into Spanish-American War (1899 – 1901)

1900s - 1980s

1901 Harold Cornwall (b) Brockton, Massachusetts

1903 Margaret Melton (b) in Norfolk Virginia

1903 Robert H Murphy (b) in Norfolk, Virginia

1905 Niagara Movement

1907 Marie Howell (b) Brockton, Massachusetts

1941 Japan attacks Pearl Harbor

1941 U.S. entered into World War II

1945 End of World War II

1948 President Harry Truman desegregates the U.S. military

1950 Start of Korean War

1945 End of Korean War

1914 Panama Canal

1914 World War I - Begins

1917 U.S. entered into World War I (1917 – 1918)

1918 ▪ End of World War I
    ▪ Spanish American Flu

1939 World War II - Begins

1941 Japan attacks Pearl Harbor

1941 U.S. entered into World War II

1945 End of World War II

1948 President Harry Truman desegregates the U.S. military

1950 Start of Korean War

1945 End of Korean War

1954 Start of Civil Rights Movement

1955 Start of Vietnam War

1964 Civil Rights Act

1965 Voting Rights Act

1970 End of Civil Rights Movement

1975 ▪ End of Vietnam War
    ▪ Evacuation of Saigon

1982 The researching and documentation begins for the history of the Cornwall Murphy family

Source Notes and Selected Bibliography

Books

Adams, Catherine and Pleck, Elizabeth H., *Love of Freedom, Black Women in Colonial and Revolutionary New England*, published by Oxford University Press, 2010. ISBN 978-0-19-538909.

Advovasio, J.M., *The First American's In Pursuit of Archaeology's Greatest Mystery*, published by Modern Library, New York, New York, 2002. ISBN 0-375-75704-X.

Allardice, Bruce S., *Confederate Colonels, A Biographical Register*, published by The University of Missouri Press, Columbia, Missouri, 2008. ISBN 978-0-8262-1809.

Altoff, Gerald T., *Amongst My Best-Men, African Americans and The War of 1812*, published by The Perry Group, Put-In-Bay, Ohio, 1996. ISBN 1-887794-02-6.

Aptheker, Herbert, *American Negro Slave Revolts, 40th Anniversary Edition*. International Publishers. 5th Edition, 1987. ISBN 0-7178-0605-7.

Axtell, James, *After Columbus, Essays in the Ethnohistory of Colonial North America*, published by Oxford University, Press Inc. 1988 ISBN 0-19-505375-3.

Axtell, James, *The Rise and Fall of the Powhatan Empire, Indians in Seventeenth-Century Virginia*, published by The Colonial Williamsburg Foundation, 1995. ISBN 978-0-87935-153-3.

Berlin, Ira, Reidy, Joseph P., Rowland, Leslie S., *Freedom, A Documentary History of Emancipation, 1861-1867, Series II, The Black Military Experience*, published by Cambridge University Press, Cambridge, England, 1982. ISBN 0-521-22984-7.

Binkin, Martin, Eitelberg, Mark J., *Blacks and the Military* published by the Brookings Institution, Washington, DC. 1982.

Blackmon, Douglas A., *Slavery by Another Name, The Re-Enslavement of Black Americans from the Civil War to World War II*, published by Double Day New York, New York, 2008. ISBN 978-0-385-50625-0.

Borneman, Walter R., *1812, The War that Forged a Nation*, published by HarperCollins Publishers, New York, New York, 2004. ISBN 0-06-053112-6.

Bowers, William T., *Black Solider, White Army: the 24th Infantry Regiment in Korea*, published by the Center of Military History, United States Army, Washington, District of Columbia, 1996. ISBN 0-16-048803-6.

Broadnax, Samuel L., *Blue Skies, Black Wings, African American Pioneers of Aviation*, published by University of Nebraska Press, Lincoln, Nebraska, 2008. ISBN 978-0-8032-1774-4.

Brown, Alexander Crosby, *Steam Packets on the Chesapeake*, published by Cambridge, Maryland: Cornell Maritime Press, 1961 LCCN 61-012580

Buchanan, John, The *Road to Guildford Courthouse, The American Revolution in the Carolinas*, published by John Wiley and Sons, Inc. New York, New York, 1997. ISBN 0-471-169402-X.

Buchloz, Robert O., *London, A Social and Cultural History, 1550 – 1750*, published by Cambridge University Press, New York, New York, 2012. ISBN 978-0-521-89652.

Budiansky, Stephen, *Perilous Fight, America's Intrepid War with Britain on the High Seas, 1812 – 1815*, published by Borzoi Books a Division of Random House, New York, New York, 2010. ISBN 978-0-307-27069-6.

Burgess, Robert H., and Wood, H. Graham, *Steamboats Out of Baltimore*, published by Tidewater Publishers, Cambridge, Maryland, 1968. LCCCN: 68-58859.

Busch, Noel F., *Winter Quarters, George Washington and the Continental Army at Valley Forge*, published by Liveright, New York, New York, 1974. ISBN 0-87140-587-3.

Butterfield, Kenneth C., Supervisor. *Manumission Book of the Town of Huntington and Babylon Long Island 1800 - 1824, New York*. Published by Town of Huntington New York Historical Society. 1980.

Cannon, John, *Dictionary of British History*, published by Oxford University Press, New York, New York, 2001. ISBN 978-0-19-955037-1.

Castel, Albert E., *The Presidency of Andrew Johnson*, published by The Regents Press of Kansas, Lawrence, Kansas, 1979. ISBN 0-7006-0190-2.

Catchpole, Brian, *The Korean War, 1950-53*, Carroll & Graff Publishers, New York, New York, 2000. ISBN 0-7867-0939-1.

Cawthorne, Nigel, *Kings and Queens of England, From the Saxon Kings to the House of Windsor*, published by Arcturus Publishing Ltd., London, England, 2009.

Chadwick, Bruce, *The Forging of a Revolutionary Leader and the American Presidency, George Washington's War*, published Sourcebooks, Inc. Naperville, Illinois, 2004. ISBN 1-4022-0222-9.

Chalmers, David M., *Hooded Americanism, The History of the Ku Klux Klan*, published by Duke University Press, Durham, North Carolina, 1987. ISBN 0-8223-0730-8.

Churchill, Winston S., *The Birth of Britain, A History of Speaking Peoples, Volume I*, published by Dodd, Mead & Company, New York, New York, 1956. LCCCN 56-6868.

Colaiaco, James A., *Frederick Douglass and the Fourth of July*, published by Palgrave Macmillan, New York, New York, 2006. ISBN 1-4039-7033-5.

Cook, Adrian, *The Armies of the Streets, The New York City Draft Riots of 1863*, published by The University Press of Kentucky, Lexington, Kentucky, 1974. ISBN 0-8131-1298-2.

Cornell, Rev. John, *Genealogy of the Cornell Family*, published by published by T.A. Wright Press, New York, 1902

Craven, Avery, *Reconstruction: The Ending of the Civil War*, published by Holt, Rinehart and Winston, Inc., New York, New York, 1969. SBN 03-073245-X.

Cruden, Robert, *The Negro in Reconstruction*, published by Prentice-Hall, Inc., Englewood Cliffs, New Jersey, 1969. LCCC 69-17370.

Cumings, Bruce, *The Korean War, A History*, published by The Modern Library, New York, New York. ISBN 978-0-679-64357-9

Daughan, George C., *1812, The Navy's War*, published by Basic Books, New York, New York, 2011. ISBN 978-0465-02046-1.

De Villers, Marq and Hirtle, Shelia, *Into Africa, A Journey through Ancient Empires*, published by Key Porter Books Limited, Toronto, Ontario, 1997. ISBN 1-55013-884-7.

Donald, David Herbert, *Lincoln*, Simon & Schuster, New York, New York, 1995. ISBN 0-684-80846-3.

Egerton, Douglas R., *Death of Liberty, African Americans and Revolutionary America*, published by Oxford University Press, New York, New York, 2009. ISBN 978-0-530669-9.

Egerton, Douglas, *Gabriel's Rebellion: the Virginia Slave Conspiracies of 1800 and 1802*, published by The University of North Carolina Press, Chapel Hill, North Carolina, 1993. ISBN 0-8078-2113-6.

Elting, John R., *Amateurs, To Arms: A Military History of the War of 1812*, published by Algonquin Books of Chapel Hill, Chapel Hill, North Carolina, 1991. ISBN 0-945575-08-4.

Ferling, John, *Independence, The Struggle to Set America Free*, published by Bloombury Press, New York, New York, 2001. ISBN 978-1-60819-008-9.

Fireside, Harvey, *Separate and Unequal, Homer Plessey and the Supreme Court Decision that Legalized Racism*, published by Carroll & Graf Publishers, New York, New York, 2004. ISBN 0-7867-1293-7.

Fleming, Thomas, *Washington's Secret War, the Hidden History of Valley Forge*, published by Smithsonian Books, HarperCollins, New York, New York, 2005. ISBN 978-0060872939.

Fligstein, Neil, *Going North, Migration of Blacks and Whites from the South, 1900-1950, Quantitative Studies in Social Research*, Academic Press, New York, New York, 1981. ISBN 0-12-2670720-1.

Foote, Shelby, *The Civil War, A Narrative: Red River To Appomattox*. published by Random House Inc., New York, New York, 1974. ISBN 0-394-74623-6.

Franklin, John H. and Moss, Alfred A., *From Slavery to Freedom: A History of Negro Americans*, published by McGraw-Hill, New York, New York. ISBN 0-394-56362-X.

Gardiner, Sarah Diodati, *Early Memories of Gardiners Island: The Isle of Wight*, New York, published by East Hampton Star, East Hampton, New York, 1947.

Gillette, William, *Retreat from Reconstruction, 1869-1879*, published by Louisiana State University Press, Baton Rouge, Louisiana, 1979. ISBN 0-8071-0569-4.

Greene, Robert Ewell, *Black Courage, 1775-1783, Documentation of Black Participation in the American Revolution*, published by National Society of the American Revolution, Washington, District of Columbia, 1984. ISBN 0*9602528-4-3.

Grossman, James R., *Land of Hope: Chicago, Black Southerners and the Great Migration*, The University of Chicago Press, Chicago, Illinois, 1989. ISBN 0-226-30994-0.

Grundset, Eric G., *Forgotten Patriots, African American and American Indian Patriots in the Revolutionary War, A Guide to Services, Sources and Studies*, published by The National Society Daughters of the American Revolution, 2008. ISBN 978-1-892237-10-1.

Guelzo, Allen C., *Lincoln and Douglas, The Debates That Defined America*, printed by Simon & Schuster, New York, New York, 2008. ISBN 13-978-0-7432-7320-6.

Guiteras. Gertrude Elizabeth, Guiteras, *Wardwell and Allied Families, Genealogical and Biographical*, published by The American Historical Society, New York, New York, 1926.

Gwathmey, John H., *Historical Register of Virginians in the Revolution*, published by Genealogical Publishing Company, 1996. ISBN 978-0806305578.

Hahn, Steven, *A Nation Under Our Feet, Black Political Struggles in the Rural South from Slavery to the Great Migration*, published by Belknap Press of Harvard University, Cambridge, Massachusetts, 2003. ISBN 0-674-01169-4.

Hainer, Pattie, *Uncommon Sufferings and Surprising Deliverances: The Black Community of Situate-Norwell, 1633 to 1800*, grant funded by the Massachusetts Foundation for the Humanities and the Bay State Historical League, 1996.

Hale, Robert R., *Early Brunswick Probate Records, 1785 – 1835*, published by Heritage Books, Inc., Bowie, Maryland. ISBN 1-55613-240-9. 1989.

Hardesty, Von, *Black Wings, Courageous Stores of African Americans in Aviation and Space History*, published by HarperCollins, New York, New York, 2008. ISBN 978-0-06-126138-1.

Harrison, Alferdteen, *Black Exodus, The Great Migration for the American South*, published by University Press of Mississippi, Jackson, Mississippi, 1991. ISBN 0-87805-491-X.

Hart, Albert Bushnell (editor), *Life at Valley Forge (1777-1778), American History told by Contemporaries, Volume II: Building of the Republic, 1689-1783*, published by The MacMillan Companies, New York, New York, 1901.

Hashaw, Tim, *Children of Perdition, Melungeons and the Struggle of Mixed America*, published by Mercer University Press, Macon, Georgia, First edition, 2006. ISBN-13: 978-0-88146-013-1.

Hashaw, Tim, The *Birth of Black America, the First African Americans and the Pursuit of Freedom at Jamestown.* Published by Carroll and Graf Publishers, New York, New York, in 2007. ISBN-13: 978-0-78671-781-7.

Heinegg, Paul, Free *African Americans of North Carolina, Virginia and South Carolina from the Colonial Period to About 1820,* published by Clearfield Co; printed 2005, reprinted: 2008, Fifth Edition. Two Volumes. ISBN 0-8063-5281-7.

Henry, Robert Selph, *The Story of Reconstruction,* published by Konecky & Konecky, New York, New York, 1999. ISBN 1-56852-254-1.

Hickey, Donald R., *The War of 1812, A Forgotten Conflict,* published by University of Illinois Press, Chicago, Illinois, 1989. ISBN 0-252-01613-0.

Higginbotham, Don, *The War of American Independence, Military Attitudes, Policies, and Practice, 1763 – 1789,* published by The Macmillan Company, New York, New York, 1971. Library of Congress Card Catalog Number, 74-132454..

Hine, Darlene Clark; Hine, William C.; and Harold, Stanley, *African Americans, a Concise History, Second Edition.* Printed by Pearson, Prentice Hall, Saddle River, New Jersey, 2006. ISBN: 0-13-192583-0.

Horsman, Reginald, *The Causes of the War of 1812,* printed by Octagon Books, New York, New York, 1975. ISBN 0-374-93960-8.

Ilgenfritz, Elizabeth, *Anne Hutchinson, Religious Leader,* published by Chelsea House Publishers. New York, New York. ISBN 1-55546-660-5.

Jakeman, Robert J., *The Divided Skies, Establishing Segregated Flight Training at Tuskegee,* Alabama, 1934-1942., published by The University of Alabama Press, Tuscaloosa, Alabama, 1992. ISBN 0-8173-0527-0.

James, Bill, Popular *Crime, Reflections on the Celebration of Violence,* published by Scribner Publishing, Division of Simon & Schuster, Inc., 2011. ISBN 978 1-4165-5273-4

Kagey, Deedie, *When Past is Prologue: A History of Roanoke County,* published Walsworth Press Inc., LC No. 88-51691, 1988,

Kaplan, Sidney, *The Black Presence in the Era of the American Revolution, 1770 – 1800,* published the New York Graphic Society, LTD, 1973. ISBN 0-812-0541-2.

Kendrick, Paul and Kendrick, Stephen, *Douglass and Lincoln, How a Revolutionary Black Leader and a Reluctant Liberator Struggled to End Slavery and Save the Union,* published by Walker & Company Publishing, New York, New York, 2008. ISBN 10-0-8027-1523-0.

Ketchem, Richard M., Saratoga, *Turning Point of Americas Revolutionary War,* published by Henry Holt and Company, New York, New York, 1997. ISBN 0-8050-4681-X.

Kingsbury, Susan Myra (Editor), *The Records of the Virginia Company of London: Documents, I, 1607-1622, Volume 3, from the Court Book, from the Manuscript in the Library of Congress,* published by Heritage Books, Bowie, Maryland. ISBN 0-7884-0210-2.

Kirchberger, Joe H., The *Civil War and Reconstruction, An Eyewitness History*, published by Facts on File, Inc., New York, New York, 1991. ISBN 0-8160-2171-6.

Klein, Maury, *History of the Louisville & Nashville Railroad*, published by University Press of Kentucky, 2003. ISBN 10: 0813122635.

Klingaman, William K. *Abraham Lincoln and the Road to Emancipation, 1861 – 1865*, published by Viking Penguin Books, New York, New York, 2001. ISBN 0-670-86754-3.

Langguth, A J., *Union 1812, The Americans Who Fought the Second War of Independence*, published by Simon & Schuster, New York, New York, 2006. ISBN 978-0-7432-2618-9.

Lanning, Lt. Col (Ret) Michael Lee, The *African American Solider, from Crispus Attucks to Colin Powell*, published by Carol Publishing Group, Secaucus, New Jersey, 1997. ISBN 1-55972-404-8.

LaPlante, Eve, *American Jezebel, the Uncommon Life of Anne Hutchinson, the Woman Who Defied the Puritans*. published by Harper Collins Publishing, New York, New York, 2004. ISBN 0-056233-1.

Leary, Helen F. M., and Stirewalt, Maurice R., *North Carolina Research, Genealogy and Local History*, published by The North Carolina Genealogical Society, 1980. ISBN 0936370009.

Leckie, Robert, *George Washington's War, The Saga of the American Revolution*, published by Harper Perennial, New York, New York, 1993. ISBN 0-06-016289-9.

Lindon, Mary Elizabeth, *Virginia's Montgomery County*, published by Montgomery Museum and Lewis Miller Regional Art Center, Christiansburg, Virginia, 2009. ISBN 978-0-970648-2-7.

Litwack, Leon F., *Trouble in Mind, Black Southerners in the Age of Jim Crow*, published by Alfred A. Knopf Inc., New York, New York, 1998. ISBN 0-394-52778-x.

Lockhart, Paul, *The Drillmaster of Valley Forge, the Baron De Steuben and the Making of the American Army*, published by Hollier Collins Publishers, New York, New York, 2008. ISBN 13-978-0-06-145163-8.

Lomask, Milton, *Andrew Johnson, President on Trial*, published by Octagon Books, New York, New York, 1973. ISBN 0-374-95082-2.

MacGregor, Morris J., Jr., *Integration of the Armed Forces, 1940-1965*, published by the Center of Military History, United States Army, Washington, D.C., 1981. Superintendent Documents Number D-114.2: In 8/940-65.

MacNutt, Stewart W., *New Brunswick, A History 1784 – 1867*, published by Macmillan of Canada, Toronto, Canada. 1963. ISBN 0-7715-9818-1.

Mann, Kenny, African *Kingdoms of the Past, Kongo, Ndongo, West Central Africa*, published by Dillon Press, Parsippany, New Jersey, 1996. ISBN 0-87518-658-0.

Marcus, Dr. Grania Bolton, *Discovering the African American Experience in Suffolk County, 1620 – 1860*, published by N.Y. Society for the Preservation, Mad Printers, Mattituck, NY 1988.

Marius, Richard, *Thomas More*, published by Alfred A. Knopf, New York, New York, 1984. ISBN 0-394-45982-2.

Maruyama, Susan J., *African Americans, Voices of Triumph, Perseverance*, published by the Editors of Time-Life Books, Alexandria, Virginia, 1993. ISBN 0-7835-2250-9.

McCary, Ben C., *Indians in Seventeenth- Century* Virginia, published by The Virginia 350th Anniversary Celebration Corporations, MCMLVII

McKanan, Dan, *Prophetic Encounters, Religion and the American Radial Tradition*, published by Beacon Press, Boston, Massachusetts, 2011. ISBN 978-0-8070-1315-1.

McManus, Edgar J., *Black Bondage in the North*, published by Syracuse University Press, Syracuse, New York, printed 2001. ISBN 0-8156-2893-5.

McPherson, James M., *Ordeal by Fire, The Civil War, Volume II*, published by McGraw Hill, 2001. ISBN 0-07-231736-1.

McPherson, James M., *The Struggle for Equality, Abolitionists and the Negro in the Civil War and Reconstruction*, published by Princeton University Press, Princeton, New Jersey, 1964. Library of Congress Card 63-23411.

Mersky, Peter and Polmar, Norman, *The Naval Air War in Vietnam*, published by The Nautical and Aviation Publishing Company, Annapolis, Maryland. ISBN 0-933852-13-4.

Middlekauff, Robert, *The Glorious Cause, the American Revolution, 1773-1789*, published by Oxford University Press, New York, New York, 1982. ISBN 0-19-502921-6.

Moche, Joanne Spiers, *Families of Grace through 1900, Remembering Radford, Volume I*, published by Heritage Books, Westminster, Maryland, 2008. ISBN 978-0-7884-3744-1.

Moretti, Lynne Geever, *Slavery in Situate, Massachusetts 1673 –1790: Benign Servitude, Master Thesis*, submitted to the Office of Graduate Studies and research, University of Massachusetts Boston. December, 2002.

Mossiker, Frances, Pocahontas, *The Life and the Legend*, published by Da Capo Press, Inc. New York, New York, 1996. ISBN 0-306-806991-1.

Mullin, Gerald, W., *Flight and Rebellion: Slave Resistance in Eighteenth Century Virginia*, published by Oxford University Press, New York, New York, 1972. Library of Congress Card Number 73:173327.

Musciant, Ivan, *Empire by Default, The Spanish-American War and the Dawn of the American Century*, published by Henry Holt and Company, Inc., New York, New York, 1998. ISBN 0-8050-3500-1.

Nichols, Roger L., *Indians in the United States, A Comparative History*, published by University of Nebraska Press, Lincoln, Nebraska, 1998. ISBN 0-8032-3341-8.

Nock, O. S., *Railways of the USA*, published by Hastings House Publishes, New York, New York. ISBN 0-8038-6359-4.

Othow, Helen Chavis, *John Chavis, African American Patriot, Preacher, Teacher and Mentor (1763 – 1838)*, published by McFarland & Company, Inc., Jefferson, North Carolina, 2001. ISBN 978-0786408184.

Parker, J. Roy, *The Ahoskie Era of Hertford County*, published by Parker Brothers, Inc., Ahoskie, North Carolina, 1939.

Parker, Roy, Jr. *Cumberland County, A Brief History*, published by the North Carolina Department of Cultural Resources, Division of Archives and History, in 1990. ISBN 0-86526-243-8.

Parramore, Thomas C., Trial *Separation: Murfreesboro, North Carolina and the Civil War*, published by Murfreesboro Historical Association, Inc, Murfreesboro, North Carolina:. LCCN TX-5-007-748.

Pickett, Margaret F. and Pickett, Dwayne W., *The European Struggle to Settle North America: Colonizing Attempts by England, France and Spain, 1521-1608*, published by McFarland and Company, Inc., 2011 Jefferson, North Carolina, and London, ISBN 978-0-7864-5932-2.

Piersen, William D., *Black Yankees, The Development of and Afro-American Subculture in Eighteenth-Century New England*, published by The University of Massachusetts Press, Amherst, Massachusetts, 1988. ISBN 0-87023-586-9.

Pratt, Harvey Hunter, *Early Planters of Situate, Massachusetts*, published by the Situate Historical Society, Situate, Massachusetts, 1929. ISBN 0-7884-0885-2.

Purcell, L. Edward, *Immigration, Social Issues in American History Series*, published by Oryx Press, Phoenix, Arizona, 1995. ISBN 0-89774-873-5.

Pybus, Cassandra, *Jefferson's Faulty Math: The Question of Slave Defections in the American Revolution*, William and Mary Quarterly, April 2005. Volume LXII Number 2.

Reef, Catherine, *African Americans in the Military*, published by InfoBase Publishing, New York, New York, 2010. ISBN 978-0-8160-7839-4.

Reynolds, E.E., *Thomas More & Erasmus*, published by Fordham University Press, New York, New York, 1965. LOCCN 65-26739.

Richardson, Heather Cox, West *From Appomattox, the Reconstruction of America after the Civil War*, published by Yale University Press, New Haven, Connecticut, 2007. ISBN 978-0-300-11052-4.

Riendeau, Roger, *A Brief History of Canada*, published by Facts On File, Inc., New York, New York, 2000. ISBN 0-8160-3157-6.

Sandler, Stanley, *The Korean War, No Victors, No Vanquished*, published by The University Press of Kentucky, Lexington, Kentucky, 1999. ISBN 0-8131-2119-1.

Schneller, Robert J., *Blue & Gold and Black: Racial Integration of the U.S. Naval Academy*, published by Texas A&M University Press, 2007. ISBN 978-1-60344-000-4.

Shaw, G.C., D.D., *John Chavis, 1763-1838, A Remarkable Negro Who Conducted a School in North Carolina for White Boys and Girls*, published by Yail-Ballou Press, Bingham, New York, 1931.

Shillington, Kevin, *History of Africa*, published by Macmillan Publishers, Oxford, Malaysia, ISBN 0-333-59957-8.

Smith, Douglas, J., *Managing White Supremacy, Race, Politics and Citizenship in Jim Crow Virginia*, published by The University of North Carolina Press, Chapel Hill, North Carolina. ISBN 0-8078-2756-8.

Smith, Paul H., *Loyalists and Redcoats, A Study in British Revolutionary Policy*, published by the University of North Carolina Press, Chapel Hill, North Carolina, 1964. Library of Congress Catalog Card Number, 64-22526.

Smith, Philip H., *Curiosities in American History, The Green Mountain Boys: or Vermont and the New York Land - Jobbers*, published by Philip H. Smith, Publisher, Pawling, New York, 1885. Library of Congress 16765-Q2.

Starkey, Larry, *Wilkes Booth Came to Washington*, published by Random House, New York, New York, 1976. ISBN 0-394-48894-6.

Stauffer, John, *The Black Hearts of Men, Radical Abolitionists and the Transformation of Race*, published by Harvard University Press, Cambridge, Massachusetts, 2002. ISBN 0-674-00645-3.

Stewart MacNutt, Stewart W., *New Brunswick, A History 1784 – 1867*, published by Macmillan of Canada, Toronto, Canada. 1963. ISBN 0-7715-9818-1.

Stewart, David O., *The Summer of 1787*, published by Simon & Schuster, New York, New York, 2007. ISBN 978-0-7432-8692.

Stokesbury, James L., *A Short History of the Civil War*, published by William Morris and Company, Inc., New York, New York, 1995. ISBN 0-688-11523-3.

Talty, Stephan, *Mulatto America, Crossroads of Black and White Culture A Social History*, published by Harper Collins Publishers, New York New York. 1999. ISBN 0-06-018517-1.

Taylor, Alan, The *Civil War of 1812, American Citizens, British Subjects, Irish Rebels and Indian Allies*, published by Alfred A. Knopf, New York, New York, 2010. ISBN: 978-1-4000-4265-4.

Taylor, Rosser Howard, *The Free Negro in North Carolina*, published by The James Sprunt Historical Publications, under The North Carolina Historical Society, Vol. 17, No.1, and the University of Chapel Hill, North Carolina. 1920.

Traxel, David, 1898, *The Tumultuous Years of Victory, Invention, Internal Strife and Industrial Expansion that Saw the Birth of the American Century*, published by Alfred A. Knopf, New York, New York, 1998. ISBN 0-679-45497-5.

Trelease, Allen, W., *White Terror, The Ku Klux Klan, Conspiracy and Southern Reconstruction*, published by Greenwood Press Publishers, Westport, Connecticut, 1971. ISBN 0-31321168-X.

Tye, Larry, *Rising form the Rails, Pullman Porters and the Making of the Black Middle Class*, published by the Henry Holt and Company, New York, New York, 2004. ISBN 0-8050-7075-3.

Tyler, D. Gardiner, *A History and Pictorial Review of Charles City County, Virginia*, published by Philip Council, 1990. LOC 90-63386.

Viorst, Milton, Fall *From Grace, the Republican Party and the Puritan Ethic*, published by the New American Library Inc., New York, New York, 1968. Library of Congress catalog Number: 68-20115.

Walker Frank S., Jr., *Remembering: A History of Orange County, Virginia*, published by the Orange County Historical Society, Inc., Orange, Virginia

Walton, Ben L., *Great Black War Fighters, Profiles in Service*, published by Strategic Book Publishing and Rights Co., Houston, Texas. 2012. ISBN 978-1-61897-108-1

Wesley, Charles H., *Prince Hall, Life and Legacy*, published by United Supreme Council, Southern Jurisdiction, Prince Hall Affiliation, Washington, DC. 1977.

White, Margaret Anne, *The Early Years at Cedar Grove Friends Meeting in Woodland, North Carolina*, published by in The Southern Friend, Journal of the North Carolina Friends Historical Society, Vol. 1, No. 1, 1979.

White, Richard, *The Middle Ground: Indians, Empires, and Republics in the Great Lakes Region*, published by Cambridge University Press, in 1991. ISBN 0521424607

Williams, David, *A People's History of the Civil War, Struggles for the Meaning of Freedom*, published by The New Press, New York, New York, 2005. ISBN 1-59558-018-2.

Williams, Selma R., *Divine Rebel, the Life of Anne Marbury Hutchinson*. published by Holt, Rinehart and Winston, New York, 1981. ISBN: 0-03-055846-8.

Wood, Martin, *The Family and Descendants of St Thomas More*, published by Gracewing Ltd, London, England, 2008. ISBN 978-0-85244-681.

Wood, Sudie Rucker, *The Rucker Family Genealogy: with their Ancestors, Descendants and Connections*, published by Old Dominion Press, Inc., Richmond, Virginia, 1932.

Wood-Holt, B.. *Early Marriage Records of New Brunswick, Saint John City and County from the British Conquest to 1839*. Holland House, Inc. Saint John, N.B. Canada. 135606. 1986.

Woodward, Grace Steele, *Pocahontas*, published by University of Oklahoma Press, Norman, Oklahoma, 1969. LCCC 68-15687.

Worrell, Anne Lowry, *A Brief of Wills and Marriages in Montgomery and Fincastle Counties, Virginia, 1773-1831*, published by Virginia Book Company, Berryville, Virginia, 1932.

Electronic Sources

Harper, Douglas. Slavery in the North. http://www.slavenorth.com/massachusetts.htm

http://query.nytimes.com/gst/abstract.html?res=9E03EEDB1E30E333A25751C2 A9679C946196D6CF, The New York Times, January 22, 1910, New York Times.

http://query.nytimes.com/gst/abstract.html?res=9E03EEDB1E30E333A25751C2 A9679C946196D6CF, The New York Times, January 22, 1910, New York Times.

http://www.larcomfamilytree/documents/lineage.html

U.S. National Archives and Records Administration, Black Soldiers in the Civil War. http://www.archives.gov/education/lessons/blacks-civil-war/douglass-sons.html

U.S. Department of State, Office of the Historian, Milestones: 1945-1952, The Truman Doctrine, 1947. http://history.state.gov/milestones/1945-1952/TrumanDoctrine. Accessed May, 6, 2013.

Government Publications

Brockton City Directory. Brockton, Massachusetts

Commonwealth of Massachusetts, *State Department of Public Health, Registry of Vital Records and Statistics, Record of Marriage, Year 1891.*

Commonwealth of Massachusetts, Secretary of the Commonwealth, *Massachusetts Archives Collection*

Commonwealth of Massachusetts, *Vital Records of Beverly, Massachusetts, Births, Marriages, Deaths until 1850.*

Commonwealth of Massachusetts, *Vital Records of Bridgewater, Massachusetts, Births, Marriages, Deaths until 1850.*

Commonwealth of Massachusetts, *Vital Records of Cambridge, Massachusetts, Births, Marriages, Deaths until 1850.*

Commonwealth of Massachusetts, *Vital Records of Situate, Massachusetts, Deaths until 1850.*

Commonwealth of Massachusetts, *Vital Records of Taunton, Massachusetts, Births, Marriages, Deaths until 1850.*

Commonwealth of Massachusetts, *Vital Records of Wilmington, Massachusetts, Births, Marriages, Deaths until 1850.*

Commonwealth of Virginia Department of Historic Resources, Historical Markers, D-11 Ruckersville, Orange County, Virginia

Daggett, Stephen, Congressional Research Service, *Costs of Major U.S. Wars*, June 29, 2010.

Dumont, William H. *Some Virginia Revolutionary Veterans and Their Heirs*. Washington, D.C.: Fiscal Section of the National Archives.

Free Inhabitants in Southern District, in the County of Hertford, State of North Carolina.

Granville County, *North Carolina Marriages, 1753 -1855*

Granville County, *North Carolina Vital Statistics*, Annual Edition: 1880

Hening, William W., ed. 1809-23. *The Statutes at Large: Being a Collection of All the Laws of Virginia, from the First Session of the Legislature, in the Year 1670 – Extracts.*

McFadden, Terri, Research Assistant, Beverly Historical Society Collections, Beverly, Massachusetts. 2012

Norfolk City Directory, Norfolk Virginia

Oxford, N.C. Vital Statistics, Annual Edition:

Secretary of the Commonwealth of Massachusetts. *Massachusetts Soldiers and Sailors in the War of the Revolution*. Boston, MA. Wright and Potter Printing Co., 1896. 17 Vols.

Swasey, Charles W., *Historical Collections of the Essex Institute*, published by the Essex Institute, Salem, Massachusetts, 1864. Volume XXXXIV.

The Virginia Magazine of History and Biography, Council and General Court Records, published by the Virginia Historical Society, Richmond, Virginia Dorman, Frederick. 1958-1995. *Virginia Revolutionary Pension Applications, Volumes 1-45.* Washington, D.C.

U.S. Census, Smithtown, Suffolk County, New York

U.S. Special Census Schedule: Distribution of Slaves in United States History

U.S. Special Census Schedule: Surviving Soldiers, Sailors, and Marines, and Widows

United States Census Bureau: 1790 Schedule; 1800 Schedule; 1810 Schedule; 1820 Schedule; 1830 Schedule; 1840 Schedule; 1850 Schedule; 1860 Schedule; 1870 Schedule; 1880 Schedule; 1890 Schedule; 1900 Schedule; 1910 Schedule; 1920 Schedule; 1930 Schedule.

United States Revolutionary War Pension Bounty Land Warrant Applications

United States, National Archives and Records Administration, *Confederate Applications for Presidential Pardons*

York County, *Virginia Deeds, Orders, and Wills, 1657-1659.*

Magazines and Newspaper Articles

Jet Magazine *Admiral Chambers Heads Persian Gulf Naval Force*, March 13, 1980, Published by Johnson Publishing Company, Chicago, IL.

Sluiter, Engel, *New Light on the "20 and Odd Negroes" Arriving in Virginia in 1619*, published by William and Mary Quarterly, 3rd Series, Volume 54, No. 2, April 1997.

Study of Afro-American Life Report and History in conjunction with the Association for the Study of Negro Life and History. *"Science and Invention"*

The Crisis Magazine, National Association for the Advancement of Colored People, 1940. Vol.47, No. 11, Cover Image.

The Crisis Magazine, Wilkins, Roger, Editor, *The Black Solider and The Civil War*, Baltimore, Maryland, 21215, Volume 106, Number 1, January-February 1999

The Virginia Magazine of History and Biography, *Council and General Court Records*, published by the Virginia Historical Society, Richmond, Virginia, Vol XI-No.1, July 1903.

Thornton, John K, *Warfare in Atlantic Africa, 1500-1800*, published by University College London, London, England, 1999

Thornton, John, *The African Experience of the "20 and Odd Negroes" Arriving in Virginia in 1619*, published by William and Mary Quarterly College Quarterly – Historical Magazine, 3rd Series, Volume 55, No.3, Williamsburg, Virginia, July 1998.

Walker, Jesse, Staff Correspondent, The Afro-American Newspaper, *D.C. Grad Ranks High at U.S. Naval Academy, Ensign Lawrence Chambers Jr. Stands 119 in Class of 783*. June 14, 1952.

Wilkins, Major Fred J., *"Steuben Screamed but Things Happened and an Army Was Born at Valley Forge Just One Hundred and Seventy Years Ago,"* The Picket Post, January 1948, published by The Valley Forge Historical Society.

O'Donnell, Richard, Yankee Magazine, *There Have Been Thousands of Department Store Santa's since 1800, but None Quite Like The First Department Store Santa Claus, December 1969*, published by Yankee Publishing Inc., Dublin, NH., 1969

Young, Joe and Lewis, Sam, music by Donaldson, Walter, *How 'Ya Gonna Keep 'Em Down on the Farm? (After They've Seen Paree)*, published by Waterson, Berlin & Snyder Co., Music Publishing, New York, New York, 1919.

Notes

1. Based on DNA evidence from descendants, the ancestors of Benjamin Brooker, Cuffe Grandison and Caesar Russell probably came from the northwest coast of Africa, to include the present day countries of Nigeria, Senegal and the people from the nations along Africa's west coast, from Gambia to Equatorial Guinea.

2. Commonwealth of Massachusetts, *Vital Records of Scituate, Massachusetts*, Marriages until 1850. Page 392.

3. McCary, Ben C., *Indians in Seventeenth Century Virginia*. Published by The Virginia 350th Anniversary Celebration Corporations, MCMLVII Page 1.

4. Axtell, James, *The Rise and Fall of the Powhatan Empire, Indians in Seventeenth-Century Virginia*, published by The Colonial Williamsburg Foundation, 1995. ISBN 978-0-87935-153-3. Page 5.

5. Ibid., Page 7.

6. McCary, Ben C., *Indians in Seventeenth- Century Virginia*. Published by The Virginia 350th Anniversary Celebration Corporations, MCMLVII. Page 6

7. Commonwealth of Massachusetts, Vital Records of Scituate, Massachusetts, Deaths until 1850. Page 392.

8. National Day of Mourning Plaque at Coles Hill, Post Office Square, Plymouth, Massachusetts. Erected by the Town of Plymouth on behalf of the United American Indians of New England, 1999.

9. Shillington, Kevin, *History of Africa*, published by Macmillan Publishers, Oxford, Malaysia, ISBN 0-333-59957-8. Page 198.

10. De Villers, Marq and Hirtle, Shelia, *Into Africa, A Journey through Ancient Empires*, published by Key Porter Books Limited, Toronto, Ontario, 1997. ISBN 1-55013-884-7. Page 160.

11. Shillington, Kevin, *History of Africa*, published by Macmillan Publishers, Oxford, Malaysia, ISBN 0-333-59957-8. Page 198.

12. The Historic Dates for the Kingdoms of Kongo and Angola are largely pieced together from the dates from Mann, Kenny, *African Kingdoms of the Past, Kongo, Ndongo, West Central Africa*, published by Dillon Press, Parsippany, New Jersey, 1996. ISBN 0-87518-658-0. Page 5.

13. De Villers, Marq and Hirtle, Shelia, *Into Africa, A Journey through Ancient Empires*, published by Key Porter Books Limited, Toronto, Ontario, 1997. ISBN 1-55013-884-7. Page 162.

14. Shillington, Kevin, *History of Africa*, published by Macmillan Publishers, Oxford, Malaysia, ISBN 0-333-59957-8. Page 201.

15   De Villers, Marq and Hirtle, Shelia, *Into Africa, A Journey through Ancient Empires*, published by Key Porter Books Limited, Toronto, Ontario, 1997. ISBN 1-55013-884-7. Page 165.

16   De Villers, Marq and Hirtle, Shelia, *Into Africa, A Journey through Ancient Empires*, published by Key Porter Books Limited, Toronto, Ontario, 1997. ISBN 1-55013-884-7. Page 166-167.

17   Thorton, John K, *Warfare in Atlantic Africa, 1500-1800*, published by University College London, London, England, 1999. Page 102.

18   Thorton, John, *The African Experience of the "20 and Odd Negroes" Arriving in Virginia in 1619*, published by <u>William and Mary Quarterly</u>, 3rd Series, Volume 55, No.3, July 1998. Page 424, 431-434.

19   Hashaw, Tim, *The Birth of Black America, the First African Americans and the Pursuit of Freedom at Jamestown, published by* Carroll and Graf Publishers, New York, New York, in 2007. ISBN-13: 978-0-78671-781-7, Page 69.

20   Ibid., Pages 72-73.

21   Ibid., Page 73.

22   Sluiter, Engel, *New Light on the "20 and Odd Negroes" Arriving in Virginia in 1619*, published by William and Mary Quarterly, 3rd Series, Volume 54, No. 2, April 1997. Page 397.

23   Ibid., Pages 398.

24   Ibid., Page 397.

25   Kingsbury, Susan Myra (ed.), *The Records of the Virginia Company of London: Documents, I, 1607-1622*, Volume 3, from the Court Book, from the Manuscript in the Library of Congress, published by Heritage Books, Bowie, Maryland. ISBN 0-7884-0210-2. Page 243.

26   McCartney, Martha W., *Jamestown People to 1800, Landowners, Public Officials, Minorities and Native Leaders*, published by Genealogical Publishing Company, Baltimore Maryland, 2012. ISBN 978-0-8063-1872-1. Page 9.

27   The Virginia Magazine of History and Biography, *Council and General Court Records*, published by the Virginia Historical Society, Richmond, Virginia, Volume XI, No.8, Page 281.

28   Tim Hashaw, *The Birth of Black America, the First African Americans and the Pursuit of Freedom at Jamestown, published by* Carroll and Graf Publishers, New York, New York, in 2007. ISBN-13: 978-0-78671-781-7, Page 169.

29   The Virginia Magazine of History and Biography, *Council and General Court Records*, published by the Virginia Historical Society, Richmond, Virginia, Vol XI-No.1, July 1903. Page 281.

30   Marie Howell Cornwall is descended from John Geaween as evidenced by a number of primary and secondary sources. Marie Howell Cornwall was the

daughter of William Howell; who was the son of Harriet Gowen Howell; who was the daughter of Henry Gowen; who was the son of Edward Gowen V; who was the son of Edward Gowen IV; who was the son of Edward Gowen III; who was the son of Edward Gowen, Jr.; who was the son of Edward Gowen, Sr.; who was the son of William Gowen; who was the son of Michael Gowen; and who was the son of John Geaween (Gowen).

31 The Virginia Magazine of History and Biography, *Council and General Court Records*, published by the Virginia Historical Society, Richmond, Virginia, Vol XI-No.1, July 1903. Page 281.

32 York County, Virginia Deeds, Orders, and Wills, 1657-1659, Page 18.

33 Ibid.

34 Ibid.

35 York County, Virginia Deeds, Orders, and Wills

36 Charles County, Virginia Deeds, Orders, and Wills

37 Mason, Polly Cary, *Records of Colonial Gloucester County Virginia*, A collection of abstracts from original documents concerning the lands and people of Colonial Gloucester County, 1946, Newport News, Virginia. Page ix.

38 Ibid., Page 84.

39 Hashaw, Tim, *Children of Perdition, Melungeons and the Struggle of Mixed America*, published by Mercer University Press, Macon, Georgia, First edition, 2006. ISBN- 13: 978-0-88146-013-1. Page 31 - 32.

40 McManus, Edgar J., *Black Bondage in the North*, Syracuse University Press, Syracuse, New York, 2001..ISBN 0-8156-2893-5. Page 17.

41 Margaret Melton Murphy is descended from Joshia Melton as evidenced by a number of primary and secondary sources. Margaret Melton Murphy was the daughter of Abner Melton; who was the son of David Melton; who was the son of James Melton; who was he son of Joshia Melton (AKA as Milton); and the son or Robert Melton.

42 Heinegg, Paul, *Free African Americans of North Carolina, Virginia and South Carolina from the Colonial Period to About 1820*. Clearfield Co; printed 2005, reprinted: 2008, Fifth Edition. Two Volumes. ISBN 0-8063-5281-7. Page 832-833.

43 Land Patents of Virginia, Book 1, Part 2. Page 570.

44 Brown, Genealogical Abstracts, Revolutionary War Veterans Script Act, 1852, 139; Gwathmey, Historical Register of Virginians in the Revolution

45 Heinegg, Paul, *Free African Americans of North Carolina, Virginia and South Carolina from the Colonial Period to About 1820*. Clearfield Co; printed 2005, reprinted: 2008, Fifth Edition. Two Volumes. ISBN 9780-8063-52800. Page 833.

46 Ibid.

47   Hening, William W., *The Statutes at Large: Being a Collection of All the Laws of Virginia, in the Year 1684 to 1710.* Act XVI, An Act for Suppressing Outlying Slaves. For the Jamestown Foundation of the Commonwealth of Virginia by the University Press of Virginia, Charlottesville, Facsimile Reprint 1969. Standard Book Number: 8139-0254-1. Volume III, Pages 86-87.

48   Ibid.

49   Ibid., Page 252.

50   Leary, Helen F. M., and Stirewalt, Maurice R., *North Carolina Research, Genealogy and Local History,* published by The North Carolina Genealogical Society, 1980. ISBN 0936370009. Page 232

51   Ibid.

52   Heinegg, Paul, *Free African Americans of North Carolina, Virginia and South Carolina from the Colonial Period to About 1820.* Clearfield Co; printed 2005, reprinted: 2008, Fifth Edition. Two Volumes. ISBN 0-8063-5281-7. Page 282.

53   Marie Howell Cornwall is descended from Elizabeth Owell as evidenced by a number of primary and secondary sources. Marie Howell Cornwall was the daughter of William Howell; who was the son of Christopher Howell; who was the son of John Howell; who was the son of Freeman Howell; who was the son of Mathew Howell; who was the son of Judith Howell; and who was the daughter of Elizabeth Owell (Howell).

54   Heinegg, Paul, *Free African Americans of North Carolina, Virginia and South Carolina from the Colonial Period to About 182*0. Clearfield Co; printed 2005, reprinted: 2008, Fifth Edition. Two Volumes. ISBN 0-8063-5281-7. Page 651.

55   Hashaw, Tim, *Children of Perdition, Melungeons and the Struggle of Mixed America.* Mercer University Press, Macon, Georgia, First edition, 2006. ISBN- 13: 978-0-88146-013-1. Page 27.

56   Hening, William W., The Statutes at Large: Being a Collection of All the Laws of Virginia, from the First Session of the Legislature, in the Year 1670 – Extracts. Published for the Jamestown Foundation of the Commonwealth of Virginia by the University Press of Virginia, Charlottesville, Facsimile Reprint 1969. Standard Book Number: 8139-0254-1. Volume II, Page 515.

57   Ibid.

58   Ibid., Page 283.

59   Ibid., Page 170.

60   Descendants of the English born Thomas and Rebecca (Briggs) Cornell and their 3rd great-grandson, Mansfield Cornwall who settled in St. John Parish, New Brunswick, Canada, have the same DNA profile that matches descendants of the English and Native American Flushing Cornwall of St. John Parish, New Brunswick, Canada and his great-grandson Harold Cornwall. Based on DNA

there is no doubt that Thomas and Rebecca (Briggs) Cornell and Flushing Cornwall (1810 – 1888) share common ancestors. Based on the autosomal DNA, Thomas and Rebecca (Briggs) Cornell are the 6th great-grandparents Harold Cornwall of Brockton, Massachusetts.

61 Harold Cornwall is believed to be descended from Sir Thomas More (1478-1535); who is believed to be grandfather of Cecily More (1526-1615); who is the mother of Thomas Briggs (1554-1593) as evidenced by the publication *Genealogy of the Cornell Family*. Thomas Briggs is the father of Henrie Briggs (1570-1625); who is the father of Rebecca Briggs (1600 – 1673); who is the mother of Richard Cornwell (1624 – 1694); who was the father of Jacob Cornwell (1698 – unknown); who was the father of Daniel Cornwell (1702 – 1769); who was the father of Samuel Cornwell (1752 – 1840); who was the father of Mansfield Cornwell (1784 – unknown); who was the father of Flushing Cornwell (1810 – 1888); who was the father of William Cornwell (1844 – 1926); who was the father of Benjamin Cornwall (1869 – 1918); who was the father of Harold Cornwall.

62 Guiteras, Gertrude Elizabeth, *Guiteras, Wardwell and Allied Families, Genealogical and Biographical*, published by The American Historical Society, New York, New York, 1926. Page 67.

63 "Sir Thomas More, Knight, Lord Chancellor of England, was an English statesman, lawyer, writer and social philosopher. Born on February 7, 1478, he was the son of Sir John More (1451–1530) and Agnes Graunger (d 1499). Thomas More was knighted by King Henry VIII in May, 1521 and appointed Lord Chancellor in October 1529. He was executed on July 6, 1535 and buried in the Chapel of St. Peter in Chains in the London Tower. He was Beatified by Pope Leo III on December 29, 1886, and Canonized by Piux XI on May 19, 1935. His Feast Day is celebrated in the Catholic Church on June 22nd. Already the Patron Saint of Lawyers, he was declared Patron Saint of Statesmen and Politicians by Pope Paul II on October 31, 2000." Wood, Martin, *The Family and Descendants of St Thomas More*, published by Gracewing Ltd, London, England, 2008. ISBN 978-0-85244-681. Page 2.

64 Portrait by Hans Holbein the Younger

65 Ilgenfritz, Elizabeth, *Anne Hutchinson, Religious Leader*. Chelsea House Publishers. New York, New York. ISBN 1-55546-660-5. 1991. Page 20

66 Cornell, Rev. John, *Genealogy of the Cornell Family,"* Published by T.A. Wright Press, New York, 1902. Page 63

67 Ibid.

68 Williams, Selma R. *Divine Rebel, the Life of Anne Marbury Hutchinson*. Published by Holt, Rinehart and Winston, New York, 1981. ISBN: 0-03-055846-8. Page 11.

69   Cornell, Rev. John, *Genealogy of the Cornell Family,*" Published by T.A. Wright Press, New York, 1902. Page 17.

70   Williams, Selma R. *Divine Rebel, the Life of Anne Marbury Hutchinson.* Published by Holt, Rinehart and Winston, New York. ISBN: 0-03-055846-8. Page Pages 95-96.

71   LaPlante, Eve. *American Jezebel, the Uncommon Life of Anne Hutchinson, the Woman Who Defied the Puritans.* Published by Harper Collins Publishing, New York, New York, 2004. ISBN 0-056233-1. Pages 232 – 233.

72   Ibid., Page 234 – 235.

73   Ibid., Page 239.

74   Cornell, Rev. John, *Genealogy of the Cornell Family,*" Published by T.A. Wright Press, New York, 1902. Page 63

75   Cornell, Rev. John, *Genealogy of the Cornell Family,* published by T.A. Wright Press, New York, 1902. Page 31

76   McManus, Edgar J., *Black Bondage in the North.* Published by Syracuse University Press, Syracuse, New York, printed 2001. ISBN 0-8156-2893-5. Page 1.

77   Pratt, Harvey Hunter, *Early Planters of Scituate, Massachusetts.* Published by the Scituate Historical Society, Scituate, Massachusetts, 1929. ISBN 0-7884-0885-2. Page 306.

78   Commonwealth of Massachusetts, Vital Records of Scituate, Massachusetts, Marriages until 1850. Page 341.

79   Hainer, Pattie, *Uncommon Sufferings and Surprising Deliverances: The Black Community of Scituate-Norwell, 1633 to 1800,* grant funded by the Massachusetts Foundation for the Humanities and the Bay State Historical League, 1996. Page 20.

80   Pratt, Harvey Hunter, *Early Planters of Scituate, Massachusetts,* published by the Scituate Historical Society, Scituate, Massachusetts, 1929. ISBN 0-7884-0885-2. Page 306.

81   Commonwealth of Massachusetts, *Vital Records of Scituate, Massachusetts.* Deaths until 1850. Page 392. It is speculated that the date transcribed from the handwritten town record to the printed town books incorrectly stated the year of the marriage. If Cuffe married in 1755 he would have been eleven and Ruth would have been eight. It is further speculated that the correct date was 1765 and that the 65 was transposed to 55.

82   Harper, Douglas, *Slavery in the North.* http://www.slavenorth.com/massachusetts.htm

83   Swasey, Charles W., Historical Collections of the Essex Institute, published by the Essex Institute, Salem, Massachusetts, 1864. Volume XXXXIV. Page 205.

84   McFadden, Terri, Research Assistant, Beverly Historical Society Collections, Beverly, Massachusetts. 2012.

85   Adams, Catherine and Pleck, Elizabeth H., *Love of Freedom, Black Women in Colonial and Revolutionary New England*, published by permission of Oxford University Press, 2010. ISBN 978-0-19-538909. Pages 138 – 139.

86   Adams, Catherine and Pleck, Elizabeth H., *Love of Freedom, Black Women in Colonial and Revolutionary New England*, published by permission of Oxford University Press, 2010. ISBN 978-0-19-538909. Pages 138 – 139.

87   Grundset, Eric G., Forgotten Patriots, African American and American Indian Patriots in the Revolutionary War: A Guide to Services, Sources and Studies. Published by The National Society Daughters of the American Revolution, 2008. ISBN 978-1-892237-10-1. Page 133.

88   Vital Records of Taunton, Massachusetts, 1862, Page 142

89   Descendants of the German born William and Catherine Rucker and their 2nd great-grandson, John Rucker who settled in St. Marks Parish, Orange County, Virginia have the same DNA profile that matches descendants of the African American Lucy Rucker of Big Lick Township, Roanoke County, Virginia. John Rucker (1680 – 1742) and Lucy Rucker Lamkin (1815 – 1891) share a common ancestor. Based on DNA William and Catherine Rucker are the 8th great-grandparents (first generation), and either an unknown male or a female is the parent of Lucy Rucker Lamkin, who is the 2nd great-grandmother of Robert Murphy.

90   McManus, Edgar J., *Black Bondage in the North*, Syracuse University Press, Syracuse, New York printed 2001. ISBN 0-8156-2893-5, Page 2.

91   Wood, Sudie Rucker, *The Rucker Family Genealogy: with their Ancestors, Descendants and Connections*, published by Old Dominion Press, Inc., Richmond, Virginia, 1932. Page 1.

92   Different historians stated that Susanna Ruckers' maiden name was Philips instead of Coghill. In the book *The History of the Rucker Family*, dated 1927, by Edythe Johns Rucker Whitley, she postulates that Susanna Rucker (Page 9) was formerly Susannah Phillips. However, based on subsequent study as evidenced by the more recent publication, *The Rucker Family Genealogy: with their Ancestors, Descendants and Connections, by* Sudie Rucker Wood, date 1932, states that Mrs. Ruckers maiden name was Coghill, daughter of Fredrick and Sarah Coghill of Orange County, Virginia.

93   Walker, Frank S., Jr., *Remembering: A History of Orange County*, Virginia, published by the Orange County Historical Society, Inc., Orange, Virginia, 2004. Page 40 – 41.

94   Will of John Rucker, Orange County, Virginia, Will Book 1, p. 248, Probated Jan. 28, 1742

95   Egerton, Douglas R., *Death of Liberty, African Americans and Revolutionary America*, published by permission of Oxford University Press, New York, New York, 2009. ISBN 978-0-530669-9. Page 56.

96   Ibid., page 6.

97   Grundset, Eric G., *Forgotten Patriots, African American and American Indian Patriots in the Revolutionary War: A Guide to Services, Sources and Studies*. Published by The National Society Daughters of the American Revolution, 2008. ISBN 978-1-892237-10-1. Page v.

98   Pension Records: Samuel Cornwell. *Revolutionary War Pension and Bounty-Land Warrant Application Files*. United States Archives, Washington, DC. 1836.

99   Leckie, Robert, *George Washington's War, The Saga of the American Revolution*, Published by Harper Perenial, New York, New York, 1993. ISBN 0-06-016289-9. Page 198

100   Ibid., pages 198 and 199

101   Ketchem, Richard M., *Saratoga, Turning Point of Americas Revolutionary War*. Published by Henry Holt and Company, New York, New York, 1997. ISBN 0-8050-4681-X. Page 14.

102   Pension Records: Samuel Cornwell. *Revolutionary War Pension and Bounty-Land Warrant Application Files*. United States Archives, Washington, DC. 1836.

103   Ferking, John, *Independence, The Struggle to Set America Free*, published by Bloombury Press, New York, New York, 2001. ISBN 978-1-60819-008-9. Page 138.

104   Chadwick, Bruce, *The Forging of a Revolutionary Leader and the American Presidency, George Washington's War*, published Sourcebooks, Inc. Naperville, Illinois, 2004. ISBN 1-4022-0222-9. Page 116 – 118.

105   Busch, Noel F., *Winter Quarters, George Washington and the Continental Army at Valley Forge*, published by Liveright, New York, New York, 1974. ISBN 0-87140-587-3. Pages 49.

106   Ibid., pages 59-60.

107   Fleming, Thomas, *Washington's Secret War, the Hidden History of Valley Forge*, published by Smithsonian Books, HarperCollins, New York, New York, 2005. Page 130.

108   Hart, Albert Bushnell (editor), *Life at Valley Forge (1777-1778)*, American History told by Contemporaries, Volume II: Building of the Republic, 1689-1783, published by The MacMillan Companies, New York, New York, 1901. Page 570.

109   Ibid.

110   Lockhart, Paul, *The Drillmaster of Valley Forge, the Baron De Steuben and the Making of the American Army*, published by Hollier Collins Publishers, New York, New York, 2008. ISBN 13-978-0-06-145163-8. Page 77.

111   Wilkins, Major Fred J., "Steuben Screamed but Things Happened and an Army Was Born at Valley Forge Just One Hundred and Seventy Years Ago," The Picket Post, January 1948, published by The Valley Forge Historical Society

112 Wilkins, Major Fred J., "*Steuben Screamed but Things Happened and an Army Was Born at Valley Forge Just One Hundred and Seventy Years Ago*," The Picket Post, January 1948, published by The Valley Forge Historical Society, January 1948. Page 7-8.

113 Ibid.

114 Wilkins, Major Fred J., "*Steuben Screamed but Things Happened and an Army Was Born at Valley Forge Just One Hundred and Seventy Years Ago*," The Picket Post, January 1948, published by The Valley Forge Historical Society, January 1948. Page 7.

115 Benjamin Brooker (Id. No: 180). Secretary of the Commonwealth of Massachusetts. *Massachusetts Soldiers and Sailors in the War of the Revolution*. Boston, MA. Wright and Potter Printing Co., 1896. 17 Vols.

116 Ibid.

117 Smith, Philip H., *Curiosities in American History, The Green Mountain Boys: or Vermont and the New York Land - Jobbers*, published by Philip H. Smith, Publisher, Pawling, New York, 1885. Library of Congress 16765-Q2. Page 9.

118 Military Record: Cuffee Grandison. Secretary of the Commonwealth. *Massachusetts Soldiers and Sailors in the War of the Revolution. Vol. III.* Boston, MA, USA: Wright and Potter Printing Co., 1896. Page 479.

119 Secretary of the Commonwealth. *Massachusetts Soldiers and Sailors in the War of the Revolution. Vol. VI.* Boston, MA, USA: Wright and Potter Printing Co., 1896. Page 715.

120 Ibid.

121 Smith, Paul H., *Loyalists and Redcoats, A Study in British Revolutionary Policy*, published by The University of North Carolina Press, Chapel Hill, North Carolina, 1964. Library of Congress Catalog Number 64-22526. Page 141.

122 Ibid., page 168.

123 Pybus, Cassandra, *Jefferson's Faulty Math: The Question of Slave Defections in the American Revolution*, William and Mary Quarterly, 2005, Volume LXII Number 2. Pages 243-264.

124 Pension Records: Edward Going. *Revolutionary War Pension and Bounty-Land Warrant Application Files.* United States Archives, Washington, DC. 1836.

125 Ibid.

126 Military Record: Caesar Russell. Secretary of the Commonwealth. *Massachusetts Soldiers and Sailors in the War of the Revolution. Vol. I-XVII.* Boston, MA, USA: Wright and Potter Printing Co., 1896.

127 Lockhart, Paul, *The Drillmaster of Valley Forge, the Baron De Steuben and the Making of the American Army*, published by Hollier Collins Publishers, New York, New York, 2008. ISBN 13-978-0-06-145163-8. Page 282.

128   Ibid., pages 203-205.

129   Edward Going Pension Records. *Revolutionary War Pension and Bounty-Land Warrant Application Files.* United States Archives, Washington, DC. 1836.

130   Pruitt, Albert Bruce, Abstracts of Land Entries: Caswell County, North Carolina, 1778-1795, 1841-1863 and Person County, North Carolina, 1792-1795. Published by Dr. A.B. Pruitt, 1990. ISBN 0-944992-31-5. Page 89.

131   North Carolina Genealogical Society Journal

132   Edward Going is listed as Edward Gains in this record. Caswell County, North Carolina Tax List, 1777, 1780, and 184. As listed in Pruitt, Albert Bruce, *Abstracts of Land Entries: Caswell County, North Carolina, 1778-1795, 1841-1863 and Person County, North Carolina, 1792-1795.* Published by Dr. A.B. Pruitt, 1990. ISBN 0-944992-31-5. Page 89.

133   Ibid.

134   Granville County, North Carolina Marriages, 1753 -1855

135   The Gowen Family Newsletter, published by the Gowen Research Foundation, Lubbock, Texas. Volume 8, No. 2 October 1996, Page 6; and The Gowen Manuscript, published by the Gowen Research Foundation, Lubbock, Texas. Page 116-117.

136   Ibid.

137   Ibid.

138   Caesar Russell (Id. No: 182) and Sally Richardson Russell (Id. No: 183). Wilmington Records of Birth, Marriages and Deaths from 1730 to 1898, page 179.

139   Caesar Russell family, Commonwealth of Massachusetts, Vital Records, 1633 to 1850, Beverly, Massachusetts. Page 287.

140   McFadden, Terri, Researcher, Beverly Historical Society, Beverly, Massachusetts, Interview, March 2012

141   Ibid.

142   Caesar Russell, United States 1850 Census, Taunton, County of Bristol, Massachusetts, Page 493, line 30.

143   U.S. Department of Commerce, Census Bureau, 1790 Census, Census of Population and Housing.

144   Ibid.

145   Members of the Cornwall Murphy family recorded in the 1790 Census: Freeman Howell; James Ballard; Benjamin Brooker; Joshia Melton, Free Person of Color in Hertford, NC; Caesar Russell, Free Person of Color in Wilmington, MA, along with wife and newborn daughter.

146   Middlekauff, Robert, *The Glorious Cause, the American Revolution,* 1773-1789. Published by Oxford University Press, New York, New York, 1982. ISBN 0-19-502921-6. Page 328

147 Daniel Shays, Secretary of the Commonwealth of Massachusetts. *Massachusetts Soldiers and Sailors in the War of the Revolution*. Boston, MA. Wright and Potter Printing Co., 1896. 17 Vols.Vol.14, Page 76.

148 Higginbotham, Don, *The War of American Independence, Military Attitudes, Policies, and Practice, 1763 – 1789*, published by The Macmillan Company, New York, New York, 1971. Library of Congress Card Catalog Number, 74-132454. Page 447-448.

149 Ibid.

150 Kaplan, Sidney, *The Black Presence in the Era of the American Revolution, 1770 – 1800*, published the New York Graphic Society, LTD, 1973. ISBN 0-812-0541-2. Page 181.

151 Wesley, Charles H., *Prince Hall, Life and Legacy*, published by United Supreme Council, Southern Jurisdiction, Prince Hall Affiliation, Washington, DC. 1977. Pages 66-70.

152 Commonwealth of Massachusetts, Secretary of the Commonwealth, Massachusetts Archives Collection

153 Middlekauff, Robert, *The Glorious Cause, the American Revolution, 1773-1789*. Published by Oxford University Press, New York, New York, 1982. ISBN 0-19-502921-6. Page 627.

154 Egerton, Douglas, *Gabriel's Rebellion: the Virginia Slave Conspiracies of 1800 and 1802*, published by The University of North Carolina Press, Chapel Hill, North Carolina, 1993. ISBN 0-8078-2113-6. Page 21.

155 Ibid.

156 Ibid., pages 32-39.

157 Ibid.

158 Mullin, Gerald, W., *Flight and Rebellion: Slave Resistance in Eighteenth Century Virginia*, published by permission of Oxford University Press, New York, New York, 1972. Library of Congress Card Number 73:173327. Page 147.

159 Ibid., Page 151.

160 Williams, David, *"A People's History of the Civil War, Struggles for the Meaning of Freedom,"* published by The New Press, New York, New York, 2005. ISBN 1-59558-018-2. Page 18.

161 Ibid., Page 150.

162 Franklin, John H. and Moss, Alfred A., *From Slavery to Freedom: A History of Negro Americans*, published by McGraw-Hill, New York, New York. ISBN 0-394-56362-X. Page 133.

163 Riendeau, Roger, *A Brief History of Canada*, published by Facts On File, Inc., New York, New York, 2000. ISBN 0-8160-3157-6. Page 81.

164   Wood-Holt, B. *Early Marriage Records of New Brunswick, Saint John City and County from the British Conquest to 1839*, Holland House, Inc. Saint John, N.B. Canada. 135606. 1986. Page 8.

165   Ibid., page 1.

166   MacNutt, Stewart W., *New Brunswick, A History 1784 – 1867*, published by Macmillan of Canada, Toronto, Canada. 1963. ISBN 0-7715-9818-1. Page 16.

167   Ibid., page 58

168   Hale, Robert R., *Early Brunswick Probate Records, 1785 – 1835*, published by Heritage Books, Inc., Bowie, Maryland. ISBN 1-55613-240-9. 1989. Pages 478.

169   Ibid., page 517.

170   Horsman, Reginald, *The Causes of the War of 1812*, printed by Octagon Books, New York, New York, 1975. ISBN 0-374-93960-8. Pages 24 – 25.

171   Ibid., pages 26 - 27.

172   Daughan, George C., 1812, *The Navy's War*, published by Basic Books, New York, New York, 2011. ISBN 978-0465-02046-1. Pages 20-21.

173   Hickey, Donald R., *The War of 1812, A Forgotten Conflict*, published by University of Illinois Press, Chicago, Illinois, 1989. ISBN 0-252-01613-0.Page 10.

174   Ibid.

175   Daughan, George C., *1812, The Navy's War*, published by Basic Books, New York, New York, 2011. ISBN 978-0465-02046-1. Pages 20-21.

176   Budiansky, Stephen, *Perilous Fight, America's Intrepid War with Britain on the High Seas, 1812 – 1815*, published by Borzoi Books a Division of Random House, New York, New York, 2010. ISBN 978-0-307-27069-6. Page 36- 37.

177   Borneman, Walter R., *1812, The War that Forged a Nation*, published by HarperCollins Publishers, New York, New York, 2004. ISBN 0-06-053112-6. Page 21 - 23.

178   Ibid.

179   Altoff, Gerald T., *Amongst My Best-Men, African Americans and The War of 1812*, published by The Perry Group, Put-in-Bay, Ohio, 1996. ISBN 1-887794-02-6. Page 4-5.

180   Budiansky, Stephen, *Perilous Fight, America's Intrepid War with Britain on the High Seas, 1812 – 1815*, published by Borzoi Books a Division of Random House, New York, New York, 2010. ISBN 978-0-307-27069-6. Page 83- 85.

181   Ibid., page 83.

182   "John Lyon Gardiner Dead.; Owner of Gardiner's Island, Associated with Capt. Kidd, the Pirate." *The New York Times*, January 22, 1910, page 9.

183   Ibid.

184 Butterfield, Kenneth C., Supervisor. *Manumission Book of the Town of Huntington and Babylon Long Island 1800 - 1824, New York*. Published by Town of Huntington New York Historical Society. 1980. Page i.

185 Marcus, Dr. Grania Bolton, *Discovering the African American Experience in Suffolk County, 1620 – 1860*. N.Y. Society for the Preservation, Mad Printers, Mattituck, NY 1988. Page 56

186 Ibid., page 157

187 Butterfield, Kenneth C., Supervisor. *Manumission Book of the Town of Huntington and Babylon Long Island 1800 - 1824, New York*. Published by Town of Huntington New York Historical Society. 1980. Page 28.

188 Gardiner, Sarah Diodati, *Early Memories of Gardiners Island: The Isle of Wight, New York*, published by East Hampton Star, East Hampton, New York, 1947. Page 75.

189 Ibid., page 76.

190 MacNutt, Stewart W., *New Brunswick, A History 1784 – 1867*. Published by Macmillan of Canada, Toronto, Canada. 1963. ISBN 0-7715-9818-1. Page 16.

191 Gardiner, Page 79.

192 Ibid., pages 9 - 11.

193 Lewis Gardiner (Id. No: 54) U.S. Census, Smithtown, Suffolk County, New York, Page 41, Line 8.

194 Samuel Cornwell, Pension Records. *Revolutionary War Pension and Bounty-Land Warrant Application Files*. United States Archives, Washington, DC. 1836.

195 Daughan, George C., *1812, The Navy's War*, published by Basic Books, New York, New York, 2011. ISBN 978-0465-02046-1. Pages 39-40.

196 Altoff, Gerald T., *Amongst My Best-Men, African Americans and The War of 1812*, published by The Perry Group, Put-in-Bay, Ohio, 1996. ISBN 1-887794-02-6., Page xi - xvi.

197 Elting, John R., *Amateurs, To Arms, A Military History of the War of 1812*, published by Algonquin Books of Chapel Hill, Chapel Hill, North Carolina, 1991. ISBN 0-945575-08-4. Page 71.

198 Ibid., pages 71 – 74.

199 Samuel Cornwell, Pension Records. *Revolutionary War Pension and Bounty-Land Warrant Application Files*. United States Archives, Washington, DC. 1836.

200 Samuel Cornwell, United States Revolutionary War Pension Bounty Land Warrant Application, File Number 201374490. June 13, 1827.

201 Budiansky, Stephen, *Perilous Fight, America's Intrepid War with Britain on the High Seas, 1812 – 1815*, published by Borzoi Books a Division of Random House, New York, New York, 2010. ISBN 978-0-307-27069-6. Page 243- 245.

202 Ibid.

203   Horsman, Reginald, *The Causes of the War of 1812*, printed by Octagon Books, New York, New York, 1975. ISBN 0-374-93960-8. Page 158–159.

204   Taylor, Alan, *The Civil War of 1812, American Citizens, British Subjects, Irish Rebels and Indian Allies*. Published by Alfred A. Knopf, New York, New York, 2010. ISBN: 978-1-4000-4265-4. Page 125.

205   Hickey, Donald R., *The War of 1812, A Forgotten Conflict*, published by University of Illinois Press, Chicago, Illinois, 1989. ISBN 0-252-01613-0. Page 72 - 73.

206   Horsman, Page 267.

207   Taylor, Alan, *The Civil War of 1812, American Citizens, British Subjects, Irish Rebels and Indian Allies*. Published by Alfred A. Knopf, New York, New York, 2010. ISBN: 978-1-4000-4265-4. Page 180 – 189.

208   Taylor, Page 206 – 207.

209   Ibid., page 210.

210   Ibid., pages 180 – 189.

211   Ibid., pages 210 – 214.

212   Borneman, Walter R., *1812, The War that Forged a Nation*, published by HarperCollins Publishers, New York, New York, 2004. ISBN 0-06-053112-6. Page 105.

213   Ibid., pages 104 - 106.

214   Ibid., page 223 and pages 110 - 111.

215   Altoff, Gerald T., *Amongst My Best-Men, African Americans and The War of 1812*, published by The Perry Group, Put-in-Bay, Ohio, 1996. ISBN 1-887794-02-6. Page 37.

216   Ibid.

217   Daughan, George C., *1812, The Navy's War*, published by Basic Books, New York, New York, 2011. ISBN 978-0465-02046-1. Pages 210.

218   Hickey, Donald R., *The War of 1812, A Forgotten Conflict*, published by University of Illinois Press, Chicago, Illinois, 1989. ISBN 0-252-01613-0. Page 131 – 135.

219   Borneman, Page 177 - 178.

220   Elting, John R., *Amateurs, To Arms, A Military History of the War of 1812*, published by Algonquin Books of Chapel Hill, Chapel Hill, North Carolina, 1991. ISBN 0-945575-08-4. Page 199 – 200.

221   Proclamation, April 2, 1814. Admiralty Archives 1/508,579, London Public Records Office. Printed in Easton, Md., Republican Star, May 3, 1814

222   Budiansky, Stephen, *Perilous Fight, America's Intrepid War with Britain on the High Seas, 1812 – 1815*, published by Borzoi Books a Division of Random House, New York, New York, 2010. ISBN 978-0-307-27069-6. Page 330 - 332.

223 Altoff, Gerald T., *Amongst My Best-Men, African Americans and The War of 1812*, published by The Perry Group, Put-in-Bay, Ohio, 1996. ISBN 1-887794-02-6. Page 118.

224 Ibid., page 120.

225 Hickey, Donald R., *The War of 1812, A Forgotten Conflict*, published by University of Illinois Press, Chicago, Illinois, 1989. ISBN 0-252-01613-0. Page 208.

226 Daughan, Pages 377 - 379.

227 Elting, Page 309.

228 Taylor, Page 414 - 419.

229 Samuel Cornwell, Pension Records. *Revolutionary War Pension and Bounty-Land Warrant Application Files.* United States Archives, Washington, DC. 1836.

230 Aptheker, Herbert, *American Negro Slave Revolts, 40th Anniversary Edition.* International Publishers. 5th Edition, 1987. ISBN 0-7178-0605-7. Page 298.

231 Ibid., page 300.

232 Parramore. Thomas C., *Trial Separation: Murfreesboro, North Carolina and the Civil War.* Murfreesboro, North Carolina: Murfreesboro Historical Association, Inc.. LCCN TX-5-007-748. Page 10

233 Ibid.

234 Purcell, L. Edward, *Immigration, Social Issues in American History Series*, published by Oryx Press, Phoenix, Arizona, 1995. ISBN 0-89774-873-5. Page 23.

235 Ibid., Page 29.

236 Distribution of Slaves in United States History, United States Census Bureau, Ancestry.com

237 McKanan, Dan, *Prophetic Encounters, Religion and the American Radial Tradition*, published by beacon Press, Boston, Massachusetts, 2011. ISBN 978-0-8070-1315-1. Page 30.

238 McPherson, James M., *The Struggle for Equality, Abolitionists and the Negro in the Civil War and Reconstruction*, published by Princeton University Press, Princeton, New Jersey, 1964. Library of Congress Card 63-23411. Page 6.

239 Ibid.

240 Samuel Brooker, United States Census Bureau, 1820, Boston, Massachusetts, Page 47.

241 Obituary of Samuel Cornwell, Brockton Daily Enterprise, Brockton, Massachusetts, Saturday, July 25, 1953.

242 Pearl Ashport Brooks interview, Brockton, Massachusetts, November 1975. Mrs. Brooks provided extensive insight and information on the times and life of Flushing Cornwall and the life of his wife Harriet Brooker Cornwall. Pearl Ashport Brooks interview, Brockton, Massachusetts, November 1975.

243 Ibid.

244 Harriet Brooker (Id. No. 49), Commonwealth of Massachusetts Vital Records and Statistics, Annual Edition: 1901; Records of Bridgewater, Ma 1850.

245 Pearl Ashport Brooks interview, November 2005.

246 1870 U.S. Census, Fayetteville, Cumberland, County, North Carolina. Page 19, line 24.

247 Parker, Roy, Jr. *Cumberland County, A Brief History*, published by the North Carolina Department of Cultural Resources, Division of Archives and History, in 1990. ISBN 0-86526-243-8. Page 43.

248 Worrell, Anne Lowry, *A Brief of Wills and Marriages in Montgomery and Fincastle Counties, Virginia, 1773-1831*, published by Virginia Book Company, Berryville, Virginia, 1932. Page 5.

249 Moche, Joanne Spiers, *Families of Grace through 1900, Remembering Radford*, Volume I, published by Heritage Books, Westminster, Maryland, 2008. ISBN 978-0-7884-3744-1. Page 48.

250 Ibid.

251 1860 United States Federal Census, *Schedule 2. Slave Inhabitants in Montgomery County, Virginia*. Page 19, Line 4, Column B.

252 Lindon, Mary Elizabeth, *Virginia's Montgomery County*, published by Montgomery Museum and Lewis Miller Regional Art Center, Christiansburg, Virginia, 2009. ISBN 978-0-970648-2-7. Page 57.

253 1860 United States Federal Census, *Schedule 2. Slave Inhabitants in Montgomery County, Virginia*. Page 19, Line 4, Column B.

254 Ibid., Page 188.

255 Ibid. Page 192.

256 Marcus, Dr. Grania Bolton, *Discovering the African American Experience in Suffolk County, 1620 – 1860*. N.Y. Society for the Preservation, Mad Printers, Mattituck, NY 1988. Page 156.

257 James Melton, Schedule I. – Free Inhabitants in Southern District, in the County of Hertford, State of North Carolina. September 1850, Page 653. Line 12

258 James Melton, Schedule I. – Free Inhabitants in Southern District, in the County of Hertford, State of North Carolina. September 1850, Page 653. Line 12

259 Jane (sic) Adkins, Schedule I. – Free Inhabitants in Southern District, in the County of Hertford, State of North Carolina. September 1850, Page 653. Line 8

260 Abner Melton, United States Census Bureau, 1900, North Carolina; United States Census Bureau, 1870, North Carolina.

261 Colaiaco, James A., *Frederick Douglass* and the Fourth of July, published by Palgrave Macmillan, New York, New York, 2006. ISBN 1-4039-7033-5. Page 60 -

262 Guelzo, Allen C., *Lincoln and Douglas, The Debates That Defined America*, printed by Simon & Schuster, New York, New York, 2008. ISBN 13-978-0-7432-7320-6. Page 12 – 13.

263 Stauffer, John, *The Black Hearts of Men, Radical Abolitionists and the Transformation of Race*, published by Harvard University Press, Cambridge, Massachusetts, 2002. ISBN 0-674-00645-3. Page 20 – 21.

264 Klingaman, William K. Abraham *Lincoln and the Road to Emancipation, 1861 – 1865*, published by Viking Penguin Books, New York, New York, 2001. ISBN 0-670-86754-3. Page 28 - 29.

265 Ibid., Page 9.

266 Guelzo, Allen C., *Lincoln and Douglas, The Debates That Defined America*, printed by Simon & Schuster, New York, New York, 2008. ISBN 13-978-0-7432-7320-6. Page 93 – 96.

267 Klingaman, Page 29.

268 Guelzo, Page 307.

269 United States Naval History Division, United States Navy Department, Civil War Naval Chronology, 1861 – 1865, published by the U.S. Government Printing Office, Washington, D.C., 1971. Library Card No. 71-609471. Page II-24.

270 Ibid., Page III-18.

271 Ibid., pages 362 – 363.

272 Taylor, Rosser Howard, *The Free Negro in North Carolina*, published by The James Sprunt Historical Publications, under The North Carolina Historical Society, Vol. 17, No.1, and the University of Chapel Hill, North Carolina. 1920. Page 23.

273 Ibid., page 24.

274 Kendrick, Paul and Kendrick, Stephen, *Douglass and Lincoln, How a Revolutionary Black Leader and a Reluctant Liberator Struggled to End Slavery and Save the Union*, published by Walker & Company Publishing, New York, New York, 2008. ISBN 10-0-8027-1523-0. Page 63.

275 McPherson, James M., *The Struggle for Equality, Abolitionists and the Negro in the Civil War and Reconstruction*, published by Princeton University Press, Princeton, New Jersey, 1964. Library of Congress Card 63-23411. Page 195 -196.

276 Stokesbury, James L., *A Short History of the Civil* War, published by William Morris and Company, Inc., New York, New York, 1995. ISBN 0-688-11523-3. Page 220.

277 Binkin, Martin, Eitelberg, Mark, Schexnider, Alvin, and Smith, Marvin, *Blacks and the Military*, published by the Brookings Institute, Washington, DC., 1982. ISBN 0-8157-0974-9. Page 14-15.

278 Cook, Adrian, *The Armies of the Streets, The New York City Draft Riots of 1863*, published by The University Press of Kentucky, Lexington, Kentucky, 1974. ISBN 0-8131-1298-2. Page 56-67.

279 Ibid., pages 77 - 78.

280 McPherson, James M., *Ordeal by Fire, The Civil War, Volume II*, published by McGraw Hill, 2001. ISBN 0-07-231736-1. Page 388 – 389.

281 Hine, Darlene Clark; Hine, William C.; and Harold, Stanley, *African Americans, A Concise History*, Second Edition. Printed by Pearson, Prentice Hall, Saddle River, New Jersey, 2006. ISBN: 0-13-192583-0. Page 185.

282 Ibid., pages 171.

283 Charles R. Douglas, Private Company F, 54th Massachusetts Colored Infantry to 1st Sargent, 5th Massachusetts Colored Calvary. War Department, Adjutant General's Office, Military Record, Copyists, March 19, 1863. Bookmark V. 14, Page 93, '68, Crenshaw, Copyist.

284 Lewis H. Douglas, Sargent Major, Company D, 54th Massachusetts Colored Infantry. War Department, Adjutant General's Office, Military Record, Copyists, March 25, 1863. Shaughan, Copyist.

285 McPherson, James M., *Ordeal by Fire, The Civil War, Volume II*, Page 389.

286 Stokesbury, James L., *A Short History of the Civil War*, published by William Morris and Company, Inc., New York, New York, 1995. ISBN 0-688-11523-3. Page 220

287 McPherson, James M., *The Struggle for Equality, Abolitionists and the Negro in the Civil War and Reconstruction*, published by Princeton University Press, Princeton, New Jersey, 1964. Library of Congress Card 63-23411. Page 207.

288 Klingaman, William K., *Abraham Lincoln and the Road to Emancipation, 1861 – 1865*, published by Viking Penguin Books, New York, New York, 2001. ISBN 0-670-86754-3. Page 276.

289 Ibid.

290 Ibid.

291 Kendrick, Paul and Kendrick, Stephen, *Douglass and Lincoln, How a Revolutionary Black Leader and a Reluctant Liberator Struggled to End Slavery and Save the Union*, published by Walker & Company Publishing, New York, New York, 2008. ISBN 10-0-8027-1523-0. Page184.

292 Foote, Shelby, *The Civil War, A Narrative: Red River To Appomattox*. Published by Random House Inc., New York, New York, 1974. ISBN 0-394-74623-6. Page 430 – 431.

293 William Cornwall personal account of his granddaughter, Mrs. Martha Cornwall Royster of Brockton, Massachusetts

294 Stokesbury, James L., *A Short History of the Civil War*, published by William Morris and Company, Inc., New York, New York, 1995. ISBN 0-688-11523-3. Page 28.

295 Ibid., pages 27-28.

296 Isabella Fraction. United States Military Pension, October 21, 1895. United States Colored Troops Military Record, 18611865. Record Number 47518843.

297 Thomas Fraction. United States Colored Troops Military Record, 18611865. Record Number 47518850.

298 John Jackson, Commonwealth of Massachusetts, Vital Records and Statistics 1928; United States Census Bureau, 1850, N.Y.

299 Aaron Jackson, personal account of Mrs. Martha Cornwall Royster of Brockton, Massachusetts

300 Aaron Jackson, personal account of his granddaughter, Mrs. Martha Cornwall Royster of Brockton, Massachusetts

301 Aaron Jackson, U.S. Special Census Schedule – Surviving Soldiers, Sailors, and Marines, and Widows, S.D. 67; E.D. 1051; Minor Civil Division: Massachusetts. Line 20.

302 Kirchberger, Joe H., *The Civil War and Reconstruction, An Eyewitness History*, published by Facts on File, Inc., New York, New York, 1991. ISBN 0-8160-2171-6. Page 202.

303 Henry, Robert Selph, *The Story of Reconstruction*, published by Konecky & Konecky, New York, New York, 1999. ISBN 1-56852-254-1. Page 9.

304 Starkey, Larry, *Wilkes Booth Came to Washington*, published by Random House, New York, New York, 1976. ISBN 0-394-48894-6. Page 70-71.

305 Ibid., page 68.

306 Ibid., page 87.

307 Donald, David Herbert, *Lincoln*, published by Simon & Schuster, New York, New York, 1995. ISBN 0-684-80846-3. Page 588.

308 Richardson, Heather Cox, *West From Appomattox, the Reconstruction of America after the Civil War*, published by Yale University Press, New Haven, Connecticut, 2007. ISBN978-0-300-11052-4. Page 41.

309 Cruden, Robert, *The Negro in Reconstruction*, published by Prentice-Hall, Inc., Englewood Cliffs, New Jersey, 1969. LCCC 69-17370. Page 9 -10.

310 Cruden, Robert, *The Negro in Reconstruction*, published by Prentice-Hall, Inc., Englewood Cliffs, New Jersey, 1969. LCCC 69-17370. Page 5.

311 Binkin, Martin, Eitelberg, Mark, Schexnider, Alvin, and Smith, Marvin, *Blacks and the Military*, published by the Brookings Institute, Washington, DC., 1982. ISBN 0-8157-0974-9. Page 15.

312 Berlin, Ira, Reidy, Joseph P., Rowland, Leslie S., *Freedom, A Documentary History of Emancipation, 1861-1867, Series II, The Black Military Experience*, published by Cambridge University Press, Cambridge, England, 1982. ISBN 0-521-22984-7. Page 808-810.

313 Pearl Ashport Brooks, first cousin to Harriet Brooker Cornwall (mothers were Russell sisters), stated that her father Colonel Lemuel A. Ashport was one of the models for the sculpture. She stated that her father "likeness" was in the fourth row, directly behind the horse the second man in with the beard. Upon her death, she willed to the Brockton, Massachusetts Historical Society her father's Massachusetts 54th canteen and sword, each used in battle with the Regiment's insignia, and the flag that draped her father's casket.

314 Roger Wilkins, Editor, *The Black Solider and The Civil War*, The Crisis Magazine, January-February 1999, Baltimore, Maryland, 21215, Volume 106, Number 1 Page 32.

315 Craven, Avery, *Reconstruction: The Ending of the Civil War*, published by Holt, Rinehart and Winston, Inc., New York, New York, 1969. SBN 03-073245-X. Page 39.

316 Ibid., Page 88-89.

317 Castel, Albert E., *The Presidency of Andrew Johnson*, published by The Regents Press of Kansas, Lawrence, Kansas, 1979. ISBN 0-7006-0190-2. Page 26.

318 Craven, Avery, *Reconstruction: The Ending of the Civil War*, published by Holt, Rinehart and Winston, Inc., New York, New York, 1969. SBN 03-073245-X. Page 89.

319 Ibid.

320 Robert T. Preston, United States, National Archives and Records Administration, Confederate Applications for Presidential Pardons, 1865-1867. Image 319-322.

321 Lomask, Milton, *Andrew Johnson, President on Trial*, published by Octagon Books, New York, New York, 1973. ISBN0-374-95082-2. Page 134.

322 Castel, Albert E., *The Presidency of Andrew Johnson*, published by The Regents Press of Kansas, Lawrence, Kansas, 1979. ISBN 0-7006-0190-2. Page 47.

323 Chalmers, David M., *Hooded Americanism, The History of the Ku Klux Klan*, published by Duke University Press, Durham, North Carolina, 1987. ISBN 0-8223-0730-8. Page 8 -11.

324 The World Book Encyclopedia; Historical Statistics of the United States: Colonial Times to 1970, U.S. Department of Commerce, Bureau of the Census, 1975; and The United States Civil War Center.

325   The World Book Encyclopedia; Historical Statistics of the United States: Colonial Times to 1970, U.S. Department of Commerce, Bureau of the Census, 1975; and The United States Civil War Center.

326   Kirchberger, Joe H., *The Civil War and Reconstruction, An Eyewitness History*, published by Facts on File, Inc., New York, New York, 1991. ISBN 0-8160-2171-6. Page 269.

327   The World Book Encyclopedia; Historical Statistics of the United States: Colonial Times to 1970, U.S. Department of Commerce, Bureau of the Census, 1975; and The United States Civil War Center.

328   Ibid.

329   McPherson, James M., *Ordeal by Fire, The Civil War, Volume II*, Page 435.

330   Ibid., Page 39.

331   Lomask, Milton, *Andrew Johnson, President on Trial*, published by Octagon Books, New York, New York, 1973. ISBN0-374-95082-2. Page 139.

332   Ibid., Page 142.

333   Trelease, Allen, W., *White Terror, The Ku Klux Klan, Conspiracy and Southern Reconstruction*, published by Greenwood Press Publishers, Westport, Connecticut, 1971. ISBN 0-31321168-X. Page xxiii.

334   McPherson, James M., *Ordeal by Fire, The Civil War, Volume II*, Page 435.

335   Castel, Albert E., *The Presidency of Andrew Johnson*, published by The Regents Press of Kansas, Lawrence, Kansas, 1979. ISBN 0-7006-0190-2. Page 208.

336   Allardice, Bruce S., *Confederate Colonels, A Biographical Register*, published by The University of Missouri Press, Columbia, Missouri, 2008. ISBN 978-0-8262-1809. Page 313.

337   Berlin, Ira, Reidy, Joseph P., Rowland, Leslie S., Freedom, A Documentary History of Emancipation, 1861-1867, Series II, The Black Military Experience, published by Cambridge University Press, Cambridge, England, 1982. ISBN 0-521-22984-7. Page 808-810.

338   Ibid.

339   Allardice, Bruce S., *Confederate Colonels, A Biographical Register*, published by The University of Missouri Press, Columbia, Missouri, 2008. ISBN 978-0-8262-1809. Page 313.

340   Nock, O. S., *Railways of the USA*, published by Hastings House Publishes, New York, New York. ISBN 0-8038-6359-4. Page 44.

341   Kagey, Deedie, *When Past is Prologue: A History of Roanoke County*, published Walsworth Press Inc., LC No. 88-51691, 1988, Page 279-280.

342   Viorst, Milton, *Fall From Grace, the Republican Party and the Puritan Ethic*. Published by the New American Library Inc., New York, New York, 1968. Library of Congress catalog Number: 68-20115. Page 86 – 87.

343 Trelease, Allen, W., *White Terror, The Ku Klux Klan, Conspiracy and Southern Reconstruction*, published by Greenwood Press Publishers, Westport, Connecticut, 1971. ISBN 0-31321168-X. Page 189.

344 Ibid., Page 190.

345 Ibid., Page 217.

346 Gillette William, *Retreat from Reconstruction, 1869-1879*, published by Louisiana State University Press, Baton Rouge, Louisiana, 1979. ISBN 0-8071-0569-4. Page 94.

347 Viorst, age 90 – 91.

348 Gillette Page 24.

349 Ibid., Page 44.

350 Viorst, Page 94 – 95.

351 Advertisement taken out by the Cornwell Brothers, Charles, Philip, and Samuel in the 1866 Brockton City Directory. The name Cornwell and Cornwall was interchangeable throughout the 1880's.

352 O'Donnell, Richard, Yankee Magazine, *There Have Been Thousands of Department Store Santa's since 1800, but None Quite Like The First Department Store Santa Claus*, December 1969, published by Yankee Publishing Inc., Dublin, NH., 1969. Page 104.

353 Picture of Hanford Cornwell (circa 1890), courtesy from the private collection of Constance Curts.

354 Study of Afro-American Life Report and History in conjunction with the Association for the Study of Negro Life and History. *"Science and Invention"* Page 4.

355 Benjamin Cornwell, Commonwealth of Massachusetts, State Department of Public Health, Registry of Vital Records and Statistics, Record of Marriage, Year 1891. Volume 416, Page 501, Number 6.

356 Obituary of Samuel Cornwell, Brockton Daily Enterprise, Brockton, Massachusetts, Saturday, July 25, 1953.

357 Othow, Helen Chavis, *Personal Interview on the Life of John Chavis*, March 21, 2013, Oxford Township, Granville County, North Carolina.

358 Grundset, Eric G., Forgotten Patriots, African American and American Indian Patriots in the Revolutionary War, A Guide to Services, Sources and Studies. Published by The National Society Daughters of the American Revolution, 2008. ISBN 978-1-892237-10-1. Page 515.

359 Othow, *Personal Interview on the Life of John Chavis*, March 21, 2013.

360 Othow, Helen Chavis, *John Chavis, African American Patriot, Preacher, Teacher and Mentor (1763 – 1838)*, published by McFarland & Company, Inc., Jefferson, North Carolina, 2001. ISBN 978-0786408184. Page 15 -17.

361 Ibid., page 25.

362 Heinegg, Paul, *Free African Americans of North Carolina, Virginia and South Carolina from the Colonial Period to About 1820*. Clearfield Co; printed 2005, reprinted: 2008, Fifth Edition. Two Volumes. ISBN 0-8063-5281-7.

363 Freeman Howell, United States 1820 Census, Mecklenburg County, Virginia. Page 48, Line 27.

364 Matthew Howell, United States 1820 Census, Mecklenburg County, Virginia. Page 48, Line 26.

365 Ibid.

366 John Howell, Oxford, N.C. Vital Statistics, Annual Edition: 1830; United States Census Bureau, 1880, N.C.

367 Jane Harris, Ibid; personal account of Mrs. Marie Cornwall.

368 Heinegg, Paul *Free African Americans of North Carolina, Virginia and South Carolina from the Colonial Period to About 1820*. Clearfield Co; printed 2005, reprinted: 2008, Fifth Edition. Two Volumes. ISBN 0-8063-5281-7.

369 Christopher Howell, Granville County, North Carolina Vital Statistics, Annual Edition: 1880; United States Census Bureau, 1880, N.C.; picture courtesy of Mrs. Marie Cornwall.

370 Harriet Gowen, Granville County, North Carolina Vital Statistics.

371 James Fraction, United States Census Bureau, 1870, N.C. and 1880, N.C. James Fraction U.S. Military Pension Avadavat. Commonwealth of Massachusetts, Vital Records and Statistics 1919. Personal account of Mr. Paul Chapman (Son-in-Law), of Attleboro Massachusetts.

372 Lucy Rucker Lampkin, U.S. James Fraction U.S. Military Pension Avadavat.

373 Burgess, Robert H., and Wood, H. Graham, *Steamboats Out of Baltimore*, published by Tidewater Publishers, Cambridge, Maryland, 1968. LCCCN: 68-58859. Page xvii.

374 Brown, Alexander Crosby *Steam Packets on the Chesapeake, published by* Cambridge, Maryland: Cornell Maritime Press, 1961 LCCN 61-012580 Page xiii.

375 Julia's brother, William Utley, was a businessman in St. Paul, living with his wife Dora and their children. Many of William and Dora's descendants still live in the St. Paul and Minneapolis metropolitan communities today.

376 James Fraction. *U.S. Military Pension Deposition*, November 21, 1918, Washington, D.C. William T. Tyler, Senior Assistant Director, Division of Operation, U.S. Railroad Administration, Interstate Commerce Building.

377 Great Northern Railway Historical Society

378 James Fraction. *U.S. Military Pension Deposition*, November 21, 1918, Washington, D.C. William T. Tyler, Senior Assistant Director, Division of Operation, U.S. Railroad Administration, Interstate Commerce Building.

379 Paul Chapman Interview, Attleboro, Massachusetts, 1976. Much of the information on the life of James Fraction and his wife Julia Utley was chronicled in an interview with their son-in-law, Paul Chapman.

380 Paul Chapman Interview, Attleboro, Massachusetts, 1976.

381 Paul Chapman Interview, Attleboro, Massachusetts, 1976.

382 Maruyama, Susan J., *African Americans, Voices of Triumph, Perseverance*, published by the Editors of Time-Life Books, Alexandria, Virginia, 1993. ISBN 0-7835-2250-9. Page 183.

383 Fireside, Harvey, *Separate and Unequal, Homer Plessey and the Supreme Court Decision that Legalized Racism*, published by Carroll & Graf Publishers, New York, New York, 2004. ISBN 0-7867-1293-7. Page 4-5.

384 Harrison, Alferdteen, *Black Exodus, The Great Migration for the American South*, published by University Press of Mississippi, Jackson, Mississippi, 1991. ISBN 0-87805-491-X. Page vi.

385 Litwack, Leon F., *Trouble in Mind, Black Southerner in the Age of Jim Crow*, published by Alfred A. Knopf Inc., New York, New York, 1998. ISBN 0-394-52778-x. Page 244.

386 Blackmon, Douglas A., *Slavery by Another Name, The Re-Enslavement of Black Americans from the Civil War to World War II*, published by Double Day New York, New York, 2008. ISBN 978-0-385-50625-0. Page 147.

387 Fireside, Page 232-233.

388 Ibid., page 233.

389 Litwack, Leon F., *Trouble in Mind, Black Southerner in the Age of Jim Crow*, published by Alfred A. Knopf Inc., New York, New York, 1998. ISBN 0-394-52778-x. Page 244.

390 Musciant, Ivan, *Empire by Default, The Spanish-American War and the Dawn of the American Century*, published by Henry Holt and Company, Inc., New York, New York, 1998. ISBN 0-8050-3500-1. Page 246.

391 Burgess, Robert H., and Wood, H. Graham, *Steamboats Out of Baltimore*, published by Tidewater Publishers, Cambridge, Maryland, 1968. LCCCN: 68-58859. Page 164-166.

392 Paul Chapman Interview, Attleboro, Massachusetts, 1976.

393 Young, Joe and Lewis, Sam, music by Donaldson, Walter, *How 'Ya Gonna Keep 'Em Down on the Farm? (After They've Seen Paree)*, published by Waterson, Berlin & Snyder Co., Music Publishing, New York, New York, 1919.

394 James Fraction, Military Pension Records. United States Archives, Washington, DC. October, 1917.

395 Parker, J. Roy, *The Ahoskie Era of Hertford County*, published by Parker Brothers, Inc., Ahoskie, North Carolina, 1939. Page 492 -493.

396   Ibid.

397   Sally Ballard, United States Census Bureau, North Carolina, 1880.

398   White, Margaret Anne, *The Early Years at Cedar Grove Friends Meeting in Woodland, North Carolina*, published by in The Southern Friend, Journal of the North Carolina Friends Historical Society, Vol. 1, No. 1, 1979.

399   Prior to the Civil War the shipyard was known as the Gosport Shipyard. After the capture of the city the shipyard was renamed by the Union Army as the Norfolk Shipyard after the city in which it was located. In 1917, after the United States entered into World War I, the federal government purchased the property and adjoining land and renamed it the Naval Station Norfolk.

400   Traxel, David, *1898, The Tumultuous Years of Victory, Invention, Internal Strife and Industrial Expansion that Saw the Birth of the American Century*, published by Alfred A. Knopf, New York, New York, 1998. ISBN 0-679-45497-5. Page 32.

401   Defined as a person from a northern state who went to the South after the Civil War to profit from the Reconstruction.

402   William Howell (1879 – 1946), Commonwealth of Massachusetts, Registry of Vital Records and Statistics Year.

403   Harrison, Alferdteen, *Black Exodus, The Great Migration for the American South*, published by University Press of Mississippi, Jackson, Mississippi, 1991. ISBN 0-87805-491-X. Page 31.

404   Hahn, Steven, *A Nation Under Our Feet, Black Political Struggles in the Rural South from Slavery to the Great Migration*, published by Belknap Press of Harvard University, Cambridge, Massachusetts, 2003. ISBN 0-674-01169-4. Page 467.

405   Grossman, James R., *Land of Hope: Chicago, Black Southerner and the Great Migration*, The University of Chicago Press, Chicago, Illinois, 1989. ISBN 0-226-30994-0. Page 13.

406   Ibid.

407   Ibid., page 48-49.

408   Harrison, Alferdteen, *Black Exodus, The Great Migration for the American South*, published by University Press of Mississippi, Jackson, Mississippi, 1991. ISBN 0-87805-491-X. Page 22.

409   Tye, Larry, *Rising form the Rails, Pullman Porters and the Making of the Black Middle Class*. Published by the Henry Holt and Company, New York, New York, 2004. ISBN 0-8050-7075-3. Pages 8 – 18.

410   Tye, Larry, *Rising form the Rails, Pullman Porters and the Making of the Black Middle Class*. Published by the Henry Holt and Company, New York, New York, 2004. ISBN 0-8050-7075-3. Page 77.

411   Margaret Melton, personal account of Mrs. Margaret (Melton) Murphy

412   Margaret Melton, personal account of Mrs. Margaret (Melton) Murphy

413 Account of Margaret Melton Murphy and Odie Melton Rocha; and Junious Melton's 1917 U.S. Draft Registration Card.

414 Robert H. Murphy, Sr., Commonwealth of Massachusetts, Vital Records and Statistics, 1969. Personal account of Mrs. Margaret Murphy of Boston, Massachusetts

415 Landers, Warren P., Editor, *Brockton and Its Centennial, The Organization and Story of its One Hundredth Anniversary, June 12-18, 1921*, published by the City of Brockton, Massachusetts, Brockton, Massachusetts, 1921.

416 Gray, Leo R. Personal Interview, February 23, 2012.

417 Broadnax, Samuel L., *Blue Skies, Black Wings, African American Pioneers of Aviation*, published by University of Nebraska Press, Lincoln, Nebraska, 2008. ISBN 978-0-8032-1774-4. Page 10-11.

418 Ibid., page 11.

419 Maruyama, Susan J., *African Americans, Voices of Triumph, Perseverance*, published by the Editors of Time-Life Books, Alexandria, Virginia, 1993. ISBN 0-7835-2250-9. Page 158.

420 Jakeman, Robert J., *The Divided Skies, Establishing Segregated Flight Training at Tuskegee, Alabama, 1934-1942.*, published by The University of Alabama Press, Tuscaloosa, Alabama, 1992. ISBN 0-8173-0527-0. Page 62.

421 Broadnax, Samuel L., *Blue Skies, Black Wings, African American Pioneers of Aviation*, published by University of Nebraska Press, Lincoln, Nebraska, 2008. ISBN 978-0-8032-1774-4. Page 9-10.

422 Hardesty, Von, *Black Wings, Courageous Stores of African Americans in Aviation and Space History*, published by HarperCollins, New York, New York, 2008. ISBN 978-0-06-126138-1. Page 63.

423 Ibid., page 63.

424 Jakeman, Robert J., *The Divided Skies, Establishing Segregated Flight Training at Tuskegee, Alabama, 1934-1942.*, published by The University of Alabama Press, Tuscaloosa, Alabama, 1992. ISBN 0-8173-0527-0. Page 184-185.

425 Ibid., page 65.

426 Ibid., page 197.

427 Ibid., page 191.

428 Hardesty, Von, *Black Wings, Courageous Stores of African Americans in Aviation and Space History*, published by HarperCollins, New York, New York, 2008. ISBN 978-0-06-126138-1. Page 65.

429 Gray, Leo R. Personal interview. February 23, 2012.

430 Bowers, William T., *Black Solider, White Army: the 24ᵗʰ Infantry Regiment in Korea*, published by the Center of Military History, United States Army, Washington, District of Columbia, 1996. ISMB0-16-048803-6. Page 36-37.

431 Sandler, Stanley, *The Korean War, No Victors, No Vanquished*, published by The University Press of Kentucky, Lexington, Kentucky, 1999. ISBN 0-8131-2119-1. Page 18 – 19.

432 Ibid., pages 24 – 25.

433 Catchpole, Brian, *The Korean War, 1950-53*, Carroll & Graff Publishers, New York, New York, 2000. ISBN 0-7867-0939-1. Page 4-5.

434 Cumings, Bruce, *The Korean War, A History*, published by The Modern Library, New York, New York. ISBN978-0-679-64357-9 Page 11.

435 Catchpole, Page 7-13

436 Cumings, Page 11.

437 U.S. Department of State, Office of the Historian, *Milestones: 1945-1952, The Truman Doctrine, 1947*. http://history.state.gov/milestones/1945-1952/TrumanDoctrine. Accessed May, 6, 2013.

438 Sandler, Stanley, *The Korean War, No Victors, No Vanquished*, published by The University Press of Kentucky, Lexington, Kentucky, 1999. ISBN 0-8131-2119-1. Page 171.

439 U.S. Department of Army Corp of Engineers, official website http://www.usace.army.mil/About/History/HistoricalVignettes/MilitaryConstruction Combat/098KoreanWar.aspx

440 Ibid.

441 Catchpole, Brian, *The Korean War, 1950-53*, Carroll & Graff Publishers, New York, New York, 2000. ISBN 0-7867-0939-1. Page 259.

442 Cumings, Bruce, *The Korean War, A History*, published by The Modern Library, New York, New York. ISBN978-0-679-64357-9 Page 16.

443 Catchpole, Brian, *The Korean War, 1950-53*, Carroll & Graff Publishers, New York, New York, 2000. ISBN 0-7867-0939-1. Page 258-260.

444 Karnow, Staney, *Vietnam A History, the First Complete Account of Vietnam at War*, published by Viking Press, New York, New York, 1983. ISBN 0-670-74604-5. Page 169.

445 Minh, Bui Cong, *A Distant Cause, A History and the Vindication of the Viet Nam War*, published by Xlibris Publishers, Bloomington, Indiana, 2006. ISBN 1-4134-8163-9. Page 41-54.

446 Ibid., page 54.

447 Daggett, Stephen, Congressional Research Service, *Costs of Major U.S. Wars*, June 29, 2010. Page 2.

448 Reef, Catherine, *African Americans in the Military*, published by InfoBase Publishing, New York, New York, 2010. ISBN 978-0-8160-7839-4. Page 69.

449   Walker, Jesse, "D.C. Grad Ranks High at U.S. Naval Academy, Ensign Lawrence Chambers Jr. Stands 119 in Class of 783" *The Afro-American Newspaper*,. June 14, 1952.

450   Schneller, Robert J., *Blue & Gold and Black: Racial Integration of the U.S. Naval Academy*, published by Texas A&M University Press, 2007. ISBN 978-1-60344-000-4. Page 99.

451   Reef, Catherine, *African Americans in the Military*, published by InfoBase Publishing, New York, New York, 2010. ISBN 978-0-8160-7839-4. Page 69.

452   Mersky, Peter and Polmar, Norman, *The Naval Air War in Vietnam*, published by The Nautical and Aviation Publishing Company, Annapolis, Maryland. ISBN 0-933852-13-4. Page 213-214.

453   Jet Magazine *Admiral Chambers Heads Persian Gulf Naval Force*, March 13, 1980, Published by Johnson Publishing Company, Chicago, IL. Page 57.

454   Picture courtesy of the *USS Midway* 1989 Calendar Memorabilia Collection.

455   Jet Magazine *Admiral Chambers Heads Persian Gulf Naval Force*, March 13, 1980, Published by Johnson Publishing Company, Chicago, IL. Page 57.

456   Reef, Catherine, *African Americans in the Military*, published by InfoBase Publishing, New York, New York, 2010. ISBN 978-0-8160-7839-4. Page 69.

457   Walton, Ben L., *Great Black War Fighters, Profiles in Service*, published by Strategic Book Publishing and Rights Co., Houston, Texas. 2012. ISBN 978-1-61897-108-1. Page 53.

458   Lanning, Lt. Col (Ret) Michael Lee, *The African American Solider, from Crispus Attucks to Colin Powell*, published by Carol Publishing Group, Secaucus, New Jersey, 1997. ISBN 1-55972-404-8. Page 241.

459   Bravin, Jess. "Court Upends Voting Rights Act." *Wall Street Journal*. http://online.wsj.com, retrieved 06/27/13

Index